The psychology of gender

THE PSYCHOLOGY OF GENDER

THE PSYCHOLOGY OF GENDER

EDITED BY
ANNE E. BEALL
ROBERT J. STERNBERG

FOREWORD BY
ELLEN BERSCHEID

GUILFORD PRESS
New York   London

© 1993 The Guilford Press
A Division of Guilford Publications, Inc.
72 Spring Street, New York, NY 10012

Printed in the United States of America

This book is printed on acid-free paper.

Last digit is print number: 9 8 7 6 5 4 3 2 1

Library of Congress Cataloging-in-Publication Data

The psychology of gender / edited by Anne E. Beall and
    Robert J. Sternberg.
        p.   cm.
    Includes bibliographical references and index.
    ISBN 0-89862-286-7. — ISBN 0-89862-283-2 (pbk.)
    1. Sex differences (Psychology) 2. Gender identity.   3. Sex
(Psychology)   I. Beall, Anne E.   II. Sternberg, Robert J.
    [DNLM: 1. Gender Identity.   2. Sex Behavior—psychology.   3. Sex
Characteritics.   BF 692 P467 1993]
BF692.2.P437   1993
155.3'3 — dc20
DNLM/DLC
for Library of Congress   93-11508
                                                               CIP

Contributors

Mahzarin R. Banaji, Ph.D., Department of Psychology, Yale University, New Haven, Connecticut

Anne E. Beall, M.S., M.Phil., Department of Psychology, Yale University, New Haven, Connecticut

Deborah L. Best, Ph.D., Department of Psychology, Wake Forest University, Winston-Salem, North Carolina

Ellen Berscheid, Ph.D., Department of Psychology, University of Minnesota, Minneapolis, Minnesota

Susan E. Cross, Ph.D., Department of Educational Psychology, University of Texas at Austin, Austin, Texas

Irene Fast, Ph.D., Department of Psychology, University of Michigan, Ann Arbor, Michigan

Florence L. Geis, Ph.D., Department of Psychology, University of Delaware, Newark, Delaware

Carol Nagy Jacklin, Ph.D., Department of Psychology, University of Southern California, Los Angeles, California

Douglas T. Kenrick, Ph.D., Department of Psychology, Arizona State University, Tempe, Arizona

Bernice Lott, Ph.D., Department of Psychology, University of Rhode Island, Kingston, Rhode Island

Diane Maluso, Ph.D., Department of Psychology and Department of Women's Studies, University of Hawaii at Manoa, Honolulu, Hawaii

Hazel Rose Markus, Ph.D., Department of Psychology, University of Michigan, Ann Arbor, Michigan

Chandra Reynolds, M.A., Department of Psychology, University of Southern California, Los Angeles, California

Robert J. Sternberg, Ph.D., Department of Psychology, Yale University, New Haven, Connecticut

Melanie R. Trost, Ph.D., Communication Department, Arizona State University, Tempe, Arizona

John E. Williams, Ph.D., Department of Psychology, Wake Forest University, Winston-Salem, North Carolina

Foreword

I wish I could say I have a completely dispassionate and solely scholarly interest in the questions addressed in this book. But I cannot. On the other hand, who can? Matters of gender concern everyone. Every aspect of an individual's life, including all those elements of the human condition associated with "life, liberty, and the pursuit of happiness," are deeply intertwined with questions of gender. Moreover, matters of gender actively engage virtually every issue of concern and controversy in the United States at this time, and those in many other societies across the planet as well.

As a consequence, I believe this book to be one of the most important I have read in the past decade, and, as editor of *Contemporary Psychology* during many of those years, I have read, sampled, or rifled through thousands of books believed to be of interest to scholars in psychology and thus worthy of review in the American Psychological Association's official book review journal. It is not that this book reveals the "truth" about gender. Rather, what makes this book important is that the tentative answers these leading scholars of the psychology of gender give to the questions they pose about gender phenomena will have a great deal of impact on a great many people and, eventually, on society itself.

Some of the research on gender is already beginning to enter the bloodstream of American society. Isolated driblets appear now and again in the media, and some of the available evidence is beginning to filter into judicial proceedings, including those of the Supreme Court (Fiske, Bersoff, Borgida, Deaux, & Heilman, 1991). Yet the findings and perspectives offered in this book cannot be said to be widely known. For one thing, most research on gender is of relatively recent vintage within psychology. For another, much of this research has been a by-product of wider, and more traditional, issues of concern to psychologists, not the central focus. What the contributors to this book do is extract and distill from their own larger areas of expertise that theory and research which bears either directly or indirectly on psychological questions of gender. The result, concentrated and contained within the covers of a single book, is powerful—some will even find it disturbing.

This text is especially likely to be unsettling for those to whom the findings of the psychology of gender are new. Such was the experience of the senior professor of mathematics at the University of Minnesota who asked to read one the chapters lying on my desk. Incredulous, her reaction to the research presented in the chapter was, "Why don't people know about this?" Perhaps now they will. Most of the information that is now available on the subject is represented here, all in one place. And, although the issues are complex, there is little in this book that is not accessible to the average person interested in the psychology of gender.

The distinction between biological sex and gender, often confused in the media and popular writings and even sometimes in professional discourse on "sex differences," is fundamental. As Lott and Maluso succinctly put it in Chapter 4, "Whereas sex denotes a limited set of innate structural and physiological characteristics related to reproduction, and divides animal species into female and male, gender is specific to humans and connotes all the complex attributes ascribed by culture(s) to human females and males, respectively" (p. 99). And, as Sternberg observes in his introductory chapter (Chapter 1), while everyone agrees that an individual's sex is biologically determined, "what is uncertain is whence came the similarities and differences we observe in male versus female emotions, motivations, thoughts, and behavior" (p. 2). Although their possible permutations are many, and the issues each joins are complex, the basic alternatives are obvious and just two in number: innately determined biological predispositions, on the one hand, and social environmental forces, on the other.

What several of the contributors to this book document is that the source of many of the similarities and differences we observe in male and female humans is not quite as much a matter for discussion as it once was, or as it was even just a few decades ago. With the advances that have been made in the psychology of social cognition and perception—the study of how the mind perceives and processes information about ourselves and other people—has come overwhelming evidence of the potency, and insidious subtlety, of the social–environmental forces associated with gender upon human behavior.

A person's sexual identity, male or female, is usually the first bit of information we notice about him or her, and that information is often received and begun to be mentally processed in the blink of an eye. As Cross and Markus discuss in Chapter 3, an individual's sexual identity is a primary category of human social perception. Thus, we usually notice that the stranger is male or female in the first microseconds of our encounter. Sometimes, when the image of the other on our retina has been so fleeting that we cannot even report exactly what it was that we saw, we still can report that we know the stranger is male or female. "How do you know?," the experimenter asks. "I just know," we say. "It's a gut feeling."

Not only does the mind sometimes see more than it can tell, it often makes much more of it than we know. Knowledge of another's biological sexual identity is the master key that immediately unlocks a trove of other information about that person, a vast array of beliefs about that person's nature along almost every dimension on which a human can be placed. With lightening speed, and as a result of mental processes that are not directly accessible to us through introspection and conscious reflection—and of which, as a consequence, we are frequently unaware—we are ready to act appropriately toward the person if action should be required to protect our interests and well-being. In the service of survival, the efficiency of the human's mental equipment for preparing us to act quickly in response to others of the species has been honed to staggering proportions over evolutionary time.

Everyone agrees that an individual's sex is biologically determined. And most everyone familiar with the evidence agrees that in many cultures, and certainly in current American culture, many important human attributes are consistently and differentially ascribed to males and females. Ours, in other words, is not a "gender-free" society. However, what makes the study of gender both controversial and of consequence is not that the attributes of men and women are widely believed to be different; rather, it is because these different attributes are differentially valued. Most of the attributes ascribed to males are those that society, both its male and female members, often regard as better, superior, or more admirable for a human being to possess than are the qualities typically ascribed to females. Thus, not only is our society not gender-free, gender in our society is neither value-free nor value-equal.

It follows, but perhaps it should be spelled out, that the qualities associated with the male of the species are not only widely regarded as more desirable qualities for a human to have, but they also are the very qualities that, most people would agree, are especially desirable for persons in positions of responsibility in a society to possess. "Competent," "logical," and "rational"—it is people who possess qualities such as these to whom we are willing to entrust our fate and award our esteem. Thus, the human attributes differentially associated with gender systematically, some would say relentlessly, correspond to those generally regarded as prerequisites for occupying positions of power and status in society. Therein lies the rub of gender, and the reason why this book, which presents what psychologists know, think they know, and what they suspect about gender, is not destined for a dusty shelf in the back bins of the library.

While agreeing that the human qualities associated with males and females are differentially valued, some have argued that the size of the value differential inherent in the social construction of gender is not great and, thus, it is without practical consequence. "Women are, after all, highly valued," the argument goes, "though perhaps not always valued quite as highly as males overall." The evidence, however, suggests that the negative—or "less positive," if one prefers—value placed on the qualities ascribed to females may have serious consequences, not simply for women, but for all members of a society.

To take an example far enough away from home so as to not immediately stir up the controversies simmering in our own country, consider the consequences of the value differential for China. In 1992, an item out of the Associated Press's Beijing bureau was headlined "China Drafts Measure Declaring Women Are Equal to Men." That was about it. No enforcement mechanisms, no explanation, just "men and women are equal" from now on. The government's admission that sex discrimination exists in China was unusual because the Chinese government has long regarded sex discrimination as a capitalist problem, the article said, and went on to speculate that the proclamation may have been made in response to Western criticism of human rights problems in China. My guess, however, is that the government might have had something of much greater consequence for China's future in mind. In 1990, Reuters News Service released the astonishing report that currently there were 689 single men for every 100 single women in China! A sex ratio of 689 (expressed as the number of men per 100 women, with a sex ratio of 100 being balanced) is extraordinary (see Guttentag & Secord, 1983). One suspects, in fact, that such a sex ratio has never before in human history characterized such a large collective—1.1 billion people, the most populous society the world has ever seen. It seems likely that centuries of Chinese custom, predicated on the belief that females are inferior in quality to males, has collided with the government's recent "one child per set of parents" rule and with advances in medical technology to produce an unprecedented degree of selective abortion and female infanticide.

China thus appears to have stumbled into a social experiment of brave new world proportions. The family in China is the foundation of that society, just as it is in our own and most other societies. But now, if the sex ratio is strongly imbalanced (it is difficult to know what the true figures are for *The New York Times* ["China's Crackdown," 1993] recently reported that "Ms. Peng refused to release the sex ratio" from the 1992 census), many men will not be able to marry, to have children, and to establish a family of their own within the current social order and tradition. One does not need a Ph.D. in social psychology to predict that some changes in China's social structure are on the horizon. In addition to a social experiment, the present situation also represents a colossal biological experiment, for as Charles Darwin (1952) noted a long time ago, in matters of human mating and reproduction "It is not the weal or woe of any one individual, but that of the human race to come, which is here at stake" (p. 578).

If the Chinese government believes it can erase the negative value their society places on females by a simple declaration that men and women are equal, it is in for a nasty surprise. The government of the United States made its own declaration almost 30 years ago in Title VII of the 1964 Civil Rights Act banning sex discrimination in the public sector. But unlike the Chinese government, whose proclamation of equality was made deliberately and, it would seem, with specific aims in mind, our own declaration appears to have been made without much forethought. Some say it even came about accidentally—the work of a machiavellian legislator who balked at the idea of racial equality and sneaked the word "sex" into the Civil Rights Act at the last minute to guarantee its defeat in Congress. Whether or not this story is apocryphal, it is clear that few people foresaw its consequences for American society and its institutions, especially the family.

The deterioration of the family is often regarded as the root of every social problem currently confronting American society. Throughout the tangled skein of forces that have acted and interacted over the past 30 years to produce our present societal ills, including the plight of American children, questions, suspicions, and assertions about sex differences in behavior and about gender thread through like a bright red ribbon. It is not surprising, then, that many look to psychology—the core of the social, behavioral, and biological sciences—for some clear answers to the confusing questions in which gender is importantly implicated. Thus it also should not be surprising to gender scholars if even their tentative answers to the question "whence came the differences?" are used—and misused—for purposes far afield of those typical of most academic exercises.

The contributors to this volume largely step around the social controversies that surround their subject matter. It is safe to say, however, that none is ignorant of them or unmindful of the implications of the hypotheses they entertain. If, for example, the differences we see in the behavior of men and women primarily have their source in genetically programmed differences associated with biological sex, then declarations of equality—at least equality on the dimensions currently associated with positions of status and power in human society—are swimming upstream against a strong biological current. Even if we could magically create a gender-free social world, newly born males and females would soon exhibit the behavioral sex differences we currently see, if the biological hypothesis is correct.

Shorn of its elaborations and stated baldly, this is the argument of sociobiology, "the systematic study of the biological bases of all social behaviors" (Crawford, Smith, & Krebs, 1987). As this characterization suggests, sociobiological studies of the biological bases of social behavior begin with the assumption that all social behavior does have a biological base and, thus, it is the job of the sociobiologist to guess just what that biological base might be. The result has been that there appear to be very few, if any, sex differences in social behavior that the creative mind of some sociobiologist somewhere has not attributed to the evolutionary forces of natural and sexual selection operating differentially on male and female humans. Unfortunately for sociobiologists, however, Mother Nature did not videotape the evolution of the human species for our analysis—which leaves a great deal of current sociobiological discourse about the genesis of sex differences in behavior on a par with science fiction.

Although often as entertaining as science fiction, some sociobiological treatises on the genesis of sex differences in behavior are not as innocuous. Biological determinism is sometimes used both as an explanation and as a justification for the current status and power differences between men and women. Sociobiology, in fact, has earned its reputation for being the psychology of sex, violence, and oppression (see Scarr, 1989), with the presumed differential biological bases of behavior being both the reason ("it's only natural") and the excuse ("they can't help it") for male domination and violence toward women.

The zeal with which some male sociobiologists have pursued their thesis in the area of sex differences in social behavior has raised the issue of bias in scholars' study of gender. Although scientists "have promoted the presentation of themselves as antiseptic drones, whose work is uncorrupted by influences [that] . . . muddy life for the rest of us," as *Time's* essayist Overbye (1993) observes, "science is done by real people who do not check their humanity at the lab door." The classic textbook illustration of that assertion in contemporary psychology is provided by the study of gender. For example, Beall (Chapter 5) argues convincingly that "contemporary psychology engages in the construction of gender through the questions that are researched, the kinds of research that get published, the types of experimental designs that are used, and the gender of the subjects who are studied" (p. 143), with the higher value attached to males manifesting itself in all of these activities. Had she wished, Beall could have documented the same assertions for physics (as Capra, 1982, has done), medical science, or virtually any of the sciences populated largely by males, which is to say all of them. All are inadvertently—for one need assume no malice or even awareness of the effect, simply tunnel vision for the kinds of questions and possible answers that are important— engaged in the social construction of gender.

But that saw is now ripping both ways these days in the psychology of gender. Ex cathedra advocacy of the sociobiological argument, for example, is becoming matched in frequency by ex cathedra condemnation of it. Take, for example, a review of a popular sociobiological book on gender differences in mating behaviors that appeared in *Contemporary Psychology* in 1991. The overweening enthusiasm and shoddy scholarship with which the author weaved his sociobiological interpretation of behavioral differences between men and women caused the reviewer, a careful evolutionary and comparative scholar of impeccable credentials, to writhe in embarrassment (Dewsbury, 1991). In order to systematically critique the book, however, the reviewer had to tell the reader what it said, and to do that he quoted some of its egregiously specious passages. As editor, I placed this excellent and timely criticism of arguments that currently appear in popular writings, and in not a few university classrooms as well, toward the front of the journal where it was most likely to be read. The first objection came even before the review was published, from several women on the journal's production staff who wondered if it was wise to publish the review because it called attention to the book and its repugnant assertions, and its publication was followed by much the same protest from some women scholars. The assumption seemed to be that if socially irresponsible and personally odious sociobiological tracts running under cover of "science" are studiously ignored by serious evolutionary and gender scholars, they will disappear. Not likely; they delight and fuel the prejudices of too many.

Because sociobiology is in "bad odor" due to the excesses of some of its advocates, and because many psychologists find evolutionary theory a useful source of testable hypotheses (as Kenrick & Trost demonstrate in Chapter 6), attempts are currently being made to distance both sociobiology and behavior genetics from what is being called "evolutionary social psychology." Envisioned as a hybrid of evolutionary psychology and social psychology, Buss (1990) describes several "pitfalls" that must be avoided by practioners of evolutionary social psychology, specifically: "we must jettison notions of genetic determinism and behavioral unmodifiability, eliminate false dichotomies between 'genetic' and 'learned,' and place cross-cultural variability in a sensible theoretical context" (p. 265). Just as a rose by any other name would smell as sweet, one suspects that evolutionary social psychology itself will be casting about for another name if it is not successful in avoiding these familiar traps.

All of the current contributors do avoid these traps, including Best and Williams in Chapter 10 on cross-cultural perspectives of gender, and thus the extreme form of the sociobiological argument is not represented here. In fact, in his introductory chapter, Sternberg takes some pains to note that the questions posed by the current contributors about the sources of sex differences in behavior are sophisticated and complex; deceptively simple theories of biological determinism and methods that partition behavioral variance into a tidy "genetic" pile and an equally neat "learned" pile do not appear in this book. New readers in the psychology of gender might have been wondering why this disclaimer is pointedly made in the introductory chapter. The wariness of many behavioral scientists toward simplistic applications of sociobiology and behavior genetics to the origins of sex differences in behavior is the answer.

The current sophistication and complexity in current approaches to questions of gender has been forced, not by an intrinsic implausibility of the sociobiological argument—for it is plausible, although often too narrowly conceived even on its own grounds (e.g., see Brewer & Caporeal, 1990)—but rather by evidence that has substantially increased the plausibility of the argument that social–environmental forces are strong and pervasive contributors to sex differences in behavior. The social–environmental explanation for sex differences in behavior, again in bald and extreme form, is that if we took two genetically identical humans and tatooed the label "male" on the forehead of one and the label "female" on the other and then parachuted them into our society, each would soon start showing the usual differences in behavior even though there could be no biological basis for those differences. They would start showing these differences because no person is immune from the potent influence that gender beliefs and expectations exert on human behavior.

The evidence relevant to the social–environmental proposition, much of which is presented in the first section of this book, has several different levels of implication—for society, for psychology, and for the individual's own life and aims—and many readers will be absorbing the chapters on all three levels simultaneously. The pertinent societal issues will spring to mind with every turn of the page. At the same time, many psychologists will be thinking about the implications of the theory and research on gender for their own areas of inquiry.

For example, my own area of interest, interpersonal relationships, is saturated with differences between men and women in relationship behaviors. These differences are often attributed to personality differences between men and women, or to other stable dispositional differences, including possible physiological differences between men and women along such dimensions as autonomic reactivity. Many sex differences in relationship behavior, for example, are "explained" by the greater affiliative and nurturant predispositions of women and thus their greater sensitivity to interpersonal relationships and to the needs of others. But one clear implication of the evidence presented in this book is that many of these traditional sex differences in relationship behavior—especially within opposite-sex relationships—are not sex differences per se; rather, they may reflect status and power differences that are usually confused with sex. There is no body of evidence relevant to this proposition; the implications of the power and status differential between men and women have been drawn almost exclusively for the workplace or the schoolroom, not for close relationships which usually carry a presumption of the partners' approximate equality in power and status within the relationship. But too many of the known sex differences in relationship behavior, especially within marriage, appear to fit the power alternative far too well for this possibility not to be systematically examined by relationship scholars. To take just one example of many, consider Levenson and Gottman's (1986) findings that in discussions of conflict, the husbands' negative affect consists primarily of anger and contempt, while the wives' negative affect is overwhelmingly fear, sadness, and "whining." Are anger and contempt "masculine" emotions that society teaches males it is acceptable to display? Or are anger and contempt "power" emotions, more likely to be displayed by anyone, male or female, toward those of lesser power than they are to be expressed by those of lesser status toward their superiors? Both of these explanations derive from gender, but the causal dynamics of the behavioral difference are different, as would be their implications for marital intervention.

In addition to their implications for the study of human behavior, many readers will be thinking about the personal implications of the contents of these chapters, perhaps not with respect to themselves but rather those they love. For example, when I read Jacklin and Reynolds' chapter on the socialization of gender differences (Chapter 8), and Lott and Maluso's chapter about the social learning of gender (Chapter 4), both of which underscore how quickly and thoroughly gender permeates a child's mind, my thoughts turned to a spring afternoon 15 years ago when my niece returned home from kindergarten and proudly sang a song she had learned that day. The song—about how a sick little boy called the doctor, and *she* arrived with *her* black bag, from which *she* took *her* stethoscope and so forth—prompted my sister and me to marvel at the wonderul new world my niece would be living in, a world in which she would meet her destiny unfettered by the assumptions of gender. Our happy reveries were interrupted by the doorbell, which my niece ran to answer. When she returned, she looked very puzzled. "Someone wants Dr. Berscheid," she said. "Who's he?"

Geis's chapter, detailing how gender becomes a self-fulfilling prophecy (Chapter 2), will be stunning to many readers. It was to me. And it prompted an odd reaction. As I read this chapter, my thoughts turned again to my niece, now about to graduate from college and embark on her career. But when I put this chapter down, it was with the thought, voiced aloud, "I hope she never reads this!" An unworthy wish for an educator, but perhaps not quite as unreasonable as I first guiltily assumed. I feared my niece would find the evidence of how subtly the cards are stacked against her as persuasive as I did, and abandon her ambitions, much too fragilely held to withstand gratuitous assault. An individual's aspirations, psychologists know, are largely a multiplicative function of two quantities: the desirability of a goal and the probability of reaching it should the attempt be made. Because something multiplied by nothing equals nothing, even a very desirable goal will not be attempted unless there is a reasonable chance of achieving it.

What the reactions of young women to the Geis chapter will be, I do not know. But wondering about its impact, I realized for the first time that the rhetoric of equal opportunity—hollow though it may sometimes seem to many—also has served as a self-fulfilling prophecy. Although most young women are aware that men in this society currently enjoy far more power and status than women do, many of them, such as my niece and her friends, talk as though this difference is merely a remnant of conditions that prevailed in times past—not the present. Acting on that belief, they help make it come true. But, on the other hand of course, it is painful to see them blindsided and confused by the invisible treachery of gender, a treachery in which they themselves often become unwitting accomplices.

Few will leave this book thinking about issues of gender in quite the same way as they did before they picked it up. Many readers will find that most questions about gender are more complex than they thought. And most will leave it with a heightened appreciation of how difficult, perhaps impossible, it will be for researchers to clearly determine the extent to which, and how, biological predisposition and social influence contribute to each specific behavioral difference between males and females we currently see. Thus those of us who want answers now to many questions of gender may have a very long wait.

That being my personal conclusion, I left these perspectives on the psychology of gender, and the questions about the existence of biological predispositions, social environmental forces, and their interaction, thinking about Pascal's perspective on the question of the existence of God. If there isn't a God, Pascal argued, then it does not matter what we believe. But if there is a God, it does matter. Therefore, he concluded, we should believe that God exists, and act accordingly. Similarly, if the behavioral differences we currently observe between human males and females are the result of biologically based dispositions, then it does not matter if we adopt the belief that they are primarily the result of social–environmental forces because these biologically based differences will assert themselves even in a gender-free society. But if there are no biologically based sex differences in behavior—or, more likely, if these differences are limited both in number and magnitude—then it does very much matter that we believe that sex differences in behavior are the result of social environmental forces. Therefore, we should believe that the current social construction of gender is primarily responsible for the sex differences we see in behavior, and act accordingly to try to achieve a gender-free society.

But let the reader decide what now is a matter of evidence—and what must be left to faith, philosophy, and personal value—in the realm of gender.

REFERENCES

Brewer, M. B., & Caporael, L. R. (1990). Selfish genes vs. selfish people: Sociobiology as origin myth. *Motivation and Emotion, 14*, 237–243.

Buss, D. (1990). Evolutionary social psychology: Prospects and pitfalls. *Motivation and Emotion, 14*, 265–286.

Capra, F. (1982). *The turning point: Science, society and the rising culture.* New York: Simon & Shuster.

China's crackdown on births: A stunning, and harsh, success. (1993, April 25). *The New York Times*, p. 1.

Crawford, C., Smith, M., & Krebs, D. (Eds.). (1987). *Sociobiology and psychology: Ideas, issues, and applications.* Hillsdale, NJ: Erlbaum.

Darwin, C. (1952). The origin of species by means of natural selection. The descent of man and selection in relation to sex. In *Great books of the western world* (Vol. 49). Chicago: Encyclopedia Britannica.

Dewsbury, D. A. (1991). Monogamy and the "wimplification" of America. *Contemporary Psychology, 36*, 949–950.

Fiske, S. T., Bersoff, D. N., Borgida, E., Deaux, K., & Heilman, M. E. (1991). Social science research on trial: Use of sex stereotyping research on *Price Waterhouse v. Hopkins, American Psychologist, 46*, 1049–1060.

Gottman, J. M., & Levenson, R. (1986). Assessing the role of emotion in marriage. *Behavioral Assessment, 8*, 31–48.

Guttentag, M., & Secord, P. F. (1983). *Too many women: The sex ratio question.* Beverly Hills: Sage.

Overbye (1993, April 26). *Time.*

Scarr, S. (1989). Sociobiology: The psychology of sex, violence, and oppression? *Contemporary Psychology, 34*, 440–443.

ELLEN BERSCHEID
University of Minnesota
April, 1993

Preface

> The omnipresent process of sex, as it is woven into the whole
> texture of our man's or woman's body, is the pattern of all the
> process of our life.
>
> —HAVELOCK ELLIS (*The New Spirit*)

Havelock Ellis wrote these words during the last century. He was most
noted for his work on sexuality, but he clearly recognized the importance
of gender in society. Ellis was not the first to recognize this fact. People
throughout the ages have discussed the importance of gender and the
nature of gender differences. Gender is discussed in legal codes, in literature, and in religious texts. Gender has probably been discussed as long
as it has been around.

But why have people always been so interested in the nature of gender
and gender differences? Perhaps because there is no clear answer to most
of the questions we have about gender. Is gender a biological distinction
or is it just a social one? Does one's gender imply certain abilities or certain
deficits? These are the questions that have been debated throughout the
centuries and these questions still interest us today. These questions are
interesting from a scholarly point of view, but they are important because
the answers to them have tremendous social implications. The belief that
men and women are different has in the past led to differential treatment
of males and females, treatment that has sometimes been especially detrimental to women. As a result, few fields of study have such political
overtones as the study of gender.

Gender is also an interesting topic because it affects one's daily life.
We live in a society in which most people work, socialize, and become
intimate with the other gender. And yet, many people feel that the other
gender is somehow "different" and that "they" sometimes act in strange
and mysterious ways. Perhaps that is the reason there has been such an
explosion of self-help books that claim to give the reader an understanding
of the opposite sex. People want to know how they should relate to
members of the other gender, how they can become intimate with them,

and how they can speak the other gender's language. We have heard people
say: "Men/women are so strange. I just don't understand them sometimes."

It is for all these reasons that we edited this book. We have an
interest in understanding gender and in understanding the nature of gender
differences. We believe strongly that the questions that remain unan-
swered about the nature of gender are some of the most interesting questions about humanity. We also believe that the answers that people have
offered to these questions could have profound societal and personal
implications

In editing this book we did not give a preference to a certain point
of view or a certain approach to gender. We used the title "The Psychology
of Gender" with the goal of gathering numerous, different perspectives
on gender into one volume. Far too often, only one perspective is offered
in a book on gender and many worthwhile perspectives are never addressed. We invite you as the reader to evaluate these chapters and to
decide which perspective or perspectives you find the most compelling.

We believe the work represented in this book is some of the most
compelling on gender that is currently being done. The authors vary both
in how they view gender and in how they support their view. Some
authors discuss broad, sweeping theories of gender, whereas other authors
focus on a particular question that they have about gender. Some authors
approach the field with cross-cultural methodology, whereas other authors
approach gender within a particular social context. We believe that each
chapter in this book has something unique to offer.

The book begins with a Foreword by Ellen Berscheid. In the Foreword, Berscheid discusses her view of the field of gender. In Chapter 1,
Robert J. Sternberg suggests that the way investigators view gender depends on the kinds of questions they ask about it.

Part I of the book comprises three chapters that address how gender
affects our thoughts and behavior. In Chapter 2, Florence L. Geis discusses
how gender stereotypes can sometimes lead to self-fulfilling prophecies
whereby people confirm a gender stereotype that is detrimental to them.
Her work is particularly concerned with how self-fulfilling prophecies
operate in the workplace. In Chapter 3, Susan E. Cross and Hazel Rose
Markus discuss how one's knowledge about gender can influence the way
that people perceive the world and the way people feel about themselves.
In Chapter 4, Bernice Lott and Diane Maluso discuss how people learn
about gender and gender roles and how other people influence our
adult behavior.

Part II comprises three chapters that address broad theories of why
the two genders appear to be different. In Chapter 5, Anne E. Beall
discusses a social–constructionist account of gender and suggests that the
division of people into male and female is more of a perceptual and social

division than a practical one. In Chapter 6, Douglas T. Kenrick and Melanie R. Trost examine the nature of gender differences and suggest that many of these differences are due to evolutionary processes. In Chapter 7, Irene Fast discusses how people develop self-concepts that incorporate gender identities. She is particularly concerned with very early events in a child's life that influence one's identity as a man or a woman.

Part III comprises two chapters that address how gender operates in biological and cultural ways. In Chapter 8, Carol Nagy Jacklin and Chandra Reynolds discuss the ways that children become gendered, or rather, masculine and feminine. Jacklin and Reynolds review theories that attribute differences to biological or environmental components. They suggest that gender typing may potentially be due to both genetic and environmental components and that the child may actually control his or her identity development. In Chapter 9, Deborah L. Best and John E. Williams discuss their cross-cultural research on whether people in all countries share the same gender stereotypes and gender-role ideologies and whether most people incorporate these beliefs into their self-concepts. This chapter explicitly discusses how gender is perceived all over the world.

Finally, in Part IV, an overview, Mahzarin R. Banaji discusses her view of the field of gender and attempts to integrate all of the different perspectives on the psychology of gender into one framework.

The book as outlined is more than a description of different theories of gender. The authors have taken great pains to discuss the research that supports their view and the implications of a particular theory for the society at large. There are numerous ways that one can think about gender and these different views are collected within this volume. Each of these views suggests a different way of thinking about men and women and a different way of relating to them. You will find that there are many provocative questions and issues within each chapter.

This book is intended for anyone who has an interest in gender, regardless of that interest. The chapters cover a broad array of life stages and social contexts. The chapters discuss children, adults, work issues, romantic relationships, and many other topics, which we found fascinating to read. We hope you also find them fascinating.

REFERENCE

Ellis, H. (1890). *The new spirit*. London: Chiswick Press.

ANNE E. BEALL
ROBERT J. STERNBERG

Contents

THE PSYCHOLOGY OF GENDER

What Is the Relation of Gender to Biology and Environment?: An Evolutionary Model of How What You Answer Depends on Just What You Ask

ROBERT J. STERNBERG

Few truisms are more obvious than that the answer one gives to a question depends on just what the question is. What may be somewhat less obvious is how differences in answers to psychological questions may only appear to be contradictory when in fact they are not strictly comparable because they are answers to differently framed questions. In this introductory chapter, I consider how answers to the question of the relation of gender to biology and environment, discussed either explicitly or implicitly in all of the chapters of this book, depend in large part on how the question is framed. I argue that the question of the relation between gender and biology and environment has gone through five rough "stages." The stages are rough in the sense that they represent a loose rather than a strict chronological progression. Progress through the stages has not always been in the forward direction. A given theorist may alternate among framings of a question, even within a single work. Moreover, earlier levels are not "bad" in any sense. Rather, they represent simpler framings of a question. One could argue as to how complexly questions of gender should be framed.

What do I mean by the "framing of a question?" I mean that different versions of what superficially might sound like the same question reveal themselves at a deeper level to be different questions. How we frame questions about the relation between gender and other things may largely determine how we answer questions about this relation.

The proposed model has five levels, which I consider in turn. The successive levels represent successively more complex framings of the question of the relation between a psychological construct, such as gender, and the dual influences of biology and environment. The model is shown in Figure 1.1. In illustrating the model, I quote from chapters of this book. These quotes are illustrative of formulations at each level but do not necessarily indicate that the authors of the quoted chapters hold general views at that level. Indeed, a given investigation may formulate questions at different times at different levels. The levels here apply to forms of questioning, not to people.

In discussing the model, I need to define what I mean by its terms. I use the term *gender*, as do the chapter authors, to refer to conceptions of socially defined sex roles. Thus, everyone agrees that sex is biologically determined. What is uncertain is whence came the similarities and differences we observe in male versus female emotions, motivations, thoughts, and behavior. Although there are both similarities and differences across genders, I focus on differences here. The term *biology* refers to sources of variation that are genetically preprogrammed. Their effects are determined at the moment of conception, although it may take any amount of time for these effects to manifest themselves and play themselves out. The term *environment* refers to the physical as well as the social–cultural milieu in which a person lives. Such effects start to be seen primarily after birth, although even *in utero* they may start to be felt through the mother's nutrition, exposure to environmental hazards, and the like. By *interaction*, I mean the effects that result from the interplay between biology and the environment. If exposure of the fetus to radiation results in genetic damage *in utero*, for example, such an effect would be due to the interaction of biology and environment.

Consider now four levels of questioning about the relation of gender to biology and environment.

Level 1: Are gender differences due to biology or to environment?

In Level 1, the relation between gender on the one hand and biology and environment on the other is seen as an either–or question. For example, Cross and Markus (Chapter 3, this volume) state:

> [B]iological sex dictates one's role in reproduction, but the conceptions of gender held by one's significant sociocultural contexts influence everything

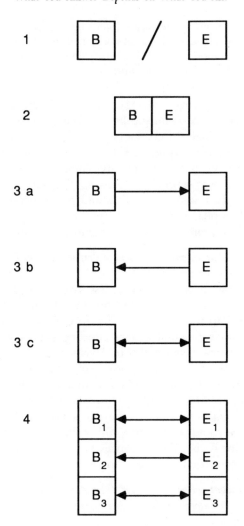

FIGURE 1.1. A model of the evolution of the framing of questions about the relation of gender to biology and environment. In Level 1, gender is believed to be due to biology or environment—the question is, Which? In Level 2, gender is believed to be due to biology and environment—the question is, How much is it due to each? In Level 3, gender is believed to be due to interaction between biology and environment, and it is realized that main effects are virtually inseparable from the interaction—the question is, In what direction(s) does the interaction proceed? In Level 4, gender is believed to be due to biology–environment interactions, but it is realized that the nature of the interaction varies over time and space—the question is, What are the mechanisms that lead to both interaction and its spatiotemporal variation?

else—from one's name to one's occupation, choices, preferences, and aspirations. Beliefs about gender are based not in biological reality but instead in
a pervasive and complex belief system that "little boys" and "little girls" (as
the nursery rhyme goes) are made of fundamentally different essences. (p. 56)

This statement represents a biology versus environment formulation of
gender. In this view, sex is biologically determined, whereas gender beliefs
are based not on biological facts but on sociocultural factors. Others, cited
by Lott and Maluso (Chapter 4, this volume), view aspects of gender
beliefs and practices as biologically determined (e.g., toy preferences).
The environment may amplify preexisting biological tendencies, but in
doing so it is only reinforcing beliefs and preferences that are already
there. Again, I emphasize that Level 1 conceptualizations are not "right"
or "wrong." They represent a way of framing a question.

*Level 2: To what extent are gender differences due to biology and to what
extent are they due to environment?*

In Level 2, the theorist takes the view that gender differences are due
in part to biology and in part to environment. The question then becomes
one of the extent to which they are due to each. One might list sets of
biological and environmental factors affecting gender and compare the
numbers of each and their weights in development. When Fast (Chapter
7, this volume) refers to "Stoller's (1968) explorations of the relative importance of internal (libido) forces and environmental factors in the developmental sequence Freud proposed" (p. 176), the stage is set for a partitioning
of factors according to whether they are biological or environmental. Or
as Jacklin and Reynolds (Chapter 8, this volume) note, "The behavioral
genetic viewpoint is that the influences on behavior can be classified as
genetic or environmental in nature" (p. 203).

*Level 3: To what extent are gender differences due to biology, to what extent
are they due to environment, and to what extent are they due to the interaction
between the two?*

In Level 3, the concept of interaction is introduced. Thus, it is recognized that there is some dynamism in the relation between biology and
environment. Enlightened behavioral–genetic studies of the kind reviewed
by Jacklin and Reynolds may recognize the existence of interaction between heredity and environment: For example, if parents of identical twins
treat their twins more alike than do parents of nonidentical twins, heredity
and environment are interacting. In this example, a biological factor increases environmental similarity. Freud's views, discussed by Fast, also
show how biology can affect environment: According to Freud, the presence of the penis in the boy and its absence in the girl lead to very different
experiencing of the environment and to the development of different gender conceptions.

As noted by Kenrick and Trost (Chapter 6, this volume), interactions between biology and environment can go in both directions:

> Cultural customs . . . can exaggerate [genetic] predispositions, they can act against them, or they can be irrelevant. If the members of a culture set up training experiences for athletics, martial arts, and military training that excludes females, the inherent sex differences will be exaggerated. (p. 165)

In this case, biology affects culture. However, if men are sent off to war and many of them are killed and thereby prevented from reproducing, culture will be affecting biology.

These examples make clear the extent to which the nature of the interaction is culturally modifiable, if not fully controllable. As noted by Geis (Chapter 2, this volume):

> [B]iological factors may well predispose men and women to different behavior, but the elaborate human cognitive system, with its attunements to learning, social expectations, and role models, and its susceptibility to biases and foibles, heavily influences biological predispositions and frequently overrides them. (p. 36)

Level 4: To what extent are gender differences due to biology, to what extent to environment, and to what extent interaction between the two, as a function of time and place?

Finally, in Level 4 we recognize that it is not possible to assign fixed universal percentages of variation to the effects of biology and culture, because their effects vary over time and place. As Beall (Chapter 5, this volume) notes, "A particular culture's experiences of the world . . . is not the only experience that a person can have of the world" (p. 128). Best and Williams (Chapter 9, this volume) give numerous examples of how biology and environment might *interact differentially* across cultures. Indeed, an analysis of sex-role ideologies led them to conclude that cultural effects were greater than were gender effects. If one culture, for example, sends all its ablest young men off to war and another instead sends both men and women not selected for warring ability, the cultural custom of warring will have differential effects on who is left to spread his/her genes to the next generation. Best and Williams give examples of cultures in which both men and women act aggressively, neither does, primarily men do, or primarily women do. Unless one postulates different genetic levels of aggression across cultures, which seems unlikely, culture is operating to channel biological drives in different ways in the different cultures.

I believe, then, that as we pose the question of the relation between biology and environment in increasingly complex ways, our answers become increasingly sophisticated and removed from the idea that there is "an answer" to the question of how gender is influenced by biology and environment. The recognition that there will be no single quantitative apportioning of variance leads us to ask more productive further questions, in particular, about the *mechanisms* underlying the interaction between biology and environment on gender views.

The model of levels that I have discussed is applied here to views on gender, but the same kind of model applies equally well to other constructs, such as personality or intelligence. Although the study of gender is relatively newer than the study of personality or of intelligence, in one respect, at least, it seems to have moved beyond those fields. We do not see in this book the kinds of absolutist attempts to partition variance that we still see in those literatures. None of the contributors to this book has set as a research goal to calculate h^2 (proportion of variation due to heredity) as though it were a fixed, forever unchanging number waiting to be discovered.

GENDER IN THOUGHT AND ACTION

Self-Fulfilling Prophecies: A Social Psychological View of Gender

FLORENCE L. GEIS

Gertie Go-Getter felt elated. She had just been promoted to manager of her company's Customer Liaison Department. Anticipating the increased autonomy, she relished the chance to develop and pursue her own ideas. Unfortunately, the same could not be said for Tim Typical, the manager of Public Relations and Gertie's immediate supervisor. Tim had opposed Gertie's promotion. Customer Liaison was in the doldrums, making his whole department look bad. Tim knew just what was needed—a "bright, aggressive young man" who would step in, take over, and *do* something. Somehow, Gertie just didn't fit this image. Tim was no bigot though. He would be the first to tell you (if you asked him) that he had always believed women were as competent as men; he just couldn't see Gertie taking the *initiative*. Resigned, Tim resolved to help Gertie as much as he could. So in the months that followed, he constantly supplied her with projects to work on—thus leaving her no time to develop any of her own initiatives.

This is a self-fulfilling prophecy—an initially false belief that itself causes the very behavior that makes it come true. Believing Gertie lacked initiative, Tim kept her busy with his projects, thereby preventing her from displaying the initiative she actually possessed, and thus seemingly confirming his initially mistaken belief. Social psychology studies the mutual influence between one individual and another, or others. For clarity, the person whose behavior is the focus of interest is called the actor; the other is called the perceiver, observer, or evaluator. Actually, of course, both parties in an interaction are simultaneously actors and perceivers, of themselves as well as of each other. In the Gertie and Tim example, Gertie was the actor and Tim the perceiver.

"Gender" is socially defined masculinity and femininity. Social psychology studies how gender is defined, created, and maintained through social influence, especially in the course of social interaction (Deaux & Major, 1987; Henley & Freeman, 1989; Maccoby, 1990; West & Zimmerman, 1987). It analyzes the present, immediate determinants of behavior—the beliefs, expectations, goals, thought processes, and actions of the perceiver and actor; the demands, opportunities, and informational cues of the situation; and how these factors influence each other. In this view, "sex" is biological—being male or female—but gender is a social construction (Hare-Mustin & Marecek, 1988; Lorber & Farrell, 1991; Unger, 1989; Weisstein, 1968; Wittig, 1985). Obviously, not all behavior is influenced by gender. This chapter focuses on the factors involved when it is. Finally, although social learning theory is part of this perspective, it is covered in a separate chapter, so this one focuses on the social cognition and role theory contributions of social psychology.

The self-fulfilling prophecy (James, 1916; Merton, 1948) consists of two basic elements (see Figure 2.1). One is a mental or cognitive element consisting of knowledge, beliefs, expectations, feelings, attitudes, intentions, goals, and values. The other consists of overt, observable behavior—including actions, words, pictures, facial expressions, and body language. The main idea of the self-fulfilling prophecy is that beliefs cause behaviors *and* behaviors cause beliefs, as represented by the causal arrows

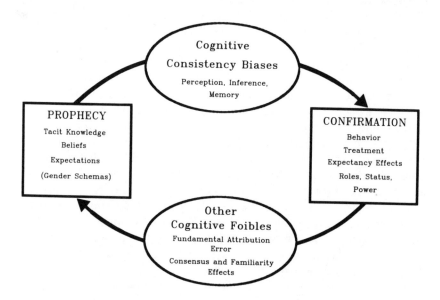

FIGURE 2.1. The self-fulfilling prophecy of gender beliefs and behavior.

in Figure 2.1. Specifically, stereotypical beliefs about men and women cause biased perceptions and discriminatory treatment of them, including discriminatory role and status assignments, and the resulting sex differences in behavior and achievement then seemingly confirm that the initial expectations were true. Thus, this perspective can also be called expectancy-role theory. The forces that keep this self-perpetuating system going are social and mental processes called consistency biases and other cognitive foibles. This chapter describes the self-fulfilling prophecy of Figure 2.1, focusing in turn on the causal elements of gender beliefs, cognitive consistency biases, both perceivers' and actors' behavior, including the influence of roles and status, and finally some additional cognitive foibles that transform behavior observations into gender stereotypes to complete the cycle.

GENDER BELIEFS: CONSCIOUS AND UNCONSCIOUS

The first important point to grasp is that for most educated people, conscious and unconscious gender beliefs do not match. Prejudice and stereotypes are socially undesirable, so when our mind is focused on the topic, conscious beliefs are egalitarian (Duncan, 1982; McBroom, 1984). In contrast, when our attention is focused on other matters, as it is virtually all of the time, our general store of knowledge about the world shapes and guides our perceptions and actions automatically and without our awareness (Devine, 1989; Wilson, 1985). Everyone's knowledge about the world includes all of the old gender stereotypes as tacit or implicit beliefs. The stereotypes include personality traits, role behavior, physical appearance, and occupations (Ashmore & Del Boca, 1979; Deaux & Lewis, 1984). They described men as dominant, rational, objective, independent, decisive, competitive, aggressive, capable of leadership, good at science and mathematics, and interested in business, sports, and politics. They described women as submissive, deferent (toward men), emotional, subjective, gullible, dependent, sensitive to others, caring, nurturant, able to devote themselves to others, and good at domestic tasks and childrearing (Bem, 1974; Bergen & Williams, 1991; Spence & Helmreich, 1978; Williams & Best, 1982).

Most important, and contrary to fact, both sexes were considered peculiarly deficient in the characteristic traits of the other sex (Foushee, Helmreich, & Spence, 1979). Thus the stereotypes portrayed women as valuable to men for sex and domestic service but less competent than men and unsuited for authority or leadership (Bass, Krusell, & Alexander, 1971; Deaux & Lewis, 1984; Schein, 1973, 1975; Spence, Helmreich, & Stapp, 1975).

Like our knowledge in other domains, gender stereotypes are organized together in our mind into mental structures called schemas (Taylor & Crocker, 1981). A schema is an organized body of knowledge about a concept or category containing all of its attributes and the relations among the attributes. For example, one's schema for fast-food restaurants might include the attributes of "fast counter service," "limited menu," "food served in plastic containers," and so on. Similarly, most people's schema for women includes all of the feminine stereotypes. Because the category label and all of the attributes are associated with each other, as soon as someone is recognized as a woman, all of the stereotypes are also activated (Deaux & Lewis, 1984; Kessler & McKenna, 1978). Most important, although our conscious attitudes tend to be abstract principles, our gender schema includes scripts for specific situations. As a result, behavior only sometimes follows conscious beliefs, but reliably reflects activated schemas.

Although we disavow gender stereotypes, they influence our self-concepts. According to social identity theory (Hogg & Abrams, 1988; Tajfel, 1981) much of one's personal identity is derived from such social group memberships as one's nationality, ethnicity, religion, and occupation—as well as from one's sex. We adopt and internalize the norms, values, and attributes of our groups. Gender identity theory (Spence, 1985) proposes that because sex and gender distinctions are central, important, and pervasive in our culture, gender is the earliest, most central and most organizing component of everyone's self-concept. Thus, both perceivers and actors bring gender-coded expectations for themselves and their partners into their interactions, although the gender distinction is stronger for some individuals than for others (Bem, 1985).

THE COGNITIVE CONSISTENCY BIASES: FROM BELIEFS TO BEHAVIOR

These unacknowledged gender stereotypes unconsciously influence our perceptions, inferences, and memory of women and men. In general, they enhance perceptions, interpretations, and memories that are consistent with stereotypical attributes and obscure, diffuse, or cause us to disregard or forget information that is inconsistent with them (Broadbent, 1973; White & Carlston, 1983; Zadney & Gerard, 1974). Thus, even when women and men behave alike, we see them as different.

Perceptual Bias: When Believing Is Seeing

In the example of Tim and Gertie, it was Gertie's actual behavior that confirmed Tim's expectations about her. However, self-fulfilling prophecies can also occur entirely in the mind of the perceiver (Ickes, Patterson, Rajecki, & Tanford, 1982). If Gertie had presented some ideas to Tim, he might have failed to "hear" or recognize them, or might have discounted them as irrelevant or inadequate. Thus, in Tim's mind, his expectations would still have been confirmed, in spite of Gertie's actually disconfirming behavior. This distortion of reality is called perceptual bias, although actually it also involves interpretation or inference.

The idea of perceptual bias is difficult to accept. Like Tim, we all think that what we see or hear is what is actually out there. Our experience is that our perceptions are accurate representations of external reality. But in fact, perceptions are constructed by the brain. They are representations of reality *as it is interpreted* by our relevant prior knowledge (Taylor & Crocker, 1981). It is this interpretation that identifies and gives meaning to the perception. The interpretation occurs rapidly, automatically, and unconsciously in neural processing (Rock, 1983). Although much of our world knowledge can be made conscious when we focus on it, its *use* in interpretation is unconscious. By the time we are aware of a perception, it has already been categorized and interpreted (Bodenhausen, 1990; Erber & Fiske, 1984; Watkins & Peynircioglu, 1984; Winter & Uleman, 1984).

Now recall that the gender stereotypes are part of everyone's knowledge about the world. It is this implicit knowledge, reflecting cultural assumptions, not our conscious beliefs, that interprets events in our daily life (Basow, 1986; Hunt, 1987; Miller, 1984; Wilson, 1985). This implicit knowledge operates as an expectation (Jones & McGillis, 1976). In addition to shaping interpretations, expectations also cause selective perception. We are more likely to see what we expect to see, sometimes even if it is not actually there, and not see or reinterpret what we do not expect, sometimes even if it is there (Bodenhausen, 1988; Darley & Gross, 1983; Hirt, 1990; Stangor, 1988; Zadney & Gerard, 1974). Although Tim consciously believed women were competent, the stereotype that they lack initiative could have caused him not to notice or recognize Gertie's actual initiatives, even if she had found time to develop some and present them to him.

Which schema will be used in a situation depends on perceivers' previous experience. More frequently and recently used schemas are primed, and thus more likely to be activated (Bargh & Pietromonaco, 1982; Higgins, Rholes, & Jones, 1977). Because sex and gender distinctions are so pervasive in society, our gender schemas are chronically primed (Higgins, King, & Mavin, 1982; Spence, 1985). Actors' sex is the first and most automatically recognized information about them (Brewer, 1988; Grady, 1979; Kessler & McKenna, 1978; Klatzky, Martin, & Kane, 1982). Further, frequently practiced inferences like the person–gender association become even faster and more automatic (Smith, 1984, 1989). These "proceduralized" inferences then preempt other more reasonable bases of judgment (Zarate & Smith, 1990).

For example, Fidell (1970) sent resumé summaries of eight psychologists to psychology department chairpersons across the country asking the academic rank at which each should be considered for hiring. Each resumé bore a man's name for some evaluators but a woman's for others. The average rank suggested for the resumés when they were identified as a woman's was assistant professor, the entry-level rank in academia. However, the identical evidence attributed to a man elicited recommendations of associate professor, a higher rank usually associated with the job security of tenure and always associated with a higher salary. The department chairs were not intentionally discriminating against women. Rather, their implicit gender stereotypes caused them to actually "see" the evidence differently, depending on the sex of the person described. Similarly, evaluators rate men's applications for professional and managerial positions higher than identical applications from women (Gutek & Stevens, 1979; Rosen, Jerdee, & Prestwick, 1975).

Implicit beliefs interpret perceptions of males and females from the moment they are born. Newborn sons were judged as larger, stronger, firmer, and more alert by their parents than were newborn daughters, even though objective measurements revealed no differences between the infants (Rubin, Provenzano, & Luria, 1974). In elementary school, teachers see boys as more prominent than girls (Ben Tsvi-Mayer, Hertz-Lazarowitz, & Safir, 1989). A man at the head of the table in a mixed-sex group is seen as the leader of the group, but not a woman (Porter & Geis, 1981). Men's leadership is judged better than identical leadership by women (Bartol & Butterfield, 1976; Dobbins, Stuart, Pence, & Sgro, 1985). A woman who performs well on an intellectual task is judged as less competent than a man performing at the same level (Deaux & Taynor, 1973; Vaughn & Wittig, 1981). Men's solutions to problems are seen as more logical (Taynor & Deaux, 1975) or acceptable (Sterling & Owen, 1982) than the identical solutions by women. Women who succeed academically or in high-status careers are seen as less successful in romance and marriage, and when careers conflict with domestic responsibilities, the wife is expected to give up her career for child care or to move when her husband is transferred (Janman, 1989).

There are three qualifications to the perceptual devaluation of women. First, women are rated more competent than men for stereotypically "feminine" tasks, discussion topics (e.g., sewing or child care), or occupations (Etaugh & Riley, 1983). Second, pro-male bias can be overcome by external, authoritative validation of the woman's excellence (Brown & Geis, 1984; Pheterson, Kiesler, & Goldberg, 1971). Finally, the bias may be diminishing. The original study involved product evaluations. College students judged male authors' essays as more profound and persuasive and their authors as more prestigious than the identical essays attributed to female authors (Goldberg, 1968; Paludi & Strayer, 1985). In a review of such studies, Lott (1985) concluded that pro-male bias prevails, but a later review (Swim, Borgida, Maruyama, & Myers, 1989) found less bias. However, most of the later studies used evaluators with less status or expertise than the product authors. Obviously, in natural settings, evaluators have higher status and expertise than their subordinates, and it is precisely those with more status or expertise who are more likely to be biased (Fiske & Kinder, 1981; Ward, 1981).

Inference: Interpreting the Evidence

Inferences, like perceptions, make the evidence more consistent with prior beliefs, including gender beliefs. Because all perception involves interpretation, inference operates from the instant of preconscious perception (Klatzky et al., 1982). These inferences automatically fill in the gaps in the actual evidence and enable us to make sense of incoming information (Higgins & King, 1981; Uleman & Bargh, 1989). For example, consider a short story: "Mary heard the ice cream truck coming down the street. Remembering her birthday money, she ran into the house." As soon as you read the story you knew that Mary was a child, not an adult; that she was a girl, not a boy; and you probably imagined her running up the front walk and in through the door rather than taking off across the lawn and crashing into the side of the house—even though none of these facts was included in the actual evidence. Similarly, as soon as one knows a person's sex, one's mind automatically interprets all of the information about the person in terms of gender stereotypes, as illustrated by the perceptual bias studies discussed earlier. Because the stereotypes operate preconsciously, we are unaware of their influence. Instead, we attribute our perceptions and judgments to other socially plausible factors in the evidence (Nisbett & Wilson, 1977).

Stereotypes also shape inferences at a later, more conscious stage of information processing. Attribution is how we explain the causes of people's behavior. Because of intelligence and competence stereotypes, attributions for success and failure at intellectual tasks depend on whether the actor is a woman or a man. People explain a man's success by attributing it to his ability, an internal, stable factor that is likely to continue into the future. However, the same success by a woman is more likely to be attributed to "luck," an external, unstable factor implying little likelihood of repeat performances (Deaux & Emswiller, 1974; Frieze, Fisher, Hanusa, McHugh, & Valle, 1978; Josefowitz, 1985, Offerman, 1986). One study (Feather & Simon, 1975) even found a woman's success in medical school attributed to cheating! Failures follow the opposite pattern. Men's failures are attributed to external factors but women's to lack of ability. Thus, men's successes are seen as indicative of future performance and their failures discounted as temporary, but women's successes are discounted and their failures interpreted as diagnostic. This means that a man will be seen as more likely to succeed in the future than a woman with the identical record of previous successes and failures.

The same stereotypes lower women's self-confidence in their ability to succeed at intellectual or "masculine"-typed tasks, college courses, and occupations (Basow & Medcalf, 1988; Bridges, 1988; Erkut, 1983; Lippa & Beauvais, 1983; Vollmer, 1984, 1986), and lower self-confidence diminishes performance (Lenney & Gold, 1982). Note the self-fulfilling prophecies: Because of the biased attributions, employers are less likely to hire or promote women. Then, because people believe that decisions are fair (Baron & Hershey, 1988), women's lesser success seemingly confirms the initial stereotypes. The double whammy is that the same beliefs lower women's self-confidence, causing actually poorer performance and giving the stereotypes a grain of truth.

Blaming the Victim

The consistency bias may account for another prevalent attribution—blaming the victim, especially when the victim is a woman (Howard, 1984). Women tend to blame themselves when something goes wrong—in a personal relationship, marriage, or at work. Men tend to blame someone or something else (Bar Tal & Frieze, 1977). When a woman is raped, beaten, or sexually harassed, the popular first inference is that somehow "she asked for it." It was she who caused the man's behavior, not he. The alternative inference, also victim blaming, is that she is lying or neurotic. Finally, until the 1970s, it was tacitly assumed that women did not make contributions in science, art, politics, or business because *they* lacked both interest and ability. All these victim-blaming attributions reflect implicit gender stereotypes.

Fighting the Bias

Although stereotypical inferences are unconscious and automatic, their influence on our final, conscious perceptions is not inevitable. Perception is a two- or three-stage process, proceeding from an earlier automatic and unconscious stage to a later more controlled and conscious product (Gilbert, Krull, & Malone, 1990; Quattrone, 1982; Trope, 1986). The early stage categorizes and identifies the target person ("It's a woman"; "It's Sally Sly") and characterizes her behavior on the basis of relevant schemas and situational cues ("What she's saying is trivial"). The later, more conscious stage revises and corrects the initial result in light of conscious information. At this later stage, perceivers may—or may not—revise their perceptions to correct the stereotypes' influence (Devine, 1989; Devine, Monteith, Zuwerink, & Elliot, 1991). Thus, educating people about the influence of stereotypes may help overcome them. Similarly, reminding people of their conscious gender beliefs produces perceptions and behavior more in line with those beliefs (Porter, Geis, Cooper, & Newman, 1985; Sherman, Ahlm, Berman, & Lynn, 1978; Snyder & Swann, 1976).

Remembering Consistencies and Forgetting Inconsistencies

Just as we are more likely to perceive and infer information consistent with the stereotypes, we are also more likely to remember it. First, we are more likely to remember our own inferences and labels ("male chauvinist," "team player") than the actual information (Fiske & Pavelchak, 1986). Second, we remember those parts of the information that are consistent with our schemas (Bodenhausen, 1988; Cohen, 1981). If Vera's letter of recommendation said she was a leader and Vernon's letter said the same about him, the employer would be more likely to remember Vernon's leadership and forget Vera's. Third, we sometimes "remember" attributes or behaviors implied by our schema even if they were not actually present (Bellezza & Bower, 1981; Cantor & Mischel, 1977). As we register information about a person, we encode the activated stereotypical attributes along with the actual information. The inferred and experienced elements are then stored together in the mind and become indistinguishable, so the inferred is "remembered" as experienced (Graesser & Nakamura, 1982; O'Sullivan & Durso, 1984).

The memory consistency bias has one possible qualification. People are more likely to remember information that is *in*consistent with schemas for traits known to vary from one person to another (e.g., schemas for extroversion or honesty) than they are to remember either schema-consistent or irrelevant information (Hastie, 1981). The inconsistency bias presumably reflects greater mental processing. If gender stereotypes become recognized as more variable, they could produce inconsistency biases. However, the memory advantage of inconsistent information decreases when the perceiver is cognitively busy, as in an ongoing social interaction (Gilbert, Pelham, & Krull, 1988). In addition, even when inconsistent information is well recalled, overall impressions, especially evaluations, can still remain consistent with the initial stereotypes (Dreben, Fiske, & Hastie, 1979; Erber & Fiske, 1984; Hastie & Kumar, 1979; Hemsley & Marmurek, 1982; Sherman & Gorkin, 1980).

BEHAVIOR: TREATMENT, CONFIRMATION, ROLES, AND STATUS

Although laboratory research (Maccoby & Jacklin, 1974) and elaborate statistical meta-analysis (Eagly, 1987; Hyde & Linn, 1986) can discern a few characteristics on which men and women actually differ in the stereotyped ways, the differences are few in number and small in size. However, the laboratory results do not mean that men and women do not behave differently in their daily lives. Stereotypical assumptions influence the behavior of both perceivers and actors, and sex differences in social roles and status are both cause and effect of the differential expectations.

Treating Women and Men Differently: The Perceiver's Behavior

Although most people believe that they treat men and women the same, in fact they often treat them differently. Gender-biased perceptions and inferences cause discriminatory behavior (Heilman & Guzzo, 1978), an extension of the consistency bias from perceivers' cognitions to their treatment of the actor. Because of his stereotypes, Tim Typical falsely perceived Gertie Go-Getter as lacking initiative. Thus, he treated her as if she had none. Needless to say, if Tim had been dealing with Gus rather than Gertie, his perception and treatment of his subordinate would have been different. The differential treatment begins early in life. Consistent with the stereotypes, males are treated as more important and more competent (Hansen & O'Leary, 1985; Lott, 1985; Pugh & Wahrman, 1983; Wallston & O'Leary, 1981). Discriminatory treatment advantaging males has been found in nursery schools (Fagot, 1984), elementary schools (Fagot & Hagan, 1985; Sadker & Sadker, 1985), and college classrooms (Basow & Silberg, 1987; Brooks, 1982; Hall & Sandler, 1982). At work, women, especially black women, are more likely to be targets of sexual harassment (Fitzgerald, Weitzman, Gold, & Ormerod, 1988; Gutek, 1985).

Differential treatment is rampant in group tasks and discussions. When researchers secretly gave a man the correct problem solution in advance, the group quickly accepted it and applauded his insight. But when the same solution was given to a woman, it was ignored or rejected (Altemeyer & Jones, 1974). In group discussions, women's contributions are interrupted, overlooked, ignored, or "unheard" (Bunker & Seashore, 1975). When women do offer leadership, others react negatively. Group members of both sexes responded to women leaders' contributions with fewer facial expressions of approval and more disapproval than to the same contributions from men leaders (Butler & Geis, 1990). These nonverbal signals could discourage and inhibit a potential woman leader. Students voted to exclude a competent woman from their group, preferring both a competent man and an incompetent woman (Hagen & Kahn, 1975). In a later replication (Deutsch & Leong, 1983), competent women were liked as much as competent men—except when the task was competitive. On a joint task, men distanced themselves from a woman partner by turning their face or body away from her, but did not distance themselves from male partners (Lott, 1987). In dividing tasks among themselves, both women and men assigned feminine tasks to women and masculine ones to men (Lewis, 1985).

Studies of organizations tell the same story of increasingly egalitarian conscious attitudes but continuing discriminatory treatment (Gribbons & Lohnes, 1982; Kahn & Crosby, 1987). In most organizations of all types, women are less likely to be hired for nontraditional jobs—including professional and managerial positions—than are men with identical qualifications (Cohen & Bunker, 1975; Futoran & Wyer, 1986; Glick, Zion, & Nelson, 1988; Olson & Frieze, 1987; Vetter, 1986). When women are hired, they receive a lower salary than equally qualified men doing the same job (Cannings, 1988; Nieva & Gutek, 1981; Olson & Frieze, 1987; Persell, 1983). On the job, women are given less support, authority, autonomy, credence, and resources (Helmreich, Spence, Beane, Lucker, & Matthews, 1980; Jacobs, 1989; Rosen & Jerdee, 1974). As both cause and result, they are rated lower on competence, effectiveness, knowledgeability, or managerial skill (Bartol & Butterfield, 1976; Frank, 1988; Gutek, 1985; Nieva & Gutek, 1981). Not surprisingly, women are less likely or slower to be promoted (Aisenberg & Harrington, 1988; Blau & Ferber, 1985), producing a "glass ceiling" on their advancement (Morrison, White, Van Velsor, & Center for Creative Leadership, 1987). In fact, in one field study, the women received higher performance evaluations but the men received more promotions (Gupta, Jenkins, & Beehr, 1983).

Most sex discrimination is probably unconscious and unintended. Evaluators can always find plausible facts to justify their decisions. However, the particular facts perceived as the reasons for the decision may not be those that actually caused it (Nisbett & Wilson, 1977; Quattrone & Tversky, 1984). Similarly, most women are well aware of discrimination against "women in general," but deny that they personally have experienced it (Crosby, 1982). Without a matched sample for comparison, discrimination is difficult to detect. Note the self-fulfilling prophecies. Because of the stereotypes, boys and men are treated as more important and more competent. They are given more help, opportunities, support, resources, autonomy, and promotions than are equally qualified girls and women. As a result of their social advantages, they "go further," thus seemingly confirming the initial stereotypes.

Expectancy Confirmation: The Actor's Behavior

Perceivers' stereotypes also influence actors' actual behavior. People tend to behave in accord with others' expectations, especially others such as teachers and supervisors who control their rewards (Jones & Jones, 1964), because perceivers' expectations lead them to treat the actor in a way that elicits the confirming behavior. This was the case with Tim and Gertie. Falsely expecting Gertie to lack initiative, Tim filled her hours with his projects. As a result, Gertie actually showed no initiative. Behavioral confirmation is well documented (Fazio, Effrein, & Falender, 1981; Kite & Deaux, 1986; Miller & Turnbull, 1986; Snyder, 1984; Word, Zanna, & Cooper, 1974).

A few studies have addressed gender-related expectations. One is that beautiful women are more warm, receptive, and sociable toward men than are unattractive women. Snyder, Tanke, and Berscheid (1977) falsely led some men to believe (from a fake photograph) that their female partner in a get-acquainted phone conversation was beautiful; the others that she was unattractive. Judges rated the conversations of women whose partner believed they were beautiful as warmer, more receptive, and sociable. The men's expectations led them to treat their partners in a way that caused the women to confirm the initially false beliefs. Here is a major basis for the grain of truth in stereotypes. If men treat beautiful women in a way that elicits warmth and sociability, then, over a lifetime of such experiences, beautiful women will indeed behave more warmly and sociably toward them. Once the process is set in motion, it is impossible to tell which comes first, the chicken or the egg, the stereotypical belief or the behavior that is both cause and effect of the belief.

Perceivers' expectations also work on men. Two men played a competitive game involving a "noise weapon." Before the game, one, the perceiver, was falsely informed that his opponent was very aggressive. Anticipating a heavy attack, he used the weapon liberally. His partner, the actor, then duly reciprocated. After several rounds, the perceiver was replaced by a third man. With a new partner who had never behaved aggressively, actors who had been led to attribute their game behavior to their disposition continued their heavy use of the weapon. The perceivers' expectations had made them actually aggressive (Snyder & Swann, 1978). Confirmation of dominance and ability stereotypes has also been documented. A college man and woman in different rooms used a signaling system to negotiate a division of labor on gender-typed tasks. Men who believed their partner was a woman assigned her more of the feminine tasks and were less yielding to her preferences than those who falsely believed they were dealing with a man. And women whose partners knew they were women chose more feminine tasks for themselves than those whose partners believed they were men (Skrypnek & Snyder, 1982). These studies suggest that at least some of the differences in men's and women's aggressiveness, dominance, and task choices are caused by the difference in expectations and treatment of them.

Actors' and perceivers' gender expectations, reinforced by differential treatment, can also explain other sex differences in behavior. For example, consistent with male dominance and competence expectations, men interrupt women more than women interrupt men. When women offer an idea, they are more likely to hesitate or apologize (Brooks, 1982; Zimmerman & West, 1975). Men make more task-oriented contributions and fewer socioemotional ones than women do (Yamada, Tjosvold, & Draguns, 1983). However, when groups falsely believed a woman had expertise, she offered more task contributions and fewer socioemotional ones (Wood & Karten, 1986), showing that these behaviors are the result of social expectations, not innate disposition. A patent example of confirming social expectations is that a wife with a full time job outside the home spends more time on housework than does her similarly employed husband (Hartmann, 1981).

When actors confirm others' false expectancies, they sometimes change their beliefs about themselves to be consistent with their behavior (Fazio et al., 1981; Snyder & Swann, 1978). As Mead (1934) and Lofland (1969) noted, people internalize definitions of themselves conveyed by others' attitudes toward them and treatment of them. The greater the consistency, clarity, and duration over time, and the greater the consensus among different interaction partners, the greater the internalization. Because compliance with gender expectations operates over our entire lifetime, even people who consciously reject gender stereotypes are influenced by them. Nonnormative expectancies are powerful but not inevitable (Swann, 1987). Actors can sometimes resist perceivers' expectations (Lewis, 1985) or even disconfirm them (Swann & Ely, 1984). However, gender expectations are normative, so violations may be punished. (See the "damned if she does, damned if she doesn't" dilemma described later.) In addition, gender expectations may be more difficult to disconfirm than other schemas because they are consensual in society (Swann, 1984).

Roles, Status, Power, and Gender Stereotypes

Gender expectations lead us to prefer men for authority positions and assign women to subordinate roles. In families, groups, and organizations throughout society, men have higher status than women (Betz & Fitzgerald, 1987; England, 1979; Kanter, 1977; Lovdal, 1989; Needleman & Nelson, 1988; Scanzoni, 1982). But status inequality is a cause of the stereotypes, as well as a result of them. Social roles, status, and power are important situational determinants of behavior.

Just as people behave according to others' expectations, they also behave according to the opportunities and requirements of their social and occupational roles (Sherif, 1979). Although people hope to choose roles compatible with their interests, roles shape personality more than personal dispositions influence how a given role will be played (Baumeister, Chesner, Senders, & Tice, 1988; Epstein, 1981; Kiotas, 1987; Kohn & Schooler, 1978; Lieberman, 1965; Taylor, 1983; Yount, 1986). People internalize the implications of their roles (Fazio et al., 1981; Lofland, 1969; Offerman, 1984). Here lies a major source of differences in behavior between men and women (Miller, 1986). High-status roles require dominance, intelligence, rationality, objectivity, initiative, leadership, and decision making (Secord, 1982). Note that these characteristics sound suspiciously similar to the masculine stereotypes. Because only men have been seen in authority roles, their behavioral requirements appear to us to be "characteristically masculine."

In contrast, subordinate roles offer little opportunity for these behaviors; instead, they require or encourage dependence (superiors control subordinates' salaries and work conditions, and subordinates must await their superiors' directions), accommodation, and deference to the superiors' decisions and time schedules; sensitivity to the superiors' needs, preferences, and idiosyncracies; and nurturance of them (Secord, 1982; Snodgrass, 1985, 1992). In the past, virtually all women were seen in subordinate roles. Thus, the behavioral requirements of subordinate roles came to be seen as "characteristically feminine" (cf. Rothbart, Fulero, Jensen, Howard, & Birrell, 1978; both Unger, 1976, 1978, and Henley, 1977, pointed out the status implications of behavioral sex differences).

Obviously, not all men hold authority positions. Most of them are subordinates because society offers few authority positions. The important distinction is that virtually all the authorities we see are men and virtually none are women. Note the self-fulfilling prophecies. Because women were assigned subordinate roles (and chose them because they were socially expected), they displayed the subordinate traits and not the authority traits, thereby defining the feminine stereotypes. As a result of the stereotypes (and their role behavior), women were seen as "naturally" suited only to subordinate positions, thus perpetuating the cycle. Similarly, because only men were assigned to high-status roles, those traits came to be viewed as masculine, and thus only men were considered suitable for authority positions.

Research supports this analysis. Geis, Brown, Jennings, and Corrado-Taylor (1984) had college students view two replicas of three television commercials featuring a a man and woman. One set of replicas duplicated the network versions with verbatim scripts portraying an implicit assumption that the man's preference was all that mattered; the woman's was never mentioned. The man was shown as the important person, the woman as bent only on serving his wishes. In the second set of replicas the same scripts were used, but the two actors reversed roles in the scenarios. Thus, in these reversed versions the woman was shown as the high-status partner in the relationship. Viewers described the men in the first set as "rational, independent, dominant, ambitious leaders" and the women as "emotional, dependent, submissive, contented followers." The traditional status inequality between the sexes produced the traditional masculine and feminine personality attributions. However, in the reversed-role versions, the personality descriptions also reversed. The masculine characteristics followed the high-status role, not the male actor, and the feminine ones followed the low-status role. Similarly, attributions of influenceability followed low-status role occupants regardless of their sex (Eagly & Wood, 1982).

Status in a relationship determines not only the actors' perceived trait, but also the display of them. Women's deference, smiling, being interrupted, and occupying little space with their body define them as lower in status than men who display dominance by talking and interrupting more, smiling less, and occupying more body space (Henley, 1977). These behaviors are not only a cause of the status difference but also a result of it, another self-fulfilling prophecy. For example, people assigned the superior role talked more, interrupted their partner more, smiled less, used more body space, or showed more dominance than those assigned the subordinate role, regardless of sex (Deutsch, 1990; Leffler, Gillespie, & Conaty, 1982) and regardless of actual personal dominance (Kiotas, 1987). Entrepreneurial assignments increased girls' as well as boys' entrepreneurial ability (Kourilsky & Campbell, 1984). And neither women nor men in dead-end jobs express interest in advancement. Desire for advancement depends on realistic opportunity for it (Kanter, 1977).

Status and Power

Status and power go together. One begets the other (Unger, 1978), so men also have more power than women. Men use direct power to influence others—reward, coercion, authority, expertise—but women use "weak tactics"—wheedling, manipulation, supplication, or helplessness (Howard, Blumstein, & Schwartz, 1986). Most social psychologists have focused on power rather than status as the cause of sex differences (Johnson, 1976; Lips, 1991; Morawski, 1987; Paludi, 1990; Sherif, 1982; Unger, 1976, 1978). Power is control, influence, and authority (Lips, 1991):

> Control of resources, including human resources, and of core social institutions that enables (a) *effective* [italics in original] initiation of action, decisions,

policies and propaganda and (b) use of *effective* [italics in original] sanctions, e.g., opening or closing others' access to power, rewards or punishments, including the ultimate punishment of force or its threat. (Sherif, 1982, p. 388)

Like status, relative power in a relationship also overrides participants' sex in determining behavior. While speaking, high-status people look their low-status partner in the eye but are less attentive when the partner is speaking. Low-status partners use the opposite pattern (Exline, Ellyson, & Long, 1975). When pairs of women and men discussed a neutral topic, traditional status assumptions prevailed. The men used the high-status visual behavior and women the low-status pattern. However, when the experimenter assigned the pairs a discussion topic on which the woman had more expertise than the man, thereby giving her situational power, it was she, not the man, who used the high-status gaze patterns (Dovidio, Ellyson, Keating, Heltman, & Brown, 1988). Similarly, women as well as men in groups given the high-power position in an intergroup negotiation expressed more direct hostility toward the low-power group, less covert, indirect hostility, and less anxiety than low-power groups of either sex (Siderits, Johannsen, & Fadden, 1985). But if women are no worse than men at displaying power when they have it, they are also no better. Groups of women given power over another group were as quick and ruthless as advantaged male groups to exploit the disadvantaged group. However, disadvantaged male groups resisted exploitation more effectively than did disadvantaged female groups (Insko et al., 1983).

Power and control provide personal as well as social advantages. Greater power and autonomy lead to increased motivation and interest, less pressure and tension, greater creativity and cognitive flexibility, better learning, better performance, a more positive emotional tone, higher self-esteem, trust, persistence at a task, and better physical and mental health (Deci & Ryan, 1987; Langer & Benevento, 1978; Miller, Schooler, Kohn, & Miller, 1979). The greater incidence of depression in women has been attributed to their lesser power and autonomy, especially in the housewife role (Gove, 1972). Wives who work outside the home, especially in high-level careers, report greater satisfaction and feelings of well-being (Betz & Fitzgerald, 1987; Birnbaum, 1975).

Three Variations on the Status and Power Theme

The theory of status characteristics and expectation states (Berger & Zelditch, 1985; Ridgeway, 1991; Webster & Foschi, 1988) proposes that the unequal status of men and women in society is carried as an automatic, unconscious expectation into situations in which men's and women's actual competence is unknown. Because status is equated with competence, men are expected to provide the major contributions and leadership—and to

reap the deserved rewards of respect and prestige. Because task contributions can be interpreted as status seeking, they are not accepted from
women (Ridgeway, 1982), thus producing a self-fulfilling prophecy. This
theory does not identify status as defining stereotypical gender traits, but
rather as the source of differential expectations for how men and women
should behave and be treated.

A second variation (Eagly, 1987) proposes that women's "communal"
traits versus men's "agentic" ones are due not to status differences but to
their different primary roles of homemaker versus employee. For example,
college students given descriptions of women and men as either employees
or homemakers attributed the feminine traits to the homemakers and the
masculine ones to the employees, regardless of the role occupant's sex
(Eagly & Steffen, 1984). Similarly, Hoffman and Hurst (1990) concluded
that gender stereotypes do not represent perceptions of actual differences
between the sexes but rather rationalizations for assigning women and
men to different social roles. A third variation related to power (Leidig,
1981) proposes that the feminine traits are caused by women's fear of
violence such as rape and wife beating. This fear keeps them dependent
on men for protection and therefore submissive.

Implications

It was traditionally assumed that women gravitate to subordinate roles
because they are passive and dependent. In contrast, the research on roles,
status, and power suggests that women are passive and dependent because
they occupy subordinate roles. These studies show that both men and
women know both the high- and low-status behaviors. Which set of traits
they display depends on their relative status in the situation, not on
their personalities. Thus, the prevailing status inequality produces another
grain of truth in the stereotypes and another self-fulfilling prophecy. The
influence of roles and status can also explain why laboratory studies revealed so few and small sex differences in behavior. In research on sex
differences, men and women are assigned the same role and status; thus
they behave the same. Roles, status, and power are probably the strongest
and most pervasive situational determinants of gender beliefs and behavior.
Other situational cues such as stereotypically masculine or feminine tasks,
discussion topics, or situations also influence behavior because they evoke
differential expectations of expertise (hence power or status relevant to
the situation).

Female Authority Role Models

Because expectations for women depend on their roles and status, as
women increasingly occupy employee and higher-status roles, other

women's expectations for themselves change accordingly (Fiorentine, 1988). Employed and high-status women serve as role models for other women. For example, young girls whose mother was employed outside the home gave more diverse and higher-status occupational choices (Selkow, 1984). The percentages of women alumnae in *Who's Who in America* reflected the percentages of female faculty at the colleges they had attended (Tidball, 1973), and young psychologists of both sexes who had same-sex research sponsors in graduate school had published more 5 years after their degree than those with opposite-sex sponsors (Goldstein, 1979).

Even brief exposure to a few female authorities in the laboratory increased college women's career aspirations. Students viewed either the traditional television commercials described previously, in which a man and woman were shown both treating him as the important partner in the relationship, or the reversed-role versions in which the male and female actors switched roles in the same scenario, and then wrote an essay describing their life and concerns as they imagined them 10 years in the future. The women who had seen the traditional commercials mentioned many more domestic than career themes. In contrast, those who had seen the reversed-role commercials showing women as authorities gave equal emphasis to careers and domestic life, as did male viewers of both versions. (Geis, Brown, Jennings, & Porter, 1984). Similarly, consistent with the idea that women already know the high-status role behaviors, the same reversed-role commercials also increased women's display of the behavioral skills of self-confidence and independence of judgment. Women who had been exposed to the female authorities in the reversed-role commercials showed more self-confidence (fewer signs of nervousness such as fidgeting, self-comforting gestures, lack of eye contact, and rigid posture) while delivering an extemporaneous speech, and also moved their own judgments of the humorousness of previously rated cartoons farther away from a false consensus toward the cartoon's true humorousness than did those who had just viewed the traditional commercials showing women as subordinate helpmates (Jennings, Geis, & Brown, 1980). Similarly, exposure to female competence models increased women's confidence in their own abilities (Ozer & Bandura, 1990). These studies showed that women's career aspirations and actual behavioral skills are not simply matters of individual abilities and interests. Rather, they can be raised or lowered very quickly by expectations and possibilities implicit in the visible roles of women in the social environment.

Most important, female authority models also counteract evaluators' perceptual bias. Viewing a half-hour videotape of female authorities decreased children's gender stereotypes (Eisenstock, 1984). In discussion groups that saw the traditional male authority commercials described previously and then had a male experimenter as the live authority for their session, the women and men actually contributed equally, but they both rated the men higher on leadership. Perceptual bias prevailed. However, in groups that saw the female authority commercials and then had a female experimenter, the women and men were evaluated as equal in leadership, reflecting reality (Geis, Boston, & Hoffman, 1985). Similarly, evaluators rated female managerial applicants higher when there were more of them, and exposure to successful women eliminated sex discrimination in applicant screening decisions (Heilman, 1980; Heilman & Martell, 1986). Experience working for a woman decreased subordinates' prejudice against women as bosses (Ezell, Odewahn, & Sherman, 1981; Tsui & Gutek, 1984), and a female supervisor's remarks about a female subordinate influenced observers' evaluations of her more than did the same comments by a male supervisor (Geis, Brown, & Wolfe, 1990).

Female authority models may even overcome the dislike of competent women. After watching videotaped scenes of mostly male managers interacting with subordinates, viewers rated male managers on a second videotape as more competent and likable than the females. However, when the first tape showed mostly female managers, viewers rated the women on the second tape higher than the men (Geis, Dietz, Brofee, & Fennimore, 1992). In natural settings, individuals who are seen as more likable are more likely to be advanced (Regan, Straus, & Fazio, 1974). Both supervisors and subordinates evaluate women leaders as more successful—more effective, competent, liked, and respected—when there are more female authorities in the organizational environment (Tsui & Gutek, 1984). Similarly, male students at the Coast Guard Academy became more favorable toward women in the Coast Guard about 3 years after women were first admitted to the Academy (Cheatham, 1984).

Pornography as Role Modeling

Role-modeling research has focused on issues relevant to careers and achievement, but the same general principle—the modeling effect, that people tend to behave as they see others behaving and find such behavior acceptable—could also account for the effects of pornography depicting rape in which men are shown as dominating (high-status) and women as low-status (actually, *no*-status) targets of their hostility and aggression. In both laboratory and field studies, men exposed to more pornography or other violence against women were more accepting of rape myths, for example, that rape is motivated by sexual desire (actually it is motivated by hostility), less upset about an actual rape, less sympathetic to the victim, more accepting of violence against women, and more sexually callous in general, or they responded more sexually to a woman in a professional setting (Bierre, Corne, Runtz, & Malamuth, 1984; Donnerstein, 1984; Linz, Donnerstein, & Penrod, 1988; McKenzie-Mohr & Zanna, 1990). And attitudes condoning rape and violence predict both self-reported violence against women and actual aggression (e.g., delivering more purported painful punishments to a woman than to a man partner) in both field and laboratory studies (Malamuth, 1981, 1983, 1984).

Role-Modeling Implications

In the past it was easy to assume that men's ability to "succeed in business without really trying" (and in the professions, science, and politics) was due to their mysterious masculine characteristics. However, contrary to the stereotypes, men and women, including black men and women, do not differ in achievement motivation (Crew, 1982; Stewart & Chester, 1982). The studies reviewed above suggest that a better explanation for men's past achievements may be the traditional prevalence of male authority models throughout society. The research suggests that when women are given the same social advantage previously enjoyed only by men, they show similar aspirations and performances and reap the same acceptance, recognition, and success. Although the effects of roles and role models in laboratory studies are probably temporary, repeated exposures may be cumulative. Like drops of water falling on a stone, effects of habitual roles and a lifetime of exposure to male or female authority models would presumably be deeper and more lasting.

The role-model studies have two important qualifications. First, the female authorities were shown as accepted and supported by co-participants, just as male authorities are in society. In contrast, in the studies discussed earlier in this chapter, when women assumed authority or were shown without social support, they were devalued, disliked, or both. Second, there must be *multiple* female authorities in the situation. Accepted female authorities disconfirm gender stereotypes by their behavior and by the way others treat them, and disconfirmations dispersed among a number of exemplars break the stereotypes more than if they were all displayed by the same person (Weber & Crocker, 1983). Recall that the frequency and recency of using a schema strengthen it. More female authorities in the environment increase the frequency of disconfirmations, and therefore their likely recency. Most important, multiple models are more effective because they create a consensus effect (discussed later). A lone female authority, or one of only a few, can be discounted as an exception (Lord, Lepper, & Mackie, 1984; Rothbart & Lewis, 1988). In addition, because the lone or token woman is distinctive in the group specifically due to her sex (McArthur, 1981), perceivers' gender schemas are more activated, leading to increased stereotyping. Thus, the token woman is often doomed to failure (Gutek & Morasch, 1982; Kanter, 1977).

OTHER COGNITIVE FOIBLES CLOSE THE CIRCLE:
FROM BEHAVIOR TO BELIEFS

The research discussed above shows that changing women's roles and status, and thus changing how they behave and how they are treated, does in fact change perceivers' gender stereotypes. This section outlines the processes that translate behavior observations into beliefs.

From Behavior to Disposition: The Fundamental
Attribution Error

The fundamental attribution error is attributing actors' behavior to their internal personality dispositions and underestimating the influence of situational constraints (Jones & Davis, 1965; Ross, 1977). For example, when we see Marcia waiting for Marc's directions, we assume that Marcia is dependent and Marc is dominant, ignoring the situational constraint that Marcia is Marc's secretary. Recall that perception always involves interpretation and that initial inferences are preconscious, automatic, and dispositional. The fundamental attribution error is a failure to make sufficient conscious correction of the initial inference (Gilbert, et al., 1988). For example, Ross, Amabile, and Steinmetz (1977) had three Stanford University students draw lots for roles in a questioner–contestant game. Questioners prepared general-knowledge questions from their own areas of expertise to pose to the contestants who, as expected, were able to answer relatively few of them. The third student served as the audience. After the game, both contestants and audience rated the questioners as more intelligent than themselves or than each other. Failing to take sufficient account of the special advantage conferred on the questioner by the situational role, they committed the fundamental attribution error.

Men's and women's traditional difference in roles and status would presumably have the same effect. Recall that high-status roles require dominance, initiative, and objectivity; low-status roles do not permit such behavior and instead foster dependence, submissiveness, and sensitivity. It is the fundamental attribution error that makes the high-status characteristics appear to be internal personality traits of men and the subordinate characteristics dispositions of women. In addition, we compound the initial error by further assuming that the traits are innate and sex linked (Campbell, 1967). Thus, the erroneously inferred dispositions are then further mistakenly attributed to the actors' sex.

Attributions for women's and men's behavior are subject to a further qualification. With no prior beliefs about actors we attribute *any* behavior to their dispositions. That explains how high- and low-status behavior came to be seen as masculine and feminine and also how female authority models break the stereotypes. However, when perceivers do have prior beliefs about the actor, as in the case of gender stereotypes, they attribute behavior consistent with their expectations to the actor's disposition, but inconsistent behavior to situational constraints (Kulik, 1983)—another self-fulfilling prophecy. Thus, as noted earlier, because of the stereotypes, people attribute men's successes to ability and their failures to external causes but do the opposite for women. It is also because of this qualification that the female model effect requires multiple models to create a consensus effect that redefines stereotypical expectations.

Defining Truth and Adding Value: Consensus Effects

Gender Stereotypes: Consensus Defines "the Truth"

The stereotypical gender attributes are assumed to be "true" not only because they are perceived as internal dispositions but also because they are consensual in society. When there is an objective, physical criterion to decide an issue, we usually use it. If we want to know our weight, we get on a scale. But for many issues there is no objective criterion. Is thin more attractive than fat? How good a manager is Carol? To decide such issues, we use social consensus—agreement among the relevant or important people, or a majority of them, on a matter of opinion. Deciding which personality characteristics are masculine or feminine falls into this category. Behavior relevant to all traits, including gender stereotypes, is always more or less ambiguous. Trait attribution is always an inference, as noted earlier. When the evidence is ambiguous, social consensus defines "the truth." Thus, it simultaneously defines and validates individuals' beliefs (Festinger, 1954; Sherif, 1935). If you doubt this, think of entering a crowded elevator and singing *The Star Spangled Banner* out loud. This act is neither illegal nor immoral; it is "unthinkable" because it violates the social consensus of what is appropriate for the situation.

Gender stereotypes are consensual throughout society (Bem, 1974; Spence & Helmreich, 1978) because even while we disavow them consciously, we still enact them and see others enact them in the unequal roles and status of our daily life. Similarly, gender stereotypes are still portrayed in the media (Lovdal, 1989; Signorielli, 1989; Sullivan & O'Connor, 1988), and fictional information, although consciously discounted, nevertheless penetrates our judgments and beliefs as real (Gerrig & Prentice, 1991). As a result, men and women are seen or assumed to possess the stereotypical traits. Even when objective evidence disconfirms the consensus, we still see the consensus as true (Asch, 1956). The consensus effect, along with the fundamental attribution error, explains the impact of multiple female authority models. When a number of women are seen as authorities, they create a consensus effect, redefining "the truth"—the stereotypes—of what is characteristic and acceptable for women. The frequency of occurrences serves as the criterion of their validity (Hasher, Goldstein, & Toppino, 1977).

Consensus can also define particular truths. College students who saw a videotape of a group discussion showing a male leader with group members responding to him with facial expressions of approval rated him as showing more leadership and competence than those who saw a woman leader using the same script, but with disapproving group members, rated her. Similarly, students who saw the same woman's performance embedded in group approval evaluated her higher than those who saw the man encountering disapproval rated him. The members' facial expressions communicated a nonverbal social consensus that defined the quality of the leader's performance, but the students were not aware of this influence on their ratings (Brown & Geis, 1984).

Gender Stereotypes: From "Facts" to Values

Because consensus defines "the truth," it also transforms gender stereotypes from assumed facts into values. Because there is no objective criterion of what a "true feminine personality" actually is, if everyone agrees that women are emotional, dependent, and nurturant, then emotionality, dependence, and nurturance became hallmarks of "true femininity." As a result, these traits become normative and valued for women because displaying them both defines and validates their "true femininity." The consensus acquires value *because* it serves as the criterion of truth and validity (Lewin, 1951). Similarly, the consensual observation that authorities have always been men creates the norm that authorities *should be* men. "What is" becomes "what is desirable"; descriptions become prescriptions.

Because the stereotypes are implicit if not explicit values, men and women strive to cultivate them. These pressures for desirable behavior are further reinforced by the pressures of unequal status and perceivers' expectations described earlier. In fact, people try to maintain a self-image that is both socially desirable (Baumeister, 1982; Tesser, 1988; Tetlock & Manstead, 1985) and also consistent with their self-beliefs (Lecky, 1945; Swann, 1983; Swann & Read, 1981). Although these motives may conflict, they frequently converge on promoting gender-stereotypical behavior, providing another grain of truth for the stereotypes and another self-fulfilling prophecy. For example, when pairs of college students had to decide which of them would be leader in a forthcoming task, dominant women became leaders when paired with a nondominant woman, but used their dominance to make a nondominant male partner the leader

(Megargee, 1969; Nyquist & Spence, 1986). And because the stereotypes are values, both women and men behave more stereotypically in public than in private (Eagly & Crowley, 1986; Eagly, Wood, & Fishbaugh, 1981; Gould & Slone, 1982).

The "Damned if She Does, Damned if She Doesn't" Dilemma

Also because gender stereotypes are values as well as assumed facts, violations of them are punished. Women are disapproved for assertiveness as well as believed incapable of it. As a result, professional and managerial women often find themselves in a "damned if she does, damned if she doesn't" dilemma (Wolman & Frank, 1975). Conscious standards for their positions require competence, assertiveness, independence, and leadership. At the same time, supervisors and associates also expect them to be feminine (Kemper, 1984). Recall that stereotypical femininity requires lower levels of the masculine traits of competence, assertiveness, independence, and leadership, as well as more sensitivity and accommodation. The emotional, less intelligent, and sex-object stereotypes are especially incompatible with career success. As a result, women who act in a feminine manner are liked but their professional efforts go unrecognized; those who act professionally may be recognized as competent but they are disliked (Carli, 1990; Crawford, 1988; Keating, 1985; O'Leary, 1974).

Examples of these reactions are the studies mentioned earlier in which fellow group members showed disapproving facial expressions in response to women leaders or voted to exclude a competent woman from their group. The glass ceiling on women's promotions is probably another example. In other studies, women who were recognized as competent, assertive, or leaders (without social support) were also seen as cold, unfeminine, aggressive, abrasive, arrogant, or neurotic (Costrich, Feinstein, Kidder, Marecek, & Pascale, 1975; Denmark, 1979; Feather & Simon, 1975; Horner, 1972; Porter & Geis, 1981; Seyfried & Hendrick, 1973).

Adding Emotional Investment: Familiarity and Liking

A final factor that strengthens both beliefs and perceptions is familiarity, also called the mere exposure or repeated exposures effect. As we encounter particular objects, ideas, events, or people more frequently, we come to like them more, providing the encounters are not aversive. Familiarity does not define beliefs or perceptions, but rather makes them easier, more likable, acceptable, or comfortable. Zajonc (1968) identified the effect and reviewed relevant studies. For example, college students liked the men whose photographs they had seen several times more than they liked those seen only once—regardless of which particular men they had seen more frequently. Liked coworkers are evaluated as more competent than disliked ones, regardless of actual competence (Regan, et al., 1974). Repetition of ideas or principles leads to greater acceptance of them (Wilson & Miller, 1968). And pursuing the same strategy or procedure repeatedly creates false belief in its efficacy and validity (Kiesler & Mathog, 1971).

The familiarity effect suggests that when stereotyped behavior and assumptions are prevalent in society, they will be considered likable, acceptable, and valid. Violation of the stereotypes arouses negative affect (Butler & Geis, 1990) and may be threatening (Mandler, 1982). Such effects would reinforce all of the cognitive and behavioral processes described in this chapter and thus reinforce the self-fulfilling prophecies. For example, the familiarity effect could heighten the "damned if she does, damned if she doesn't" dilemma. Because we are familiar with women as subordinates displaying the stereotypical traits, we dislike and reject women in authority displaying high-status (masculine) characteristics. Familiarity could also heighten the impact of female authority models. Exposure to multiple female authorities makes them and their behavior not only consensual but also more familiar and therefore more acceptable, both to women as actors and to their perceivers and evaluators.

Although familiarity effects would appear to be relevant to both gender-stereotypical behavior and perceivers' evaluations of it, virtually no research exists on the topic. The only relevant study located is one mentioned earlier in which evaluators previously exposed to a majority of either male or female managers on a videotape later rated either male or female managers, respectively, on a second tape as more likable. Familiarity effects would appear to be a topic ripe for exploration by gender researchers.

Because high- and low-status role behaviors are misperceived as dispositional, because the perceptions are consensual in society, implicitly defining them as both "true" and desirable, and because their familiarity makes them likable, stereotypical gender beliefs are constantly reinforced even while they are consciously denied. These processes complete the self-fulfilling prophecy cycle and bring us back to the beginning of this chapter.

PERSPECTIVE: SOME IMPLICATIONS AND CONCLUSIONS

In the past, both psychologists and other people assumed that individuals' behavior and achievements reflected their stable, internal personality traits. In contrast, current research shows that behavior and achievement, and even our personality traits, are heavily influenced by others' beliefs, perceptions, expectations, and treatment, as well as by our knowledge of expectations for members of our sex. For example, our display of stereotypical masculine or feminine traits depends on expectations for and assignments to high- versus low-status roles. Expectations and role assignments can change behavior rapidly. In the laboratory, perceivers' expectations, high-status role assignments, and exposure to female authority models changed women's behavior and evaluators' sex discrimination in less than an hour. The stereotypical personality traits appeared stable in the past because the differential expectations touched so many areas of life and were consensual in society. This chapter suggests that both women's and men's behavior, achievements, and personality traits are far more quickly responsive to social situational forces than was previously supposed.

Most organizations, including colleges, advertise their equal opportunity policies. However, opportunities always depend on recognition of credentials or performance (Haslett, Geis, & Carter, 1992). The research reviewed in this chapter shows that women's credentials and performances are unconsciously devalued compared to identical information about a man. The result is sex discrimination in hiring, salary, support, and promotion. Until organizations put teeth in their policies, equal opportunity remains a hollow promise at best. At worst, it strengthens the self-fulfilling prophecy by creating the false belief that women had a fair chance, leading to the false conclusion that lower levels of success reflect their own inadequacies.

Three Qualifications

First, although the self-fulfilling prophecy was described as a sequence of processes, actually all the processes operate simultaneously. Our history of many repetitions of all the processes and outcomes forms the context for each new occurrence. Second, in the classic self-fulfilling prophecy, the initial belief is false. However, in the case of gender stereotypes and behavior, because the process is repeated over and over, there is a kernel of truth in the "initial" beliefs. But a kernel of truth is not the whole truth, or even a major part of it. No particular stereotypical trait is true of every woman or every man, or in every situation for any woman or man. The problem of stereotypes and self-fulfilling prophecies is that they cause us to assume the stereotypes even when they do not exist. Finally, there is continual interplay between the individual perceiver or actor and society at large. Individuals' perceptions and actions are conditioned by their knowledge of social expectations and practices, which are simultaneously defined by the aggregate of individuals' behaviors.

Making Self-Fulfilling Prophecies Work for Equality

Although self-fulfilling prophecies are strong, countertrends are also evident. First, despite the many pressures encouraging stereotypical behavior, men and women behave the same more often than differently, especially given the same situational constraints and advantages. Second, stereotypical beliefs have virtually disappeared at the conscious level, at least among the educated, and may also be diminishing in our unconscious schemas. Sensitivity is becoming more acceptable for men; paid employment for women. Finally, family roles are also changing. Employed wives now do less housework and husbands more (33%) than 20 years ago (Robinson, 1988).

Like the traditional self-fulfilling prophecies, these countertrends are both causes and consequences of each other (Smith, 1985). Self-fulfilling prophecies can also work to break the stereotypes. Human cognitive processes will not change. We will still use our world-knowledge schemas to interpret and guide our perceptions and behavior; our consistency biases and other foibles will still operate, but the *results* of the processes will change if the contents of our schemas change, specifically, if our conscious beliefs filter down into our operating schemas and replace the stereotypes. For example, if Tim's stereotype that "women lack initiative" were replaced in his automatic operating schemas by his conscious belief that women are as competent as men (e.g., "people who get promoted are competent" might be the operating phrase), his consistency biases would still operate but now lead him to see and treat Gertie as more competent than she actually was. And with the increased support, autonomy, and authority, Gertie would live up to the "competence" expectation just as participants in the studies reviewed earlier confirmed their perceivers' expectations. This change has not happened yet, at least not on a broad scale, as this chapter has documented, but it may be in progress.

There are two major ways to break the traditional cycle. One is educational—making people aware of their unconscious stereotypical assumptions and their unintended effects, probably with frequent reminders in relevant situations. This awareness permits people, with some effort, to make conscious allowance for their biases and to correct them, in effect to consciously "rethink" their perceptions. This strategy is difficult. It requires genuine egalitarian intentions, accepting the idea that one's perceptions are not accurate but biased, and remembering to interrupt one's thoughts to make the required corrections. With the best of intentions, such efforts are unreliable.

The easier way to break the cycle is to provide multiple, socially supported female authority models in the social environment. The environment can be a group, an organization, or society at large, but the more widespread these models are, the more effective they become because of the increasing consensus effect. As women perform in these roles, and others behaviorally acknowledge their authority, the high-status characteristics come to be seen as possible and acceptable for women. Thus, other women aspire and perform accordingly, and evaluators recognize and accept women's competence. Indeed, the recent decrease in conscious stereotypes may be a result of the role-model effect created by women's move into the paid labor force and higher-status positions over the past 20 years. The role-model solution is easier because it does not require conscious understanding or effort. It works automatically, simply changing the content of the preconscious assumptions. Its problem is getting enough women promoted to authority positions and supported in them to serve as role models in the first place. Thus, a combination of education and affirmative action (to provide role models) would probably be most effective. To the extent that either solution succeeds, it makes the other easier. More aware decision makers are more amenable to affirmative action because they understand its rationale, and increasing the number of female authorities reduces discriminatory perceptions and treatment, with or without awareness.

Biological Influences

From the perspective of the present chapter, biological factors may well predispose men and women to different behavior, but the elaborate human cognitive system, with its attunements to learning, social expectations, and role models, and its susceptibility to biases and foibles, heavily influences biological predispositions and frequently overrides them (cf. Diamond, 1988). For practical purposes, the stereotypical masculine and feminine traits are socially defined, created, and perpetuated. They are neither intrinsically masculine nor feminine, but human. This is not to say that there are no biological influences on personality. There are (Reinisch, Rosenblum, & Sanders, 1987). Individuals are born with predispositions for different levels of intelligence, dominance, and timidness, for example. However, all the predispositions occur in both sexes. Differences, again, are social: Timidity is permitted for girls but discouraged in boys.

Individual Differences

The processes and outcomes described in this chapter can all be modified by real differences in personality. Whether from biological inheritance, personal experience, or both, one woman differs from another in intelligence, social skills, creativity, and a host of other traits, and so do men. Obviously, those who display more of the socially valued attributes and fewer weaknesses fare better in a given level of situational difficulty. This chapter has focused on the different social environments encountered by men and women created by different assumptions about their personalities, behavior, and "appropriate" roles and status. These factors explain why men have succeeded in high-level careers more than equally endowed women. Women have faced a less accepting social environment. Obviously, also, some particular environments are less discriminatory than others. Perceivers also differ in how strongly their gender stereotypes influence their perceptions and treatment of men and women (Martin, 1987; Spence & Helmreich, 1972). Thus, any particular woman's success depends on both her individual assets and the discriminatory level of her particular situation, as well as that of society at large.

SUMMARY

From the social psychological perspective, gender beliefs and behavior can be understood as an overall self-fulfilling prophecy consisting of a cluster of related and mutually reinforcing specific self-fulfilling prophecies. Gender stereotypes operate as unconscious expectations or prophecies. The fulfillments or confirmations consist of perceptions, behaviors, or their outcomes. In the broadest outline, gender stereotypes operating as implicit expectations bias perception and treatment of women and men, and the results of the discriminatory perceptions and treatment—sex differences in behavior and achievement—then seemingly confirm that the stereotypes were true all along.

In spite of conscious beliefs in gender equality, traditional stereotypes remain encoded in the knowledge structures or schemas that automatically, without our awareness, interpret and guide our perceptions, inferences, memories, and treatment of men and women. The stereotypes described men as competent and suited for authority, women as sensitive and responsive, and both sexes as deficient in the traits of the other. We are more likely to notice, infer, and remember schema-consistent information; consider it more relevant, informative, and credible; and see it as dispositional. We often cannot distinguish inference from evidence. These schema-consistency biases produce self-fulfilling prophecies.

First, we "see" men and women as possessing the stereotypical traits, whether they do or not, thus mistakenly "confirming" the stereotypical prophecies in our own mind. Second, we treat women and men as if they possessed the stereotypical traits. Because actors tend to comply with perceivers' expectations, the prophecies are confirmed in reality by their actual behavior, and the stereotypes acquire a kernel of truth. Third, the stereotypes lead us to prefer men for authority positions and expect subordinate status for women. As a result, the behavior required by authority roles appears characteristically masculine, and that required by subordinate positions as feminine. The traditional "gender" stereotypes are actually status characteristics. Because men and women are still unequal in status, we all enact the stereotypes in our social encounters and see others model them on a daily basis. These behaviors and observations are a major confirmation of the stereotypical prophecies. The stereotypes reflect the status difference and also perpetuate it.

Three additional cognitive foibles convert observations of behavior into implicit stereotypical beliefs. Committing the fundamental attribution error, we assume that high-status behavior is dispositional in men and subordinate behavior in women. The differential expectations, perceptions, roles, and consequent behavior are consensual in society, defining them as the truth and further endowing them with value. One result is that women and men strive to display the "desirable" attributes. Another is that those who violate the stereotypes are disliked, producing a "damned if she does, damned if she doesn't" dilemma for professional and managerial women. Both results add to the stereotypes' grain of truth and produce self-fulfilling prophecies. Finally, familiarity makes stereotypical beliefs and behavior more liked and discriminatory practices seem more valid. As a result of the real and imagined confirmations, the stereotypes remain active as schemas in our store of knowledge about the world, and so the self-fulfilling prophecies continue.

Self-fulfilling prophecies can also create and perpetuate equal opportunity for women and men. Human cognitive processes will not change, but their outcomes can. People can be educated about their biases so they can consciously correct their perceptions, interpretations, and decisions. The more reliable method is changing the content of the gender knowledge that automatically and unconsciously interprets information and guides behavior. Providing multiple socially supported female authority models uses the status, attribution error, consensus, and familiarity effects to break the feminine stereotype. Presumably, male sensitivity models would also break the masculine stereotype.

In this social psychological perspective, the stereotypical behavioral traits, interests, and abilities, mislabeled masculine or feminine, are primarily results of social expectations and the situational opportunities and constraints of high- versus low-status social roles and power. The traits themselves are neither masculine nor feminine, but human. Which traits are displayed can change rapidly in response to situational demands, social support, and the sex of authority models. Men's achievements in the past no doubt reflected high ability, but they also reflected social advantages still not available to most women.

REFERENCES

Aisenberg, N., & Harrington, M. (1988). *Women of academe: Outsiders in the sacred grove*. Amherst, MA: University of Massachusetts Press.

Altemeyer, R. A., & Jones, K. (1974). Sexual identity, physical attractiveness and seating position as determinants of influence in discussion groups. *Canadian Journal of Behavioural Science, 6*, 357–375.

Asch, S. E. (1956). Studies of independence and conformity. A minority of one against a unanimous majority. *Psychological Monographs, 70* (9, Whole No. 416).

Ashmore, R. D., & Del Boca, F. K. (1979). Sex stereotypes and implicit personality theory: Toward a cognitive-social psychological conception. *Sex Roles, 5,* 219–248.

Bargh, J. A., & Pietromonaco, P. (1982). Automatic information processing and social perceptions: The influence of trait information presented outside of conscious awareness on impression formation. *Journal of Personality and Social Psychology, 43,* 437–449.

Baron, J., & Hershey, J. C. (1988). Outcome bias indecision evaluation. *Journal of Personality and Social Psychology, 54,* 569–579.

Bar Tal, D., & Frieze, I. H. (1977). Achievement motivation for males and females as a determinant of attributions for success and failure. *Sex Roles, 3,* 301–314.

Bartol, K. M., & Butterfield, D. A. (1976). Sex effects in evaluating leaders. *Journal of Applied Psychology, 61,* 446–454.

Basow, S. (1986). *Gender stereotypes: Traditions and alternatives.* Monterey, CA: Brooks/Cole.

Basow, S. A., & Medcalf, K. L. (1988). Academic achievement and attributions among college students: Effects of gender and sex-typing. *Sex Roles, 19,* 555–567.

Basow, S. A., & Silberg, N. T. (1987). Student evaluations of college professors: Are female and male professors rated differently? *Journal of Educational Psychology, 79,* 308–314.

Bass, B. M., Krusell, J., & Alexander, R. A. (1971). Male managers' attitudes toward working women. *American Behavioral Scientist, 15,* 221–236.

Baumeister, R. (1982). A self-presentational view of social phenomena. *Psychological Bulletin, 91,* 3–26.

Baumeister, R. F., Chesner, S. P., Senders, P. S., & Tice, D. M. (1988). Who's in charge here? Group leaders do lend help in emergencies. *Personality and Social Psychology Bulletin, 14,* 17–22.

Bellezza, F. S., & Bower, G. H. (1981). Person stereotypes and memory for people. *Journal of Personality and Social Psychology, 41,* 856–865.

Bem, S. L. (1974). The measurement of psychological androgyny. *Journal of Consulting and Clinical Psychology, 42,* 155–162.

Bem, S. L. (1985). Androgyny and gender schema theory: A conceptual and empirical integration. In T. B. Sonderegger (Ed.), *Nebraska symposium on motivation: Psychology of gender* (pp. 179–226). Lincoln, NB: University of Nebraska Press.

Ben Tsvi-Mayer, S., Hertz-Lazarowitz, R., & Safir, M. P. (1989). Teachers' selections of boys and girls as prominent pupils. *Sex Roles, 21,* 231–245.

Bergen, D. J., & Williams, J. E. (1991). Sex stereotypes in the United States revisited: 1972–1988. *Sex Roles, 24,* 413–424.

Berger, J., & Zelditch, M. Jr. (1985). *Status, rewards, and influence: How expectations organize behavior.* San Francisco: Jossey-Bass.

Betz, N. E., & Fitzgerald, L. F. (1987). *The career psychology of women.* Orlando, FL: Academic Press.

Bierre, J., Corne, S., Runtz, M., & Malamuth, N. M. (1984, August). *The rape arousal inventory: Predicting actual and potential sexual aggression in a university population.* Paper presented at the annual meeting of the American Psychological Association, Toronto, Canada.

Birnbaum, J. A. (1975). Life patterns and self-esteem in gifted family-oriented and career-committed women. In M. Mednick, S. Tangri, & L. Hoffman (Eds.), *Women and achievement* (pp. 396–419). New York: Halsted.

Blau, F. D., & Ferber, M. A. (1985). Women in the labor market: The last twenty years. In L. Larwood, A. H. Stromberg, & B. A. Gutek (Eds.), *Women and work: An annual review* (Vol. 1, pp. 19–49). Beverly Hills, CA: Sage.

Bodenhausen, G. V. (1988). Stereotypic biases in social decision making and memory: Testing process models of stereotype use. *Journal of Personality and Social Psychology, 55,* 726–737.

Bodenhausen, G. V. (1990). Stereotypes as judgmental heuristics: Evidence on circadian variations in discrimination. *Psychological Science, 1,* 319–322.

Brewer, M. B. (1988). A dual-process model of impression-formation. In T. K. Srull & R. S. Wyer, Jr. (Eds.), *Advances in social cognition* (Vol. 1, pp. 1–36). Hillsdale, NJ: Erlbaum.

Bridges, J. S. (1988). Sex differences in occupational performance expectations. *Psychology of Women Quarterly, 12,* 75–90.

Broadbent, D. E. (1973). *In defense of empirical psychology.* London: Methuen.

Brooks, V. R. (1982). Sex differences in student dominance behavior in female and male professors' classrooms. *Sex Roles, 8,* 683–690.

Brown, V., & Geis, F. L. (1984). Turning lead into gold: Leadership by men and women and the alchemy of social consensus. *Journal of Personality and Social Psychology, 46,* 811–824.

Bunker, B. B., & Seashore, E. W. (1975). Breaking the sex role stereotypes. *Public Management, 57,* 5–11.

Butler, D., & Geis, F. L. (1990). Nonverbal affect responses to male and female leaders: Implications for leadership evaluation. *Journal of Personality and Social Psychology, 58,* 48–59.

Campbell, D. T. (1967). Stereotypes and the perception of group differences. *American Psychologist, 22,* 817–829.

Cannings, K. (1988). The earnings of female and male middle managers. *Journal of Human Resources, 23,* 34–56.

Cantor, N., & Mischel, W. (1977). Traits as prototypes: Effects on recognition memory. *Journal of Personality and Social Psychology, 35,* 38–48.

Carli, L. L. (1990). Gender, language, and influence. *Journal of Personality and Social Psychology, 59,* 941–951.

Cheatham, H. E. (1984). Integration of women in the U.S. military. *Sex Roles, 11,* 141–153.

Cohen, C. E. (1981). Person categories and social perception: Testing some boundaries of the processing effects of prior knowledge. *Journal of Experimental Social Psychology, 40,* 441–452.

Cohen, S. I., & Bunker, K. A. (1975). Subtle effects of sex role stereotypes on recruiter hiring decisions. *Journal of Applied Psychology, 60,* 566–567.

Costrich, N., Feinstein, J., Kidder, L., Marecek, J., & Pascale, L. (1975). When stereotypes hurt: Three studies of penalties for sex-role reversals. *Journal of Experimental Social Psychology, 11*, 520–530.

Crawford, M. (1988). Gender, age, and the social evaluation of assertion. *Behavior Modification, 12*, 549–564.

Crew, J. C. (1982). An assessment of needs among black business majors. *Psychology, 19*, 18–22.

Crosby, F. (1982). *Relative deprivation and working women.* New York: Oxford University Press.

Darley, J. M., & Gross, P. H. (1983). An hypothesis-confirming bias in labeling effects. *Journal of Personality and Social Psychology, 44*, 20–33.

Deaux, K., & Emswiller, T. (1974). Explanations of successful performance on sex-linked tasks: What is skill for the male is luck for the female. *Journal of Personality and Social Psychology, 29*, 80–85.

Deaux, K., & Lewis, L. L. (1984). The structure of gender stereotypes: Interrelationships among components and gender label. *Journal of Personality and Social Psychology, 46*, 991–1004.

Deaux, K., & Major, B. (1987). Putting gender into context: An interactive model of gender-related behavior. *Psychological Review, 94*, 369–389.

Deaux, K., & Taynor, J. (1973). Evaluation of male and female ability: Bias works two ways. *Psychological Reports, 32*, 261–262.

Deci, E. L., & Ryan, R. M. (1987). The support of autonomy and the control of behavior. *Journal of Personality and Social Psychology, 53*, 1024–1037.

Denmark, F. L. (1979). The outspoken woman: Can she win? Paper presented to the New York Academy of Sciences, New York, NY.

Deutsch, F. M. (1990). Status, sex and smiling: The effect of role on smiling in men and women. *Personality and Social Psychology Bulletin, 16*, 531–540.

Deutsch, F. M., & Leong, F. T. (1983). Male responses to female competence. *Sex Roles, 9*, 79–91.

Devine, P. G. (1989). Stereotypes and prejudice: Their automatic and controlled components. *Journal of Personality and Social Psychology, 56*, 5–18.

Devine, P. G., Monteith, M. J., Zuwerink, J. R., & Elliot, A. J. (1991). Prejudice with and without compunction. *Journal of Personality and Social Psychology, 60*, 817–830.

Diamond, M. C. (1988). *Enriching heredity: The impact of the environment on the anatomy of the brain.* New York: Free Press.

Dobbins, G. H., Stuart, C., Pence, E. C., & Sgro, J. A. (1985). Cognitive mechanisms mediating the biasing effects of leader sex on ratings of leader behavior. *Sex Roles, 12*, 549–560.

Donnerstein, E. (1984). Pornography: Its effect on violence against women. In N. Malamuth & E. Donnerstein (Eds.), *Pornography and sexual aggression* (pp. 53–84). Orlando, FL: Academic Press.

Dovidio, J. F., Ellyson, S. L., Keating, C. F., Heltman, K., & Brown, C. E. (1988). The relationship of social power to visual displays of dominance between men and women. *Journal of Personality and Social Psychology, 54*, 233–242.

Dreben, E. K., Fiske, S. T., & Hastie, R. (1979). The independence of evaluative and item information: Impression and recall order effects in behavior-based impression formation. *Journal of Personality and Social Psychology, 37*, 1758–1768.

Duncan, D. D. (1982). Recent cohorts lead rejection of sex typing. *Sex Roles, 8*, 127–132.

Eagly, A. H. (1987). *Sex differences in social behavior: A social role interpretation.* Hillsdale, NJ: Erlbaum.

Eagly, A. H., & Crowley, M. (1986). Gender and helping behavior: A meta-analytic review of the social psychological literature. *Psychological Bulletin, 100*, 283–308.

Eagly, A. H., & Steffen, V. J. (1984). Gender stereotypes stem from the distribution of women and men into social roles. *Journal of Personality and Social Psychology, 46*, 735–754.

Eagly, A. H., & Wood, W. (1982). Inferred sex differences in status as a determinant of gender stereotypes about social influence. *Journal of Personality and Social Psychology, 43*, 915–928.

Eagly, A. H., Wood, W., & Fishbaugh, L. (1981). Sex differences in conformity: Surveillance by the group as a determinant of male nonconformity. *Journal of Personality and Social Psychology, 40*, 384–394.

Eisenstock, B. (1984). Sex-role differences in children's identification with counterstereotypical televised portrayals. *Sex Roles, 10*, 417–430.

England, P. (1979). Women and occupational prestige: A case of vacuous sex equality. *Signs, 5*, 252–265.

Epstein, C. F. (1981). *Women in law.* New York: Basic Books.

Erber, R., & Fiske, S. T. (1984). Outcome dependency and attention to inconsistent information. *Journal of Personality and Social Psychology, 47*, 709–726.

Erkut, S. (1983). Exploring sex differences in expectancy, attribution, and academic achievement. *Sex Roles, 9*, 217–231.

Etaugh, C., & Riley, S. (1983). Evaluating competence of women and men: Effects of marital and parental status and occupational sex typing. *Sex Roles, 9*, 943–952.

Exline, R. V., Ellyson, S. L., & Long, B. (1975). Visual behavior as an aspect of power role relationships. In P. Pliner, L. Kramer, & T. Alloway (Eds.), *Nonverbal communication of aggression* (pp. 21–52). New York: Plenum Press.

Ezell, H. F., Odewahn, C. E., & Sherman, J. D. (1981). The effects of having been supervised by a woman on perception of female managerial competence. *Personnel Psychology, 34*, 291–299.

Fagot, B. I. (1984). Teacher and peer reactions to boys' and girls' play styles. *Sex Roles, 11*, 691–702.

Fagot, B. I., & Hagan, R. (1985). Aggression in toddlers: Responses to the assertive acts of boys and girls. *Sex Roles, 12*, 341–351.

Fazio, R. H., Effrein, E. A., & Falender, V. J. (1981). Self-perceptions following interaction. *Journal of Personality and Social Psychology, 41*, 232–242.

Feather, N. T., & Simon, J. F. (1975). Reactions to male and female success and failure in sex-linked occupations: Impression of personality, causal attributions, and perceived likelihood of different consequences. *Journal of Personality and Social Psychology, 31*, 20–31.

Festinger, L. A. (1954). Theory of social comparison processes. *Human Relations*, 7, 117–140.

Fidell, L. S. (1970). Empirical verification of sex discrimination in hiring practices in psychology. *American Psychologist*, 25, 1094–1098.

Fiorentine, R. (1988). Increasing similarity in the values and life plans of male and female college students? Evidence and implications. *Sex Roles*, 18, 143–158.

Fiske, S. T., & Kinder, D. R. (1981). Involvement, expertise, and schema use: Evidence from political cognition. In N. Cantor & J. Kihlstrom (Eds.), *Personality, cognition, and social interaction* (pp. 171–190). Hillsdale, NJ: Erlbaum.

Fiske, S. T., & Pavelchak, M. A. (1986). Category-based versus piecemeal-based affective responses: Developments in schema-triggered affect. In R. M. Sorrentino, & E. T. Higgins (Eds.), *Handbook of motivation and cognition: Foundations of social behavior* (pp. 167–203). New York: Guilford Press.

Fitzgerald, L. F., Weitzman, L. M., Gold, Y., & Ormerod, M. (1988). Academic harassment: Sex and denial in scholarly garb. *Psychology of Women Quarterly*, 12, 329–340.

Foushee, H. C., Helmreich, R. L., & Spence, J. T. (1979). Implicit theories of masculinity and femininity: Dualistic or bipolar. *Psychology of Women Quarterly*, 3, 259–269.

Frank, E. J. (1988). Business students perceptions of women in management. *Sex Roles*, 19, 107–118.

Frieze, I. H., Fisher, J., Hanusa, B., McHugh, M., & Valle, V. (1978). Attributing the causes of success and failure: Internal and external barriers to achievement in women. In J. Sherman & F. Denmark (Eds.), *Psychology of women: Future directions of research*. New York: Psychological Dimensions.

Futoran, G. C., & Wyer, R.J., Jr. (1986). The effects of traits and gender stereotypes on occupational suitability judgments and the recall of judgment-relevant behavior. *Journal of Experimental Social Psychology*, 22, 475–503.

Geis, F. L., Boston, M., & Hoffman, N. (1985). Sex of authority role models and achievement by men and women: Leadership performance and recognition. *Journal of Personality and Social Psychology*, 49, 636–653.

Geis, F. L., Brown, V., Jennings, J., & Corrado-Taylor, D. (1984). Sex vs. status in sex-associated stereotypes. *Sex Roles*, 11, 771–786.

Geis, F. L., Brown, V., Jennings, J., & Porter, N. (1984). T. V. commercials as achievement scripts for women. *Sex Roles*, 10, 513–525.

Geis, F. L., Brown, V., & Wolfe, C. (1990). Legitimizing the leader: Endorsement by male versus female authority figures. *Journal of Applied Social Psychology*, 20, 943–970.

Geis, F. L., Dietz, B. L., Brofee, E., & Fennimore, E. (1992). How to succeed in business without really trying: Same-sex authority models. Unpublished manuscript, University of Delaware, Newark, DE.

Gerrig, R. J., & Prentice, D. A. (1991). The representation of fictional information. *Psychological Science*, 2, 336–340.

Gilbert, D. T., Krull, D. S., & Malone, P. S. (1990). Unbelieving the unbelievable. Some problems in the rejection of false information. *Journal of Personality and Social Psychology*, 59, 601–613.

Gilbert, D. T., Pelham, B. W., & Krull, D. S. (1988). On cognitive busyness: When person perceivers meet persons perceived. *Journal of Personality and Social Psychology, 54*, 733–740.

Glick, P., Zion, C., & Nelson, C. (1988). What mediates sex discrimination in hiring decisions? *Journal of Personality and Social Psychology, 55*, 178–186.

Goldberg, P. (1968, April). Are women prejudiced against women? *Transaction, 5*, 28–30.

Goldstein, E. (1979). Effect of same-sex and cross-sex role models on the subsequent academic productivity of scholars. *American Psychologist, 23*, 407–410.

Gould, R. J., & Slone, C. G. (1982). The "feminine modesty" effect: A self-presentational interpretation of sex differences in causal attribution. *Personality and Social Psychology Bulletin, 8*, 477–485.

Gove, W. (1972). The relationship between sex roles, mental illness and marital status. *Social Forces, 51*, 34–44.

Grady, K. E. (1979). Androgyny reconsidered. In J. H. Williams (Ed.), *Psychology of women: Selected readings* (pp. 172–177). New York: W. W. Norton.

Graesser, A. C., & Nakamura, G. V. (1982). The impact of a schema on comprehension and memory. In G. H. Bower (Ed.), *The psychology of learning and motivation* (Vol. 16, pp. 60–109). New York: Academic Press.

Gribbons, W. D., & Lohnes, P. R. (1982). *Careers in theory and experience: A twenty year longitudinal study*. Albany, NY: State University of New York Press.

Gupta, N., Jenkins, G. D. Jr., & Beehr, T. A. (1983). Employee gender, gender similarity, and supervisor–subordinate cross-evaluations. *Sex Roles, 8*, 174–184.

Gutek, B. A. (1985). *Sex and the workplace: The impact of sexual behavior and harrassment on women, men, and organizations*. San Francisco: Jossey-Bass.

Gutek, B. A., & Morasch, B. (1982). Sex-ratios, sex-role spillover, and sexual harassment of women at work. *Journal of Social Issues, 38*, 55–74.

Gutek, B. A., & Stevens, D. A. (1979). Differential responses of males and females to work situations which evoke sex role stereotypes. *Journal of Vocational Behavior, 14*, 23–32.

Hagen, R. L., & Kahn, A. (1975). Discrimination against competent women. *Journal of Applied Psychology, 5*, 363–376.

Hall, R. M., & Sandler, B. R. (1982). *The classroom climate: A chilly one for women*. Washington, DC: Association of American Colleges.

Hansen, R. D., & O'Leary, V. E. (1985). Sex determined attributions. In V. E. O'Leary, R. K. Unger, & B. S. Wallston (Eds.), *Women, gender and social psychology* (pp. 67–99). Hillsdale, NJ: Erlbaum.

Hare-Mustin, R. T., & Marecek, J. (Eds.). (1988). *Making a difference: Psychology and the construction of gender*. New Haven, CT: Yale University Press.

Hartmann, H. I. (1981). The family as the locus of gender, class, and political struggle: The example of housework. *Signs, 6*, 366–394.

Hasher, L., Goldstein, D., & Toppino, T. (1977). Frequency and the conference of referential validity. *Journal of Verbal Learning & Verbal Behavior, 16*, 107–112.

Haslett, B., Geis, F. L., & Carter, M. (1992). *The organizational woman: Power and paradox*. New York: Ablex.

Hastie, R. (1981). Schematic principles in human memory. In E. T. Higgins, C. P. Herman, & M. P. Zanna (Eds.), *Social cognition: The Ontario symposium* (Vol. 1, pp. 39–88). Hillsdale, NJ: Erlbaum.

Hastie, R., & Kumar, P. A. (1979). Person memory: Personality traits as organizing principles in memory for behavior. *Journal of Personality and Social Psychology*, 37, 25–38.

Heilman, M. (1980). The impact of situational factors on personnel decisions concerning women: Varying the sex composition of the applicant pool. *Organizational Behavior and Human Performance*, 26, 386–395.

Heilman, M. E., & Guzzo, R. A. (1978). The perceived cause of work success as a mediator of sex discrimination in organizations. *Organizational Behavior and Human Performance*, 21, 346–357.

Heilman, M. E., & Martell, R. F. (1986). Exposure to successful women: Antidote to sex discrimination in applicant screening decisions? *Organizational Behavior and Human Decision Processes*, 37, 376–390.

Helmreich, R. L., Spence, J. T., Beane, W. E., Lucker, G. W., & Matthews, K. A. (1980). Making it in academic psychology: Demographic and personality correlates of attainment. *Journal of Personality and Social Psychology*, 39, 896–908.

Hemsley, G. D., & Marmurek, H. H. C. (1982). Person memory: The processing of consistent and inconsistent person information. *Personality and Social Psychology Bulletin*, 8, 433–438.

Henley, N. M. (1977). *Body politics: Power, sex and nonverbal communication*: Englewood Cliffs, NJ: Prentice-Hall.

Henley, N. M., & Freeman, J. (1989). The sexual politics of interpersonal behavior. In J. Freeman (Ed.), *Women: A feminist perspective* (4th ed.) (pp. 457–469). Mountainview, CA: Mayfield.

Higgins, E. T., & King, G. A. (1981). Accessibility of social constructs: Information-processing consequences of individual and contextual variability. In N. Cantor & J. F. Kihlstrom (Eds.), *Personality, cognition, and social interaction* (pp. 69–122). Hillsdale, NJ: Erlbaum.

Higgins, E. T., King, G. A., & Mavin, G. H. (1982). Individual construct accessibility and subjective impressions and recall. *Journal of Personality and Social Psychology*, 43, 35–47.

Higgins, E. T., Rholes, W. S., & Jones, C. R. (1977). Category accessibility and impression formation. *Journal of Experimental Social Psychology*, 13, 141–154.

Hirt, E. R. (1990). Do I see only what I expect? Evidence for an expectancy-guided retrieval model. *Journal of Personality and Social Psychology*, 58, 937–951.

Hoffman, C., & Hurst, N. (1990). Gender stereotypes: Perception or rationalization? *Journal of Personality and Social Psychology*, 58, 197–208.

Hogg, M. A., & Abrams, D. (1988). *Social identifications: A social psychology of intergroup relations and group processes*. London: Routledge.

Horner, M. S. (1972). Toward an understanding of achievement related conflicts in women. *Journal of Social Issues*, 28, 157–175.

Howard, J. A. (1984). Societal influences on attribution: Blaming some victims more than others. *Journal of Personality and Social Psychology*, 47, 494–505.

Howard, J. A., Blumstein, P., & Schwartz, P. (1986). Sex, power, and influence tactics in intimate relationships. *Journal of Personality and Social Psychology*, 51, 102–109.

Hunt, D. E. (1987). *Beginning with ourselves: In practice, theory, and human affairs.* Cambridge, MA: Brookline Books.

Hyde, J. S., & Linn, M. C. (1986). *The psychology of gender: Advances through meta-analysis.* Baltimore, MD: Johns Hopkins University Press.

Ickes, W., Patterson, M. L., Rajecki, D. W., & Tanford, S. (1982). Behavioral and cognitive consequences of reciprocal versus compensatory responses to preinteraction expectancies. *Social Cognition, 1,* 160–190.

Insko, C. A., Gilmore, R., Drenan, S., Lipsitz, A., Moehle, D., & Thibaut, J. (1983). Trade versus expropriation in open groups: A comparison of two types of social power. *Journal of Personality and Social Psychology, 44,* 977–999.

Jacobs, J. A. (1989). *Revolving doors: Sex segregation and women's careers.* Stanford, CA: Stanford University Press.

James, W. (1916). *The varieties of religious experience.* New York: Longmans Green.

Janman, K. (1989). One step behind: Current stereotypes of women, achievement, and work. *Sex Roles, 21,* 209–230.

Jennings (Walstedt), J., Geis, F. L., & Brown, V. (1980). The influence of television commercials on women's self-confidence and independent judgment. *Journal of Personality and Social Psychology, 38,* 203–210.

Johnson, P. (1976). Women and power: Toward a theory of effectiveness. *Journal of Social Issues, 32,* 99–110.

Jones, E. E., & Davis, K. E. (1965). From acts to dispositions: The attribution process in person perception. In L. Berkowitz (Ed.), *Advances in experimental social psychology* (Vol. 2, pp. 220–266), New York: Academic Press.

Jones, E. E., & McGillis, D. (1976). Correspondent inferences and the attribution cube: A comparative reappraisal. In J. H. Harvey, W. J. Ickes, & R. F. Kidd (Eds.), *New directions in attribution research* (Vol. 2, pp. 389–420). Hillsdale, NJ: Erlbaum.

Jones, R. G., & Jones, E. E. (1964). Optimum conformity as an ingratiation tactic. *Journal of Personality, 32,* 436–458.

Josefowitz, N. (1985). Women and power: A new model. In A. G. Sargent (Ed.), *Beyond sex roles* (pp. 199–214). St. Paul, MN: West.

Kahn, W. A., & Crosby, F. (1987). Discriminating between attitudes and discriminatory behaviors. In L. Larwood, B. A. Gutek, & A. H. Stromberg (Eds.), *Women and work: An annual review* (Vol. 1, pp. 215–328). Beverly Hills, CA: Sage.

Kanter, R. M. (1977). *Men and women of the corporation.* New York: Basic Books.

Keating, C. F. (1985). Gender and the physiognomy of dominance and attractiveness. *Social Psychology Quarterly, 48,* 61–70.

Kemper, S. (1984). When to speak like a lady. *Sex Roles, 10,* 435–443.

Kessler, S. J., & McKenna, W. (1978). *Gender: An ethnomethodological approach.* New York: Wiley.

Kiesler, C. A., & Mathog, R. (1971). Resistance to influence as a function of number of prior consonant acts. In C. A. Kiesler (Ed.), *The psychology of commitment* (pp. 66–73). New York: Academic Press.

Kiotas, A. J. (1987). *The effect of assigned status and dominance-trait upon paralinguistic behavior in simulated groups: A test of situation versus disposition.* Unpublished master's thesis, University of Delaware, Newark, DE.

Kite, M. E., & Deaux, K. (1986). Attitudes toward homosexuality: Assessment and behavioral consequences. *Basic and Applied Social Psychology, 7*, 137–162.

Klatzky, R. L., Martin, G. L., & Kane, R. A. (1982). Influence of social-category activation on processing of visual information. *Social Cognition, 1*, 95–109.

Kohn, M. L., & Schooler, C. (1978). The reciprocal effects of the substantive complexity of work and intellectual flexibility: A longitudinal assessment. *American Journal of Sociology, 84*, 24–52.

Kourilsky, M., & Campbell, M. (1984). Sex differences in a simulated classroom economy: Children's beliefs about entrepreneurship. *Sex Roles, 10*, 53–66.

Kulik, J. A. (1983). Confirmatory attributions and the perpetuation of social beliefs. *Journal of Personality and Social Psychology, 44*, 1171–1181.

Langer, E. J., & Benevento, A. (1978). Self-induced dependence. *Journal of Personality and Social Psychology, 36*, 886–893.

Lecky, P. (1969). *Self-consistency: A theory of personality*. Garden City, NY: Doubleday.

Leffler, A., Gillespie, D. L., & Conaty, J. C. (1982). The effects of status differentiation on nonverbal behavior. *Social Psychology Quarterly, 45*, 153–161.

Leidig, M. W. (1981). Violence against women: A feminist-psychological analysis. In S. Cox (Ed.), *Female psychology: The emerging self* (pp. 190–205). New York: St. Martin's Press.

Lenney, E., & Gold, J. (1982). Sex differences in self-confidence: The effects of task completion and of comparison to competent others. *Personality and Social Psychology Bulletin, 8*, 74–80.

Lewin, K. (1951). *Field theory in social science*. New York: Harper.

Lewis, L. L. (1985). *The influence of individual differences in gender stereotyping on the interpersonal expectancy process*. Unpublished doctoral dissertation, Purdue University, West Lafayette, IN.

Lieberman, S. (1965). The effects of changes in roles on the attitudes of role occupants. In H. Proshansky & B. Seidenberg (Eds.), *Basic studies in social psychology* (pp. 485–494). New York: Holt, Rinehart & Winston.

Linz, D. G., Donnerstein, E., & Penrod, S. (1988). Effects of long-term exposure to violent and sexually degrading depictions of women. *Journal of Personality and Social Psychology, 55*, 758–768.

Lippa, R., & Beauvais, C. (1983). Gender jeopardy: The effects of gender, assessed femininity and masculinity and false success/failure feedback on performance in an experimental quiz game. *Journal of Personality and Social Psychology, 44*, 344–353.

Lips, H. (1991). *Women, men, and power*. Mountain View, CA: Mayfield.

Lofland, J. (1969). *Deviance and identity*. Englewood Cliffs, NJ: Prentice-Hall.

Lorber, J., & Farrell, S. A. (Eds.). (1991). *The social construction of gender*. Newbury Park, CA: Sage.

Lord, C. G., Lepper, M. R., & Mackie, D. M. (1984). Attitude prototypes as determinants of attitude-behavior consistency. *Journal of Personality and Social Psychology, 46*, 1254–1266.

Lott, B. (1985). The devaluation of women's competence. *Journal of Social Issues, 41*, 43–60.

Lott, B. (1987). Sexist discrimination as distancing behavior: I. A laboratory demonstration. *Psychology of Women Quarterly, 11*, 47–58.

Lovdal, L. T. (1989). Sex role messages in television commercials: An update. *Sex Roles, 21*, 715–724.

Maccoby, E. E. (1990). Gender and relationships: A developmental account. *American Psychologist, 45*, 513–520.

Maccoby, E. E., & Jacklin, C. N. (1974). *The psychology of sex differences.* Stanford, CA: Stanford University Press.

Malamuth, N. M. (1981). Rape proclivity among males. *Journal of Social Issues, 37*, 138–157.

Malamuth, N. M. (1983). Factors associated with rape as predictors of laboratory aggression against women. *Journal of Personality and Social Psychology, 45*, 432–442.

Malamuth, N. M. (1984). Aggression against women: Cultural and individual causes. In N. M. Malamuth & E. Donnerstein (Eds.), *Pornography and sexual aggression* (pp. 19–52). Orlando, FL: Academic Press.

Mandler, G. (1982). The structure of value: Accounting for taste. In M. S. Clark & S. T. Fiske (Eds.), *Cognition and affect: The 17th annual Carnegie symposium* (pp. 3–36). Hillsdale, NJ: Erlbaum.

Martin, C. L. (1987). A ratio measure of sex stereotyping. *Journal of Personality and Social Psychology, 52*, 489–499.

McArthur, L. Z. (1981). What grabs you? The role of attention in impression formation and causal attribution. In E. T. Higgins, C. P. Herman, & M. P. Zanna (Eds.), *Social cognition: The Ontario symposium* (Vol. 1, pp. 201–246). Hillsdale, NJ: Erlbaum.

McBroom, W. H. (1984). Changes in sex-role orientations: A five year longitudinal comparison. *Sex Roles, 11*, 583–592.

McKenzie-Mohr, D., & Zanna, M. P. (1990). Treating women as sexual objects: Look to the (gender schematic) male who has viewed pornography. *Personality and Social Psychology Bulletin, 16*, 296–308.

Mead, G. H. (1934). *Mind, self, and society.* Chicago: University of Chicago Press.

Megargee, E. E. (1969). Influence of sex roles on the manifestation of leadership. *Journal of Applied Psychology, 53*, 377–382.

Merton, R. K. (1948). The self-fulfilling prophecy. *Antioch Review, 8*, 193–210.

Miller, D. T., & Turnbull, W. (1986). Expectancies and interpersonal processes. *Annual Review of Psychology, 37*, 233–256.

Miller, J. B. (1986). *Toward a new psychology of women.* Boston: Beacon Press. (Original work published 1976)

Miller, J. G. (1984). Culture and the development of everyday social explanation. *Journal of Personality and Social Psychology, 46*, 961–978.

Miller, J., Schooler, C., Kohn, M. L., & Miller, K. A. (1979). Women and work: The psychological effects of occupational conditions. *American Journal of Sociology, 85*, 66–94.

Morawski, J. G. (1987). The troubled quest for masculinity, femininity, and androgyny. In P. Shaver & C. Hendrick (Eds.), *Sex and gender* (pp. 44–69). Newbury Park, CA: Sage.

Morrison, A. M., White, R. P., Van Velsor, E., & Center for Creative Leadership. (1987). *Breaking the glass ceiling: Can women reach the top of America's largest corporations?* Reading, MA: Addison-Wesley.

Needleman, R., & Nelson, A. (1988). Policy implications: The worth of women's work. In A. Statham, E. M. Miller, & H. O. Mauksch (Eds.), *The worth of women's work: A qualitative synthesis* (pp. 293–307). Albany, NY: State University of New York Press.

Nieva, V. F., & Gutek, B. A. (1981). *Women and work: A psychological perspective.* New York: Praeger.

Nisbett, R. E., & Wilson, T. D. (1977). Telling more than we can know: Verbal reports on mental processes. *Psychological Review, 84,* 231–259.

Nyquist, L. V., & Spence, J. T. (1986). Effects of dispositional dominance and sex role expectations on leadership behaviors. *Journal of Personality and Social Psychology, 50,* 87–93.

Offerman, L. R. (1984). Short-term supervisory experience and LPC score: Effects of leader sex and group sex composition. *Journal of Social Psychology, 123,* 115–121.

Offerman, L. R. (1986). Visibility and evaluation of female and male leaders. *Sex Roles, 14,* 533–543.

O'Leary, V. (1974). Some attitudinal barriers to occupational aspirations in women. *Psychological Bulletin, 81,* 809–826.

Olson, J. E., & Frieze, I. H. (1987). Income determinants for women in business. In A. H. Stromberg, L. Larwood, & B. A. Gutek (Eds.), *Women and work: An annual review* (Vol. 2, pp. 173–206). Newbury Park, CA: Sage.

O'Sullivan, C. S., & Durso, F. T. (1984). Effects of schema-incongruent information on memory for stereotypical attributes. *Journal of Personality and Social Psychology, 47,* 55–70.

Ozer, E. M., & Bandura, A. (1990). Mechanisms governing empowerment effects: A self-efficacy analysis. *Journal of Personality and Social Psychology, 58,* 472–486.

Paludi, M. A. (Ed). (1990). *Ivory power: Sexual harassment on campus.* Albany, NY: State University of New York Press.

Paludi, M. A., & Strayer, L. A. (1985). What's in an author's name? Differential evaluations of performance as a function of author's name. *Sex Roles, 12,* 353–361.

Persell, C. H. (1983). Gender, rewards and research in education. *Psychology of Women Quarterly, 8,* 33–47.

Pheterson, G. I., Kiesler, S. B., & Goldberg, P. A. (1971). Evaluation of the performance of women as a function of their sex, achievement and personal history. *Journal of Personality and Social Psychology, 19,* 114–118.

Porter, N., & Geis, F. L. (1981). Women and nonverbal leadership cues: When seeing is not believing. In C. Mayo & N. Henley (Eds.), *Gender and nonverbal behavior* (pp. 39–61). New York: Springer-Verlag.

Porter, N., Geis, F. L., Cooper, E., & Newman, E. (1985). Androgyny and leadership in mixed-sex groups. *Journal of Personality and Social Psychology, 49,* 803–823.

Pugh, M. D., & Wahrman, R. (1983). Neutralizing sexism in mixed-sex groups. Do women have to be better than men? *American Journal of Sociology, 88,* 746–762.

Quattrone, G. A. (1982). Over attribution and unit formation. When behavior engulfs the person. *Journal of Personality and Social Psychology, 42*, 593–607.

Quattrone, G. A., & Tversky, A. (1984). Causal versus diagnostic contingencies: On self-deception and on the voter's illusion. *Journal of Personality and Social Psychology, 46*, 237–248.

Regan, D. T., Straus, E., & Fazio, R. (1974). Liking and the attribution process. *Journal of Experimental Social Psychology, 10*, 385–397.

Reinisch, J. M., Rosenblum, L. A., & Sanders, A. S. (Eds). (1987). *Masculinity/femininity: Basic perspectives*. New York: Oxford University Press.

Ridgeway, C. L. (1982). Status in groups: The importance of motivation. *American Sociological Review, 47*, 76–88.

Ridgeway, C. L. (Ed.). (1991). *Gender, interaction and inequality*. New York: Springer-Verlag.

Robinson, J. P. (1988, December). Who's doing the housework? *American Demographics, 63*, 24–48.

Rock, I. (1983). *The logic of perception*. Cambridge, MA: MIT Press.

Rosen, B., & Jerdee, T. H. (1974). Influence of sex-role stereotypes on personnel decisions. *Journal of Applied Psychology, 59*, 9–14.

Rosen, B., Jerdee, T. H., & Prestwick, T. L. (1975). Dual career mutual adjustment: Potential effects of discriminatory managerial attitudes. *Journal of Marriage and the Family, 37*, 565–572.

Ross, L. (1977). The intuitive psychologist and his shortcomings. In L. Berkowitz (Ed.), *Advances in experimental social psychology* (Vol. 10, pp. 174–221). New York: Academic Press.

Ross, L., Amabile, T., & Steinmetz, J. L. (1977). Social roles, social control, and biases in social perception processes. *Journal of Personality and Social Psychology, 35*, 484–494.

Rothbart, M., Fulero, S., Jensen, C., Howard, J., & Birrell, B. (1978). From individual to group impressions: Availability heuristics in stereotype formation. *Journal of Experimental Social Psychology, 14*, 237–255.

Rothbart, M., & Lewis, S. (1988). Inferring category attributes from exemplar attributes: Geometric shapes and social categories. *Journal of Personality and Social Psychology, 55*, 961–972.

Rubin, J. Z., Provenzano, F. J., & Luria, Z. (1974). The eye of the beholder: Parents' views on sex of newborns. *American Journal of Orthopsychiatry, 44*, 512–519.

Sadker, M., & Sadker, D. (1985, March). Sexism in the schoolroom of the '80's. *Psychology Today*, 54–57.

Scanzoni, J. (1982). *Sexual bargaining: Power politics in the American marriage* (2 nd ed.). Chicago: University of Chicago Press.

Schein, V. E. (1973). Relationship between sex role stereotypes and requisite management characteristics. *Journal of Applied Psychology, 57*, 95–100.

Schein, V. E. (1975). Relationships between sex-role stereotypes and requisite management characteristics among female managers. *Journal of Applied Psychology, 60*, 340–344.

Secord, P. F. (1982). The origin and maintenance of social roles: The case of sex roles. In W. Ickes & F. S. Knowles (Eds.), *Personality, roles, and social behavior* (pp. 33–53). New York: Springer-Verlag.

Selkow, P. (1984). Effects of maternal employment on kindergarten and first-grade children's vocational aspirations. *Sex Roles, 11*, 677–690.

Seyfried, B. A., & Hendrick, C. (1973). When do opposites attract? When they are opposite in sex and sex-role attitudes. *Journal of Personality and Social Psychology, 25*, 15–20.

Sherif, C. W. (1979). Bias in psychology. In J. A. Sherman & E. T. Beck (Eds.), *The prism of sex: Essays in the sociology of knowledge* (pp. 93–133). Madison, WI: University of Wisconsin Press.

Sherif, C. W. (1982). Needed concepts in the study of gender. *Psychology of Women Quarterly, 6*, 375–398.

Sherif, M. (1935). A study of some social factors in perception. *Archives of Psychology, 187*.

Sherman, S. J., Ahlm, K., Berman, L., & Lynn, S. (1978). Contrast effects and their relationship to subsequent behavior. *Journal of Experimental Social Psychology, 14*, 340–350.

Sherman, S. J., & Gorkin, L. (1980). Attitude bolstering when behavior is inconsistent with central attitudes. *Journal of Experimental Social Psychology, 16*, 388–403.

Siderits, M. A., Johannsen, W. J., & Fadden, T. F. (1985). Gender, role, and power: A content analysis of speech. *Psychology of Women Quarterly, 9*, 439–450.

Signorielli, N. (1989). Television and conceptions about adult sex roles: Maintaining conventionality and status quo. *Sex Roles, 21*, 341–360.

Skrypnek, B. J., & Snyder, M. (1982). On the self-perpetuating nature of stereotypes about women and men. *Journal of Experimental Social Psychology, 18*, 277–291.

Smith, E. R. (1984). Model of social inference processes. *Psychological Review, 91*, 392–413.

Smith, E. R. (1989). Procedural efficiency: General and specific components and effects on social judgment. *Journal of Experimental Social Psychology, 25*, 500–523.

Smith, P. (1985). *Language, the sexes and society.* Oxford, UK: Blackwell.

Snodgrass, S. E. (1985). Women's intuition: The effect of subordinate role on interpersonal sensitivity. *Journal of Personality and Social Psychology, 49*, 146–155.

Snodgrass, S. E. (1992). Further effects of role versus gender on interpersonal sensitivity. *Journal of Personality and Social Psychology, 62*, 154–158.

Snyder, M. (1984). When belief creates reality. In L. Berkowitz (Ed.), *Advances in experimental social psychology* (Vol. 18, pp. 248–306). New York: Academic Press.

Snyder, M., & Swann, W. B., Jr. (1976). When actions reflect attitudes: The politics of impressions management. *Journal of Personality and Social Psychology, 34*, 1034–1042.

Snyder, M., & Swann, W. B., Jr. (1978). Behavioral confirmation in social interaction: From social perception to social reality. *Journal of Experimental Social Psychology, 14*, 148–162.

Snyder, M., Tanke, E. D., & Berscheid, E. (1977). Social perception and interpersonal behavior: On the self-fulfilling nature of social stereotypes. *Journal of Personality and Social Psychology, 35*, 656–666.

Spence, J. T. (1985). Gender identity and its implications for concepts of masculinity and femininity. In T. B. Sonderegger (Ed.), *Nebraska symposium on motivation: Psychology of gender* (pp. 59–95). Lincoln, NB: University of Nebraska Press.

Spence, J. T., & Helmreich, R. L. (1972). The Attitudes toward Women Scale: An objective instrument to measure attitudes toward the rights and roles of women in contemporary society. *JSAS Catalog of Selected Documents in Psychology, 2*, 66.

Spence, J. T., & Helmreich, R. L. (1978). *Masculinity and femininity: The psychological dimensions, correlates and antecedents.* Austin, TX: University of Texas Press.

Spence, J. T., Helmreich, R. L., & Stapp, J. (1975). Ratings of self and peers on sex-role attributes and their relations to self-esteem and conceptions of masculinity and femininity. *Journal of Personality and Social Psychology, 32*, 29–39.

Stangor, C. (1988). Stereotype accessibility and information processing. *Personality and Social Psychology Bulletin, 13*, 694–708.

Sterling, B. S., & Owen, J. W. (1982). Perceptions of demanding versus reasoning male and female police officers. *Personality and Social Psychology Bulletin, 8*, 336–340.

Stewart, A. J., & Chester, N. L. (1982). Sex differences in human social motives: Achievement, affiliation, and power. In A. J. Stewart (Ed.), *Motivation and society* (pp. 172–218). San Francisco: Jossey-Bass.

Sullivan, G. L., & O'Connor, P. J. (1988). Women's role portrayals in magazine advertising: 1958–1983. *Sex Roles, 18*, 181–188.

Swann, W. B., Jr. (1983). Self-verification: Bringing social reality into harmony with the self. In J. Suls & A. G. Greenwald (Eds.), *Psychological perspectives on the self* (Vol. 2, pp. 33–66). Hillsdale, NJ: Erlbaum.

Swann, W. B., Jr. (1984). Quest for accuracy in person perception: A matter of pragmatics. *Psychological Review, 91*, 457–477.

Swann, W. B., Jr. (1987). Identity negotiation: Where two roads meet. *Journal of Personality and Social Psychology, 53*, 1038–1051.

Swann, W. B., Jr., & Ely, R. J. (1984). A battle of wills: Self-verification versus behavioral confirmation. *Journal of Personality and Social Psychology, 46*, 1287–1302.

Swann, W. B., Jr., & Read, S. J. (1981). Self-verification processes: How we sustain our self-conceptions. *Journal of Experimental Social Psychology, 17*, 351–370.

Swim, J., Borgida, E., Maruyama, G., & Myers, P. G. (1989). Joan McKay versus John McKay: Do gender stereotypes bias evaluations? *Psychological Bulletin, 105*, 409–429.

Tajfel, H. (1981). *Human groups and social categories: Studies in social psychology.* Cambridge, England: Cambridge University Press.

Taylor, S. E. (1983). Adjustment to threatening events: A theory of cognitive adaptation. *American Psychologist, 38*, 1161–1173.

Taylor, S. E., & Crocker, J. (1981). Schematic bases of social information processing. In E. T. Higgins, C. P. Herman, & M. P. Zanna (Eds.), *Social cognition: The Ontario symposium* (Vol. 1, pp. 89–134). Hillsdale, NJ: Erlbaum.

Taynor, J., & Deaux, K. (1975). Equity and perceived sex differences: Role behavior as defined by the task, the mode, and the actor. *Journal of Personality and Social Psychology, 32*, 381–390.

Tesser, A. (1988). Toward a self-evaluation maintenance model of social behavior. In L. Berkowitz (Ed.), *Advances in experimental social psychology* (Vol. 21, pp. 181–227). New York: Academic Press.

Tetlock, P. E., & Manstead, A. S. R. (1985). Impression management versus intrapsychic explanations in social psychology. A useful dichotomy? *Psychological Review, 92*, 59–77.

Tidball, M. E. (1973). Perspective on academic women and affirmative action. *Educational Record, 54*, 130–135.

Trope, Y. (1986). Identification and inferential processes in dispositional attribution. *Psychological Review, 93*, 239–257.

Tsui, A. S., & Gutek, B. A. (1984). A role set analysis of gender differences in performance, affective relationships, and career success of industrial middle managers. *Academy of Management Journal, 27*, 619–635.

Uleman, J. S., & Bargh, J. A. (1989). *Unintended thought.* New York: Guilford Press.

Unger, R. K. (1976). Male is greater than female: The socialization of status inequality. *Counseling Psychologist, 6*, 2–9.

Unger, R. K. (1978). The politics of gender: A review of relevant literature. In J. A. Sherman & F. L. Denmark (Eds.), *The psychology of women: Future directions of research* (pp. 461–518). New York: Psychological Dimensions.

Unger, R. K. (1989). Sex in psychological paradigms: From behavior to cognition. In R. K. Unger (Ed.), *Representations: Social constructions of gender* (pp. 1–12, 15–20). Amityville, NY: Baywood.

Vaughn, L. S., & Wittig, M. A. (1981). Women's occupations, competence, and role over-load as determinants of evaluation by others. *Journal of Applied Social Psychology, 10*, 398–415.

Vetter, B. (1986). The last two decades. *Science 86, 7*, 62–63.

Vollmer, F. (1984). Sex differences in personality and expectancy. *Sex Roles, 11*, 1121–1139.

Vollmer, F. (1986). Why do men have higher expectancy than women? *Sex Roles, 14*, 351–362.

Wallston, B. S., & O'Leary, V. E. (1981). Sex makes a difference: Differential perceptions of women and men. In L. Wheeler (Ed.), *Review of personality and social psychology* (pp. 9–41). Beverly Hills, CA: Sage.

Ward, C. (1981). Prejudice against women: Who, when, and why. *Sex Roles, 7*, 163–171.

Watkins, M. J., & Peynircioglu, Z. F., (1984). Determining perceived meaning during impression formation: Another look at the meaning change hypothesis. *Journal of Personality and Social Psychology, 46*, 1005–1016.

Weber, R., & Crocker, J. (1983). Cognitive processes in the revision of stereotypic beliefs. *Journal of Personality and Social Psychology, 45*, 961–977.

Webster, M., Jr., & Foschi, M. (Eds.). (1988). *Status generalization: New theory and research.* Stanford, CA: Stanford University Press.

Weisstein, N. (1968). *Kinder, kirche, kuche as scientific law: Psychology constructs the female.* Boston: New England Free Press.

West, C., & Zimmerman, D. H. (1987). Doing gender. *Gender and Society, 1,* 125–151.

White, J. D., & Carlston, D. E. (1983). Consequences of schemata for attention, impression, and recall in complex social interactions. *Journal of Personality and Social Psychology, 45,* 536–549.

Williams, J. E., & Best, D. L. (1982). *Measuring sex stereotypes: A thirty nation study.* Beverly Hills, CA: Sage.

Wilson, T. D. (1985). Strangers to ourselves: The origins and accuracy of beliefs about one's own mental states. In J. H. Harvey & G. Weary (Eds.), *Attribution: Basic issues and applications* (pp. 9–36). New York: Academic Press.

Wilson, W., & Miller, H. (1968). Repetition, order of presentation, and timing of arguments and measures as determinants of opinion change. *Journal of Personality and Social Psychology, 9,* 184–188.

Winter, L., & Uleman, J. S. (1984). When are social judgments made? Evidence for the spontaneousness of trait inferences. *Journal of Personality and Social Psychology, 47,* 237–252.

Wittig, M. A. (1985). Metatheoretical dilemmas in the psychology of gender. *American Psychologist, 40,* 800–811.

Wolman, C., & Frank, H. (1975). The solo woman in a professional peer group. *American Journal of Orthopsychiatry, 45,* 164–171.

Wood, W., & Karten, S. J. (1986). Sex differences in interaction style as a product of perceived sex differences in competence. *Journal of Personality and Social Psychology, 50,* 341–347.

Word, C. O., Zanna, M. P., & Cooper, J. (1974). The nonverbal mediation of self-fulfilling prophecies in interracial interaction. *Journal of Experimental Social Psychology, 10,* 109–120.

Yamada, E. M., Tjosvold, D., & Draguns, J. G. (1983). Sex-role scripts. *Sex Roles, 9,* 541–553.

Yount, K. R. (1986). A theory of productive activity: The relationships among self-concept, gender, sex role stereotypes, and work-emergent traits. *Psychology of Women Quarterly, 10,* 63–87.

Zadney, J., & Gerard, H. B. (1974). Attributed intentions and informational selectivity. *Journal of Experimental Social Psychology, 10,* 34–52.

Zajonc, R. B. (1968). Attitudinal effects of mere exposure. *Journal of Personality and Social Psychology Monograph Supplement, 9,* 1–27.

Zarate, M. A., & Smith, E. R. (1990). Person categorization and stereotyping. *Social Cognition, 8,* 161–185.

Zimmerman, D., & West, C. (1975). Sex roles, interruptions, and silences in conversation. In B. Thorne & N. Henley (Eds.), *Language and sex: Difference and dominance* (pp. 105–129). Rowley, MA: Newbury House.

Gender in Thought, Belief, and Action: A Cognitive Approach

SUSAN E. CROSS

HAZEL ROSE MARKUS

During the early 1990s, the comedy television program *Saturday Night Live* regularly featured a segment titled "Pat". In most respects Pat was a rather average person except that Pat's gender was not readily apparent. The humor of the skit came from empathizing with the predicaments of people who tried to interact naturally with Pat without this all-important knowledge. Quite believably, those in the skit were depicted as desperate to resolve the ambiguity of Pat's gender. They searched for subtle or hidden clues to his/her gender identity. They asked leading questions to determine his/her group membership, carefully phrasing their questions in gender-neutral language. They struggled to avoid the embarrassment of using the wrong pronoun. They devised elaborate plans in an attempt to "trap" Pat into revealing his/her "biological" sex. The question of the androgynous character's gender status was never answered in the skits; many of them ended by portraying the other actors' palpable relief in escaping the situation.

The "Pat" skit played on viewers' intolerance for gender ambiguity and people's clear and present need always to know another's gender. With such knowledge one can interact appropriately; without this seemingly basic information, the simplest encounter is markedly strained. Even the most superficial of social exchanges ("Hello, M— Jones") cannot be negotiated. There are no norms for interacting with gender-neutral others, only for interacting with men or women. The example highlights the way in which gender is not just a variable that influences the "basic" processes of thinking, feeling, appreciating, striving, and acting, but also a social fact that conditions and governs these very processes.

People are socialized to consider gender a primary piece of information about a person, and gender knowledge significantly influences most subsequent interactions and thoughts about the person. Biological sex dictates one's role in reproduction, but the conceptions of gender held in one's significant sociocultural contexts influence everything else—from one's name to one's occupation, choices, preferences, and aspirations. Beliefs about gender are based not in biological reality but instead in a pervasive and complex belief system that "little boys" and "little girls" (as the nursery rhyme goes) are made of fundamentally different essences.

The issue of why gender matters is currently being pursued everywhere—in the humanities, in the social sciences, in philosophy, and in the popular media. Answers to why gender matters can be found at all levels of analysis—the individual, the societal, the cultural, the historical. This chapter examines gender as it is constructed and represented at the *individual* level and focuses on the cognitive approach to understanding how gender constrains and affords experience in the social world. We will approach gender by inquiring how gender is represented in the mind—by exploring how gender functions as a category of tremendous significance when thinking about others and when thinking about the self, and how gender influences both *what* one thinks and *how* one thinks. A cognitive perspective claims that some of the most important aspects of the differences in the behavior of men and women can be linked to how gender is mentally represented and to how it is given meaning.

GENDER AS A SOCIAL AND COGNITIVE CREATION

A cognitive perspective on gender has as its cornerstone the idea that gender is a basic category used to understand and engage one's social environment. But gender is far from being solely a cognitive creation; in most respects it is a social creation built on a foundation of physical difference. Although future research may paint a different picture, recent reviews suggest that the influences of biology on gender differences are relatively minor (Baker, 1987; Jacklin, 1989). Yet culture reifies and amplifies these differences many times over, creating a sense of a pervasive difference between men and women. Although some aspects of the traditional social stereotypes of men and women have been questioned and rejected, many social patterns, beliefs, expectations, or assumptions that are based on these traditional views remain, and they are pervasively represented and realized in institutional functioning, in legal codes as well as in cultural habits, norms, values, and everyday social practices

(Crawford & Hamilton, 1989; Geertz, 1973; Ruble, 1983). Indeed, because the social practices and the social norms, expectations, and values regarding men and women in our society are so divergent, some have described the sexes as inhabiting very different worlds or cultures (Tannen, 1990).

A cognitive perspective on gender can illuminate why gender is such a powerful category and why it seems so important in social interaction. For almost 40 years, researchers have examined Allport's (1954) assertion that "the human mind must think with the aid of categories" (p. 20). A great deal of research has supported his claim, finding that human cognitive capacity is limited, and so the wealth of incoming information and stimuli that each person encounters in the course of a day, hour, or even moment must be simplified in order to ease the demands on our cognitive abilities. This "cognitive miser" approach (Taylor, 1981) has elaborated the way people use categories, schemas, or stereotypes in everyday interactions with others in order to guide their interactions, to make swift judgments and inferences about others, and to facilitate their memory for these social interactions.[1]

Grouping people into simple categories reduces the amount of effort needed to understand or interact with them (Allport, 1954; Taylor, 1981). People appear to automatically assign others to easily observable categories (black male, businessman, senior citizen) and then to allow the generalizations or characterizations invoked by this category to direct their thoughts, feelings, and behaviors toward that person. The cognitive perspective of the last two decades has helped explain *why* this categorization process occurs (e.g., the information processing capacity of the human mind is limited and so people seek shortcuts), *how* it occurs (i.e., how information processing proceeds and how heuristics or biases influence this process), and the factors that may reduce an overreliance on categories or generalizations or that may even result in their change (for reviews, see Deaux & Major, 1987; Fiske & Taylor, 1991; Hamilton & Trolier, 1986; Higgins & Bargh, 1987; Markus & Zajonc, 1985; Rothbart & John, 1985; Schneider, 1991; Sherman, Judd, & Park, 1989). The first part of this chapter briefly summarizes findings from the research on social cognition and schemas, illustrating their relevance to gender as a social category.

The cognitive perspective also helps explain how gender categories and labels are sustained in the social world. Even though women perform

---

[1] In this chapter, we use category to indicate a social group, while a stereotype includes the social consensus about the characteristics that define that group. Schemas are an individual's idiosyncratic, internalized representations of stereotypes. As such they may faithfully mirror the general belief of the wider society, or they may deviate from the stereotype. Since much of the recent understanding of stereotyping has resulted from schema research, we will use the latter term whenever we refer to an internal, mental representation.

competently in many traditionally male roles—as astronauts, lawyers, chief of police, or state governors, for example—the stereotypes of men and women have changed very little in the last 20 years. The cognitive perspective helps explain the processes that support and maintain those stereotypes and reveals what is necessary for these stereotypes to change. Cognitive perspectives and approaches have also informed our understanding of gender as an important aspect of thinking about the self. Using the tools provided by cognitive psychology, researchers have been able to uncover the central role of the self in mediating thought and behavior (for reviews, see Greenwald & Pratkanis, 1984; Kihlstrom & Cantor, 1984; Markus & Wurf, 1987). Recent research points to differences in this society in men and women's self-concepts, and to the consequences of these differences for thinking, feeling, and action (Markus & Oyserman, 1989). We will review this research and its implications for understanding the influence of gender on thought and behavior.

GENDER AND THINKING ABOUT OTHERS

Gender as a Central Category for Understanding the World

Gender is one of the primary categories that people use to understand and think about their social world. It is what Bruner (1957) has termed a *primitive categorization*. The anthropological literature suggests that every known culture has some gender role differentiation, and that all languages have gender terms. Anthropologists claim that this is currently the case throughout the world and that it has always been so (Condry, 1984; Maccoby, 1988; Mead, 1934; Rosaldo & Lamphere, 1974).

To paraphrase James (1890), gender is a basic dimension that is used to "divide" the universe, perhaps second only to the distinction between what is part of the self and what is *not* part of the self. Recent studies show that gender is one of the first social categories acquired by children (Kohlberg, 1966; Kohlberg & Ullian, 1974). As young as 24 months, children can classify objects, symbols, and adults (Cowan & Hoffman, 1986; Leinbach & Fagot, 1986; Slaby & Frey, 1975; Thompson, 1975). Between the ages of 2 and 3 children demonstrate extensive knowledge of sex-appropriate behaviors (Connor & Serbin, 1977; Kuhn, Nash, & Brucken, 1978; Maccoby, 1988; Maccoby & Jacklin, 1974); by 3 to 4 years old children may criticize others for sex-inappropriate behavior (Bem, 1989; for reviews, see Huston, 1983, 1985; Jacklin & Reynolds, Chapter 8, this volume; Katz, 1986; Maccoby, 1988; Martin & Halverson, 1983; Ruble & Ruble, 1982; Signorella & Liben, 1987). Not only is gender learned very early as a way of understanding others, but gender is one of the first components of the self-concept to be developed (Slaby & Frey, 1975; Spence, 1985; Stangor & Ruble, 1987). By the age of 2 or 3, children have acquired a sense of their gender identity (Slaby & Frey, 1975; Thompson, 1975). Once developed, one's gendered self-view will influence subsequent thought, feeling, and behavior (Sherif, 1982; for a review, see Katz, 1986). As Mussen (1969) describes, "No other social role directs more of an individual's overt behavior, emotional reactions, cognitive functioning, covert attitudes, and general psychological and social adjustment" (p. 707). So thorough is gender's influence that referring to it as a role or a category, while useful for detailing its precise behavioral consequences, runs the risk of trivializing the importance of gender identity in human experience.

Gender is a central category for thinking about others because it is easily discerned by visible cues such as physical appearance (Ashmore & Del Boca, 1981; Brewer, Dull, & Liu, 1981; Deaux & Lewis, 1983, 1984; Hamilton, 1979; McArthur, 1982; Taylor, Fiske, Etcoff, & Ruderman, 1978). Social norms still mandate substantially different styles of dress for men and women in this culture, and even in cultures in which men and women's public dress are very similar (as are the robes in a few Arab cultures), many visible cues are still available to distinguish the sexes (e.g., women's veils and men's headdresses in Saudi Arabia).

But gender is not a central category for understanding oneself and others just because it is one of the first learned or because it is easily visible. On the contrary, it may be one of the first learned precisely because it is so important for social interaction, and thus it is made salient in many situations. For example, one may expect to be waited on by female clerks in a kitchenwares store and male clerks in a hardware store. One set of gender-related schemas may be primed in a day-care center and different gender-related schemas primed in an athletic stadium. Because so many aspects of life have traditionally been associated with one gender or the other, gender-related schemas are easily primed or accessed and readily available for information processing (Bargh, Bond, Lombardi, & Tota, 1986; Bargh, Lombardi, & Higgins, 1988; Higgins, King, & Mavin, 1982). As Bem (1981) has argued, society teaches us that "the dichotomy between male and female has extensive and intensive relevance to virtually every aspect of life" (p. 362). As a result, virtually every incident or situation will be viewed through the lens of our gendered schemas.

Gender as a Stereotype or Schema

But what is the basis of this dichotomy that Bem (1981) describes? Dividing the social world into "male" and "female" is not based solely on reproductive differences, or on anatomical differences. What makes the gender category so important is that gender labels are dense with meaning. Each gender category is associated with particular traits, roles, behaviors, and occupations that comprise a stereotype, or a "picture in our heads" (Lippman, 1922) for men and women. Early work on the content of gender stereotypes showed that men are perceived to be agentic, aggressive, and instrumental, and women are viewed as passive, relational, and emotional (Ashmore, 1981; Bakan, 1966; Rosenkrantz, Vogel, Bee, Broverman, & Broverman, 1968; Spence, Helmreich, & Stapp, 1975; for reviews of gender stereotypes, see Ashmore, Del Boca, & Wohlers, 1986; Eagly, 1987; Lippa, 1990; Martin, 1987; Ruble & Ruble, 1982; Spence, Deaux, & Helmreich, 1985; Wallston & O'Leary, 1981). More recent work shows that although negative stereotypes of women may have moderated somewhat (Eagly & Mladinic, 1987; Werner & LaRussa, 1985), these stereotypes have, in fact, changed very little in the last 20 years (Bergen & Williams, 1991; Heilman, Block, Martell, & Simon, 1989; Martin, 1987; Ruble, 1983; Ruble & Ruble, 1982).

Gender stereotypes are apparently learned very early through direct teaching or observation of gender-related social roles and responsibilities (Eagly & Steffen, 1984; Hoffman & Hurst, 1990); they are also maintained and reinforced by schools, work settings, and the media (Durkin, 1985a, 1985b; Hyde, 1991), or by cognitive heuristics and biases such as illusory correlation and belief perseverance (for reviews, see Hamilton, 1981; Hamilton & Trolier, 1986; Rothbart & John, 1985; Ruble & Ruble, 1982; Stephan, 1985). The following section describes the ways that thoughts and beliefs about gender influence how we think about, judge, and interact with others.

The Role of Gender Schemas in Information Processing

Activation of Gender Schemas

Thinking of others in terms of gender is almost inescapable. When encountering an individual for the first time, we are likely to categorize the person first in terms of gender or race, and second in terms of other readily apparent features (Allport, 1954; Brewer & Liu, 1989; Fiske & Neuberg, 1990; Kessler & McKenna, 1978; McArthur & Baron, 1983; Miller, 1988). Given that gender is one of the first social categories learned, and that many elements of one's world and life are coded in terms of gender, this category may be so frequently activated and so often used that its activation becomes automatic or spontaneous for adults (Higgins & King, 1981; Nelson, Biernat, & Manis, 1990; Wyer & Srull, 1981). In one of the earliest demonstrations of the spontaneous processing of gender, Bower and Karlin (1974) demonstrated that gender judgments were made much more effortlessly than judgments of personality characteristics, suggesting that they are more easily activated (see also Brewer & Liu, 1989).

Studies of social errors also demonstrate that gender is an automatic category used in thinking about others. Imagine observing a discussion among several members of a class. Later, after class, someone asks, "Who made the comment that . . . ?" Many studies have shown that if we mis-remember, we are more likely to make a within-sex mistake than a be-tween-sex mistake (Fiske, Haslam, & Fiske, 1991; Miller, 1986; Taylor, 1981; Taylor & Falcone, 1982; Taylor, et al., 1978). In other words, if a woman initially made the comment, we are more likely to believe it was another woman than to believe it was a man, indicating that an initial categorization of the speaker by sex was made, even though further identi-fication of the speaker may be incomplete or inaccurate. These studies suggest that we use gender as a basic category to identify others and to organize information about them.

Some individuals may be especially inclined to use gender categories when thinking about others. Markus, Smith, and Moreland (1985) found that individuals who had well-elaborated self-schemas for a domain (in this study, the self-schema of being "masculine" was used) were likely to think about others in terms of this schema. While almost every person over the age of 5 will identify him/herself as a male or female, gender identity may be a more central or self-defining identity for some individu-als than for others (Bem, 1981; Markus, Crane, Bernstein, & Siladi, 1982; Sitka & Maslach, 1990). As a result, these schemas may be more easily and more frequently activated, becoming "chronically accessible" for thinking about others (Bargh et al., 1986; Bargh & Pratto, 1986; Higgins et al., 1982; for a review of automatic processing, see Bargh, 1989).

People are also more likely to use gender schemas in some situations than in others. As described earlier, many occupations have been stereo-typed as masculine or feminine (Deaux & Major, 1987; Glick, Zion, & Nelson, 1988; Heilman, 1983). For example, when children are asked to draw a scientist, virtually all of their drawings are of men (Gardner, 1986; Mason, 1986; reported in Kahle, 1988). The lone woman in a crowd of engineers (or conversely, the lone male in a group of nurses) may also activate gender schemas (see Kanter, 1977; American Psychological Asso-ciation [APA], 1991). If a situation makes one's own gender especially salient, others may also be thought of with respect to their gender. But if the situation makes other self-views salient, gender may not be as readily used in identifying others, especially if the situation makes salient member-ship in a common ingroup (Rothbart & John, 1985; Wilder & Shapiro, 1991). So the male colleagues of a female engineer may think of her in gendered terms at some times (perhaps when "the guys" are going out for a beer), but when they are trying to sell their product to potential buyers, she may be thought of in other ways (e.g., as "the silicon chip expert").

In effect, the likelihood of thinking of someone in specific gender-stereotyped terms may be somewhat reduced when other categories are made salient or when our cognitive resources are taxed. Gilbert and Hixon (1991) found that subjects who were "cognitively busy" (they had been asked to rehearse an eight-digit number while performing a task) were less likely than non-busy subjects to demonstrate that a racial category had been primed after exposure to an Asian target. Presumably, cognitively busy subjects do not have the "luxury" of attending to aspects of the target that are irrelevant to their current needs or goals. However, when some subjects were given the opportunity to activate the stereotype and subsequently were made cognitively busy, they were more likely to use the stereotype in later judgments than were nonbusy subjects (see also Bodenhausen & Wyer, 1985; Pratto & Bargh, 1991; Stangor & Duan, 1991).

Gilbert and Hixon (1991) suggest that this process may be very much like trying to locate a tool in a toolbox: "We suggest that whereas busyness may decrease the likelihood of locating the tool (activation), it may increase the likelihood of using the tool once it has been found (application)" (p. 512). For example, a female cardiac surgeon may become accustomed to looks of surprise or disbelief on the faces of patients or families who expect to see a male in her role. However, in situations in which patients or families are more likely to be cognitively busy (e.g., when they are in pain, or under extreme stress, such as in the emergency room), a doctor may observe much greater variation in the degree of this reaction: Patients who have not had the opportunity to activate or reflect on their stereotype may not even notice her gender, while those who have had time to anticipate the interaction may be more likely to react with surprise on meeting a woman. Whether it is possible to significantly decrease gender-stereotyped thinking is an open empirical question. Gender stereotypes may be so chronically activated that even extreme forms of distraction will not discourage their use.

Schema-Based Judgments

Once activated, schemas direct attention to schema-relevant stimuli. People "see" behavior that pertains to their schema; indeed such behavior often leaps out and seizes attention, while irrelevant information is ignored. Schemas work to "tune" the attentional mechanisms to selectively attend to relevant information. Once a gender schema is activated, the world it seems is organized by gender and most individuals easily make sense of it in these terms.

Interpretation of events will be influenced by the activated schema, and this is particularly likely to be the case when the situation is ambiguous or open to multiple interpretations (Asch, 1946; Bodenhausen & Wyer, 1985; Brown & Geis, 1984; Butler & Geis, 1990; Darley & Gross, 1983; Duncan, 1976; Langer & Abelson, 1974; Lingle & Ostrom, 1979; Sagar & Schofield, 1980; cf. Bodenhausen, 1988; Pavelchek, 1989). A schema becomes a lens through which individuals "view" the behavior, and the content of the schema shapes understanding of the event. A classic study of this process comes from the racial stereotyping literature (Duncan, 1976; Sager & Schofield, 1980). In this research, white subjects observed two men interacting; at a critical point, one man pushed the other. The subjects only saw the action and did not hear any of the interchange; more important, the images were degraded so that each man's race was not identifiable. When subjects were told that the instigator of the push was African-American, the event was interpreted as hostile; when the instigator was described as Caucasian, the shove was perceived as friendly horseplay.

Condry and Condry (1976) found that gender schemas function similarly to influence the evaluation of others' behavior. In their studies, subjects observed a videotape of a baby playing and were told that the child was either male or female (no identifying features were available). At one point in the tape, the baby cried when a jack-in-the-box toy popped open. Subjects who thought they were viewing a boy were more likely to label the cry as "anger," while subjects who thought they were viewing a girl were more likely to label it "fear." In this case, the subjects' beliefs about gender differences influenced their interpretations of the behavior of even a very young child.

A recent Supreme Court case (*Hopkins v. Price Waterhouse*) demonstrated this biasing effect of schemas in interpretation. In this case, the aggressive business practices of a woman accountant at a major accounting firm were negatively evaluated by her employers. When Ann Hopkins came up for review for promotion to partner, these aggressive (and very successful) strategies were interpreted as "overbearing, arrogant, self-centered, and abrasive" (APA, 1991, p. 1065). She was denied the position, despite the fact that she had more billable hours than anyone else proposed for partner that year and she had brought in business worth $25 million (Fiske, Bersoff, Borgida, Deaux, & Heilman, 1991). Hopkins's supporters described her behaviors as "outspoken, independent, self-confident, assertive, and courageous" (APA, 1991, p. 1065).

In a brief written for the court by the APA, Dr. Susan Fiske (who served as an expert for Hopkins's case, testifying to the effects of gender stereotypes) argued that had Hopkins been male, her review by the Price Waterhouse partners would have been very different. Part of her testimony recognized the consequences of sex bias in their evaluation, evidenced by statements that Hopkins's assertive behavior was seen by some partners as "overcompensa[tion] for being a woman" (Fiske, et al., 1991, p. 1051) rather than effective and successful approaches to her work. The gender schemas of the company's decision makers (who were 99% male) also resulted in different *dimensions* of evaluation for Hopkins than for her male peers. As Fiske et al. (1991) report, "The sex role appropriateness of Ann Hopkins's social skills, instead of her business-generating abilities, became the primary dimension along which she was evaluated" (p. 1051). The Supreme Court agreed and concluded: "An employer who objects to aggressiveness in women but whose positions require this trait places women in an intolerable Catch-22: out of a job if they behave aggressively and out of a job if they don't" (quoted in Fiske et al., 1991, p. 1055).

As Fiske and her colleagues argued in their court brief, several factors may have influenced the attitudes of Hopkins's superiors at Price Waterhouse. First, Hopkins was the only woman in a cohort of 88 being considered for promotion to partner at Price Waterhouse at the time. In addition, virtually all of the partners making the decision were men. Hopkins's near-solo status made her especially salient and her actions more likely to be observed (Fiske et al., 1991; see also Crocker & McGraw, 1984; Heilman, 1983; Kanter, 1977; Mullen, 1991; Pettigrew & Martin, 1987; Taylor, 1981). Hopkins may have been perceived as an outgroup member and so was stereotyped and judged more harshly than were her male peers (Kanter, 1977; Linville, 1982; Linville & Jones, 1980; Neuberg & Fiske, 1987; Pettigrew & Martin, 1987; Quattrone, 1986; Wolman & Frank 1975). This polarization effect for outgroup members (the "outgroup homogeneity bias") may be a consequence of several factors: First, the ingroup may have a less complex schema for the outgroup than for themselves.[2] In this case, one would expect the male partners to have a less complex idea of the subcategory of "female accountants" than for "male accountants." Linville has demonstrated that when one thinks less complexly about a group, one is likely to evaluate that group more extremely (Linville, 1982; Linville & Jones, 1980). So somewhat negative or irritating behaviors performed by an outgroup member will be perceived as much more negative than similar behaviors of an ingroup member (Millar & Tesser, 1986; Tesser, 1978).

This extremity effect for outgroup members may also be a function of "subjective scaling" (Biernat, Manis, & Nelson, 1991). Perceivers may evaluate men's and women's behavior on different scales and so judge the same behavior very differently. Consider, for example, a man and a woman who both hurl insults at an umpire at a baseball game. Because men are perceived as more aggressive than women (Ashmore & Del Boca, 1981;

---

[2] However, Park and Rothbart (1982) show that the outgroup homogeneity bias is not attributable solely to greater familiarity with one's own group.

Eagly & Steffen, 1984; Lippa, 1990; Martin, 1987; Ruble & Ruble, 1982; Spence et al., 1985), this behavior may be evaluated more moderately for the male target than for the female (see Brewer, 1988; Brown & Geis, 1984; Costrich, Feinstein, Kidder, Marecek, & Pascale, 1975; Deaux & Lewis, 1984; Eagly, Makhijani, & Klonsky, 1992; Heilman et al., 1989; Ruble, Cohen, & Ruble, 1984). Using this logic, Hopkins's assertive and outspoken business tactics may have been viewed as unusual for women (and in this case evaluated negatively); had she been male, these behaviors likely would have been seen as more moderate given the broader range of aggressiveness in stereotypes of men.

Finally, attributions for an individual's behavior will also be influenced by gender schemas. As Deaux and her colleagues have documented, girls' successes on masculine tasks are often attributed to luck or effort while boys are praised for their high ability when they succeed (Deaux, 1976; Deaux & Emswiller, 1974; Hanson & O'Leary, 1983; for a review, see Wallston & O'Leary, 1981). In research examining girls' participation in math and science, Eccles and her colleagues (Eccles, 1987; Eccles [Parsons], Adler, & Kaczala, 1982) have found that many parents believe that mathematics are more difficult for their daughters, and so are likely to interpret their daughter's success as a consequence of hard work, while a son's success is proof of his high ability. These different expectations of boys and girls are often demonstrated in the classroom as well. In studies in which teachers' responses to boys and girls are examined carefully, boys have received the majority of constructive teacher reactions, especially praise, criticism, and remediation (Sadker & Sadker, 1984; American Association of University Women, 1992). Whether consciously or not, some teachers appear to behave as though boys have more ability than do girls, and so their feedback to boys is more important and perhaps more effective.

Other gender-related attributions may be a function of long-standing social norms for "typical" category members. Take, for example, explanations for "gender gaps" in political attitudes. In recent elections, many commentators have remarked on the differences between men's and women's voting patterns. In most cases, the explanations for these differences have been directed toward women: Women are looking for pro-family candidates, women are disenchanted with the incumbent party, or women believe the Democratic Party is more sympathetic to women's issues. As Miller, Taylor, and Buck (1991) point out, the great majority of these commentaries have focused on how women's voting patterns deviate from the patterns of men. Very few ask the equally logical alternative question of why men's voting patterns deviate from those of women. Building on Kahneman and Miller's (1986) norm theory, Miller and his colleagues have shown that when differences exist between men and women, it is the nonprototypical gender that is seen as deviant. In the case of voting, men represent the prototype for "typical American voter," and women are seen as a variation from that prototype (study 1). Miller et al. (1991) showed that the behavior of the variant in such a case is perceived to be more mutable than the behavior of the prototypic group member. So when asked, "If the gender gap [in American voting patterns] were to disappear, whom do you think would be more likely to change their preference?" subjects believed that women would be more likely to change.[3]

Miller and his colleagues relate their findings to more general research on gender stereotyping, echoing the work of others who argue that men are treated as the prototype of the typical person, and women are viewed as the deviant from that norm (Eagly & Kite, 1987; Gilligan, 1982; Kessler & McKenna, 1978; Miller, 1976; Rosenkrantz et al., 1968). As Miller et al. (1991) suggest, this tendency may serve to maintain gender stereotypes. When a gender difference is noticed (whether in political attitudes, occupational preferences, or general characteristics), men are often assumed to represent the "average" or "typical" group member, and women are categorized as deviant. As a consequence, real or imagined characteristics of women that may explain the difference are highlighted and stigmatized. Miller, Taylor, and Buck (1991) also argue that

> . . . [W]hen explaining gender differences in voting behavior, there may be a preference for focusing on those characteristics that are lacking in women but present in men over those characteristics that are present in women but lacking in men. In other words, it may be more natural to simulate how women could "grow" to resemble men than how they could "shrink" to resemble men. (p. 11)

In sum, the characteristics of men in this culture serve as a standard against which women are measured; we attribute differences to "flaws" in women. As the Hopkins case depicts, this standard can become a dilemma for the individual woman: She is seen as inferior if she does not match the male model, and when she does, she is faulted for deviating from the stereotype of women.

---

[3] This was also the case in studies that were not related to political attitudes. In a study presenting males as the variant from the female prototype of elementary school teachers, subjects were likely to believe that a gender gap would be diminished by changes in behavior by the men, again supporting the hypothesis that the behavior of the deviant or nonprototypical group is seen as more changeable than that of the prototypical group. (Miller & Turnbull, 1990; Miller, Turnbull, & McFarland, 1990)

Schema-Related Memory

If attention is drawn to particular aspects of a person's behavior or personality because of his/her gender, one is more likely to remember those features (Brewer et al., 1981; Cohen, 1981; Zadny & Gerard, 1974). This is in part a "filtering" effect: People selectively notice, attend to, and encode stimuli that are consistent with their schema, making only those stimuli available to memory (Hastie, 1981; Markus & Zajonc, 1985; Miller & Turnbull, 1986). Information that is inconsistent with the schema may be ignored or neglected (Bodenhausen, 1988; Bodenhausen & Lichtenstein, 1987; Hastie, 1981). But schemas also influence memory in many other ways. They serve first as an organizing framework for apparently unrelated pieces of information. An observer may organize seemingly diverse behaviors such as baking cookies, petting a cat, taking long naps, and being very talkative with a convenient or stereotyped label, such as "grandmotherly type." When prompted to remember characteristics of the person, items that have been organized in relation to the schema will have greater associations in memory and so will be more easily recalled (Bransford & Johnson, 1972). When a perceiver is given another schema for the target ("college professor"), information stored in memory that is consistent with or associated with this other schema is more likely to be remembered (e.g., thoughtful, likes to read books, leaves town for the summer, or has a flexible schedule). The schema both organizes the information that is stored in memory and "tags" it for later retrieval (Cohen & Ebbesen, 1979; Lingle & Ostrom, 1979; for a review, see Markus & Zajonc 1985).

Schemas also serve a "reconstructive" role in memory (Loftus & Palmer, 1974); for example, there are times when people use their schemas to "fill in the gaps" in memory or to "go beyond the information given" (Bruner, 1957; see also Cantor & Mishel, 1977; Hamilton, Sherman, & Ruvolo, 1991; Tsumjimoto, Wilde, & Robertson, 1978). Slusher and Anderson (1987) had subjects read a list of statements about stereotyped occupations (lawyer, artist, and clergyman). Some of the statements overtly included a trait that was stereotyped for that group ("Arthur, a wealthy lawyer, is taking a swim in his backyard pool"); some sentences contained stereotype irrelevant traits ("Ben, a creative lawyer, enjoys making pottery as a hobby"); some sentences contained no trait reference ("Frank, a lawyer, is standing in front of his home") but were preselected to prompt the imagination of a trait ("wealth"). Subjects were asked to read the sentences and imagine the scene depicted; later they were asked to remember how often each of the trait terms had been paired with each occupation in the set of sentences. Subjects overestimated the frequency of stereotype-consistent terms when they had been given the opportunity to imagine a stereotype-related scene. In other words, subjects apparently used their stereotypes when picturing the scene (e.g., they imagined the lawyer in front of an expensive house) and then misremembered the actual occurrence of the descriptive term (e.g. "wealthy") in the list of sentences. They believed they had actually read what they had only seen in their mind's eye. Slusher and Anderson (1987) suggest that stereotypes for race, ethnicity, or gender are likely to be even more robust in reconstructive memory than those observed for occupational groups (see also Deaux & Major, 1987). These stronger stereotypes may lead to more frequent imagination of stereotypical actions and behaviors, and so may strengthen the stereotype or slow its modification.

Although schema-consistent information is easily generated and remembered, there are other times that we seem to best remember schema-inconsistent information (Hastie & Kumar, 1979; Srull, 1981; Wyer, Bodenhausen, & Srull, 1984). This effect can be demonstrated by asking members of a class to form an impression of "Ruth." Ruth is described as "a librarian, religious, single, owns two cats, plays the piano, visits her mother every week, goes to Las Vegas twice a year, drives a Nova, and has brown hair and green eyes." On a later recall task, what do students remember? Her trips to Las Vegas. Recent memory research shows that individuals will remember schema-inconsistent information if they must put extra effort into their thinking, as is likely to occur when they attempt to explain or rationalize an inconsistency (Hastie, 1980, 1984; Srull & Wyer, 1989; Wyer & Srull, 1986), or when they attempt to construct a global impression of a complex person (Srull, 1981; see also Branscombe & Smith, 1990; Ruble & Stangor, 1986; Stangor & Ruble, 1989; for reviews, see Fiske & Taylor, 1991; Stangor & McMillan, 1992).

Inconsistent information may reduce the effects of the schema on further thinking about the person, leading to individuation or personalization of the target rather than categorization (Brewer, 1988; Fiske & Neuberg, 1990; Fiske & Pavelchek, 1986; Locksley, Borgida, Brekke, & Hepburn, 1980; Locksley, Hepburn, & Ortiz, 1982). Such findings imply that individualization can serve as a powerful deterrent to gender stereotyping. Alternatively, however, individualized persons may be treated as atypical members of the category and recategorized with a subtype of the stereotype (Brewer, Dull, & Lui, 1981; Taylor, 1981; Weber & Crocker, 1983). For example, one may meet an atypical sorority member, Veronica. Contrary to the stereotype, one discovers that she is uninterested in fashion and is active in liberal causes. When the perceiver learns that Veronica is planning to study women's literature in graduate school, she may be recategorized as a "women's studies major." As a result, the perceiver's schema for sorority women remains unchanged. When asked later to recall information about Veronica it is likely that her membership in a sorority will not be accessed or recalled.

How Gender Schemas Direct Behavior

Thus far, we have described how the cognitive perspective helps explain the gendered nature of lived experience. Gender provides structure; it organizes and it becomes a rallying point for attention, thought, and memory. Perhaps more important, the gender schema works to provide expectancies for how people are likely to behave, for their likes or preferences, and for their characteristics or abilities. Schemas give expectations for the behavior of others; and individuals typically behave in ways that confirm these expectancies (Merton, 1948; for reviews, see Darley & Fazio, 1980; Deaux & Major, 1987; Jussim, 1986; Miller & Turnbull, 1986). This effect has been clearly demonstrated with categories other than gender. For example, Snyder and Swann (1978) told subjects that a person they were about to meet was an extrovert and that their goal was to get to know this person better. They found that subjects asked questions about parties, meeting new people, or having fun with a group of friends—the types of questions that confirmed their expectations about their partner. The Snyder and Swann study also showed that the partner's behavior was influenced by the expectancy given to the questioner; in response to questions posed to confirm the "extroverted" label, they gave more extroverted answers. In a follow-up study, Fazio, Effrein, and Falender (1981) found that the partners who were asked, and thus answered the extroverted questions, came to evaluate themselves as more extroverted than the partners in the introverted expectancy condition (even though the partners had been randomly assigned to conditions). So the expectation became a self-fulfilling prophecy: Questioners who believed that their partner was extroverted elicited confirming responses from them, and the partners came to see themselves as more extroverted as a result. Similarly, once an individual is categorized in terms of gender, people are likely to behave toward the person in ways that will elicit support for these gender schemas (Ferguson & Schmitt, 1988; Skrypnek & Snyder, 1982).

Deaux and Major (1987) argue that the likelihood that the target of our expectation will respond in a sex-typed fashion depends on his/her self-concept and goals, the social desirability of the expected behavior, and constraints in the situation. Individuals attend to those aspects of another person's expectancy that are consistent with their own self-concept (Swann, 1984; Swann & Read, 1981a) and very often attempt to disconfirm inconsistent expectancies (Swann & Ely, 1984; Swann & Hill, 1982; Swann & Read, 1981b; for a review, see Swann, 1984). For example, when in a situation where traditional sex-role behaviors are expected (perhaps when visiting relatives during Thanksgiving), the man who thinks of himself as nontraditional may go to great lengths to verify his self-concept, refusing to join the other men drinking beer and watching football and choosing instead to help clean up after the meal. (This situation has the added benefit of being socially desirable behavior in the eyes of the man's spouse and mother-in-law.) However, when the young man's choices are constrained (his father-in-law takes the dish towel out of his hands and guides him to the sofa), he is likely to comply.

Examples of gender-related self-fulfilling prophecies are pervasive. Eccles and her colleagues (Eccles, 1987; 1989; Eccles, Jacobs, & Harold, 1990; Eccles [Parsons] et al., 1982) have documented how parents' expectancies for their children influence academic strengths and achievement. After years of negative expectancies in an area like math ability, many young women may have developed fewer skills in the area and lower levels of achievement than young men. They also may have come to view themselves as less able in the domain than men, resulting in a negative self-concept for their math abilities (Markus, Cross, & Wurf, 1990).

Maintenance of Gender-Related Schemas

Is Categorization Inevitable?

The cognitive perspective has at times been used to justify stereotyping, sexism, or racial discrimination as "natural" or somehow unchangeable (Fiske, 1989). People making this argument say that cognitive capacity is limited (Fiske & Taylor, 1984; Markus & Zajonc, 1985; Nisbett & Ross, 1980) and that categorization simplifies the thinking process and so uses our cognitive resources most efficiently. It is argued that categorization processes are automatic and uncontrollable, so individuals should not be held accountable for the consequences of their normal cognitive processes (for reviews, see Jones et al., 1984; Hamilton, 1979; Brown & Geis, 1984).

However, this view overlooks other developments in social cognition that suggest that these processes can be controlled and that stereotypes and schemas can indeed be changed. Several fruitful lines of research are examining the conditions under which people choose not to let their preexisting schemas or categories automatically influence their thoughts about another person (Fiske & Neuberg, 1990; Brewer, 1988; Devine, 1989), as well as how schemas for a group or subgroup may be changed (Weber & Crocker, 1983; Rothbart & John, 1985).

In one line of work, researchers have shown that subjects may not use gender stereotypes in thinking about a target if diagnostic individuating information is available (see Deaux & Lewis, 1984; Heilman, 1983;

Krueger & Rothbart, 1988; Locksley et al., 1980; Locksley et al., 1982; Nelson, Biernat & Manis, 1990; Pratto & Bargh, 1991; Wood & Karten, 1986; for reviews, see Fiske & Taylor, 1991; Sherman, Judd, & Park, 1989). For example, neighbors who observe a housewife vociferously up-braiding a repair person over shoddy workmanship may be unlikely to apply stereotypical terms such as *passive* or *dependent* to her (and they may invite her to their house when a repair person is due). Similarly, if group tasks or roles are assigned on gender-irrelevant bases or if alternative categories are made available (e.g., a person is categorized as "my doctor" rather than as a woman), gender-based categorization may be less likely to occur (Brewer, 1988; Wilder & Shapiro, 1991).

As Brewer (1988) and others (Fiske & Neuberg, 1990; Hilton & Darley, 1991; Neuberg, 1989) argue, perceivers' goals influence the use of categories in social interaction. When perceivers are motivated to be accurate in their assessment of another (because they will reap some reward or avoid embarrassment or punishment, or for some other reason), they will be more likely to attend to schema-inconsistent information (Erber & Fiske, 1984), and may even seek out disconfirming information (Darley, Fleming, Hilton, & Swann, 1988, Neuberg, 1989; for counterexamples, see Dobbins, Cardy, & Truxillo 1988; and Nelson, Biernat, & Manis, 1990). If one is the neighbor of the woman described above, it may be important for a future interaction to have judged her nonstereotypically. Thus, in light of her stereotype-challenging assertive behavior, the possi-bility that she may say "no" to a request to borrow a tool or to cut down a tree on her property that blocks one's view increases significantly. Similarly, individuals who will be held accountable for their decisions may use more effortful or systematic processing strategies, not attending solely to schema-consistent information (Tetlock, 1983; Tetlock & Kim, 1987). Finally, the effects of schemas on judgments of others may be undermined if (1) individuals are aware of the ways that schemas may bias their thinking (Ross, Lepper, & Hubbard, 1975); and (2) they are challenged to think in schema-inconsistent ways. Anderson and others (Anderson & Sechler, 1986; Anderson, 1982; Lord, Lepper, & Preston, 1984) have found that asking subjects to "consider the opposite" or to engage in counterfactual thinking makes schema-inconsistent information more salient and reduces the tendency to confirm one's preexisting views and beliefs.

Schema Change

There are times and situations in which gender schemas may not have a compelling influence on our beliefs or evaluations of others. This means that under some conditions, one may be less likely to treat a sorority woman as though she is flighty and unintelligent or a southern man as though he were a beer-guzzling chauvinist (the "Bubba" stereotype). But are schemas ever permanently revised or undone? For many years, research in social cognition focused on the stability of our cognitive representations and investigated many ways that our schemas are maintained or protected from change. But more recent research offers some fresh perspectives on the possibilities of schema change.

One of the oldest lines of research in this area has examined the influence of contact between group members on schema or stereotype change (Allport, 1954; Amir, 1976; Cook, 1984; Miller & Brewer, 1986; Pettigrew & Martin, 1987; Rothbart & John, 1985). Beginning with the work of Sherif, Harvey, White, Hood, and Sherif (1961/1988), social scientists have observed that when competing groups are brought together to work cooperatively on superordinate goals, perceptions of the outgroup by ingroup members change. Of course, there are many constraints on this process, but further research suggests that continued contact with outgroup members and increased familiarity results in more differentiated and idiosyncratic views of an outgroup member rather than stereotyped views.

As mentioned earlier, one way that schemas may change is by the proliferation of subtypes (Weber & Crocker, 1983). When a woman with stereotyped notions of male construction workers meets one who has progressive ideas about women's rights, loves classical music, and spends his weekends perfecting his cooking skills, the perceiver may subtype him rather than change her beliefs about construction workers in general. Rothbart and John (1985) point out that repeated exposure to construction workers who disconfirm her beliefs and the creation of multiple subcategories may lead to the dissolution of the stereotype. This is most likely to happen when the target is seen to be "typical" of the category in other very important ways (for a review, see Rothbart & John, 1985).

How often do we encounter others in situations that will expose us to evidence that would lead to schema change? It takes amazingly little to confirm long-held, prior beliefs, and people are seldom in situations with outgroup members that give them opportunities to observe stereotype-discrepant behavior. Further, it is often not obvious what behavior would be associated with stereotype change (see also Reeder & Brewer, 1979; Rothbart & Park, 1986). One episode (a whistle or jeer at a nearby woman) may be enough to convince one that a man is sexist, but the behaviors that would disconfirm this belief are difficult to define. If this man let a woman open the door for herself or went "dutch-treat" on a date, would that be sufficient to change one's impression of him? If he expressed nontraditional views of women or voted for a female political candidate would these behaviors alter others' belief that he is sexist? As these examples suggest, stereotypes are very often easy to confirm but almost impossible to disconfirm.

Recent work by Mackie, Allison, Worth, and Asuncion (1992a, 1992b) suggests that exposure to many counterstereotypical outcomes may modify one's schemas over time. They suggest that schema change occurs when the outcomes (e.g., women's success in male-dominated professions) are attributed to aspects of the target individual or group (in this case, to intelligence or creativity) and then are generalized to the population as a whole. However, their research also suggests that if external attributions for the outcome are available or are made salient, they will eliminate the generalization from the subgroup to the population. So if women are believed to have achieved due to affirmative action programs or other special help, traditional categorical beliefs may be strengthened rather than changed. In sum, schemas are most likely to change if, over a period of time, one observes many members of a group behaving in stereotype-disconfirming ways and then attributes that behavior to internal or dispositional factors (Silka, 1984; Weber & Crocker, 1983; for reviews, see Fiske & Taylor, 1991; Fiske & Neuberg, 1990; Park & Hastie, 1987; Rothbart & John, 1985).

These and other recent developments in social cognition imply that traditional beliefs about men and women may be modified, and that the negative consequences of labeling and stereotyping may be reduced. However, understanding the role of categories in thinking about men and women is only a portion of a cognitive perspective on gender. In the next section, we examine the influence of gender on thinking about the self.

GENDER AND THE SELF-CONCEPT

In the previous section we outlined the ways in which gender functions as a pervasive category or schema in thinking about others. Gender-based categorization, however, begins at home. Gender is used to find coherence and meaning in the actions of others, but it is also an important means of self-categorization—and in some cases it can become a core aspect of the self-concept. Among sociocultural influences, gender appears to have almost unparalleled power to shape our thoughts, feelings, and actions (Bem, 1981; Spence, 1985). As individuals come to terms with the existence or the identity question (in this culture the "Who am I? question")—one's sex is vital information. Even though what it means to be a male or a female can differ quite dramatically throughout the world's cultures, one's sex matters everywhere.

Some version of the question, "Am I male or female?" will be asked (or even if not asked, answered by one's significant others) in all human groups. Shweder (1982) suggests that such a question is part of a package of questions about social existence. Other questions include, for example, What is me and what is not me? Who is my kind and shares my food or blood or both and who is not my kind? What is our way and what is not our way?

The questions concerning the prominence of gender in the self-concept are being answered by social and developmental psychologists, who are charting the interdependencies between gender-based expectations and early social interactions (Bem, 1989; Bigler & Liben, 1990; Maccoby, 1988). The self-concept often appears as internal and private property, but in fact, the "Who am I?" question is, in large part, answered by others. Some concept of the self appears to develop very early in life as a child comes to understand that he/she is an object in the social world (Mead, 1934). Infants are prepared from birth for interaction with a care-giver who responds to their signals. The way a mother tunes into the infant—the moment-to-moment soothing, smiling, gurgling, talking to the infant—is shaped in many important ways by the mother's understanding of what it means to be male or female.

Once a child is perceived as male or female, strikingly different assumptions can be brought to bear when responding to the child. From the moment the sex of the fetus is known (and more and more women have this information as early as 6 weeks following conception), the child's sex can become a factor in social influence. On the basis of sex, the child is cast into a gender role and a package of meanings comprising the gender schema is brought to bear when responding to the child (Eagly, 1987). Given the divergent treatment and response accorded girls and boys from their earliest experiences (Condry, 1984), it is hardly surprising that young children who are actively engaged in a search for who they are will begin to think of themselves as boys and girls, and simultaneously will begin to share many of the assumptions about the significance of being a boy or a girl.

Gender can have an impact on an individual's self-concept in at least two different ways. First, and most obvious, gender can have an impact on the *content* of the self-concept, so that gender and gender-related attributes, activities, and dispositions may become part of the self-concept. Second, an individual's gender may condition the types of social interactions that characterize one's experience, and thus gender may be instrumental in the structure and functioning of the self-system as well.

By age 4, children know whether they belong to the group of males or the group of females and they can correctly apply gender labels to themselves (Maccoby, 1988), and at an even younger age they often seem to prefer same-sex, or at least to avoid cross-sex, playmates. Gender, in fact, appears as a more powerful aspect of early identity than other social categories such as race or age (Hirschfeld, 1988). Martin and Halverson (1981), working with children, proposed that gender schemas are an outgrowth of the tendency to group information and that sex functions as an extremely salient grouping variable. They claim that all children develop an "own-sex" schema that is used to organize experience. This schema is a personalization of a superordinate sex schema that contains knowledge about how objects, traits, and roles are associated with each sex. Thus, when confronted with a truck, a child is likely to infer that trucks are for boys, and "I am a boy" and this means trucks are for me. Once the truck is marked as part of the "me" half of the universe, it will be responded to quite differently. The truck will afford approach, exploration, and information gathering. For girls, the same truck will often be categorized as "not me" because it is soon understood to be a toy that is most appropriate for boys and thus no further knowledge about the truck is acquired.

There is striking tendency for children to organize and recall information in sex-appropriate ways (Martin & Halverson, 1983, 1987). For example, when children 5 to 6 years of age are tested for their memory of sex-stereotyped pictures (a boy playing with a truck) and nonstereotyped pictures (a girl sawing wood), children misremember the pictures in a stereotypical direction so that the girl sawing wood is reconstructed as a boy sawing wood. As children develop, they will increasingly code themselves and their worlds in gender-stereotyped terms.

On the basis of current knowledge, it is reasonable to conclude that whatever form identity takes, it will include some awareness or knowledge of one's gender. Why gender becomes central or focal in the identity or the self-concept of some people but not others has not yet been given a great deal of attention (Pyke & Graham, 1983). From studies with American preschoolers, it is evident that children show considerable variation in the formation of masculine, feminine, or androgynous personality characteristics. Some little girls show an early preference for dolls and frills and some little boys for rough-and-tumble play, and likewise there are tomboy girls who consistently opt to be part of all-boy playgroups and boys who like to play predominantly with girls' toys (Thorne, 1986, 1987). Yet it is unclear what the likely consequences are of these early individual differences in stereotypically masculine or feminine behavior. Will little boys who show an early development of masculine behaviors and preferences, or those little girls who show an early development of feminine behaviors and preferences, be those who are most likely to see gender as important? Such questions are yet to be explored. Interestingly, Maccoby (1988) reports that such individual differences do not relate to same-sex preference in play. She contends that such preferences in play are the result of group dynamics of preschoolers and do not relate in any systematic fashion to sex-typed personality characteristics. To the extent that identity is also largely a group product, we can surmise that whether gender becomes a defining feature of the self-concept may likewise depend on factors beyond the early development of masculine or feminine personal attributes.

Studies of the Salience of Gender in Identity

Markus et al. (1982; Crane & Markus, 1982) hypothesized that all individuals are likely to have some explicit awareness of their gender and some understanding of what is meant by the terms *masculinity* and *femininity*. For some individuals, however, gender becomes a basic identifying feature of the self and gender is chronically used in thinking about and describing and evaluating the self. The gender self-schema is described as an interpretive framework that lends meaning and coherence to one's own experiences and to those of others. Markus et al. (1982) argued that people could have a self-schema for femininity, for masculinity, for both (as would be the case for what Bem [1981] called androgynous individuals), or for neither. People with self-schemas for masculinity or femininity will be sensitive to different information and events than people without these self-schemas, or than people who have both self-schemas as features of their self-concept.

In an exploration of the role of gender in the self-concept, Markus et al. (1982) compared people with gender self-schemas (schematics) with those without gender self-schemas (aschematics) for their performance on a variety of cognitive tasks. They found that as with other self-schemas, gender self-schemas had a marked and systematic effect on processing. Schematics recalled more schema-consistent words, evidenced more clustering in recall, endorsed more schema-congruent attributes, and did so more quickly and with greater confidence in their judgments. Similar results showing more efficient processing of gender-relevant stimuli by those with gender self-schemas have been obtained by Bem (1981), Mills (1983), and Hungerford and Sobolew-Shubin (1987) (see also Payne, Connor, & Colletti, 1987).

Bem (1981) suggested that individual differences in the robustness of gender schemas result from how much the gender dichotomy has been emphasized during socialization. People learn how to be male and how to be female and develop robust gender schemas as a result. Sex-typed people, those who identify themselves as possessing a large number of masculine or feminine attributes, are those who will partition the world in terms of male and female, and those who will use the cultural stereotype of gender as a guide for their own and others' actions. From this perspective the self-concept is assimilated into the gender schema and is subordinate to it. Bem's theory of gender schemas also differs from Markus et al.'s (1982) theory of gender schema in the assumption that masculinity and femininity are encompassed in one schema rather than in distinct masculinity and femininity schemas.

Spence (1985) also views gender as one of the central components of the self-concept and as a major organizer of individual experience. This view is somewhat less cognitively specific than other gender schema theories and argues that gender is best understood as "a primitive unarticulated concept of self" that has a powerful effect on identity even if people are unable to articulate what is meant by masculinity or femininity.

Most of the empirical research on gender and the self-concept has focused on how these schemas constrain and afford information processing about the self and others. With respect to the perception of others and gender, self-schemas are broadly and systematically used as frameworks for making sense of the thoughts, feelings, and actions of others. Markus et al. (1985) found that those with a self-schema for masculinity organized the information presented in a film depicting stereotypically masculine behavior very differently than did those who were aschematic for masculinity. The masculine schematics displayed considerable expertise with respect to masculinity and exhibited many of the qualities of expert performance. In another study of the effects of self-schemas on the perception of others, Niemi (1985) found that when gender schematics and aschematics were asked first to read and then to explain an affectively involving story in which a married couple has difficulty communicating with each other, affective and sympathetic responses were reported most frequently by those with androgynous and feminine schemas and least often by those with masculine schemas. Further, androgynous and feminine schematics saw the problem in the marriage as stemming from problems in the communication and interaction of the partners, while those with masculine self-schemas were more likely to invoke situational factors such as economic problems to explain the couple's difficulties.

Gender schemas have been examined primarily for their cognitive consequences. Although some attention has been given to the role of gender self-schemas in activity choice (Signorella, 1984), and a few studies suggest that individuals will perform best when their gender-role schema matches the gender stereotyping of a given task (e.g., Nash, 1975, 1979; Signorella & Jamison, 1986), overall, very little is known about the role of gender self-schemas in ongoing behavior. Their influence on social interaction, their role in friendship and marriage, or their place in vocations and careers remains to be determined.

In the gender schema research by Bem (1981), Markus et al. (1982), and Spence (1985) gender has been analyzed exclusively in terms of attributes related to masculinity and femininity. Yet gender is a social category as well as a personal category. Gender signifies one's membership in a group and confers a group identity. To this point virtually all research on gender identity has focused on women, and women differ in how central their group identity is to their overall sense of self. Not all women are equally invested in their group membership, and even among those who see gender as salient, some will take a traditional orientation toward gender roles, while others will assume a nontraditional orientation.

Only limited attention has been given to the precise content of gender identity or the ways in which this content may influence thought. Gurin and Markus (1988) assessed the centrality of gender identity in the self-concept by asking women, "How much do you think about being a woman?" As with other gender schema work, they found that the effects of gender centrality were strong and consistent. When those women who said they thought about being a woman "a great deal" were compared with those who did not think much about being a woman, the former were faster to endorse gender identity descriptors (e.g., "feel obligated to other women or feel close to other women"), faster to make these endorsements, and more confident that these descriptions indeed applied to them. These findings held for those women who had a nontraditional salient gender identity and those who held a traditional salient gender identity.

The cognitive structures and processes that accompany and articulate one's group identity create the link between identity and role performance. When group identity is central and thus functions schematically, it sensitizes members to group-relevant cues and events in the social environment. It allows for rapid and confident encodings, interpretations, and decisions in new situations. It also provides the basis for role performance because it contains representations of possible courses of actions that are crucial in selecting and directing the performance to be carried out. Thus, Gurin and Markus (1988) found that when gender schemas included a sense of common fate with other women, women reported more discontent with the limited power of women, were more critical of gender-based stratification, and were more supportive of collective action.

Gender and Thought

In these studies of gender self-schemas, the focus has been on how people incorporate gender-relevant attributes and identities into their self-concepts and how this influences how they interpret potentially gender relevant stimuli. The implicit assumption has been that a masculine self-schema and a feminine self-schema are essentially alike except that they are rooted in different attributes. Yet the incorporation of gender into the self-system may also have an impact on *how* one thinks. Specifically for women, key attributes in a traditional, feminine gender schema are understanding, caring, nurturance, responsibility, considerateness, and sensitivity. All of these attributes require *another* person for their expression and suggest that relations with others will be especially significant in their self-definition. In contrast, for men, key attributes of a traditional, masculine gender schema include independence, assertiveness, instrumentality, and competitiveness. All of these attributes require a separation of the self from others. If awareness and sensitivity to others are highly significant features of the psychological life of women, the structure and functioning of the self should reflect the relatively greater incorporation of others (Jordan, Kaplan, Miller, Stiver & Surrey, 1991; Jordan & Surrey, 1986; Stewart & Lykes, 1985). It follows then that women should have access to a relatively greater store of knowledge about the significant others in their life. A recent study by Josephs, Markus, and Tafarodi (1992) finds that while men have better memory for information encoded with respect to the self, women have better memory for information encoded with reference to others. As a result of these differences in the self-schema, the *content* of men and women's thought may diverge; women may spend more time thinking about relationships than do men (Wong & Csikszentmihalyi, 1991).

Markus and Oyserman (1989) explicitly suggest that masculine and feminine gender schemas may occasion different modes of processing, and that the functioning of a masculine or "separateness" schema or a feminine "connectedness" schema may help explain a diversity of studies showing gender differences in thinking. First, these two gender schemas may be "tuned" to different kinds of information. Individuals with feminine self-schemas will be especially attentive to information about others and to the connections or relationships between others. On the other hand, individuals with masculine self-schemas may attend more closely to other kinds of information. For these people, close attention to the interpersonal world may be less important because less information is needed from it to maintain or enhance the self.

A further consequence of differences in gender self-schemas is that women, in contrast to men, may often have a style or a mode of perceiving and thinking that can be characterized as *connected* in that the surrounding context is incorporated into the representation of the focal object or person. As a result of this pervasive tendency to include the self when representing the other, it may seem relatively unnatural to extract the self from the perceptual and cognitive process. Realizing the state of so-called objectivity, in many cases, may not seem a meaningful or a desirable process.

A mode of processing in which one is sensitive to the interpersonal environment may be related to what Belenky, Clinchy, Goldberger, and Tarule (1986) have referred to as "women's way of knowing." This mode of knowing starts with a premise of connection to others and avoids disagreeing, arguing, or making negative judgments because such behavior would violate the assumption of connection. In contrast, a mode of processing in which one is striving to separate from others and to become autonomous may well set up a different way of knowing, one in which doubting, challenging, arguing, and looking for an error or contradiction are desirable and necessary. Such behavior underlines the goal of separation and autonomy.

Research on gender differences from a wide range of sources provides some support for these hypotheses, although in general, the literature on gender differences is equivocal and controversial (for reviews, see Baker, 1987; Hyde & Linn, 1988; Wittig & Peterson, 1979). However, some of these findings may be organized and better understood when viewed from the perspective of the self-concept and its influence on thinking and behavior. This review must be necessarily brief; for a more complete summary of this and related literature, see Markus and Oyserman, (1989), Markus and Cross (1990), and Markus and Kitayama (1991).

Social Sensitivity and Empathy

If women's self-construal is constructed and defined in relationships, then close attention to and monitoring of others are necessary for the elaboration and understanding of the relationships between others and the self. For those with such a relational or interdependent self-construal, important others may be represented as part of the self, and so the individual may be as sensitive to stimuli relevant to these others as they will be to more purely self-relevant stimuli. Empathic responding—the vicarious cognitive or affective responding to another's state of mind—may be an unavoidable and almost automatic result.

Although the findings on gender differences in empathy have been hotly debated, recent research generally supports the notion that females have an edge on males in this area (for an opposing review, see Maccoby & Jacklin, 1974). Reviews of research on children (Hoffman, 1977) and adults (Davis & Oathout, 1987; Eisenberg & Lennon, 1983; Franzoi, Davis, & Young, 1985; Ickes, 1987) report a gender difference that favors women. However, if close others are part of the self for women, empathic responding will be more likely in situations with a spouse, family member, close friend, or child than with a stranger. Indirect evidence for this difference comes from general surveys that report that women are more likely than men to view the well-being of their parents, children, or spouse as important sources of concern (Brody, 1981; Campbell, Converse, & Rodgers, 1976), and that stressful events that occur to friends, or coworkers are more distressing to women than to men (Dohrenwend, 1977; Kessler & McLeod, 1984).

The first step in empathic responding or taking the perspective of the other is close attention to the other. There are little data on attention to social cues; however, Hall (1978) finds that females are significantly better than males in decoding or interpreting visual and auditory cues about another's affective state (for reviews, see also Hall, 1984; Haviland

& Malatesta, 1987). More recent work on social cognition in natural settings by Ickes and his colleagues (Ickes, Robertson, Tooke, & Teng, 1986)
showed that women were more likely than men to attend to their partner
and to take their partner's perspective in social interaction. Ickes et al.
(1986) suggest that adopting the perspective of their partner was, for
women, "an apparently spontaneous, empathetic [process] that may have
more to do with the communal satisfaction of sharing thoughts and feelings than with the instrumental goal of making the interaction work" (p.
74). However, Reis, Senchak, and Solomon (1985) found that men were
as intimate in relationships as women when the situation required or
demanded intimacy. The source of the difference in men's and women's
social sensitivity, empathy, or intimacy may stem from the tendency of
women to incorporate others into the self. Empathic responding may be
a "natural" or immediate result of this relational self.

Once one has carefully attended to another's thoughts and feelings,
one should be more likely to behave in a fashion that demonstrates empathy
and support. Some behavioral gender differences provide indirect evidence
for women's greater social sensitivity. For example, women show a "modesty bias" in public settings (Berg, Stephan, & Dodson, 1981; Gould &
Sloane, 1982); by downplaying or denigrating her own performance or
accomplishments, a woman may be indirectly seeking to protect the feelings and self-esteem of her friends or close associates. Research with
children has shown that girls are more likely than boys to recognize and
compliment their classmates' successes while making fewer self-congratu-
latory remarks (Frey & Ruble, 1987).

Communication Styles

Research on the communication styles of men and women suggest that
women's linguistic styles also reflect a sensitivity and connection to the
other (for reviews, see Aries, 1987, Coates, 1986; and Tannen, 1991). For
women, the goal in social interaction is often cooperation and support.
For men, the goal is often one-ups-manship (Tannen, 1991). As Coates
(1986) describes:

> [M]en typically adopt a competitive style in conversation, treating their turn
> as a chance to overturn earlier speakers' contributions and to make their own
> point as forcibly as possible. Women . . . in conversation with other women,
> typically adopt a co-operative mode: they add to rather than demolish other
> speakers' contributions, they are supportive of others, they tend not to inter-
> rupt each other. (p. 11)

For example, research on communication styles has shown that women
are more likely than men to use "minimal responses" such as *mhm* or

yeah, indicating positive attention to the speaker; women also ask more questions, and men use more imperatives (Coates, 1986; Gonzales, Pederson, Manning, & Wetter, 1990). These differences have sometimes been explained as a consequence of social power, with "women's speech" characterizing those low in power (for reviews, see Aries, 1987; Coates, 1986). However, women's desire for equality and harmony in relationships may contribute to speech patterns that minimize hierarchical relationships or status markers and instead express support for, or attentiveness to, the speaker.

Conclusion

Our appraisal of the advantages of the cognitive perspective for gender theory must be tempered by a recognition of its disadvantages. In the past, much of the cognitive social psychology research has focused on limitations or shortcomings of information processing and has made it seem that stereotyping was inevitable. Social categorization by race or gender was bound to occur, and because it was "natural" or automatic, an individual was not responsible for the consequences of these thought processes. This reading of the social information processing literature may also have been facilitated by an emphasis on the stability and constancy of schemas and stereotypes. Given this view, the possibility of unlearning old stereotypes or of reducing the effects of categorization seemed bleak. However, more recent research, such as that described above, has shown that individuals can control what were once seen as unintentional processes and can actively reduce the effects of their schemas on their interactions with others (Fiske, 1989). Researchers are now examining how new information may be considered and included in one's schemas (Krueger & Rothbart, 1990). Other work has begun to focus on motivational aspects of cognition, recognizing that "cold" cognitive processes fall short of explaining many aspects of stereotyping and prejudice (Devine, 1989; Kunda, 1990).

However, the focus of this research on schema change and control remains the individual. Most of these efforts focus on how individuals can think differently, how individuals may keep from stereotyping, or how individuals may attempt to bring their "reflexive" thoughts and feelings into concordance with nonsexist beliefs and attitudes (Devine, 1989). But gender differences are embedded in the larger fabric of our culture, and changing stereotypes and their effects requires much more than individual change. Gender stereotypes are carried in social representations or shared knowledge about the meaning of gender and what is male and what is female (Moscovici, 1984). Certainly as individuals begin to treat men and woman as equals and work on eliminating sex-typed assumptions or prejudgments, we will see further social change. But many changes will require more drastic measures—changes in institutional structures, social organization, and social policy. And such changes will require an analysis of how gender is represented and understood collectively. A future goal for research on gender from a cognitive perspective could well include an explanation of how beliefs about gender are externalized, objectified, or made "real" through social practices and institutions.

REFERENCES

Allport, G. (1954). *The nature of prejudice*. Reading, MA: Addison-Wesley.

American Association of University Women. (1982). *How schools shortchange girls: A study of major findings on girls and education*. Washington, DC: AAUW Educational Foundation and the National Education Association.

American Psychological Association. (1991). In the Supreme Court of the United States, *Price-Waterhouse v. Ann B. Hopkins: Amicus Curiae* brief for the American Psychological Association. *American Psychologist, 46*, 1061–1070.

Amir, Y. (1976). The role of intergroup contact in change of prejudice and ethnic relations. In P. A. Katz (Ed.), *Toward the elimination of racism* (pp. 245–308). New York: Pergamon Press.

Anderson, C. A. (1982). Inoculation and counter-explanation: Debiasing techniques in the perseverance of social theories. *Social Cognition, 1*, 126–139.

Anderson, C. A., & Sechler, E. S. (1986). Effects of explanation and counterexplanation on the development and use of social theories. *Journal of Personality and Social Psychology, 50*, 24–34.

Aries, E. (1987). Gender and communication. In P. Shaver & C. Hendrick (Eds.), *Sex and gender* (pp. 149–176). Newbury Park, CA: Sage.

Asch, S. E. (1946). Forming impressions of personality. *Journal of Abnormal and Social Psychology, 41*, 258–290.

Ashmore, R. D. (1981). Sex stereotypes and implicit personality theory. In D.L. Hamilton (Ed.), *Cognitive processes in stereotyping and intergroup behavior* (pp. 37–81). Hillsdale, NJ: Erlbaum.

Ashmore, R. D., & Del Boca, F. K. (1981). Conceptual approaches to stereotypes and stereotyping. In D. L. Hamilton (Ed.), *Cognitive processes in stereotyping and intergroup behavior* (pp. 1–36). Hillsdale, NJ: Erlbaum.

Ashmore, R. D., Del Boca, F. K., & Wohlers, A. J. (1986). Gender stereotypes. In R. D. Ashmore & F. K. Del Boca (Eds.), *The social psychology of female-male relations: A critical analysis of central concepts* (pp. 69–119). Orlando, FL: Academic Press.

Bakan, D. (1966). *The duality of human existence*. Boston: Beacon Press.

Baker, M. A. (1987). *Sex differences in human performance*. New York: Wiley.

Bargh, J. A. (1989). Conditional automaticity: Varieties of automatic influence in social perception and cognition. In J. S. Uleman & J. A. Bargh (Eds.), *Unintended thought* (pp. 3–51). New York: Guilford Press.

Bargh, J. A., Bond, R. N., Lombardi, W., & Tota, M. (1986). The additive nature of chronic and temporary sources of construct accessibility. *Journal of Personality and Social Psychology*, *50*, 869–878.

Bargh, J. A., Lombardi, W. J., & Higgins, E. T. (1988). Automaticity of chronically accessible constructs in person X situation effects on person perception: It's just a matter of time. *Journal of Personality and Social Psychology*, *55*, 599–605.

Bargh, J. A., & Pratto, F. (1986). Individual construct accessibility and perceptual selection. *Journal of Experimental Social Psychology*, *22*, 293–311.

Belenky, M. F., Clinchy, B. M., Goldberger, N. R., & Tarule, J. M. (1986). *Women's ways of knowing: The development of self, voice, and mind.* New York: Basic Book.

Bem, S. (1981). Gender schema theory: A cognitive account of sex typing. *Psychological Review*, *88*, 354–364.

Bem, S. (1989). Genital knowledge and gender constancy. *Child Development*, *60*, 649–662.

Berg, J. H., Stephan, W. G., & Dodson, M. (1981). Attributional modesty in women. *Psychology of Women Quarterly*, *5*, 711–727.

Bergen, D. J., & Williams, J. E. (1991). Sex stereotypes in the United States revisited: 1972–1988. *Sex Roles*, *24*, 413–423.

Biernat, M., Manis, M., & Nelson, T. (1991). Stereotypes and standards of judgment. *Journal of Personality and Social Psychology*, *60*, 485–499.

Bigler, R. S., & Liben, L. S. (1990). The role of attitudes and interventions in gender-schematic processing. *Child Development*, *61*, 1440–1452.

Bodenhausen, G. V. (1988). Stereotypic biases in social decision making and memory: Testing process models of stereotype use. *Journal of Personality and Social Psychology*, *55*, 726–737.

Bodenhausen, G. V., & Lichtenstein, M. (1987). Social stereotypes and information processing strategies: The impact of task complexity. *Journal of Personality and Social Psychology*, *52*, 871–880.

Bodenhausen, G. V., & Wyer, R. S. (1985). Effects of stereotypes on decision making and information-processing strategies. *Journal of Personality and Social Psychology*, *48*, 267–282.

Bower, G. H., & Karlin, M. B. (1974). Depth of processing pictures of faces and recognition memory. *Journal of Experimental Social Psychology*, *41*, 656–670.

Branscombe, N. R., & Smith, E. R. (1990). Gender and racial stereotypes in impression formation and social decision-making processes. *Sex Roles*, *22*, 627–647.

Bransford, J. D., & Johnson, M. K. (1972). Contextual prerequisites for understanding: Some investigations of comprehension and recall. *Journal of Verbal Learning and Verbal Behavior*, *11*, 717–726.

Brewer, M. B. (1988). A dual process model of impression formation. In T. K. Srull & R. S. Wyer, Jr. (Eds.), *Advances in social cognition* (Vol. 1, pp. 1–36). Hillsdale, NJ: Erlbaum.

Brewer, M. B., Dull, V., & Lui, L. (1981). Perceptions of the elderly: Stereotypes as prototypes. *Journal of Personality and Social Psychology*, *41*, 656–670.

Brewer, M. B., & Lui, L. L. (1989). The primacy of age and sex in the structure of person categories. *Social Cognition, 7,* 262–274.

Brody, E. M. (1981). Women in the middle and family help to older people. *Gerontologist, 21,* 471–480.

Brown, V., & Geis, F. L. (1984). Turning lead into gold: Evaluations of men and women leaders and the alchemy of social consensus. *Journal of Personality and Social Psychology, 46,* 811–824.

Bruner, J. S. (1957). On perceptual readiness. *Psychological Review, 64,* 123–152.

Butler, D. & Geis, F. L. (1990). Nonverbal affect responses to male and female leaders: Implications for leadership evaluations. *Journal of Personality and Social Psychology, 58,* 48–59.

Campbell, A., Converse, P., & Rodgers, W. (1976). *The quality of American life: Perceptions, evaluations, and satisfactions.* New York: Sage.

Cantor, N., & Mischel, W. (1977). Traits as prototypes: Effects on recognition memory. *Journal of Personality and Social Psychology, 35,* 38–48.

Coates, J. (1986). *Women, men and language: A sociolinguistic account of sex differences in language.* London: Longman.

Cohen, C. E. (1981). Person categories and social perception: Testing some boundaries of the processing effects of prior knowledge. *Journal of Personality and Social Psychology, 40,* 441–452.

Cohen, C. E., & Ebbesen, E. B. (1979). Observational goals and schema activation: A theoretical framework for behavior perception. *Journal of Experimental Social Psychology, 15,* 305–329.

Cook, S. W. (1984). Cooperative interaction in multiethnic contexts. In N. Miller & M. B. Brewer (Eds.), *Groups in contact: The psychology of desegregation* (pp. 155–185). New York: Academic Press.

Condry, J. C. (1984). Gender identity and social competence. *Sex Roles, 11,* 485–511.

Condry, J. C., & Condry, S. (1976). Sex differences: A study of the eye of the beholder. *Child Development, 47,* 812–819.

Connor, J. M., & Serbin, L. A. (1977). Behaviorally based masculine- and feminine-activity-preference scales for preschoolers: Correlates with other classroom behaviors and cognitive tests. *Child Development, 48,* 1411–1416.

Costrich, N., Feinstein, J., Kidder, L., Marecek, J., & Pascale, L. (1975) When stereotypes hurt: Three studies of penalties for sex-role reversals. *Journal of Experimental Social Psychology, 11,* 520–530.

Cowan, G., & Hoffman, C. D. (1986). Gender stereotyping in young children: Evidence to support a concept-learning approach. *Sex Roles, 14,* 211–224.

Crane, M., & Markus, H. (1982). Gender identity: The benefits of a self-schema approach. *Journal of Personality and Social Psychology, 43,* 1195–1197.

Crawford, M., & Hamilton, M. (Eds.). (1989). *Gender and thought.* New York: Springer-Verlag.

Crocker, J., & McGraw, K. M. (1984). What's good for the goose is not good for the gander: Solo status as an obstacle to occupational achievement for males and females. *American Behavioral Scientist, 27,* 357–369.

Darley, J. M., & Fazio, R. H. (1980). Expectancy confirmation processes arising in the social interaction sequence. *American Psychologist, 35,* 867–881.

Darley, J. M., Fleming, J. H., Hilton, J. L., & Swann, W. B., Jr. (1988). Dispelling negative expectancies: The impact of interaction goals and target characteristics on the expectancy confirmation process. *Journal of Experimental Social Psychology*, *24*, 19–36.

Darley, J. M., & Gross, P. H. (1983). A hypothesis-confirming bias in labeling effects. *Journal of Personality and Social Psychology*, *44*, 20–33.

Davis, M. H., & Oathout, H. A. (1987). Maintenance of satisfaction in romantic relationships: Empathy and relational competence. *Journal of Personality and Social Psychology*, *53*, 397–410.

Deaux, K. (1976). Sex: A perspective on the attribution process. In J. H. Harvey, W. J. Ickes, & R. F. Kidd (Eds.), *New directions in attribution research* (Vol. 1, ch. 15, pp. 335–352). Hillsdale, NJ: Erlbaum.

Deaux, K., & Emswiller, T. (1974). Explanations of successful performance on sex-linked tasks: What is skill for the male is luck for the female. *Journal of Personality and Social Psychology*, *29*, 80–85.

Deaux, K., & Lewis, L. L. (1983). Components of gender stereotypes. *Psychological Documents*, *13*, 25. (Ms. No. 2583).

Deaux, K., & Lewis, L. L. (1984). Structure of gender stereotypes: Interrelationships among components and gender label. *Journal of Personality and Social Psychology*, *46*, 991–1004.

Deaux, K., & Major, B. (1987). Putting gender into context: An interactive model of gender-related behavior. *Psychological Review 94*, 369–389.

Devine, P. G. (1989). Stereotypes and prejudice: Their automatic and controlled components. *Journal of Personality and Social Psychology*, *56*, 5–18.

Dobbins, G. H., Cardy, R. L., & Truxillo, D. M. (1988). The effects of purpose of appraisal and individual differences in stereotypes of women on sex differences in performance ratings: A laboratory and field study. *Journal of Applied Psychology*, *73*, 551–558.

Dohrenwend, B. S. (1977). Social status and stressful life events. *Journal of Personality and Social Psychology*, *99*, 203–214.

Duncan, B. L. (1976). Differential social perception and attribution of intergroup violence: Testing the lower limits of stereotyping of blacks. *Journal of Personality and Social Psychology*, *34*, 590–598.

Dunning, D., & Parpal, M. (1989). Mental addition versus subtraction in counterfactual reasoning: On assessing the impact of personal actions and life events. *Journal of Personality and Social Psychology*, *57*, 5–15.

Durkin, K. (1985a). Television and sex role acquisition 1: Content. *British Journal of Social Psychology*, *24*, 101–113.

Durkin, K. (1985b). Television and sex role acquisition 1: Effects. *British Journal of Social Psychology*, *24*, 191–210.

Eagly, A. H. (1987). *Sex differences in social behavior: A social-role interpretation.* Hillsdale, NJ: Erlbaum.

Eagly, A. H., & Kite, M. E. (1987). Are stereotypes of nationalities applied to both men and women? *Journal of Personality and Social Psychology*, *53*, 457–462.

Eagly, A. H., Makhijani, M. G., & Klonsky, B.G. (1992). Gender and the evaluation of leaders: A meta-analysis. *Psychological Bulletin*, *111*, 3–22.

Eagly, A. H., & Mladinic, A. (1987). Gender stereotypes and attitudes toward women and men. *Personality and Social Psychology Bulletin, 15,* 543–558.

Eagly, A. H., & Steffen, V. J. (1984). Gender stereotypes stem from the distribution of women and men into social roles. *Journal of Personality and Social Psychology, 46,* 735–754.

Eccles, J. S. (1987). Gender roles and women's achievement-related decisions. *Psychology of Women Quarterly, 11,* 135–172.

Eccles, J. S. (1989). Bringing young women to math and science. In M. Crawford & M. Gentry (Eds.), *Gender and thought: Psychological perspectives* (pp. 36–58). New York: Springer-Verlag.

Eccles (Parsons) J. E., Adler, T. F., & Kaczala, C. M. (1982). Socialization of achievement attitudes and beliefs: Parental influences. *Child Development, 53,* 310–321.

Eccles, J. S., Jacobs, J. E., & Harold, R. D. (1990). Gender role stereotypes, expectancy effects, and parents' socialization of gender differences. *Journal of Social Issues, 46,* 183–201.

Erber, R., & Fiske, S. T. (1984). Outcome dependency and attention to inconsistent information. *Journal of Personality and Social Psychology, 47,* 709–726.

Eisenberg, N., & Lennon, R. (1983). Sex differences in empathy and related capacities. *Psychological Bulletin, 94,* 100–131.

Fazio, R. H., Effrein, E. A., & Falender, V. J. (1981). Self-perceptions following social interaction. *Journal of Personality and Social Psychology, 41,* 232–242.

Ferguson, E. D., & Schmitt, S. (1988). Gender-linked stereotypes and motivation affect performance in the Prisoner's Dilemma game. *Perceptual and Motor Skills, 66,* 703–714.

Fiske, A. P., Haslam, N., & Fiske, S. T. (1991). Confusing one person with another: What errors reveal about the elementary forms of social relations. *Journal of Personality and Social Psychology, 60,* 656–674.

Fiske, S. T. (1989). Examining the role of intent: Toward understanding its role in stereotyping and prejudice. In J. S. Uleman & J. A. Bargh (Eds.), *Unintended thought* (pp. 253–283). New York: Guilford Press.

Fiske, S. T., Bersoff, D. N., Borgida, E., Deaux, K., & Heilman, M. E. (1991). Social science research on trial: Use of sex stereotyping research in *Price Waterhouse v. Hopkins. American Psychologist, 46,* 1049–1060.

Fiske, S. T., & Neuberg, S.L. (1990). A continuum of impression formation, from category-based to individuating processes: Influences of information and motivation on attention and interpretation. In M. P. Zanna (Ed.), *Advances in experimental social psychology* (Vol. 23, pp. 1–74). New York: Academic Press.

Fiske, S. T., & Pavelchek, M. A. (1986). Category-based versus piecemeal-based affective responses: Developments in schema-triggered affect. In R. M. Sorretino & E. T. Higgins (Eds.), *Handbook of motivation and cognition: Foundations of social behavior* (pp. 167–203). New York: Guilford Press.

Fiske, S. T., & Taylor, S. E. (1984). *Social cognition.* Reading, MA: Addison-Wesley.

Fiske, S. T., & Taylor, S. E. (1991). *Social cognition* (2nd ed.). New York: McGraw-Hill.

Franzoi, S. L., Davis, M. H., & Young, R. D. (1985). The effects of private self-consciousness and perspective taking on satisfaction in close relationships. *Journal of Personality and Social Psychology, 48,* 1584–1594.

Frey, K. S., & Ruble, D. N. (1987). What children say about classroom performance: Sex and grade differences in perceived competence. *Child Development, 58,* 1066–1078.

Gardner, A. L. (1986). *Effectiveness of strategies to encourage participation and retention of precollege and college women in science.* Unpublished doctoral dissertation, Purdue University, West Lafayette, IN.

Geertz, C. (1973). *The interpretation of cultures.* New York: Basic Books.

Gilbert, D. T., & Hixon, G. (1991). The trouble of thinking: Activation and application of stereotypic beliefs. *Journal of Personality and Social Psychology, 60,* 509–517.

Gilligan, C. (1982). *In a different voice: Psychological theory and women's development.* Cambridge, MA: Harvard University Press.

Glick, P., Zion, C., & Nelson, C. (1988). What mediates sex discrimination in hiring? *Journal of Personality and Social Psychology, 55,* 178–186.

Gonzales, M. H., Pederson, J. H., Manning, D. J., & Wetter, D. W. (1990). Pardon my gaffe: Effects of sex, status, and consequence severity on accounts. *Journal of Personality and Social Psychology, 58,* 610–621.

Gould, R. J., & Sloane, C. G. (1982). The "feminine modesty" effect: A self-presentational interpretation of sex differences in causal attribution. *Personality and Social Psychology Bulletin, 8,* 477–485.

Greenwald, A. G., & Pratkanis, A. R. (1984). The self. In R. S. Wyer, Jr. & T. K. Srull (Eds.), *Handbook of social cognition* (Vol. 3, pp. 129–178). Hillsdale, NJ: Erlbaum.

Gurin, P., & Markus, H. (1988). Cognitive consequences of gender identity. *Revue Internationale de Psychologie Sociale, 2,* 257–274.

Gurin, P., & Markus, H. (1989). The cognitive consequences of gender identity. In S. Skevington & D. Baker (Eds.), *The social identity of women* (pp. 152–172). Newbury Park, CA: Sage.

Hall, J. A. (1978). Gender effects in decoding nonverbal cues. *Psychological Bulletin, 85,* 845–858.

Hall, J. A. (1984). *Nonverbal sex differences: Communication accuracy and expressive style.* Baltimore, MD: Johns Hopkins University Press.

Hamilton, D. L. (1979). A cognitive-attributional analysis of stereotyping. In L. Berkowitz (Ed.), *Advances in experimental social psychology* (Vol. 12, pp. 53–84). New York: Academic Press.

Hamilton, D. L. (1981). *Cognitive processes in stereotyping and intergroup behavior.* Hillsdale, NJ: Erlbaum.

Hamilton, D. L., Sherman, S. J., & Ruvolo, C. M. (1991). Stereotype-based expectancies: Effects on information processing and social behavior. *Journal of Social Issues, 46,* 35–60.

Hamilton, D. L., & Trolier, T. K. (1986). Stereotypes and stereotyping: An overview of the cognitive approach. In J. F. Dovidio & S. L. Gaertner (Eds.), *Prejudice, discrimination, and racism* (pp. 127–163). New York: Academic Press.

Hansen, R. D., & O'Leary, V. E. (1983). Actresses and actors: The effects of sex on causal attributions. *Basic and Applied Social Psychology*, *4*, 209–230.

Hastie, R. (1980). Memory for behavioral information that confirms or contradicts a personality impression. In R. Hastie, T. M. Ostrom, E. B. Ebbesen, R. S. Wyer, D. L. Hamilton, & D. E. Carlston (Eds.), *Person memory: The cognitive basis of social perception* (pp. 141–172). Hillsdale, NJ: Erlbaum.

Hastie, R. (1981). Schematic principles in human memory. In E. T. Higgins, C. P. Herman, & M. P. Zanna (Eds.), *Social cognition: The Ontario symposium* (Vol. 1, pp. 39–88). Hillsdale, NJ: Erlbaum.

Hastie, R. (1984). Causes and effects of causal attribution. *Journal of Personality and Social Psychology*, *46*, 44–56.

Hastie, R., & Kumar, P. A. (1979). Person memory: Personality traits as organizing principles in memory for behavior. *Journal of Personality and Social Psychology*, *37*, 25–38.

Haviland, J. J., & Malatesta, C. Z. (1987). The development of sex differences in nonverbal signals: Fallacies, facts, and fantasies. In M. R. Walsh (Ed.), *The psychology of women* (pp. 183–208). New Haven, CT: Yale University Press.

Heilman, M. E. (1983). Sex bias in work settings: The lack of fit model. In L. L. Cummings & B. M. Staw (Eds.), *Research in organizational behavior* (Vol. 5, pp. 269–298). Greenwich, CN: Jai Press.

Heilman, M. E., Block, C. J., Martell, R. F., & Simon, M. C. (1989). Has anything changed? Current characterizations of men, women, and managers. *Journal of Applied Psychology*, *74*, 935–942.

Higgins, E. T., & Bargh, J. A. (1987). Social cognition and social perception. *Annual Review of Psychology*, *38*, 369–425.

Higgins, E. T., & King, G. A. (1981). Accessibility of social constructs: Information-processing consequences of individual and contextual variability. In N. Cantor & J. F. Kihlstrom (Eds.), *Personality, cognition, and social interaction* (pp. 69–121). Hillsdale, NJ: Erlbaum.

Higgins, E. T., King, G. A., & Mavin, G. H. (1982). Individual construct accessibility and subjective impressions and recall. *Journal of Personality and Social Psychology*, *43*, 35–47.

Hilton, J. L., & Darley, J. M. (1991). The effects of interaction goals on person perception. In M. P. Zanna (Ed.), *Advances in experimental social psychology* (Vol. 24, pp. 235–267). San Diego: Academic Press.

Hirschfeld, L. (1988). On acquiring social categories: Cognitive development and anthropological wisdom. *Man*, *23*, 611–638.

Hoffman, C., & Hurst, N. (1990). Gender stereotypes: Perception or rationalization? *Journal of Personality and Social Psychology*, *58*, 197–208.

Hoffman, M. L. (1977). Sex differences in empathy and related behaviors. *Psychological Bulletin*, *54*, 712–722.

Hungerford, J. K., & Sobolew-Shubin, A. P. (1987). Sex role identity, gender identity, and self-schemata. *Psychology of Women Quarterly*, *11*, 1–10.

Huston, A. C. (1983). Sex typing. In P. H. Mussen & E. M. Hetherington (Eds.), *Handbook of child psychology: Socialization, personality, and social behavior* (4th ed.) (Vol. 4, pp. 387–476). New York: Wiley.

Huston, A. C. (1985). The development of sex typing: Themes from recent research. *Developmental Review, 5,* 1–17.

Hyde, J. S. (1991, August). *Gender and sex: So what has meta-analysis done for me?* Paper presented at the American Psychological Association Annual Convention, San Francisco, CA.

Hyde, J. S., & Linn, M. C. (1988). Gender differences in verbal ability: A meta-analysis. *Psychological Bulletin, 104,* 53–69.

Ickes, W. (1987). Sex-role influences in dyadic interaction: A theoretical model. In M. R. Walsh (Ed.), *The psychology of women* (pp. 95–128). New Haven, CT: Yale University Press.

Ickes, W., Robertson, E., Tooke, W., & Teng, G. (1986). Naturalistic social cognition: Methodology, assessment, and validation. *Journal of Personality and Social Psychology, 51,* 66–82.

Jacklin, C. N. (1989). Female and male: Issues of gender. *American Psychologist, 44,* 127–133.

James, W. (1890). *Principles of psychology.* New York: Holt.

Jones, E. E., Farina, A., Hastorf, A. H., Markus, H., Miller, D. T., & Scott, R. A. (1984). *Social stigma: The psychology of marked relationships.* San Francisco: W. H. Freeman.

Jordan, J. V., Kaplan, A. G., Miller, J. B., Stiver, I. P., & Surrey, J. L. (1991). *Women's growth in connection.* New York: Guilford Press.

Jordan, J. V., & Surrey, J. L. (1986). The self-in-relation: Empathy and the mother-daughter relationship. In T. Bernay & D. W. Cantor (Eds.), *The psychology of today's women* (pp. 81–104). Cambridge, MA: Harvard University Press.

Josephs, R. A., Markus, H. R., & Tafarodi, R. W. (1992). Gender differences in the source of self-esteem. *Journal of Personality and Social Psychology, 63,* 391–402.

Jussim, L. (1986). Self-fulfilling prophecies: A theoretical and integrative review. *Psychological Review, 93,* 429–445.

Kahle, J. B. (1988). Gender and science education II. In P. Fensham (Ed.), *Development and dilemmas in science education* (Ch. 12, pp. 249–265). Philadelphia, PA: Falmer Press.

Kahneman, D., & Miller, D. T. (1986). Norm theory: Comparing reality to its alternatives. *Psychological Review, 93,* 136–153.

Kanter, R. (1977). *Men and women of the corporation.* New York: Basic Books.

Katz, P. A. (1986). Gender identity. In R. D. Ashmore & F. K. Del Boca (Eds.), *The social psychology of female-male relations.* Orlando, FL: Academic Press.

Kessler, R. C., & McKenna (1978). *Gender: An ethnomethodological approach.* New York: Wiley.

Kessler, R. C., & McLeod, J. D. (1984). Sex differences in vulnerability to undesirable life events. *American Sociological Review, 49,* 1039–1053.

Kihlstrom, J. F., & Cantor, N. (1984). Mental representations of the self. In L. Berkowitz (Ed.), *Advances in experimental social psychology* (Vol. 17, pp. 1–47). San Diego: Academic Press.

Kohlberg, L. (1966). A cognitive-developmental analysis of children's sex-role concepts and attitudes. In E. Maccoby (Ed.), *The development of sex differences* (pp. 82–172). Stanford, CA: Stanford University Press.

Kohlberg, L., & Ullian, D. Z. (1974). Stages in the development of psychosexual concepts and attitudes. In R. C. Friedman, R. M. Richart, & R. L. Vande-Wiele (Eds.), *Sex differences in behavior* (pp. 209–222). New York: Wiley.

Krueger, J., & Rothbart, M. (1988). Use of categorical and individuating information in making inferences about personality. *Journal of Personality and Social Psychology, 55*, 187–195.

Krueger, J., & Rothbart, M. (1990). Contrast and accentuation effects in category learning. *Journal of Personality and Social Psychology, 59*, 651–663.

Kuhn, D., Nash, S. C., & Brucken, L. (1978). Sex role concepts of two- and three-year-olds. *Child Development, 49*, 445–451.

Kunda, Z. (1990). The case for motivated reasoning. *Psychological Bulletin, 108*, 480–499.

Langer, E. J., & Abelson, R. P. (1974). A patient by any other name: Clinician group difference in labeling bias. *Journal of Consulting and Clinical Psychology, 42*, 4–9.

Leinbach, M. D., & Fagot, B. I. (1986). Acquisition of gender labels. *Sex Roles, 15*, 655–666.

Lifton, P. (1985). Individual differences in moral development: The relation of sex, gender, and personality to morality. *Journal of Personality, 53*, 306–334.

Lingle, J. H., & Ostrom, T. M. (1979). Retrieval selectivity in memory-based impression judgments. *Journal of Personality and Social Psychology, 37*, 180–194.

Linville, P. W. (1982). The complexity-extremity effect and age-based stereotyping. *Journal of Personality and Social Psychology, 42*, 193–211.

Linville, P. W., & Jones, E. E. (1980). Polarized appraisals of out-group members. *Journal of Personality and Social Psychology, 38*, 689–703.

Lippa, R. (1990). Gender and social behavior. In R. Lippa (Ed.), *Introduction to social psychology* (pp. 342–385). Belmont, CA: Wadsworth.

Lippman, W. (1922). *Public opinion*. New York: Harcourt, Brace.

Locksley, A., Borgida, E., Brekke, N., & Hepburn, C. (1980). Sex stereotypes and social judgment. *Journal of Personality and Social Psychology, 39*, 821–831.

Locksley, A., Hepburn, C., & Ortiz, V. (1982). Social stereotypes and judgments of individuals: An instance of the base-rate fallacy. *Journal of Experimental Social Psychology, 18*, 23–42.

Loftus, E., & Palmer, J. (1974). Reconstruction of automobile destruction. *Journal of Verbal Learning and Verbal Behavior, 13*, 585–589.

Lord, C. G., Lepper, M. R., & Preston, E. (1984). Considering the opposite: A corrective strategy for social judgment. *Journal of Personality and Social Psychology, 47*, 1231–1243.

Maccoby, E. E. (1988). Gender as a social category. *Developmental Psychology, 24*, 755–765.

Maccoby, E. E., & Jacklin, C. N. (1974). *The psychology of sex differences*. Stanford, CA: Stanford University Press.

Mackie, D. M., Allison, S. T., Worth, L. T., & Asuncion, A. G. (1992a). The generalization of outcome-biased counter-stereotypic inferences. *Journal of Experimental Social Psychology, 28*, 43–64.

Mackie, D. M., Allison, S. T., Worth, L. T., & Asuncion, A. G. (1992b). The impact of outcome biases on counterstereotypic inferences about groups. *Personality and Social Psychology Bulletin, 18*, 44–51.

Markus, H., Crane, M., Bernstein, S., & Siladi, M. (1982). Self-schemas and gender. *Journal of Personality and Social Psychology, 42*, 38–50.

Markus, H., & Cross, S. E. (1990). The interpersonal self. In L. Pervin (Ed.), *Handbook of personality: Theory and research* (pp. 576–608). New York: Guilford Press.

Markus, H., Cross, S., & Wurf, E. (1990). The role of the self-system in competence. In R. J. Sternberg & J. Kolligian, Jr. (Eds.), *Competence considered* (pp. 205–225). New Haven, CT: Yale University Press.

Markus, H., & Kitayama, S. (1991). Culture and the self: Implications for cognition, emotion, and motivation. *Psychological Review, 98*, 224–253.

Markus, H., & Oyserman, D. (1989). Gender and thought: The role of the self-concept. In M. Crawford & M. Hamilton (Eds.), *Gender and thought* (pp. 100–127). New York: Springer-Verlag.

Markus, H., Smith, J., & Moreland, R. L. (1985). Role of the self-concept in the social perception of others. *Journal of Personality and Social Psychology, 49*, 1494–1512.

Markus, H., & Wurf, E. (1987). The dynamic self-concept: A social psychological perspective. In M. R. Rosenweig & L. W. Porter (Eds.), *Annual review of psychology* (Vol. 38, pp. 299–337). Palo Alto, CA: Annual Reviews.

Markus, H., & Zajonc, R. B. (1985). The cognitive perspective in social psychology. In G. Lindzey & E. Aronson (Eds.), *Handbook of social psychology* (3rd ed.) (Vol. 1, pp. 137–230). New York: Random House.

Martin, C. L. (1987). A ratio measure of sex stereotyping. *Journal of Personality and Social Psychology, 52*, 489–499.

Martin, C. L., & Halverson, C. F., Jr. (1981). A schematic processing model of sex typing and stereotyping in children. *Child Development, 52*, 1119–1134.

Martin, C. L., & Halverson, C. F., Jr. (1983a). Gender constancy: A methodological and theoretical analysis. *Sex Roles, 9*, 775–790.

Martin, C. L., & Halverson, C. F., Jr. (1983b). The effects of sex-typing schemas on young children's memory. *Child Development, 54*, 563–574.

Martin, C. L., & Halverson, C. F., Jr. (1987). The roles of cognition in sex role acquisition. In D. B. Carter (Ed.), *Current conceptions of sex roles and sex typing: Theory and research*. New York: Praeger.

Mason, C. L. (1986). *Student attitudes toward science and science related careers: An investigation of the efficacy of a high school biology teachers' intervention program*. Unpublished doctoral dissertation, Purdue University, West Lafayette, IN.

McArthur, L. Z. (1982). Judging a book by its cover: A cognitive analysis of the relationship between physical appearance and stereotyping. In A. Hastorf & A. Isen (Eds.), *Cognitive social psychology* (pp. 149–211). New York: Elsevier.

McArthur, L. Z., & Baron, R. (1983). Toward an ecological theory of social perception. *Psychological Review, 90*, 215–238.

Mead, G. H. (1934). *Mind, self, and society*. Chicago: University of Chicago Press.

Merton, R. K. (1948). The self-fulfilling prophecy. *Antioch Review, 8*, 193–210.

Millar, M. G., & Tesser, A. (1986). Thought-induced attitude change: The effects of schema structure and commitment. *Journal of Personality and Social Psychology, 51*, 259–269.

Miller, C. T. (1986). Categorization and stereotypes about men and women. *Personality and Social Psychology Bulletin, 12*, 502–512.

Miller, C. T. (1988). Categorization and the physical attractiveness stereotype. *Social Cognition, 6*, 231–251.

Miller, D. T., Taylor, B., & Buck, M. L. (1991). Gender gaps: Who needs to be explained? *Journal of Personality and Social Psychology, 61*, 5–12.

Miller, D. T., & Turnbull, W. (1986). Expectancies and interpersonal processes. In M. R. Rosenzweig & L. W. Porter (Eds.), *Annual review of psychology* (Vol. 37, pp. 233–256). Palo Alto, CA: Annual Reviews.

Miller, D. T., & Turnbull, W. (1990). The counterfactual fallacy: Confusing what might have been with what ought to have been. *Social Justice Research, 4*, 1–16.

Miller, D. T., Turnbull, W., & McFarland, C. (1990). Counterfactual thinking and social perception: Thinking about what might have been. In M. P. Zanna (Ed.), *Advances in experimental social psychology* (Vol. 23, pp. 305–331). San Diego: Academic Press.

Miller, J. B. (1976). *Toward a new psychology of women*. Boston: Beacon Press.

Miller, N., & Brewer, M. B. (1986). Categorization effects on ingroup and outgroup perception. In J. F. Dovidio & S. L. Gaertner (Eds.), *Prejudice, discrimination, and racism*. New York: Academic Press.

Mills, C. J. (1983). Sex-typing and self-schemata effects on memory and response latency. *Journal of Personality and Social Psychology, 45*, 163–172.

Moscovici, S. (1984). The phenomena of social representations. In R. M. Farr & S. Moscovici (Eds.), *Social representations* (pp. 3–69). Cambridge, England: Cambridge University Press.

Mussen, P. H. (1969). Early sex-role development. In D. A. Goslin (Ed.), *Handbook of socialization theory and research*. Chicago: Rand McNally.

Nash, S. C. (1975). The relationship among sex-role stereotyping, sex-role preference, and the sex difference in spatial visualization. *Sex Roles, 1*, 15–32.

Nash, S. C. (1979). Sex role as a mediator of intellectual functioning. In M. A. Wittig & A. C. Petersen (Eds.), *Sex-related differences in cognitive functioning* (pp. 263–302). New York: Academic Press.

Nelson, T. E., Biernat, M. R., & Manis, M. (1990). Everyday base rates (sex stereotypes): Potent and resilient. *Journal of Personality and Social Psychology, 59*, 664–675.

Neuberg, S. L. (1989). The goal of forming accurate impressions during social interactions: Attenuating the impact of negative expectancies. *Journal of Personality and Social Psychology, 56*, 374–386.

Neuberg, S. L., & Fiske, S. T. (1987). Motivational influences on impression formation: Outcome dependency, accuracy-driven attention, and individuating processes. *Journal of Personality and Social Psychology, 53*, 431–444.

Niemi, P. (1985). The role of gender-related self-schemata in the attributions of social interaction. *Scandinavian Journal of Psychology, 26*, 170–180.

Nisbett, R. E., & Ross, L. (1980). *Human inference: Strategies and shortcomings of social judgment.* Englewood Cliffs, NJ: Prentice-Hall.

Park, B., & Hastie, R. (1987). Perception of variability in category development: Instance- versus abstraction-based stereotypes. *Journal of Personality and Social Psychology, 53*, 621–635.

Park, B., & Rothbart, M. (1982). Perception of out-group homogeneity and levels of social categorization: Memory for the subordinate attributes of in-group and out-group members. *Journal of Personality and Social Psychology, 42*, 1051-1068.

Pavelchak, M. A. (1989). Piecemeal and category-based evaluation: An idiographic analysis. *Journal of Personality and Social Psychology, 56*, 354–363.

Payne, T. J., Connor, J. M., & Colletti, G. (1987). Gender-based schematic processing: An empirical investigation and reevaluation. *Journal of Personality and Social Psychology, 52*, 937–945.

Pettigrew, T. F., & Martin, J. (1987). Shaping the organizational context for black American inclusion. *Journal of Social Issues, 43*, 41–78.

Pratto, F., & Bargh, J. A. (1991). Stereotyping based on apparently individuating information: Trait and global components of sex stereotypes under attention overload. *Journal of Experimental Social Psychology, 27*, 26–47.

Pyke, S. W., & Graham, J. M. (1983). Gender schema theory and androgyny: A critique and elaboration. *International Journal of Women's Studies, 6*, 3–17.

Quattrone, G. A. (1986). On the perception of a group's variability. In S. Worchel & W. Austin (Eds.), *The psychology of intergroup relations* (Vol. 2, pp. 25–48). New York: Nelson-Hall.

Reeder, G. D., & Brewer, M. B. (1979). A schematic model of dispositional attribution in interpersonal perception. *Psychological Review, 86*, 61–79.

Reis, H.T., Senchak, M., & Solomon, B. (1985). Sex differences in the intimacy of social interaction: Further examination of potential explanations. *Journal of Personality and Social Psychology, 48*, 1204–1217.

Rosaldo, M. Z., & Lamphere, L. (1974). *Women, culture and society.* Stanford, CA: Stanford University Press.

Rosenkrantz, P. S., Vogel, S. T., Bee, H., Broverman, I. K., & Broverman, D. M. (1968). Sex-role stereotypes and self concepts in college students. *Journal of Consulting and Clinical Psychology, 32*, 287–295.

Ross, L., Lepper, M. R., & Hubbard, M. (1975). Perseverance in self-perception and social perception: Biased attributional processes in the debriefing paradigm. *Journal of Personality and Social Psychology, 32*, 880–892.

Rothbart, M., & John, O. P. (1985). Social categorization and behavioral episodes: A cognitive analysis of the effects of intergroup contact. *Journal of Social Issues, 41*, 81–104

Rothbart, M., & Park, B. (1986). On the confirmability and disconfirmability of trait concepts. *Journal of Personality and Social Psychology, 50*, 131–142.

Ruble, D. N., & Ruble, T. L. (1982). Sex stereotypes. In A. G. Miller (Ed.), *In the eye of the beholder: Contemporary issues in stereotyping* (pp. 188–252). New York: Praeger.

Ruble, D. N., & Stangor, C. (1986). Stalking the elusive schema: Insights from developmental and social-psychological analyses of gender schemas. *Social Cognition, 4*, 227–261.

Ruble, T. L. (1983). Sex stereotypes: Issues of change in the 1970's. *Sex Roles*, *9*, 397–402.

Ruble, T. L., Cohen, R., & Ruble, D. N. (1984). Sex stereotypes: Occupational barriers for women. *American Behavioral Scientist*, *27*, 339–356.

Sadker, M., & Sadker, D. (1984). *Year 3: Final Report, Promoting effectiveness in classroom instruction.* Washington, DC: National Institute of Education.

Sagar, H. A., & Schofield, J. W. (1980). Racial and behavioral cues in black and white children's perceptions of ambiguously aggressive acts. *Journal of Personality and Social Psychology*, *39*, 590–598.

Schneider, D. J. (1991). Social cognition. In M. R. Rosenzweig & L. W. Porter (Eds.), *Annual review of psychology* (Vol. 42, pp. 527–561). Palo Alto, CA: Annual Reviews

Sherif, C. (1982). Needed concepts in the study of gender identity. *Psychology of Women Quarterly*, *6*, 375–398.

Sherif, M., Harvey, L. J., White, B. J., Hood, W. R., & Sherif, C. W. (1988). *The robbers cave experiment: Intergroup conflict and cooperation.* Middletown, CT: Wesleyan University Press. (Original work published 1961)

Sherman, S. J., Judd, C. M., & Park, B. (1989). Social cognition. *Annual Review of Psychology*, *40*, 281–326.

Shweder, R. A. (1982). Beyond self-constructed knowledge: The study of culture and morality. *Merrill-Palmer Quarterly*, *28*, 41–69.

Shweder, R. A. (1991). *Thinking through cultures: Expeditions in cultural psychology.* Cambridge, MA: Harvard University Press.

Signorella, M. L. (1984). Cognitive consequences of personal involvement in gender identity. *Sex Roles*, *11*, 923–939.

Signorella, M. L., & Jamison, W. (1986). Masculinity, femininity, androgyny, and cognitive performance: A meta-analysis. *Psychological Bulletin*, *100*, 207–228.

Signorella, M. L., & Liben, L. S. (1987). *Children's gender schemata.* San Francisco: Jossey-Bass.

Silka, L. (1984). Intuitive perceptions of change: An overlooked phenomenon in person perception? *Personality and Social Psychology Bulletin*, *10*, 180–190.

Sitka, L. J., & Maslach, C. (1990). Gender roles and the categorization of gender-relevant behavior. *Sex Roles*, *22*, 133–150.

Skrypnek, B. J., & Snyder, M. (1982). On the self-perpetuating nature of stereotypes about women and men. *Journal of Experimental Social Psychology*, *18*, 277–291.

Slaby, R. G., & Frey, K. S. (1975). Development of gender constancy and selective attention to same-sex models. *Child Development*, *46*, 849–856.

Slusher, M. P., & Anderson, C. A. (1987). When reality monitoring fails: The role of imagination in stereotype maintenance. *Journal of Personality and Social Psychology*, *52*, 653–662.

Snyder, M., & Swann, W. B. (1978). Behavioral confirmation in social interaction: From social perception to social reality. *Journal of Experimental Social Psychology*, *14*, 148–162.

Spence, J. T. (1985). Gender identity and its implications for concepts of masculinity and femininity. In T. B. Sonderegger (Ed.), *Nebraska symposium on motiva-*

tion: Psychology of gender (pp. 59–95). Lincoln, NB: University of Nebraska Press.

Spence, J. T., Deaux, K., & Helmreich, R. L. (1985). Sex roles in contemporary American society. In G. Lindzey & E. Aronson (Eds.), *Handbook of social psychology* (3rd ed.) (Vol. 2, pp. 149–178). New York: Random House.

Spence, J. T., Helmreich, R. L., & Stapp, J. (1975). Ratings of self and peers on sex role attributes and their relations to self-esteem and conceptions of masculinity and femininity. *Journal of Personality and Social Psychology, 32,* 29–39.

Srull, T. K. (1981). Person memory: Some tests of associative storage and retrieval models. *Journal of Experimental Psychology: Human Learning and Memory, 7,* 440–462.

Srull, T. K., & Wyer, R. S. (1989). Person memory and judgment. *Psychological Review, 96,* 58–83.

Stangor, C., & Duan, C. (1991). Effects of multiple task demands on memory for information about social groups. *Journal of Experimental Social Psychology, 27,* 357–378.

Stangor, C., & McMillan, D. (1992). Memory of expectancy-congruent and expectancy-incongruent information: A review of the social and social developmental literatures. *Psychological Bulletin, 111,* 42–61.

Stangor, C. S., & Ruble, D. N. (1987). Development of gender role knowledge and gender constancy. In L. S. Liben & M. L. Signorella (Eds.), *Children's gender schemata: New directions in child development* (Vol. 38, pp. 5–22). San Francisco: Jossey-Bass.

Stangor, C. S., & Ruble, D. N. (1989). Differential influences of gender schemata and gender constancy on children's information processing and behavior. *Social Cognition, 7,* 353–372.

Stephan, W. G. (1985). Intergroup relations. In G. Lindzey & E. Aronson (Eds.), *Handbook of social psychology* (3rd ed.) (Vol. 2, pp. 599–658). New York: Random House.

Stewart, A. J., & Lykes, M. B. (Eds.). (1985). Conceptualizing gender in personality theory and research. In *Gender and personality: Current perspectives on theory and research* (pp. 2–13). Durham, NC: Duke University Press.

Swann, W. B., Jr. (1984). Quest for accuracy in person perception: A matter of pragmatics. *Psychological Review, 91,* 457–477.

Swann, W. B., Jr., & Ely, R. J. (1984). A battle of wills: Self-verification versus behavioral confirmation. *Journal of Personality and Social Psychology, 46,* 1287–1302.

Swann, W. B., Jr., & Hill, C. A. (1982). When our identities are mistaken: Reaffirming self-conceptions through social interaction. *Journal of Personality and Social Psychology, 43,* 59–66.

Swann, W. B., Jr., & Read, S. J. (1981a). Acquiring self-knowledge: The search for feedback that fits. *Journal of Personality and Social Psychology, 41,* 1119–1128.

Swann, W. B., Jr., & Read, S. J. (1981b). Self-verification processes: How we sustain our self-conceptions. *Journal of Experimental Social Psychology, 17,* 351–370.

Tannen, D. (1990). *You just don't understand: Women and men in conversation.* New York: Morrow.

Taylor, S. E. (1981). A categorization approach to stereotyping. In D. L. Hamilton (Ed.), *Cognitive processes in stereotyping and intergroup behavior* (pp. 88–114). Hillsdale, NJ: Erlbaum.

Taylor, S. E., & Falcone, H. T. (1982). Cognitive bases of stereotyping: The relationship between categorization and prejudice. *Personality and Social Psychology Bulletin, 8*, 426–432.

Taylor, S. E., Fiske, S. T., Etcoff, N. L., & Ruderman, A. J. (1978). Categorical bases of person memory and stereotyping. *Journal of Personality and Social Psychology, 36*, 778–793.

Tesser, A. (1978). Self-generated attitude change. In L. Berkowitz (Ed.), *Advances in experimental and social psychology* (Vol. 11, pp. 289–338). New York: Academic Press.

Tetlock, P. E. (1983). Accountability and the perseverance of first impressions. *Social Psychology Quarterly, 46*, 285–292.

Tetlock, P. E., & Kim, J. I. (1987). Accountability and judgment processes in a personality prediction task. *Journal of Personality and Social Psychology, 52*, 700–709.

Thompson, S. K. (1975). Gender labels and early sex-role development. *Child Development, 46*, 339–347.

Thorne, B. (1986). Girls and boys together, but mostly apart. In W. W. Hartup & Z. Rubin (Eds.), *Relationship and development* (pp. 167–184). Hillsdale, NJ: Erlbaum.

Thorne, B. (1987, February). *Children and gender: Construction of difference.* Paper presented at a conference on Theoretical Perspectives on Sexual Difference, Stanford University, CA.

Tsujimoto, R. N., Wilde, J., & Robertson, D. R. (1978). Distorted memory for exemplars of social structure: Evidence for schematic memory processes. *Journal of Personality and Social Psychology, 38*, 1402–1414.

Wallston, B. S., & O'Leary, V. E. (1981). Sex makes a difference: Differential perceptions of women and men. *Review of Personality and Social Psychology, 2*, 9–41.

Weber, R., & Crocker, J. (1983). Cognitive processes in the revision of stereotypic beliefs. *Journal of Personality and Social Psychology, 45*, 961–977.

Werner, P. D., & LaRussa, G. W. (1985). Persistence and change in sex-role stereotypes. *Sex Roles, 12*, 1089–1100.

Wilder, D. A., & Shapiro, P. (1991). Facilitation of outgroup stereotypes by enhanced ingroup identity. *Journal of Experimental Social Psychology, 27*, 431–452.

Wittig, M. A., & Peterson, A. C. (1979). *Sex-related issues in cognitive functioning: Developmental issues.* New York: Academic Press.

Wolman, C., & Frank, H. (1975). The solo woman in a professional peer group. *American Journal of Orthopsychiatry, 45*, 164–171.

Wood, W. & Karten, S.J. (1986). Sex differences in interaction style as a product of perceived sex differences in competence. *Journal of Personality and Social Psychology, 50*, 341–347.

Wong, M.M., & Csikszentmihalyi, M. (1991). Affiliation motivation and daily experience: some issues on gender differences. *Journal of Personality and Social Psychology, 60*, 154–164.

Wyer, R. S., Jr., Bodenhausen, G. V., & Srull, T. K. (1984). The cognitive representation of persons and groups and its effect on recall and recognition memory. *Journal of Experimental Social Psychology, 20*, 445–469.

Wyer, R. S., Jr., & Srull, T. K. (1981). Category accessibility: Some theoretical and empirical issues concerning the processing of social stimulus information. In E.T. Higgins, C.P. Herman, & M.P. Zanna (Eds.), *Social cognition: The Ontario Symposium* (Vol. 1, pp. 161–198). Hillsdale, NJ: Erlbaum.

Wyer, R. S., Jr., & Srull, T. K. (1986). Human cognition in its social context. *Psychological Review, 93*, 322–359.

Zadny, J., & Gerard, H. B. (1974). Attributed intentions and informational selectivity. *Journal of Experimental Social Psychology, 10*, 34–52.

The Social Learning of Gender

BERNICE LOTT
DIANE MALUSO

This chapter is concerned with how the social learning approach to understanding behavior can explain the acquisition and maintenance of gender. Such an approach, as we interpret and use it here, makes a crucial distinction between sex and gender. Whereas sex denotes a limited set of innate structural and physiological characteristics related to reproduction, and divides animal species into female and male, gender is specific to humans and connotes all the complex attributes ascribed by culture(s) to human females and males, respectively. Only among humans are there girls and boys, and women and men (i.e., gendered social categories). Gender is constructed, or learned, from the particular conditions, experiences, and contingencies that a culture systematically, and differentially, pairs with human femaleness and maleness, and is a major social category used by most societies as a basis for socialization and for the ascription of social status. Members of human groups are socialized to perform behaviors appropriate to the social categories deemed important; in our society in addition to gender, these categories include age, ethnicity, skin color, social class, and sexual orientation. We also learn to respond to members of social categories with particular expectations, evaluations, and actions. An important tenet of the social learning position presented here is that the gender socialization process (the transforming of sex into gender) is not confined to the early years but continues throughout life.

The major features of social learning approaches will be considered in this chapter, and some of the variations within this broad position will be noted. Highlighted are three important propositions that guide and inform the analysis of gender presented here: (1) that socialization is a continuing, lifelong process; (2) that there is a strong compatibility between social learning and feminist viewpoints; and (3) that gender socialization in our heterogeneous, complex society is continuously affected by variations in social class and ethnicity (and other important social categories) and by idiosyncratic family and personal history variables. This results in gender being a relatively unreliable predictor of behavior, particularly in childhood and adulthood. (Gender is probably most reliably associated with behavior in adolescence, a subject for future examination.) In other words, our gender prophecies based on stereotyped expectations often fail, particularly in situations/contexts where other social categories or personal attributes are more salient or relevant. Our social institutions continue, nevertheless, to strongly support the stereotypes and to generalize behavior, thereby maintaining gender inequities in power and privilege.

Gender is discussed as a salient stimulus to which persons learn a variety of socially significant covert responses (including perceptions, attitudes, and beliefs) and overt responses. This chapter, however, is primarily focused on gender as the behavioral outcome of cultural construction or socialization. Examples are presented from the literature on children and adults; the greater number of illustrations dealing with the former reflect the greater attention that the sex typing of children's behavior has received from researchers.

The final section of this chapter considers the changes in meaning of woman and man, and girl and boy likely to accompany significant changes in our society. Just as each gender is already definable in terms of common themes and variations, and just as gender is currently a reliable predictor of behavior only under certain conditions, so can we anticipate continued reconstruction with important social changes in family, economic, and political life.

SOCIAL LEARNING BROADLY DEFINED

The term *social learning* represents a spectrum of assumptions and hypotheses relevant to the antecedents and consequences of human behavior that include, at one end, radical behaviorist positions (e.g., Staats, 1975) and, at the other end, theories in which cognition plays a predominant role (e.g., Bandura, 1977). What appears to be central to all social learning perspectives, and the unifying factor in otherwise differing approaches, is the use of general learning principles to explain human social behavior. Thus, for example, Miller and Dollard (1941) analyzed the behavior of lynch mob participants on the basis of four major variables: drive (motivational stimuli), situational stimuli, previously learned responses (habits), and response consequences. This analysis is a classic example of the "extension of liberalized S-R theory" (Miller, 1959); that is, the use of general learning principles in the interpretation of complex human behavior, a development envisaged both by Hull (1943) and by Skinner (1953).

A social learning approach assumes that social behavior is predictable from knowledge of situational events and from the individual's previous experiences with these (or similar) events (Lott & Lott, 1985). The objective is to specify the conditions that increase or decrease the probability of a particular kind of response and the likely consequences of the response. Such an approach was used by Mowrer (1960) to explain dysfunctional behavior, by Doob (1947) to explain attitudes, and by Rotter (1954) to explain a variety of social/personal behavioral choices. A social learning approach to understanding the development of sex roles, or sex-typed behavior, was clearly articulated by Mischel (1966), whose important and often cited paper has remained a useful framework for contemporary researchers.

Mischel (1966) defined sex-typed behaviors as those "that typically elicit different rewards for one sex than for the other" (p. 56), emphasizing the central role played by behavioral consequences. Reinforcements for behavior, Mischel noted, could be provided either by others or by oneself, had different values, and tended to occur with different frequencies for the two sexes. His major thesis was that the same principles that describe the acquisition of all social behaviors are relevant to understanding the development of sex-typed behaviors. Mischel called attention to the variables of reward, nonreward, and punishment (any of which could be experienced directly or vicariously through observation) and to discrimination and generalization. Persons acquire sex-typed behaviors, Mischel suggested, first by learning to discriminate between sex-typed patterns and then by generalizing from specific conditions to new situations, and finally by performing these behaviors. As Bem (1985) has noted, "Social learning theory . . . locates the source of sex-typing in the sex-differentiated practices of the socializing community" (p. 182).

As assumption basic to social learning theory is that we learn behavior by means of a relatively small number of distinguishable but related processes that operate throughout life. It is through these processes that gender is acquired and maintained. Primary attention is given to the role of positive and negative reinforcement; that is, to the consequences that follow behavior, the reactions elicited, the changes produced, and so on. Modeling or imitating the behavior of others, another continuing process, is related to the availability, likability, and power of the model, with degree of likability predictable from the positive or negative consequences or experiences associated with the model and power related to the model's access to resources or positive or negative sanctions. Labeling is clearly related to gender learning and performance; linguistic gender tags (Constantinople, 1979) that are joined to clothing, activities, and so on, act as mediators, serve an organizing function, and guide social interactions. We learn to behave in ways deemed appropriate for persons labeled similarly to ourselves.

We propose that a social learning position includes the following major components or assumptions: (1) every individual of any age has a previous learning history which provides a repertoire of responses likely to be evoked in particular situations; (2) each situation includes distinctive and general stimuli and has both specific and contextual meaning; (3) motivational factors are either brought to situations or are evoked in them; (4) new responses can be acquired if opportunities are provided for their (explicit or implicit) practice; and (5) behavior will be acquired and/or maintained if it is successful in mediating positive consequences. This framework emphasizes that behaviors once acquired must also be maintained by necessary conditions, and that what is learned is not always or necessarily performed. Bandura (1986) has argued, for example, that children learn (either directly or from observation) more behaviors than they display because they judge the behaviors inappropriate for their gender (or for other reasons) or because they anticipate negative social sanctions.

Behavioral Consequences and Opportunities for Practice

Positive consequences and opportunities for practice are considered in social learning analysis to be the primary mediators of both response performance and maintenance. The importance of consequences is highlighted in all social learning positions, including those stressing cognitive mediators and observational learning. Bandura (1977) has emphasized the necessary role played by the "experience of mastery arising from effective performance" (p. 191) in altering cognitions that mediate behavior change, but in his most recent book (Bandura, 1986) the direct consequences of reinforcement for performance are deemphasized. Not surprisingly, this newest book is subtitled "a social cognitive theory" rather than a social learning theory, a change that has been noted and discussed by a number of reviewers (e.g., Kihlstrom & Harackiewicz, 1990; Corcoran, 1991). What Bandura (1990) posits as being among the important antecedents of human motivation and action are the cognitions derived from interpretations about previous outcomes (i.e., outcome expectancies).

The effect on social behavior of positive or negative consequences, regardless of the directness of the influence, remains central to a social learning position. Consequences are often intertwined with opportunities for practice that typically precede, and provide the setting for, behavioral outcomes. Different situations provide differential opportunities to practice particular behaviors and also present demand characteristics that make some responses more probable than others. For example, a doll in a child's hands usually demands hugging, stroking, and tender, loving care in contrast to a ball, which demands bouncing, throwing, and kicking. That dolls are more often put into the hands of girls and balls into the hands of boys is, of course, crucial to the explanation of gender-related behavior in contemporary American culture. A review of gender-labeling studies (Stern & Karraker, 1989) found that while the gender label of the child had no effect on the warmth or responsiveness of the adult participants, persons reacting to children labeled a girl or a boy differed in their responses most consistently in offering dolls to the former and footballs or hammers to the latter.

Tittle (1986), after reviewing relevant literature, has argued that sex-typed play activities serve as antecedents for sex-typed social and achievement behaviors. It is particularly noteworthy, then, that Lytton and Romney (1991), in a meta-analysis of 172 studies of parental socialization practices, found a strong and consistent tendency for both mothers and fathers to encourage sex-typed activities or to "emphasize sex stereotypes in play activities and household chores" (p. 287).

Just as girls and boys find themselves encouraged to play in different situations, so too are women and men encouraged to practice behavior in "different spheres." Thus, many more women than men find themselves in kitchens and at the bedsides of sick children or adults, where certain responses are clearly more probable, more appropriate, and more likely to be rewarded than others. Bem (1985) has called attention to the common observation that "women but not men are asked to bake cookies for bake sales and are called home from work when their children get sick at school" (p. 180). Such taken-for-granted "facts of life" have enormous implications for the performance and maintenance of gender-related behavior. Mischel's (1966) example of observational learning (although somewhat outdated) is relevant to the present argument. He pointed out that

> boys and girls typically acquire many of the behaviors of both sexes. Men know how to apply face powder, and women know how to place cigars in their mouths, although through differential practise they may differ in the skill with which they execute such behaviors. (p. 59)

Similarly, men know how to diaper babies and take temperatures but have less practice in these behaviors and, consequently, typically exhibit lesser skill than women do.

Gender Socialization as a Continuing Process

It has been asserted by some writers (e.g., Deaux & Major, 1987) that, like psychoanalytic and cognitive developmental theories, social learning theory assumes that adult differences in gender-related behavior have their origins in early learning. This is an unwarranted conclusion. The social learning approach makes an important distinction between acquisition and maintenance of behavior, a distinction that is incompatible with attributing to early experiences an indelible role in gender learning. Focusing on early socialization experiences fails to acknowledge the continuing and pervasive opportunities outside the family environment, and throughout life, to practice gender-related behavior.

It may well be that parents do far less direct sex typing than do other socialization agents. Since parents tend to respond to the uniqueness of each child, and with high aspirations for their future, it is not startling to find, as reported by Lytton and Romney (1991), that the child's gender is not a significant influence on many of the parental socialization dimensions that have been studied (with the important exceptions of encouraging sex-typed activities and the tendency to show more warmth toward girls). Meyer, Murphy, Cascardi, and Birns (1991) suggest that gender-differentiated behavior in childhood is likely to be influenced not just by the parental behavior directed toward the child but also by the observations that children in two-parent heterosexual families make of "parental interaction that reflects the way most men and women relate to each other in mixed-sex dyads or groups" (p. 537). Meyer et al. (1991) argue that the way parents relate to each other and to other persons presents distinct cultural messages about the expectations for behavior by women and men.

Relevant to this discussion is the important distinction between traits and habits (Lott, 1990). A trait defines a behavioral tendency that, once acquired (e.g., through childhood socialization), remains stable, internal (psychodynamic), and cross-situational. The concept of habit, on the other hand, ties the performance of a learned response not only to the strength of that response based on prior experience but also to the situational cues and consequences present at the time. There is no assumption of consistency across situations or of intrapsychic stability unrelated to context. Personal experiences and systematically collected data support the conclusions that human behavior is not well described by traits and that individuals learn responses to, and in, situations continuously throughout their lives. As conditions and opportunities for practice change, so does our behavior. Gender socialization is a lifelong process reflecting changing circumstances and experiences. This position is asserted by many whose theory and research attend to the important influence of ethnicity on social behavior (e.g., Armstrong, 1984; LaFromboise, Heyle, & Ozer, 1990).

Recognition of within-gender and within-person variability in all social behaviors reduces the validity of positions that stress the childhood origin of gender-related traits or sex roles. Deaux and Major (1987), whose model focuses on the performance rather than the acquisition of gender-related behavior, emphasize that "the enactment of gender primarily takes place within the context of social interaction" (p. 370). Although gender in our highly gender-conscious culture is typically an important cue, it may not be the most salient factor in all interactions. The growing recognition of other social factors can be seen in conclusions such as Perry's (1991) that "class, race, and ethnicity complicate models of [gender] difference . . . in a world with an astounding variety of women" (p. 599). Fine and Gordon (1991), too, argue against the mythologizing of "women" and the "whiting out" of the rich sources of variation associated with other social constructions or categories.

Because socialization is a lifelong process, and because other social categories interact with gender, it follows that individual definitions of gender change and evolve as a function of experience and cannot be assumed always to reflect difference. Social learning theory predicts that girls and boys, and women and men, will behave similarly in similar positions and situations depending on the opportunities to practice behaviors and on the outcomes. Research on children and adults, which we discuss later in this chapter, provides support for this conclusion. As noted by Kahn and Yoder (1989), behavioral differences disappear when social forces influence both genders similarly.

RELEVANCE OF THE FEMINIST PERSPECTIVE

The social learning viewpoint seems particularly compatible with feminist psychology (e.g., Hare-Mustin & Marecek, 1990; Lott, 1985, 1990, 1991; Sherif, 1981). The major questions that feminist scholars across disciplines have asked during the past two decades have been highlighted by Perry (1991) as follows: "How is human identity constructed in different cultural contexts? How do bodies come to have the meanings they have? How are women and men fit into larger political and economic structures? [And] . . . how [is] gender . . . constructed and perpetuated?" (p. 597). Within a social learning framework such questions can be addressed, relevant empirically testable hypotheses can be formulated, and data bearing on these issues can be integrated into a theoretical network concerned with a wide variety of social phenomena.

Central to the feminist position is the conviction that "the issue of sex and gender is fundamental to an understanding of human behavior" (Deaux, 1985, p. 74). The number and variety of chapters in this volume attest to the fact that there are many approaches to the understanding of gender; however, we believe that social learning theory provides psychologists with an extremely useful and generalizable framework for research, that is, for the identification and study of meaningful variables. By contributing testable hypotheses about the conditions under which gender learning occurs and is maintained or changed, and about the consequences of gender's function as a social cue, social learning provides a theoretical and empirical framework for the most basic of feminist assumptions—that gender is a cultural construction and an ongoing process. As noted by Perry (1991), the feminist "project" is to understand "how gender . . . is constructed and how it might be re-constructed" (p. 601).

Sex denotes the anatomical and physiological distinctions between males and females in all animal species, but gender is specific to human beings and identifies women and men, and girls and boys. Gender categories are socially defined by each culture in terms of expected behavior, attributes, and values. With the exception of assumptions about reproductive capacities and roles, the meanings of girl/woman and boy/man have been found to be not fixed but to vary across time and place, supporting the conclusion that it is through socialization that sex becomes gender (Lott, 1993).

Particularly important in defining gender within each culture are interpersonal social interactions. Thus, Crawford and Marecek (1989) argue, as have others, that "gender is conceived as a principle of social organization, which structures the relations, especially the power relations, between women and men" (p. 155), and therefore "gender is thought of as a process rather than a set of attributes" (p. 156). Gender-related experiences necessarily occur within personal, political, historical, cultural, and linguistic contexts and are never independent of, but are in fact constituted by, them (Fine & Gordon, 1991; Gavey, 1989). For example, from a study of poor migrant Puerto Ricans living on the lower east side of Manhattan, Sharff (1983) concluded that children are reared to contribute to the survival of the household. Thus, while some girls are propelled toward being "child reproducers" and reinforced for traditional feminine attributes, other girls are reared to be "scholar/advocates." Training for the latter emphasizes "dominance and assertiveness . . . [and the] entire household contributes to this girl's eventual upward mobility" (Sharff, 1983; p. 58).

Despite important questions that continue to be debated among feminist theorists, there is agreement on certain broad propositions that include the following: recognition of the patriarchal, sexist nature of most aspects of contemporary social life and institutions; recognition of the negative consequences of gender inequities in power; and focus on the entire range of women's experiences (Lott, 1992). Feminists also share an openly articulated commitment to social change in alliance with others to eliminate barriers to resources based on gender, ethnicity, class, and other social categories.

A major feminist theme that is clearly compatible with a social learning analysis is that not only is gender a person variable that identifies members of two human groups, but it also signifies expected normative behavior (i.e., "sex role"). In this way, gender functions as a complex cue for the perceptions, expectations, and overt reactions of others. Several recent theoretical formulations have emphasized this stimulus function of gender and its significance in influencing behavior.

THE STIMULUS FUNCTION OF GENDER

Deaux and Major (1987) regard gender as a salient and powerful social category and posit the presence of three key elements in any social interaction in which gender-linked behaviors will be displayed: (1) perceivers and their beliefs about gender; (2) targets (or selves) and their beliefs about gender; and (3) the situation with some number of more or less salient gender-related issues or elements. Deaux and Major (1987) view gender-related behavior as flexible or adaptable and situationally influenced, since they "assume that men and women are relatively equal in their potentialities for most social behaviors and that behaviors may differ widely as a function of personal choice, the behavior of others, and the situational context" (p. 371). This cognitively oriented social learning approach focuses on performance (or display) rather than on acquisition of behavior and emphasizes the expectancies about gender that are embedded in social interaction and contribute to its context.

Gender schema theory, as formulated by Bem (e.g., 1985), includes similar assumptions and arguments. Incorporating features of both social learning and cognitive developmental theories, Bem proposes that children acquire specific information about gender and also learn "to invoke this . . . network of sex-related associations in order to evaluate and assimilate new information" (p. 186). She argues that our culture's extraordinary emphasis on the gender dichotomy encourages (or mandates) that information be encoded and organized in gender-related terms, and that gender functions as a salient and potent stimulus that has "cognitive primacy" over other social categories and evokes well-learned and widely shared responses.

The significance of gender as a stimulus is also central to the social-role analysis of gender proposed by Eagly (1983, 1987) who emphasizes that relative status is salient among the characteristics we learn to associate with, or attribute to, gender. Gender is said to function as a generalized status cue because it is observed to be correlated with power and prestige across a variety of settings and experiences. There is certainly no question that the positions of men in most groups and organizations in our society tend to be higher in authority and to offer greater access to resources than do the positions of women. Because gender covaries with power and status, persons tend to behave in ways that confirm this. Other social categories also function as generalized status cues. Ethnicity, in particular, provides cues to social standing (Landrine, 1985). Especially important are the "combined or interactive affects" of gender and ethnicity, as noted by Reid and Comas-Diaz (1990).

In addition to expectations about differential power and status associated with women and men, Eagly (1987) emphasizes differential expectations regarding communal and agentic attributes that stem from the family and work roles assigned in our culture. That people tend to find disconfirmation of such expectations unpleasant and frustrating is illustrated by findings from a meta-analysis of studies dealing with the evaluation of leaders. Eagly, Makhijani, and Klonsky (1990) found that women described as being leaders in traditionally male domains (e.g., business and high school athletics) and as behaving in task-oriented, agentic ways tended to be evaluated more negatively than were identically described men.

The stimulus function of gender has been the focus of a series of studies (Lott, 1987a, 1989; Lott, Lott, & Fernald, 1990) exploring men's distancing responses to women. This research has been guided by a social learning approach to interpersonal sexism that operationalizes face-to-face discrimination as distancing behavior and distinguishes this overt component of sexism from prejudice (affect) and stereotypes (beliefs). Three theoretically related but independently measurable components of sexism are as follows:

1. *Prejudice*, defined as *negative attitudes* toward women—for example feelings of hostility or dislike;
2. *Stereotypes*, defined as well learned, widely shared, socially validated general *beliefs* about women which reinforce, complement, or justify the prejudice, and often involve an assumption of inferiority; and
3. *Discrimination*, defined as *overt behaviors* that achieve separation from women through exclusion, avoidance, or distancing.

In a variety of settings (a laboratory situation in which pairs of strangers worked together on building a structure with dominoes, two-person interactions in popular prime-time television programs, and choice of photographed persons for service interactions), men were found to distance themselves from women significantly more than from men. Women, on the other hand, were found, in most cases, to respond similarly to both women and men.

CONSTRUCTION OF GENDER

Prediction of behavior in gender-relevant situations from knowledge of the actor's gender is sometimes possible; this follows from the cultural construction of gender. Because culture defines gender and provides opportunities for individuals to learn and display it, differences between women and men, or between girls and boys, can reliably be found for some behaviors, at some ages, in some situations, at some times and places (Lott, 1990). Such differences, however, can be understood as related more to antecedent conditions and situational determinants than to sex, since the culture has arranged experiences so that these factors covary. If a culture systematically arranges the experiences of its children and adults so that gender will be associated with differential expectations, opportunities, and consequences, it is those arrangements that we must study in order to understand their outcomes for behavior.

The literature on the sex typing of children's behavior through covariation of gender and experiences is large; here we can provide only a few examples. A social learning perspective has informed the work of Fagot, a major contributor to this literature. A general proposition central to her research is that children learn what is important from the different reactions girls and boys receive when performing the same behaviors (Fagot, 1984b). In one study (Fagot, 1978), both sets of parents were observed in their home interacting with their 20- to 24-month-old children. It was found that boys and girls were treated significantly differently in the following ways: Boys were more likely to be left alone in play or to be joined by parents, whereas girls were more likely to be verbally criticized or praised; parents responded positively to boys when they were engaged in block play and negatively to them when they were engaged in doll play or when they asked for help; and girls received positive parental reactions when they played with dolls, asked for help, watched television, or followed the parent around and negative reactions for manipulating objects, running, jumping, and climbing. These observed parental behaviors could not have been predicted from answers the parents gave to survey questions, suggesting that "parents are not fully aware of the methods they use to socialize their young children" (Fagot, 1978, p. 464), or of the specific behaviors that are socialized. Lytton and Romney (1991) found some support for this conclusion in their meta-analysis of studies dealing with parents' socialization behaviors; observational and experimental studies yielded more evidence of differential treatment of girls and boys than did self-report studies.

Teachers and peers also contribute to the sex typing of children's behavior. Fagot (1984b) found, from observations made in preschool playgroups, significantly more positive peer feedback to boys than to girls for high-activity play. Traditional sex-role behavior in other areas was followed by more positive consequences from both teachers and peers. In yet another study (Fagot, 1984a), observers of preschool playgroups reported that peers or teachers paid attention to boys' aggression (i.e., reacted to it) 81% of the time compared to 24% of the time to aggression by girls. Dependency behaviors by girls, on the other hand, were more frequently reacted to than were similar behaviors by boys. Nor surprisingly, then, aggressive conduct problems were found to be relatively stable for boys but not for girls, while dependency problems were more stable for girls. Fagot (1984a) concluded that "the pattern of reactions that children receive from peers and caregivers is very consistent with the stability of the problem behaviors. Behaviors given attention are maintained, while those that result in being ignored tend to drop out" (p. 394). Similar findings were reported from a study (Fagot & Hagan, 1985) that analyzed data on aggression collected over a 4-year period from observations of children's play during their first term of preschool attendance. While less than half of aggressive acts by girls received some response (attention), the initial aggression of boys received a response about 70% of the time, most often from another boy. The investigators concluded that "boys . . . are given responses which maintain aggressive interchanges, while girls' aggression is often ignored, which tends to terminate the interchange" (Fagot & Hagan, 1985, p. 349).

In a review of the influence of gender on relationships, Maccoby (1990) argued that children, from an early age, tend to segregate themselves into same-gender play groups. She attributes this segregation primarily to the rough-and-tumble, assertive–dominant interaction style of boys and to girls' relative passivity and difficulty in influencing boys. She does not attempt to answer the question of where these behaviors come from but notes their presence prior to the age of 3 or 4. Caplan and Larkin (1991), in commenting critically on Maccoby's paper pointed out that "by minimizing her social analysis, Maccoby made it easy to interpret her article as support for the view that these sex differences unfold developmentally for biologically based reasons" (p. 536). Caplan and Larkin, on the other hand, present the social learning argument that sex-segregated groups result from the learned dominant–aggressive behavior displayed by boys and the consequent self-protective behavior of girls. They note that the literature reviewed by Maccoby demonstrates that "boys interrupt and heckle more, talk louder, use more commands, threats, and boasts, and are generally less supportive than girls" (p. 536). Just to call these behaviors "egotistic" and "assertive," as Maccoby does, they argue, is to "fail to convey its rude, dominant and silencing qualities" (p. 536). Similar criticisms have come from Meyer et al. (1991), who point out that girls display the passivity attributed to them only when they are in the presence of boys; that is, only in mixed-gender dyads where "boys dominate and girls increasingly find these male strategies aversive" (p. 537). They propose that boys develop a sense of "entitlement" and become increasingly assertive and dominating as a result of the reactions they receive from others, and that the peer group reflects the gender separation and inequality in the family and the larger culture.

Conditions for learning an association between gender and expectations for aggressive behavior are present early in the life of a child. While Lytton and Romney (1991) found little evidence for significant differences in parental socialization of girls and boys, they acknowledge that the direction of differences were in the expected direction and that parents exhibited "more prohibition of aggression for girls" (p. 287). The consequences of such early learning is illustrated by the results of a study by Fagot, Leinbach, and Hagan (1986). They found that while some sex-typed behavior by preschoolers (e.g., preference for same-gender toys) was unrelated to whether or not the children accurately applied gender labels to pictures of children and adults, other sex-typed behavior, like aggression, varied dramatically with gender-labeling accuracy. The girls who succeeded at the labeling task showed almost no aggression in the classroom. Early sex-typed learning can occur even before the use of gender language, and sex-linked modeling has been shown not to depend on the level of a child's gender constancy cognitions (e.g., Bussey & Bandura, 1984), although the latter may certainly enhance such learning and facilitate discrimination. Children begin to use gender labels reliably between the ages of 21 months and 44 months (Hort, Leinbach, & Fagot, 1991), while gender learning begins at birth.

Other studies of aggression in children, using different research strategies, support a social learning interpretation of sex-typed behavior. Thus, for example, when a sample of teachers was asked to recommend punishment for hypothetical students (Wooldridge & Richman, 1985), more teachers recommended severe punishment for boys than for girls, especially for stealing or fighting. In another study (Perry, Perry, & Weiss, 1989), a sample of fourth- to seventh-grade boys who responded to a questionnaire were found more likely to believe that aggression increased their self-esteem and to be less likely to feel guilty about aggression than were a comparable sample of girls. Regardless of gender, fourth to seventh graders classified as aggressive were more likely than nonaggressive children to report that they expected tangible rewards from aggressive acts (Perry, Perry, & Rasmussen, 1986). Congruent findings were reported by Eron (1980) from a study of 8-year-olds; aggressive behavior in school was found to be negatively related to parental nurturance and positively related to parental punishment for children of both genders.

The conditions for practicing aggression are generally much poorer for girls than for boys. Thus, it is not surprising that in an investigation of third to fifth graders of varied racial and ethnic backgrounds, Deluty (1985) found that girls demonstrated less consistency in aggressive behavior than did boys across situations and types of response, supporting other findings of greater stability for gender-stereotypical behaviors. We know that behavior that is not reinforced by attention or other positive consequences tends not to be repeated, or to extinguish. It is not surprising, then, that a review of a number of studies of the effects of exposure to television violence (Turner, Hesse, & Preston-Lewis, 1986) led to the conclusion that television viewing is associated with a long-term increase in the aggressive behavior of boys but not of girls. In speculating about why television violence affects girls differently than it affects boys, Eron (1980) noted that in contrast to boys, "Very early in life, girls learn that physical aggression is an undesirable behavior" (p. 247) and, in addition, there are few aggressive women models on television for girls to imitate. Instead, "the more violent the programs that girls watched, the more they were exposed to female models as victims or as passive observers, and the more they may have associated aversive consequences with aggressive acts" (Eron, 1980, p. 247), decreasing the likelihood for them to behave in this way.

Explanations for gender-related behaviors that call on innate predispositions continue to appear in the psychological literature. Maccoby (1990), for example, appears to be sympathetic to such a position with respect to some behaviors. Lytton and Romney (1991) are even more explicit in strongly urging consideration of the proposition that there is "a biological substrate for toy and play preferences" (p. 287) associated with sex of the child and that parents and peers simply "reinforce and amplify existing tendencies" (p. 288). In support of this proposition, Lytton and Romney (1991) briefly cite four studies, two of which are unpublished conference papers. The weight of accumulated evidence, however, provides far more support to the conclusion of Fagot et al. (1986) that "as children begin life surrounded by exemplars of both sexes and subjected to the contingencies operating in this sex-typed world, it would be strange indeed if behavior were not affected by environmental events" (p. 443). These environmental events include the consequences that follow behavior, observation of models, and gender labeling of persons, objects, attributes, and actions.

GENDER AS AN UNRELIABLE PREDICTOR
OF BEHAVIOR

Despite the array of experiences, consequences, beliefs, observations, and opportunities for practice that support differential acquisition and maintenance of particular behaviors by girls and boys, and women and men, the amount of variation in many sex-typed behaviors turns out to be extremely large. While the meta-analyses reviewed by Eagly and Wood (1991) are interpreted by them as supporting gender differences that are generally consistent with the stereotyped beliefs about women and men, they note that "the aggregated differences are in fact extremely small" (p. 308). Gender has been found to explain no more than 5% of the variance in a variety of social behaviors, and typically less. In a complex, heterogeneous society such as ours, gender is frequently deconstructed by experiences that contradict typical, majority-culture associations. Thus, for example, gender is not a reliable predictor of aggression despite the barrage of cultural ammunition directed toward this behavior. Hyde (1984), from a meta-analysis of 143 studies of gender differences in aggression by children and adults, concluded that only about 5% of the variance in aggression could be accounted for by gender. Another meta-analysis, by Eagly and Steffen (1986), using studies only of adults in laboratory or field settings involving relatively brief encounters between strangers, found an effect size indicating that gender explains only 2% of the variance in observed aggressive behavior. An important component of Eagly's social-role theory is that gender differences in a given behavior are expected to vary "because they are contingent on the particular social norms salient in a setting" (Eagly & Steffen, 1986, p. 310); this is supported by the meta-analysis finding of a high degree of variability in the magnitude of aggression differences between women and men.

We can begin to understand the relative failure of culture to reliably construct gender (so that behavior can be predicted across situations) by studying what happens when the experiences of girls and boys, and women and men are rearranged so that the usual systematic covariation of gender and particular situations is disrupted. Some research with both children and adults relate specifically to this issue. These studies can be said to demonstrate the deconstruction of gender and perhaps represent conditions that are more veridical with life experiences than our stereotyped beliefs suggest.

Serbin, Connor, and Citron (1978), for example, had preschool teachers, over a 5-week period, reinforce the independent behavior and ignore the dependent behavior of a randomly chosen group of preschool girls and boys. As a consequence of this treatment, these children, regardless of gender, were more persistent and less likely to stay close to the teacher than were the control children. Although the treatment effect did not generalize beyond the training situation, the investigators noted that their results "suggest that the independent behaviors that were being reinforced in the training group were clearly within the repertoire of the children, but were receiving little reinforcement in the regular classroom situation" (Serbin, Connor, & Citron, 1978, p. 874).

Carpenter and her colleagues have studied the relationship between the behavior of preschoolers and the degree of structure of play activities imposed by a teacher's suggestions, instructions, or modeling. They argue that because girls are typically found in more highly structured play situations than are boys, the two groups learn different skills; girls learn to fit into structures created by others while boys learn to create their own structures. In one study (Carpenter & Huston-Stein, 1980) in which girls and boys were observed in similarly structured activities and within similarly structured classrooms, it was found that, regardless of gender, children in the highly structured (high-teacher-feedback) play situations were more compliant, less likely to use materials in a creative way, and less likely to create their own structure than children in low-teacher-feedback situations. Relevant to these findings are those from a study of 4-year-olds (Lott, 1978) in which children whose observed play behavior did not match gender expectations of teachers and parents showed greater ideational fluency on a test of creativity than did more conforming children. The less conforming boys were less likely to play in areas popular with other boys while the less conforming girls were less likely to play in indoor areas (popular with girls). An experimental study by Carpenter, Huston, and Holt (1986) assigned preschoolers to high- or low-structured activities for 15 minutes at the beginning of daily hourlong free-play periods. Each child was given both treatments for 2 to 3 weeks. The investigators found that when girls or boys were in high-structured activities they were more likely to interact with adults, but when they were in low-structured activities they were more likely to interact with peers and behave aggressively and physically, dramatically demonstrating the influence of situational factors on behavior.

With adults, too, studies have demonstrated the deconstruction of gender, and men and women have been shown to behave similarly in similar situations. For example, Snodgrass (1985) tested the hypothesis that the traditionally subordinate role of women has led to their acquisition and maintenance of greater sensitivity. In an experimental study, she randomly assigned the roles of subordinate and leader to members of same-gender or mixed-gender college student pairs who worked together on several tasks. Regardless of gender, those in the subordinate position were found to be more sensitive than leaders to the impression they were making on the other person. In a follow-up study (Snodgrass, 1992), 96 pairs of college students (half same-gender and half mixed-gender) interacted for approximately one hour on three tasks. In each pair, one person had been designated the boss, and the other the employee. No significant differences in sensitivity were found to be associated with gender; the only important variable was status. Employees were more sensitive to how their bosses felt about them, while the bosses were more sensitive to how their employees felt about themselves.

A related investigation by Deutsch (1990) also used same and mixed-gender pairs, but in this study one member was assigned the role of interviewer and the other the role of applicant for a part-time job as a news reporter. Unobtrusive observations of pair interactions revealed that in all pairs, and regardless of gender, "applicants, who presumably occupied the low-power role, smiled more than interviewers" (Deutsch, 1990, p. 537) and that gender differences in smiling were absent among applicants. Another approach to the investigation of smiling (Wilson & Lloyd, 1990) was used in a study of college students in Great Britain. A sample of students of both genders from arts schools and science schools, considered to differ in power and prestige, were photographed. The photographs were analyzed for evidence of submissive cues (smiling, head cant, and orientation away from the camera), and it was found that arts schools undergraduates displayed more submissive nonverbal behavior than did science students across all three variables with little evidence of self-presentation differences between women and men. It was the school of study and not gender that distinguished smilers from nonsmilers. Still another investigation of smiling (Brennan-Parks, Goddard, Wilson, & Kinnear, 1991) obtained evidence in support of the proposition that "gender differences . . . may not be located so much in gender roles conceived in personality terms but rather in . . . expectations that vary with the situation" (p. 382). When a group of college students were photographed individually, presumably for a facial perception study, those instructed to smile did so significantly more often than those given no instructions, and there were no differences between women and men.

Accumulated data support the conclusion that under conditions in which gender is supposed to make a difference (i.e., where social expectation for gender-related behavior is high), women and men tend to behave differently. In situations in which other social categories, roles, or demands are more relevant, however, within-gender differences will be greater than those between genders. As noted by Eagly and Karau (1991), when "other roles are salient, the expectations associated with them would tend to control behavior, and comparisons between men and women who are in the same role . . . should reveal few sex differences" (p. 8). Differences in the salience of gender should lead to variations in gender difference outcomes (Eagly & Wood, 1991). A meta-analysis by Eagly and Johnson (1990) of studies comparing women and men on leadership style found that for both interpersonal and task styles of leadership, stereotypical differences were less pronounced in studies of ongoing organizations than in assessment or laboratory studies. Organizational studies take place in real settings in which people are functioning in accord with the demands of their jobs, whereas laboratory studies utilize strangers who interact for a brief period of time under simulated conditions. Only the tendency for women to utilize a democratic (vs. autocratic) style was general across settings, but gender accounted for only 1% of the variance. Studies in natural settings over time are difficult to do and hard to find. In one example, Wheelan and Verdi (1992) content-analyzed the statements made by three ongoing conference groups which met together for from 4½ to 6 hours. No significant gender differences were found in any of seven categories of verbal content beyond the first 30 to 60 minutes of interaction. These findings underscore the need to study behavior over a longer time and in natural settings to permit the initial salience of gender to be reduced by more situation-relevant factors.

Major (1987) has proposed that women's often reported tendency to reward themselves less than men for objectively equivalent performance is a consequence of the fact that women compare their outcomes with those they have received in the past, or with those received by persons similar to themselves in gender and status. Under conditions in which women compare themselves to other social groups, however, gender differences disappear, as Major and her colleagues have demonstrated empirically. Another behavior for which there are clear expectations related to gender is performance in mathematics. A study of college students by Siegel, Galassi, and Ware (1985) found that 54.7% of the variance in math performance could be accounted for by variables predicted by a social learning model (previous performance, incentive to do well, outcome expectation, and self-efficacy). Gender, on the other hand, was not a significant variable.

Gender makes a difference when certain behaviors are reinforced for women (and others for men). In a study by Carli (1990), same-gender and mixed-gender pairs of college students were instructed to discuss a current social issue for 10 minutes. It was found that men agreed more with (i.e., were more influenced by) women who spoke tentatively than with women who spoke assertively. The style or language of men speakers, on the other hand, was not related to agreement with them by either women or men partners. It is of considerable interest that a tentative woman was perceived by the men to be more trustworthy and likable than was an assertive woman. There is good reason to assume that this differential response to the women by the men would have affected the women's behavior had the interaction continued, and that such consequences in other situations are effective shapers of behavior.

THE RECONSTRUCTION OF GENDER

The social learning approach to gender suggests that gender is a reliable predictor of social behavior only under certain conditions: where the situation provides strong expectations for gender-related behavior (i.e., where this role is most salient); where prior opportunities for practice have produced gender-associated differential skills; and where there are differential consequences to women and men for what they do and/or what they say.

Such conditions are necessary for the maintenance of sex typing. Cultural emphasis on sex typing and on gender as a way of dichotomizing human functions and attributes is universally accompanied by inequities in power and privilege. Where access to social resources is systematically and consistently greater for one group than for another, associating the different groups with particular, and differently valued, skills, attributes, interests, and behaviors would seem to be necessary.

An example can be drawn from an extensive survey of work on depression by an American Psychological Association Task Force (McGrath, Keita, Strickland, & Russo, 1990) that concluded that women are twice as likely as men to be diagnosed as suffering from depression. The authors of this report clearly identify the risk factors as including negative life experiences such as sexual and physical abuse and victimization, poverty, and marital dissatisfaction, noting the greater likelihood of such experiences for women. Since women in our society tend to occupy positions lower in status and power than do men, both within the workplace and in heterosexual relationships, their greater exposure to uncontrollable negative life experiences is predictable and not surprising. Gender differences in power are accompanied by differences in exposure to stressors and in access to moderating resources. It is understandable, therefore, why one task force member, in discussing the report, concluded that "depression is not gender-neutral" (cf. Freiberg, 1991, p. 33). Such a conclusion, however, serves to strengthen stereotypical misconceptions about women and fails to emphasize the complex relationship between gender and depression. It is the risk factors for depression that are not gender neutral, not their outcomes. Data from a national health survey in Germany are illustrative. For both employed women and employed men, depression was found to be related to high job demands and to low job decision latitude (Braun & Hollander, 1988). Both of these risk factors, however, were greater for women, as was their level of depression.

It is the accumulation of uncontrollable negative life experiences without access to mediating resources, and not the fact that one is a woman, that is causally implicated in depression. It would serve no useful purpose, and be inaccurate, to conclude that tuberculosis, for example, is not ethnic neutral because it is found more often among African-Americans. It is poverty, living in deteriorating housing, and lack of access to adequate health care that fosters the spread of tuberculosis, not ethnicity. It is differences in power (between women and men and between ethnic groups) that we must highlight in explaining differences in exposure to risk factors, whether we are talking about those leading to dysfunctions in mental or in physical health.

Can we expect that our beliefs about gender will change drastically as the greater power of men in contemporary society becomes the target of serious and effective challenge? If, at the same time, scientific studies and observations of social life challenge stereotypical beliefs about gender difference, what will gender come to mean? We already know that variables other than gender (e.g., ethnic group, occupation, sexual orientation, and social class) are more reliable predictors of behavior in certain situations, and have an interactive relationship with gender. Suppose that gender becomes less and less relevant to the work that one does and to one's participation in social networks and families. With a weakening of differential status between women and men in the workplace, and a strengthening of the factors leading to more egalitarian social/personal relationships, what will happen to our definitions of gender? These questions have been asked by others (e.g., Alpert, 1978; Bem, 1985) and have no simple answers. We can anticipate, however, that when differential power no longer distinguishes women from men, gender will not connote wide differences in expected behavior and its meaning will center on a very narrow range of attributes, providing the greatest latitude for individual differences. As Condry (1984) has noted: "Gender does not have to be a central fulcrum of our identity, and it does not have to carry the baggage it does today" (p. 506).

Bem (1985) has argued that gender has primacy over other social categories because our culture teaches us that this dichotomy has "relevance to virtually every domain of human experience" (p. 212). Such teaching, however, is not inevitable. Cultural variation in the specific meaning of "woman" and "man" has already taught the lesson that gender can be differently defined by different people, that its definition is flexible, not rigid. The meaning of woman and man can also vary in scope, from having the widest possible connotations to simply denoting two forms of the human species. Spence (1985) has already found that despite the existence of gender stereotypes, current definitions of feminine and masculine tend to be narrow and that when asked to specify the meaning of these terms, both women and men do not present a large number of agreed-upon answers. The central core of the definitions seem to be the denotation of gender identity, so that "femininity" and "masculinity" primarily identify one as a woman or a man.

In a fictional utopian look at the future, Piercy (1976) projected an egalitarian society in which women and men continued to be so identified, but in which the work that they did was not gender-typed. Adolescents of both genders went off by themselves for a time to decide on a suitable name and to contemplate their personal choices and interests, and any mixed-sex group of three adults could choose to parent a child together. We already have good reason to conclude that gender is not defined simply but is instead a complex, multifaceted concept. This is certainly true for adults and appears to be true for children as well. In a longitudinal study of preschoolers, for example, Hort, Leinbach, and Fagot (1991) found evidence for a lack of correlation between different measures of gender definition and information. Only one correlation was significant, between the salience of gender as an organizing category and amount of gender-related knowledge. The research supported the assumption that children "integrate many different components into a working conceptual and behavioral framework that revolves around the definitions and implications of 'male' and 'female'" (Hort et al., 1991, p. 196). It is likely that this continues to be the case throughout life, and that gender remains "loosely organized" and "idiosyncratic."

While we cannot predict what gender may come to mean in a changed society, we can anticipate with some certainty that its meaning in European-American culture will not be the same as it is today, just as the contemporary meaning of woman and man already differs among ethnic, socioeconomic, heterosexual, lesbian, and gay groups, and is different from what it was in our parents' time and their parents' time. Our understanding of gender is bound to change, as Perry (1991) has argued, as our culture experiences a wider variety of family forms and child-rearing practices. Fine and Gordon (1991) urge that "in order to understand gender as a relational concept full of power and possibilities, we need to disrupt prevailing notions of what is inevitable, what is natural . . . and what is impossible" (p. 24). This process is the task of psychology and represents the very essence of a social learning viewpoint that ties behavior to variable antecedents and to present situations. A future in which gender does not restrict opportunities or prescribe the directions of one's life is one that holds promise for promoting individual competencies and supporting pro-social behavior. In such a future, instead of teaching femininity and masculinity we can engage in a continuing socialization process for the maintenance of positive human qualities.

ACKNOWLEDGMENTS

Portions of this chapter were presented by the senior author as the Presidential Address for Division 35 on August 17, 1991, at the annual meeting of the American Psychological Association, San Francisco, CA.

REFERENCES

Alpert, J. L. (1978). The psychology of women: What should the field be called? *American Psychologist, 33*, 965–969.

Armstrong, M. J. (1984). Ethnicity and sex-role socialization: A comparative example using life history data from Hawaii. *Sex Roles, 10*, 157–181.

Bandura, A. (1977). *Social learning theory*. Englewood Cliffs, NJ: Prentice-Hall.

Bandura, A. (1986). *Social foundations of thought and action: A social cognitive theory*. Englewood Cliffs, NJ: Prentice-Hall.

Bandura, A. (1990). Some reflections on reflections. *Psychological Inquiry, 1*, 101–105.

Bem, S. L. (1985). Androgyny and gender schema theory: A conceptual and empirical integration. In T. B. Sanderegger (Ed.), *Nebraska symposium on motivation: Psychology of gender* (pp. 179–226). Lincoln, NB: University of Nebraska Press.

Braun, S., & Hollander, R. B. (1988). Work and depression among women in the Federal Republic of Germany. *Women & Health, 14*(2), 3–26.

Brennan-Parks, K., Goddard, M., Wilson, A. E., & Kinnear, L. (1991). Sex differences in smiling as measured in a picture taking task. *Sex Roles, 24*, 375–382.

Bussey, K., & Bandura, A. (1984). Influence of gender constancy and social power on sex-linked modeling. *Journal of Personality and Social Psychology, 47*, 1292–1302.

Caplan, P. J., & Larkin, J. (1991). The anatomy of dominance and self-protection. *American Psychologist, 46*, 536.

Carli, L. L. (1990). Gender, language, and influence. *Journal of Personality and Social Psychology, 59*, 941–951.

Carpenter, C. J., Huston, A. C., & Holt, W. (1986). Modification of preschool sex-typed behaviors by participation in adult-structured activities. *Sex Roles, 14*, 603–615.

Carpenter, C. J., & Huston-Stein, A. C. (1980). Activity structure and sex-typed behavior in preschool children. *Child Development, 51*, 862–872.

Condry, J. C. (1984). Gender identity and social competence. *Sex Roles, 11*, 485–511.

Constantinople, A. (1979). Sex-role acquisition: In search of the elephant. *Sex Roles, 5*, 121–133.

Corcoran, K. J. (1991). Efficacy, "skills," reinforcement, and choice behavior. *American Psychologist, 46*, 155–157.

Crawford, M., & Marecek, J. (1989). Psychology reconstructs the female: 1968–1988. *Psychology of Women Quarterly, 13*, 147–165.

Deaux, K. (1985). Sex and gender. *Annual Review of Psychology, 36*, 49–81.

Deaux, K., & Major, B. (1987). Putting gender into context: An interactive model of gender-related behavior. *Psychological Review, 94*, 369–389.

Delutz, R. H. (1985). Consistency of assertive, aggressive, and submissive behavior for children. *Journal of Personality and Social Psychology, 49*, 1054–1065.

Deutsch, F. M. (1990). Status, sex, and smiling: The effect of role on smiling in men and women. *Personality and Social Psychology Bulletin, 16*, 531–540.

Doob, L. W. (1947). The behavior of attitudes. *Psychological Review, 54*, 135–156.

Eagly, A. H. (1983). Gender and social influence: A social psychological analysis. *American Psychologist, 38*, 971–981.

Eagly, A. H. (1987). *Sex differences in social behavior: A social-role interpretation*. Hillsdale, NJ: Erlbaum.

Eagly, A. H., & Johnson, B. T. (1990). Gender and leadership style: A meta-analysis. *Psychological Bulletin, 108*, 233–256.

Eagly, A. H., & Karau, S. J. (1991). Gender and the emergence of leaders: A meta-analysis. *Journal of Personality and Social Psychology*, *60*, 685–710.

Eagly, A. H., Makhijani, M. G., & Klonsky, B. G. (1990). Gender and the evaluation of leaders: A meta-analysis. *Psychological Bulletin*, *111*, 3–22.

Eagly, A. H., & Steffen, V. J. (1986). Gender and aggressive behavior: A meta-analytic review of the social psychological literature. *Psychological Bulletin*, *100*, 309–330.

Eagly, A. H., & Wood, W. (1991). Explaining sex differences in social behavior: A meta-analytic perspective. *Personality and Social Psychology Bulletin*, *17*, 306–315.

Eron, L. D. (1980). Prescription for reduction of aggression. *American Psychologist*, *35*, 244–252.

Fagot, B. I. (1978). The influence of sex of child on parental reactions to toddler children. *Child Development*, *49*, 459–465.

Fagot, B. I. (1984a). The consequence of problem behavior in toddler children. *Journal of Abnormal Child Psychology*, *12*, 385–396.

Fagot, B. I. (1984b). Teacher and peer reactions to boys' and girls' play styles. *Sex Roles*, *11*, 691–702.

Fagot, B. I., & Hagen, R. (1985). Aggression in toddlers: Responses to the assertive acts of boys and girls. *Sex Roles*, *12*, 341–351.

Fagot, B. I., Leinbach, M. D., & Hagan, R. (1986). Gender labeling and the adoption of sex-typed behaviors. *Developmental Psychology*, *22*, 440–443.

Fine, M., & Gordon, S. M. (1991). Effacing the center and the margins: Life at the intersection of psychology and feminism. *Feminism and Psychology*, *1*, 19–28.

Freiberg, P. (1991, February). Media snaps up report on women, depression. *APA Monitor*, pp. 32–33.

Gavey, N. (1989). Feminist post-structuralism and discourse analysis: Contributions to feminist psychology. *Psychology of Women Quarterly*, *13*, 459–475.

Hare-Mustin, R. T., & Marecek, J. (1990). *Making a difference: Psychology and the construction of gender*. New Haven, CT: Yale University Press.

Hort, B. E., Leinbach, M. D., & Fagot, B. I. (1991). Is there coherence among the cognitive components of gender acquisition? *Sex Roles*, *24*, 195–207.

Hull, C. L. (1943). *Principles of behavior*. New York: Appleton-Century-Crofts.

Hyde, J. S. (1984). How large are gender differences in aggression? A developmental meta-analysis. *Developmental Psychology*, *20*, 722–736.

Kahn, A. S., & Yoder, J. D. (1989). The psychology of women and conservatism: Rediscovering social change. *Psychology of Women Quarterly*, *13*, 417–432.

Kihlstrom, J. F., & Harackiewicz, J. M. (1990). An evolutionary milestone in the psychology of personality. *Psychological Inquiry*, *1*, 86–100.

LaFromboise, T. D., Heyle, A. M., & Ozer, E. J. (1990). Changing and diverse roles of women in American Indian cultures. *Sex Roles*, *22*, 455–476.

Landrine, H. (1985). Race × class stereotypes. *Sex Roles*, *13*, 65–75.

Lott, B. (1978). Behavioral concordance with sex role ideology related to play areas, creativity, and parental sex-typing of children. *Journal of Personality and Social Psychology*, *36*, 1087–1100.

Lott, B. (1985). The potential enrichment of social/personality psychology through feminist research, and vice versa. *American Psychologist*, *40*, 155–164.

Lott, B. (1987a). Sexist discrimination as distancing behavior: 1. A laboratory demonstration. *Psychology of Women Quarterly*, *11*, 47–58.

Lott, B. (1989). Sexist discrimination as distancing behavior: II. Prime time television. *Psychology of Women Quarterly*, *13*, 341–355.

Lott, B. (1990). Dual natures or learned behavior: The challenge to feminist psychology. In R. T. Hare-Mustin & J. Marecek (Eds.), *Making a difference: Psychology and the construction of gender* (pp. 65–101). New Haven, CT: Yale University Press.

Lott, B. (1991). Social psychology: Humanist roots and feminist future. *Psychology of Women Quarterly*, *15*, 505–519.

Lott, B. (1993). *Women's lives: Themes and variations in gender learning* (2nd ed.). Pacific Grove, CA: Brooks/Cole.

Lott, B., & Lott, A. J. (1985). Learning theory in contemporary social psychology. In G. Lindzey & E. Aronson (Eds.), *Handbook of social psychology* (3rd ed.) (Vol. 1, pp. 109–135). New York: Random House.

Lott, B., Lott, A. J., & Fernald, J. (1990). Individual differences in distancing responses to women on a photo choice task. *Sex Roles*, *22*, 97–110.

Lytton, H., & Romney, D. M. (1991). Parents' differential socialization of boys and girls: A meta-analysis. *Psychological Bulletin*, *109*, 267–296.

Maccoby, E. E. (1990). Gender and relationships: A developmental account. *American Psychologist*, *45*, 513–520.

Major, B. (1987). Gender, justice, and the psychology of entitlement. In P. Shaver & C. Hendrick (Eds.), *Sex and gender* (pp. 124–148). Newbury Park, CA: Sage.

McGrath, E., Keita, G. P., Strickland, B. R., & Russo, N. F. (1990). *Women and depression: Risk factors and treatment issues*. Washington, DC: American Psychological Association.

Meyer, S. L., Murphy, C. M., Cascardi, M., & Birns, B. (1991). Gender and relationships: Beyond the peer group. *American Psychologist*, *46*, 537.

Miller, N. E. (1959). Extensions of liberalized S-R theory. In S. Koch (Ed.), *Psychology: A study of a science* (Vol. 2). New York: McGraw-Hill.

Miller, N. E., & Dollard, J. (1941). *Social learning and imitation*. New Haven, CT: Yale University Press.

Mischel, W. (1966). A social-learning view of sex differences in behavior. In E. E. Maccoby (Ed.), *The development of sex differences* (pp. 56–81). Stanford, CA: Stanford University Press.

Mowrer, O. H. (1960). *Learning theory and behavior*. New York: Wiley.

Perry, D. G., Perry, L. C., & Rasmussen, P. (1986). Cognitive social learning mediators of aggression. *Child Development*, *57*, 700–711.

Perry, D. G., Perry, L. C., & Weiss, R. J. (1989). Sex differences in the consequences that children anticipate for aggression. *Developmental Psychology*, *25*, 312–319.

Perry, R. (1991). Book reviews. *Signs*, *16*, 597–603.

Piercy, M. (1976). *Woman on the edge of time*. New York: Fawcett.

Reid, P. T., & Comas-Diaz, L. (1990). Gender and ethnicity: Perspectives on dual status. *Sex Roles*, *22*, 397–408.

Rotter, J. B. (1954). *Social learning and clinical psychology*. Englewood Cliffs, NJ: Prentice-Hall.

Serbin, L. A., Connor, J. M., & Citron, C. C. (1978). Environmental control of independent and dependent behaviors in preschool girls and boys: A model for early independence training. *Sex Roles, 4*, 867–876.

Sharff, J. W. (1983). Sex and temperament revisited. In M. Fooden, S. Gordon, & B. Hughley (Eds.), *Genes and gender IV: The second X and women's health* (pp. 49–62). Staten Island, NY: Gordian Press.

Sherif, C. (1981). Needed concepts in the study of gender identity. *Psychology of Women Quarterly, 6*, 375–398.

Siegel, R. G., Galassi, J. P., & Ware, W. B. (1985). Comparison of two models for predicting mathematics performance: Social learning versus math aptitude-anxiety. *Journal of Counseling Psychology, 32*, 531–538.

Skinner, B. F. (1953). *Science and human behavior.* New York: Macmillan.

Snodgrass, S. E. (1985). Women's intuition: The effect of subordinate role in interpersonal sensitivity. *Journal of Personality and Social Psychology, 49*, 146–155.

Snodgrass, S. E. (1992). Further effects of role versus gender on interpersonal sensitivity. *Journal of Personality and Social Psychology, 62*, 154–158.

Spence, J. T. (1985). Gender identity and its implications for the concepts of masculinity and femininity. In T. B. Sonderegger (Ed.), *Nebraska symposium on motivation: Psychology of gender* (pp. 59–95). Lincoln, NB: University of Nebraska Press.

Staats, A. W. (1975). *Social behaviorism.* Homewood, IL: Dorsey.

Stern, M., & Karraker, K. H. (1989). Sex stereotyping of infants: A review of gender labeling studies. *Sex Roles, 20*, 501–522.

Tittle, C. K. (1986). Gender research and education. *American Psychologist, 41*, 1161–1168.

Turner, C. W., Hesse, B. W., & Preston-Lewis, S. (1986). Naturalistic studies of the long-term effects of television violence. *Journal of Social Issues, 42*(1), 51–73.

Wheelan, S. A., & Verdi, A. (1992). Differences in male and female patterns of communication in groups: A methodological artifact? *Sex Roles.*

Wilson, A., & Lloyd, B. (1990). Gender vs. power: Self-posed behavior revisited. *Sex Roles, 23*, 91–98.

Wooldridge, P., & Richman, C. L. (1985). Teachers' choice of punishment as a function of student's gender, age, race, and IQ level. *Journal of School Psychology, 23*, 19–29.

BROAD THEORIES OF GENDER

A Social Constructionist View of Gender

ANNE E. BEALL

Chris was really angry today! Enough was enough. Chris put on the gray suit, marched into work, and went into the main boss's office and yelled: "I've brought in more money for this company than anybody else and everyone gets promoted but me! You hand out promotions like candy!" The boss saw Chris's fist slam down on the desk. There was an angry look on Chris's face. They tried to talk but it was useless. Chris just stormed out of the office in anger.

In the preceding passage, you probably envisioned a man yelling at his boss for not promoting him. However, it was never stated that Chris was a man. The image of a man yelling at his boss is an inference that was made using cultural information about gender. Thus, the gender of Chris is "constructed" by the reader to understand the previous paragraph. This chapter demonstrates how gender is constructed by cultures and by individuals. The purpose of the chapter is to discuss this social constructionist approach to gender and to argue that gender is a socially constructed category that influences our perceptions of women and men.

In this chapter, I examine several issues: (1) the central tenets of social constructionism and the historical background for this viewpoint; (2) how gender is a socially-constructed category that is maintained by various cultural and cognitive processes; and (3) how gender is socially constructed in the psychology of gender.

CENTRAL TENETS OF SOCIAL CONSTRUCTIONISM

Social constructionism is concerned with how people come to understand the world around them and with how they come to define "reality." Social constructionism differs from other approaches in its belief that people actively construct their perceptions and use culture as a guide to do so. Gergen (1985) identified the four assumptions that most social constructionists have when they use this approach. Most constructionists share at least one of the following assumptions.

1. There are many different ways that the world can be understood. A particular culture's experience of the world, in this case Western culture's understanding, is not the only experience that a person can have of the world. One's understanding of the world does not reflect an absolute reality that is simultaneously experienced by all people (Berger & Luckman, 1980). This point is supported by numerous anthropological treatises that demonstrate that cultures have many different understandings of the world. Some cultures understand the world as a place that is logical and orderly, whereas other cultures perceive the world as an arbitrary place that is governed by the whims of spirits.

There can be little doubt that different views of the world lead to different experiences of reality, which are equally "real" to the people who believe in them. For example, the Yir-Yiront of Australia do not believe that sexual intercourse leads to pregnancy, the Ndembu believe that women who are argumentative will be infertile, and the Azande believe you can consult an oracle to determine the future (Shweder, 1984). In Western cultures such as the United States, many people believe in an omniscient, omnipresent God, and there are large sections of the population who believe in astrology. All of these things are equally real to the people who experience them.

2. One's understanding of the world is a social product. Understanding involves a group of active, cooperative people who determine what constitutes reality. These understandings of the world are different across time and cultures. Investigators have found that ideas about the self vary across cultures (Shweder & Bourne, 1984). Some cultures conceptualize the self as an individual entity whereas other cultures conceptualize the self in relation to others or in terms of social roles. In addition, across time, people have conceptualized romantic love (Hunt, 1960) or the concept of the child (Aries, 1962) quite differently.

3. An understanding or conceptualization of the world may be particularly popular or persistent only because it is useful. For example, it may be useful in some cultures to believe that evil spirits inhabit the body during illness, because the culture does not have access to another understanding or because it may provide a way of coping when an illness is incurable. Conceptualizations are not necessarily persistent or popular because they are empirically valid. For example, stereotypes about particular groups may be retained even when they do not accurately describe

the group. Stereotypes may be retained because they rationalize the differential treatment of groups or the current social order.

For example, Hoffman and Hurst (1990) conducted a study in which they told subjects to imagine a planet in which there were two groups of people (Orinthians and Ackmians) who performed different jobs on the planet. Most of the members of one group were city workers who worked in the industrial centers of the cities. Thus, subjects might be told that 85% of the Orinthians and 15% of the Ackmians were city workers. Most of the members of the other group were child raisers who stayed around their home and raised children. Subjects were then asked about the personality attributes of the people in the different jobs. They were also asked why they thought there was an unequal representation of each group of people in the two jobs. Subjects reported that they believed each group had personality traits that suited its members for a particular kind of work. The fact that one group was disproportionately represented in a certain kind of work was used to assign personality traits to the members of that group. Thus, unequal representation of people led to stereotyped assessments of those people and served as a rationalization for the social order.

4. Understandings of the world are related to all kinds of social actions. Descriptions and explanations of the world influence the way that society is structured and the way that people interact. For example, if a culture believes that evil spirits inhabit the bodies of sick people, that conceptualization will affect how sick people are treated, how sick people are thought about, and how sick people interact with those around them.

The social constructionist perspective argues that human beings are not passive recipients of a set of particular events in the environment. Instead, constructionists believe that humans are actively engaged in their perceptions and thus "construct" their view of the world. Humans, however, do not engage in this enterprise alone. Human society is actively involved in determining what is "right" and "wrong," what is "moral" and "immoral," and what is "real" and what is "illusory." Thus, cultures are actively constructing social information all the time. Culture is an important concept in the social constructionist approach. Individual cultures are said to provide people with a body of knowledge referred to as "common sense" (Geertz, 1983), which explains events in the world. Thus, cultures provide people with a set of lenses through which they can observe and understand their environment (Bem, 1987). One's sense of the world is determined by the set of lenses one uses to see the world. Thus, the point of socialization is to teach children how to "see" the world, or rather, how to use the lenses the rest of the culture is using. These lenses are important because they provide people with similar understandings of the world and because they provide people with a way to interpret ambiguous information around them.

TYPES OF INFORMATION THAT ARE
SOCIALLY CONSTRUCTED

One may be arguing at this point that some ideas or beliefs are verifiable and that the social constructionist viewpoint can only go so far. I agree. Immanuel Kant has classified knowledge about the world into the following categories (Smith, 1973; Shweder, 1984): (1) *analytic*, which are statements about language, such as "a woman is a human with female secondary-sex characteristics," and (2) *synthetic*, which are statements about the world, such as "the woman is standing in the door." These types of knowledge can be: (1) *a priori*, which are statements that are established as valid without evidence, and (2) *a posteriori*, which are statements that are verified with evidence. These types of knowledge lead to four different categories: (1) *synthetic a posteriori*, which are hypotheses or laws of nature, (2) *analytic a priori*, which are syllogisms, definitions, and the like, (3) *analytic a posteriori*, which are statements about language that are established as valid through experience, and (4) *synthetic a priori*, which are statements about the world that are established as valid without evidence or experience. Synthetic a priori knowledge can be neither confirmed nor disconfirmed and therefore is socially constructed. Examples of this type of knowledge are: "Humans go to heaven or hell after death" or "Animals have souls." These beliefs cannot be confirmed or disconfirmed and people who have these beliefs use them to comprehend the world. Much social knowledge is in this category because it is established without evidence and it cannot be confirmed or disconfirmed.

HISTORICAL BACKGROUND OF THIS VIEWPOINT

According to Gergen (1982), the social constructionist viewpoint is one of two major traditions in philosophical discourse. Gergen distinguishes between what he calls the *exogenic* and the *endogenic* perspective. The exogenic perspective is that people's perceptions mirror the world around them. Thus, knowledge is the result of an environment that acts upon human beings. This perspective has been attributed to Locke, Hume, and Mill, who believed that all of human knowledge results from sensory experiences in the world or from internal thoughts about those experiences. The endogenic perspective, which is more akin to the social constructionist viewpoint, claims that knowledge depends on the processing a human brings to it. The endogenic perspective has been attributed to philosophers such as Descartes and Spinoza, who believed that perceptions of the world reveal more about human thought than about the actual world.

This debate has emerged throughout the history of psychology on a variety of topics. For example, in the field of visual perception, some theorists have claimed that one sees particular features of a stimulus because these features are present (Gibson, 1968). Other theorists have argued that perception occurs because people attempt to make sense of the world around them. Thus, perceiving may be less a function of stimulus features than of the processing a person engages in to understand the environment (Natsoulas, 1968; Rock & Victor, 1968). Of course, these positions are extreme and most theorists would probably claim that perception is a product of both stimulus features and human cognitive processing.

These two perspectives have also surfaced in cognitive psychology and have resulted in a large amount of research about how humans manipulate and use environmental stimuli. In contemporary cognitive psychology, researchers have become interested in schemas, scripts, and various heuristics that people use to process information in their environment. Gergen (1985) credits Kurt Lewin for first introducing this perspective. Lewin (1951) proposed field theory, which claims that human behavior is a function of the person and the environment. This theory was a radical departure from behaviorism and psychoanalytic theory, which located the cause of behavior in external events or personality traits respectively. Lewin's theory suggested that humans were not simply acting like robots in response to innate tendencies or environmental stimuli. Subsequent psychologists such as Festinger (1954) studied how people construe social interactions through their own social comparison processes. Other investigators have examined how emotions are socially constructed phenomena that involve the active participation of individuals in order to experience them (Averill, 1985; Harre, 1986).

SOCIAL CONSTRUCTIONISM AND GENDER

Although the social constructionist viewpoint is not a new perspective, it has been applied to the field of gender only recently. Social constructionists in the field of gender have argued that gender is a socially constructed category and that the relations between the two genders are basically social relations (Lorber, 1986). There are many reasons that theorists believe gender is a socially constructed category. Constructionists have noted that ideas about gender differ across cultures. Thus, across cultures, one's biological sex does not necessarily imply that one will engage in certain activities or that people will believe that one possesses certain attributes. In addition, there is a plethora of research that demonstrates that there are cognitive and cultural forces that maintain gender distinctions. Culture obviously influences one's beliefs and social practices and there is evidence that people actively use cultural ideas about gender to perceive and understand the social categories of male and female. I consider each of these points in this chapter.

Gender Constructions Across Cultures

Some social constructionists have pointed out how malleable the gender concept is in terms of how many genders there are supposed to be. Although people of Western cultures cannot imagine more than two genders, there are cultures that believe that there is a third gender or that a person can change his/her gender without undergoing a sex-change operation. For example, many American Indians such as the Sioux, Cheyenne, and Zuni have a category of people called *berdache*. The *berdache* are people who are physically one gender but who dress or engage in the activities of the other gender. It is unclear whether the tribes considered the *berdache* to be transformed to the other gender, or whether the tribe considered the *berdache* to be a third type of gender (Kessler & McKenna, 1985). It is likely that some American Indian tribes considered the *berdache* a separate gender while other tribes regarded them as people who had transformed their gender. Similarly, among the Navajo American Indians and the Hijara of India, there is a belief that some people are male, some people are female, and other people are intersexed, that is, they are both male and female. The Navajo and the Hijara clearly believe that there are more than two genders (Martin & Voorhies, 1975). Other societies categorize people into several gender statuses without regard to a person's genitals. For example, the Navajo have several gender statuses: males, females, males who act like females, females who act like males, and intersexed people who act like either males or females (Martin & Voorhies, 1975). It is difficult to describe these groups without referring to them in the only two names we have: male and female. However, these different gender statuses described highly different groups that were not given appellations according to their biological gender.

Anthropologists and psychologists have also documented how cultures vary in their beliefs about the nature of females and males. Mead (1935) documented that among the Mundugumour, both women and men are expected to be aggressive and unemotional whereas among the Arapesh both women and men are expected to be passive and maternal. In Western culture we believe that men are the aggressive gender and that women are the passive gender (Basow, 1986). However, among the Tchambali, men are considered the more emotional gender and women are considered the unemotional, rational members of the society (Mead, 1935).

Even ideas about birth are not necessarily associated with a specific gender. For example, although women give birth to children in all cultures, some societies have elaborate rituals where they establish that it is really the father who is the main contributor to the birth. This ritual is called *couvade* and it is practiced in Asia, Europe, Africa, North and South America, and many islands (Hall & Dawson, 1989). After the mother gives birth, the infant is delivered to the father and he rests for several days and is waited upon by relatives to overcome his fatigue. The mother returns to work immediately because the society believes that she does not need to rest like the father. Among the Koravars of Asia, one informant explained that fathers were more cared for than mothers after birth because the father's life is a more important factor than the mother's life in the birth of a child (Hall & Dawson, 1989). Among the Nayadis of India, the father would shampoo his own abdomen during labor delivery and pray to the gods of the mountain. When the delivery was over, he would thank the gods for having "got his child out" (Hall & Dawson, 1989).

The unique status of the father in childbirth is shown in many practices before and after the birth of the baby in these societies. Husbands of pregnant women must not eat certain foods, engage in certain activities, or use certain tools because it is believed that these things will harm the child (Hall & Dawson, 1989). Some societies that practice *couvade* believe that women do not experience pain during childbirth because the pain is passed to the father (Hall & Dawson, 1989). After the birth, the child rests with the father and he may engage in certain rituals that insure the baby's health and happiness. Many societies that practice couvade believe that the father gives life to the child during this period (Hall & Dawson, 1989).

In addition to different birth practices, the division of labor also varies widely in the ethnographic record. Among the Nambikwara, young women join war activities (Levi-Strauss, 1971). In some societies, women are responsible for all agriculture, whereas in other societies men are primarily responsible for farming (Levi-Strauss, 1971).

Admittedly, these examples are extreme in their demonstration of cross-cultural variability of gender roles and beliefs about gender. Recent work on cross-cultural stereotypes of gender (see Best & Williams, Chapter 9, this volume) has shown that there is evidence for pancultural similarities in gender stereotypes. However, I discuss these examples to show that cultures do vary in how they use the gender category to divide work or personality traits. Although gender is a social category in every culture, it does vary in what it means and how it is used in a society. After surveying the literature about the sexual division of labor, Levi-Strauss (1971) concluded:

> The very fact that it varies endlessly according to the society selected for consideration shows that . . . it is the mere fact of its existence which is mysteriously required, the form under which it comes to exist being utterly irrelevant at least from the point of view of any natural necessity. (p. 347)

The sexual division of labor, then, is somewhat arbitrary, but it serves an important function. Levi-Strauss (1971) argues that a sexual division of labor serves to make the two genders dependent on one another for survival. He notes that whenever one gender performs a specific task, the other gender is not allowed to perform it. This division creates a dependency between the genders because any one person will need a member of the other gender in order to survive. This sexual division of labor may have emerged because it ensures that the basic family unit consists of a male and a female who will produce children. Rubin (1975) argues that this sexual division of labor is thus a "taboo against the sameness of men and women, a taboo dividing the sexes into two mutually exclusive categories, a taboo which exacerbates the biological differences between the sexes and thereby creates [italics in the original] gender" (p. 178). Thus, the sexual division of labor may be arbitrary in terms of what is specified as the appropriate tasks for each gender, but it makes gender a salient social category because it creates a dependence between women and men.

In summary, gender appears to be a socially constructed category because it differs across cultures in its content and form. Some cultures perceive more than one gender and cultures vary in their beliefs about the nature of males and females. Gender may be a salient social category because there is a sexual division of labor that creates a dependence between women and men.

Gender Constructions by the Individual

Because gender is a salient social category, it is constantly used by individuals within any culture to understand and perceive the world. There are a number of reasons that people categorize humans into the categories male and female. First, as mentioned earlier, gender is an important social category that we learn to identify at an early age because it is useful in society. We quickly learn to categorize ourselves because we must learn which public rest room to use, which activities to engage in, and which clothes are appropriate to wear. We also learn to categorize others because we are intensely socialized by our same-gender peers (Maccoby, 1990) and our same-gender role models. One researcher found that people are greatly influenced by same-gender role models even when they have seen them only for a few minutes (Geis, 1983).

There is evidence that gender is one of the first characteristics that people encode about another person. A naturalistic study was conducted in which the researcher asked people who had purchased tokens at a subway station to describe the person selling tokens (cited in Unger & Crawford, 1992). Subjects were not given instructions about how to describe this person and they were not given information about the gender of the token seller. However, in people's descriptions, the gender of the token seller was mentioned as one of the first or second characteristics of the seller 100% of the time. Thus, subjects used gender to label a person with whom they had only interacted for a few seconds. Gender was such an important identifier that without this information one subject was unable to answer the experimenter's query and said: "I can't even remember if it was a man or a woman" (cited in Unger & Crawford, 1992, p. 148).

The gender of a person is quickly encoded and processed cognitively. Humans are highly reliant on cognitive structures such as schemas to construct their experiences (Markus & Zajonc, 1985). The gender schema is one of the ways that people understand and perceive women and men (Bem, 1987). This schema is a complex structure of information about gender. This information includes traits that supposedly describe women and men (e.g., dominant—likes math and science; passive; and independent) (Basow, 1986). The schema also includes various subtypes of stereotypical males and females such as feminist, housewife, sex kitten, lady-killer, and career man (Six & Eckes, 1991). The gender schema is important because it allows one to organize information about males and females. In addition, it helps assign gender labels to social behavior or social information.

For example, in one experiment (John & Sussman, 1985), subjects read information about two people who met at a singles bar. One person was referred to as gray buttons and the other person was referred to as brown buttons. There was no gender information in the paragraph. At some points gray buttons took the initiative and at some points brown buttons took the initiative. Subjects were asked at different points in the story to indicate the gender of each character. When gray buttons was taking the initiative, subjects thought this person was male. When brown buttons was taking the initiative, subjects thought this person was male. Most subjects even changed their judgments about the gender of the characters from one paragraph to the next, even though that choice was illogical. When the character was behaving dominantly, subjects thought the person was male and when the same character was behaving passively, they changed their mind and decided that the person was female. Thus, when gender information was not available, people used their knowledge about gender stereotypes to assign gender labels. In this case, the masculine stereotype, which includes dominance and independence, was used to understand ambiguous social information.

There are also a variety of perceptual biases that reinforce the gender schema and maintain its role in perceiving and evaluating people. One of these biases is that people tend to perceive few differences within groups and to perceive large differences between groups. Thus, people perceive women and men as two homogeneous groups that differ greatly from one another (Unger & Crawford, 1992). In one study, subjects were less able to distinguish between members of the same gender (either males or females) than to distinguish between members of different genders. People of the same gender appeared very similar, but people of a different gender were seen as dissimilar (Taylor, Fiske, Etcoff, & Ruderman, 1978). In actuality, males and females differ more among themselves than they do from one another. The only well-documented gender differences in behavior appear to be in the area of aggression (Eagly & Steffen, 1986) and helping behavior (Eagly & Crowley, 1986).

Other perceptual biases such as selective encoding, selective recall, and selective interpretation also reinforce the gender schema (Unger & Crawford, 1992). People selectively encode and remember information that confirms the gender schema. In addition, people interpret behavior in ways that are in accordance with gender schema. For example, in one study (Paludi & Strayer, 1985), the majority of subjects believed that articles about politics were written by men and that articles about the psychology of women were written by women. This judgment is fallacious because all articles that address women's issues are not written by women and all articles that address politics are not written by men.

Of course, the construction of gender is not completely perceptual. Gender distinctions are maintained by differential socialization of male and female children (see Lott & Maluso, Chapter 4, this volume), which may cause males and females to engage in different behavior and to have different aspirations. In addition, gender distinctions may be maintained through the use of different verbal and nonverbal behavior by women and by men (Henley, 1977). Gender distinctions may also be maintained by different hair styles and different clothing for the genders. Cultures often expect that men and women will not dress similarly. For example in Western culture, the Christian Bible says: "A woman must not wear men's clothing, nor a man wear women's clothing, for the Lord your God detests anyone who does this" (Deut. 22:5). Even physiological differences between women and men may sometimes be due to societal practices. Differential amounts of exercise or different types of activities by the two genders can influence their biology. For example, the smaller size of women in some cultures may be due to their poorer nutrition as compared with the men in those cultures (Jagger, 1983).

In addition, ideas and expectations about gender can influence people to confirm their gender stereotype. Thus, one's expectation that a man will be unemotional may lead to a confirmation of this expectation, because people will treat the man in an unemotional way. Expectations about people do influence the way individuals are treated and their response to this treatment may confirm the initial expectation. This process has been called the self-fulfilling prophecy (see Geis, Chapter 2, this volume, for a full explanation of how this prophecy works).

In summary, gender is socially constructed by the individual with the help of a cultural gender schema. The schema is learned at an early age because gender is a salient social category in the society. The schema is reinforced and maintained through various perceptual biases, through cultural mechanisms that may produce differences between the genders, and through the self-fulfilling prophecy.

AN EXAMPLE OF THE SOCIAL CONSTRUCTION OF GENDER

Psychology and other disciplines have engaged in the construction of gender in a variety of ways. I will first discuss the historical background of this process and then the way that psychology continues to engage in the construction of gender.

Historical Construction of Gender

Science has engaged in the construction of gender at least since the nineteenth century and probably ever since it first addressed gender issues (Shields, 1975; Weisstein, 1971). Researchers within psychology and related fields attempted experimentally to verify numerous claims about the genders, which included the idea that males were more intelligent than females. This historical review is a demonstration of how experimental science engages in the construction of cultural beliefs about gender.

Franz Joseph Gall was one of the first researchers to address the question of intelligence and gender. He was specifically interested in how the anatomical structure of the brain revealed a person's attributes, such as generosity, honesty, and intelligence. His methods of investigation have subsequently been referred to as phrenology. Gall believed, as was popular during those days, that females were less intelligent than males. He reasoned that because one could identify how intelligent people were from the structure of their brain, one could easily tell the difference between a male brain and a female brain (Shields, 1975).

Although phrenology fell into disrepute, the practice of determining intellectual abilities from brain structure continued. Scientists believed that the smaller the brain size, the less intelligent the person (Bain, 1868). Thus, scientists believed that women are less intelligent because it was thought they have a smaller brain. Other investigators believed that certain regions of the brain were responsible for intellectual functioning and they attempted to document that these areas are less developed in women. When investigators believed that the frontal lobes were responsible for intelligence, they noted that women have smaller frontal lobes. However, when investigators believed that the parietal lobes were responsible for intelligence, they then claimed that these lobes are smaller in women (Shields, 1975).

Woolley (1910) summarized the research on the anatomical differences between the genders and found that investigators had learned of female brain deficiencies in the following areas: (1) total weight of the brain, (2) weight of the frontal lobes, (3) location of the central sulcus, (4) size of the corpus callosum, (5) complexity and conformation of the gyri and sulci, and (6) development of the fetal cortex. Woolley (1910) also discussed several experiments that found that women gave more predictable answers to association tests, which was taken as evidence for women's lesser intellectual abilities by scientists.

Scientists believed not only that women are less intelligent by virtue of their brain structure, but that women are guided by instinct and emotion more than are men (Shields, 1975). Burt and Moore (1912) claimed that they had found the following:

> Women excel wherever emotions are seen to interfere with higher mental processes and to express themselves immediately and overtly in motor and organic changes; on the other hand, wherever there are differences in power of reasoning and of attention these, when well-accredited, seem to be slightly in favour of men. (p. 385)

They explained that women's greater emotionality is due to the structure of their brain. The thalamus was popularly believed to be the area where emotions are controlled and investigators proposed that women have a larger thalamus than do men, which leads to their differential emotionality. Burt and Moore (1912) stated: "Briefly and crudely, that the mental life of man is predominantly cortical; that of woman predominantly thalamic" (p. 385). Thus, it was believed that men are more rational than women and that women are more emotional than men. This belief about men and women can still be observed today (Shields, 1987).

The belief that women and men are different in terms of their intellectual and emotional functioning was further argued by individuals with evolutionary arguments. Spencer (1961) suggested that women's intellectual development was arrested at a lower stage of evolution than that of men because women need to conserve energy to bear children.

> Whereas, in man, individual evolution continues until the physiological cost of self-maintenance very nearly balances what nutrition supplies, in woman, an arrest of individual development takes places while there is yet a considerable margin of nutrition; otherwise there could be no offspring. (p. 341)

Spencer reasoned that because women are at an early stage of evolution, they are less able to reason in an abstract manner. He also argued that natural selection led to women's greater ability to understand emotions. Spencer (1961) states:

> In barbarous times a woman who could from a movement, tone or voice, or expression of face, instantly detect in her savage husband the passion that was rising, would be likely to escape dangers run into by a woman less skilled in interpreting the natural language of feeling. Hence, from the perpetual exercise of this power, and the survival of those having most of it, we may infer its establishment as a feminine faculty. (p. 343)

Although the study of gender only revealed what was popularly believed in the culture, it was used by some scholars to argue for the differential education of men and women. Hall (1906) urged that women should not be educated with men. His major argument was that coeducation would adversely affect women's menstrual periods and women's aspirations for marriage and family. However, within his article he also states that equal education with men is a poor idea because of women's lesser intellectual abilities. Hall (1906) wrote:

> I have never met or read a physician . . . who does not hold that at times girls should be metaphorically be turned out to grass, and lie fallow, so far as strenuous intellectual effort goes. The new love of freedom . . .which inclines so many girls to strive for intellectual careers has brought their sex much tension, and this is hard upon their constitution. (p. 590)

Clarke (1873), a physician, introduced a popular book that argued that women should not be educated like men. He argued that medical evidence demonstrated that intellectual endeavors would harm women physiologically. He specifically argued that women should not engage in the same intellectual activities as men because it would adversely affect the development of women's reproductive organs and would cause sterility.

Although schools did not cease educating women, many schools began programs that were designed to address women's special physiological needs, and some of Clarke's ideas were instrumental in shaping different programs of study for men and women (Rury, 1991).

Thus, science has historically engaged in the construction of gender by "scientifically verifying" popularly held beliefs about the nature of males and females. An example of this phenomenon occurred in the scientific analysis of the intellectual abilities of the two genders. Scientists attempted to verify that women were intellectually inferior to men with research on the structure of the brain and through evolutionary and functional analyses. The research about intelligence was used to argue for the differential education of men and women.

Contemporary Psychology and the Construction of Gender

Psychology has continued to engage in the construction of gender in numerous ways. Although researchers and scientists may be able to show how past investigators used faulty methodology, which they interpreted in biased ways, contemporary psychologists are subject to a whole set of other biases and problems with methodology that may help in the construction of cultural ideas about gender (Sherif, 1979).

This chapter does not argue that science is a useless tool or that one cannot study the psychology of gender. I only advocate that investigators safeguard their own investigations from their biases. I believe that in any research where scientists have hypotheses and particular beliefs about the subject matter, which is the case with most research, there are numerous ways they can bias their work. Two of the most common biases in the psychology of gender are alpha and beta biases.

Alpha Bias

One of the biases that has been prevalent in the contemporary study of gender is alpha bias, which is the exaggeration of the differences between males and females (Hare-Mustin & Marecek, 1988). This bias is seen in work that tends to emphasize that females and males are quite different in personality or in behavior. Alpha bias is not a new phenomenon. The belief that women and men are vastly different or even opposite from one another is a part of Western culture and has been proposed by Aristotle, Aquinas, Bacon, Descartes, Locke, and Rousseau (Hare-Mustin & Marecek, 1988). Males have been associated with reason and rationality, whereas females have been associated with forces that are beyond reason such as nature (Ortner, 1974).

This bias can be seen in contemporary psychology in numerous ways. In particular, psychologists have been tremendously concerned with masculinity, femininity, and androgyny, which has led to the routine inclusion of these scales in all kinds of research. In an historical review of this area, Morawski (1985) concluded that this research can best be characterized as an attempt to establish the psychological existence of masculinity and femininity rather than an attempt to discover the importance or utility of such concepts. Investigators originally constructed masculinity and femininity scales by selecting questions that men and women responded to differently and then compiling the questions into a scale. The responses that males gave were called masculine and the responses females gave were called feminine. Subsequent investigators never questioned the theoretical justification for such traits and just assumed the psychological existence of masculinity and femininity, even though many of the scales were not quantitatively reliable. In addition, although many of the scales did not predict psychological functioning as they were originally intended, the scales were still used by clinicians for diagnostic purposes. And when males and females responded similarly to such scales, researchers invented new, more "sensitive" ways to measure masculinity and femininity (Morawski, 1985).

Gilligan's theory about moral development is also an example of the emphasis on differences between men and women (Gilligan, 1982). She proposes that women and men's morality is different because the two genders are concerned with different things. Women are concerned with preserving relationships and caring for other people. Men, in contrast, are concerned with following rules of fairness. Their morality is not concerned with the preservation of relationships. Gilligan's (1982) theory is different from other theories, however, because she views female morality in a positive light.

Beta Bias

The other kind of bias prevalent in contemporary psychology of gender is beta bias (Hare-Mustin & Marecek, 1988), which is the minimization of differences between the two genders and is generally less prevalent in the field.

One example of beta bias is in the representation of women and men as similar people without regard to their differential power, status, or economic opportunities (Hare-Mustin & Marecek, 1988). Much research in psychology includes the variable of gender as an independent variable regardless of the fact that women and men cannot be randomly assigned to these groups (Unger, 1979). Men and women may differ in status and power and may not be perceived or treated similarly when they perform the same behavior. For example, Butler and Geis (1990) found that when male and female confederates both demonstrated leadership behavior in a small-group setting, subjects responded with disproportionately more displeased facial responses to the female leader than to the male leader. Even though the male and female confederates demonstrated the same behavior, subjects gave a lesser evaluation of the female leader. Clearly, the variable of gender can reflect differential status or power. Women and men cannot necessarily be viewed as similar in psychological research. Gender differences can reflect other processes that have little to do with biological sex.

A related bias is the tendency to ignore the social context in research on gender (Riger, 1992). Some gender research has attempted to separate social context from the behavior under study. Some researchers assume that people do not bring their social roles, history, or culture to the laboratory when they participate in an experiment. However, these factors may be exactly what cause men and women to behave differently in an experiment. Sociocultural factors may possibly be the most important variables to consider in gender research. Unfortunately, some researchers attempt to remove social context and then falsely to ascribe gender differences to forces within a person.

Research Design

Another way that psychologists have engaged in the construction of gender is through the types of questions investigators have asked, the subjects researchers have used, and the experimental designs researchers have employed.

One of the ways that psychology has engaged in the construction of gender is through selectivity in the research that is conducted and published in scientific journals. In the *Journal of Personality and Social Psychology*, about 5% of the articles addressed issues about women's life during the 1960s, about 11%, during the 1970s, and about 14% during the early 1980s (cited in Grady, 1981; Lott, 1985). Issues germane to a woman's life were defined as topics that addressed sex, sexuality, sex differences, sex roles, marriage, maternity, pregnancy, physical attractiveness, interpersonal attraction, achievement, and reactions to success and failure. Thus, psychologists have appeared to be relatively uninterested in research about women. However, it has been argued that these percentages do not accurately reflect the amount of research that is currently being conducted about women. These percentages may reflect how research about women is evaluated by journal editors or by the field of psychology (Grady, 1981). In addition, psychological journals will tend to publish research that finds differences between groups or, rather, when researchers reject the null hypothesis (Greenwald, 1975). Thus, researchers who find differential effects for gender tend publish their results, whereas researchers who find no differences between the genders tend not to publish their results (Grady, 1981). Thus, psychology may engage in the construction of gender by not publishing research about women or by selectively publishing research that documents gender differences.

Another way that psychology engages in the construction of gender is through the use of single-gender subject samples for experiments. Historically, males were experimental subjects approximately twice as often as females, and many of these experiments used only single-gender designs (McKenna & Kessler, 1977). Even classic experiments in psychology only used males as subjects and relatively little is known about how women would respond to the same situations. Thus, males are viewed as the standard and the results for women are assumed to be similar. An example of this phenomenon is in some of the classic research on attraction (Meyer, 1988). In this research, Dutton and Aron (1974) were interested in how arousal would influence the experience of romantic love. Male subjects crossed a shaky bridge or a steady bridge and were then interviewed by an attractive female confederate. The dependent variable of attraction was whether the subjects called the confederate after the experiment. Other studies have looked at how running in place, hearing a Steve Martin comedy, or hearing a tape of a person being mutilated influenced attraction (White, Fishbein, & Rutstein, 1981; White & Kight, 1984). The one consistent part of this research has been the gender of the subjects (male) and the gender of the confederates (female). In this case, we know a great deal about how arousal affects men's attraction to women, but we know little about the reverse.

One of the last ways that psychology engages in the construction of gender is through its operationalization of independent and dependent variables in experimental designs. McKenna and Kessler (1977) noted that when researchers are studying aggression, female subjects are treated quite differently from male subjects. Male subjects are often provoked by another person and the measure of their aggression is how many times they shock or how painful a shock they present to a confederate. In contrast, female subjects are often given vignettes and the measure of their aggression is how they would respond to this imagined person. Clearly, the differential experimental situations would lead to different types of responses that might be explained as differences between females and males.

In summary, contemporary psychology engages in the construction of gender through the kinds of questions that are researched, the kinds of research that get published, the types of experimental designs that are used, and the gender of the subjects who are studied. All these influences can lead to biased experimental results that are more congruent with cultural ideas about gender than with actual reality.

CONCLUSION

In this chapter I have argued that gender is a socially constructed category of human society. The contents of the gender schema may be different across cultures, but gender is a salient social category that is reinforced by cultural forces and by various human cognitive mechanisms. Cultures distinguish between two or more genders and organize beliefs and activities according to these categories. Individuals are influenced by the existence of these categories and their perceptions of the world are organized according to them.

Gender is also socially constructed within the scientific community through "scientific" verification of cultural beliefs about gender. Historically, scientists claimed, with evolutionary arguments and with anatomical research findings on the brain, that they had evidence of women's intellectual inferiority to men. Contemporary psychology may also engage in the construction of gender through particular biases and methodological shortcomings. However, I do not advocate discontinuing scientific inquiry about the nature of gender and gender relations, I only advocate safeguarding experiments so that unconscious biases do not creep into psychological work and interpretations of experimental results.

Gender remains an interesting and important topic that deserves special scrutiny and understanding. Research on this topic illustrates how cultures organize and understand human life, how the mind is structured, and how we can transcend gender categories and relate to one another simply as humans beings.

REFERENCES

Aries, P. (1962). *Centuries of childhood: A social history of the family life*. New York: Vintage.

Averill, J. R. (1985). The social construction of emotion: With special reference to love. In K. J. Gergen & K. E. Davis (Eds.), *The social construction of the person*. New York: Springer-Verlag.

Bain, A. (1868). *Mental science; A compendium of psychology*. New York: Appleton.

Basow, S. (1986). *Gender stereotypes*. Belmont, CA: Brooks/Cole.

Bem, S. L. (1987). Gender schema theory and the romantic tradition. In P. Shaver & C. Hendrick (Eds.), *Sex and gender: Review of personality and social psychology*. Newbury Park, CA: Sage.

Berger, P. L., & Luckman, T. (1980). *The social construction of reality*. New York: Irvington.

Burt, C., & Moore, R. C. (1912). The mental differences between the sexes. *Journal of Experimental Pedagogy*, *1*, 355–388.

Butler, D., & Geis, F. L. (1990). Nonverbal affect responses to male and female leaders: Implications for leadership evaluations. *Journal of Personality and Social Psychology*, *58*, 48–59.

Clarke, E. H. (1873). *Sex in education.* Boston: Osgood.

Deuteronomy 22:5. In the *Holy Bible.* (1984). East Brunswick, NJ: International Bible Society.

Dutton, D. G., & Aron, A. P. (1974). Some evidence for heightened sexual attraction under conditions of high anxiety. *Journal of Personality and Social Psychology, 30,* 510–517.

Eagly, A. H., & Crowley, M. (1986). Gender and helping behavior: A meta-analytic review of the social psychological literature. *Psychological Bulletin,* 100(3), 283–308.

Eagly, A. H., & Steffen, V. J. (1986). Gender and aggressive behavior: A meta-analytic review of the social psychological literature. *Psychological Bulletin,* 100(3), 309–330.

Festinger, L. (1954). A theory of social comparison processes. *Human Relations,* 7(2), 117–140

Geertz, C. (1983). *Local knowledge.* New York: Basic Books.

Geis, F. L. (1983, April). *Gender schemas and achievement: Performance and recognition.* Invited address at the Eastern Psychological Association Convention, Philadelphia, PA.

Gergen, K. J. (1982). *Toward transformation in social knowledge.* New York: Springer-Verlag.

Gergen, K. J. (1985). The social constructionist movement in modern psychology. *American Psychologist, 40*(3), 266–275.

Gibson, J. J. (1968). The theory of information pickup. In R. H. Haber (Ed.), *Contemporary theory and research in visual perception.* New York: Holt, Rinehart, & Winston.

Gilligan, C. (1982). *In a different voice: Psychological theory and women's development.* Cambridge, MA: Harvard University Press.

Grady, K. E. (1981). Sex bias in research design. *Psychology of Women Quarterly,* 5(4), 628–636.

Greenwald, A. G. (1975). Consequences of prejudice against the null hypothesis. *Psychological Bulletin, 82,* 1–20.

Hall, G. S. (1906). The question of coeducation. *Munsey's Magazine, 34,* 588–592.

Hall, N., & Dawson, W. R. (1989). *Broodmales.* Dallas, TX: Spring.

Hare-Mustin, R. T., & Marecek, J. (1988). The meaning of difference. Gender theory, postmodernism, and psychology. *American Psychologist, 43*(6), 455–464.

Harre, R. (Ed.). (1986). *The social construction of emotions.* New York: Blackwell.

Henley, N. M. (1977). *Body politics: Power, sex, and nonverbal communication.* Englewood Cliffs, New Jersey: Prentice-Hall.

Hoffman, C., & Hurst, N. (1990). Gender stereotypes: Perception or rationalization? *Journal of Personality and Social Psychology, 58*(2), 197–208.

Holy Bible. (1984). East Brunswick, New Jersey: International Bible Society.

Hunt, M. M. (1960). *The natural history of love.* London: Hutchinson & Co.

Jagger, A. M. (1983). *Feminist politics and human nature.* Totowa, NJ: Rowman & Allanheld.

John, B. A., & Sussman, L. E. (1985). Initiative taking as a determinant of role-reciprocal organization. *Imagination, Cognition and Personality, 43*(3), 277–291.

Kessler, S. J., & McKenna, W. (1985). *Gender: An ethnomethodological approach.* Chicago: University of Chicago Press.

Levi-Strauss, C. (1971). The family. In H. L. Shapiro (Ed.), *Man, culture, and society* (pp. 333–357). New York: Oxford University Press.

Lewin, K. (1951). *Field theory in social science.* New York: Harper.

Lorber, J. (1986). Dismantling Noah's ark. *Sex Roles, 14,* 567–580.

Lott, B. (1985). The potential enrichment of social/personality psychology through feminist research and vice versa. *American Psychologist, 40*(2), 155–164.

Maccoby. E. E. (1990). Gender and relationships: A developmental account. *American Psychologist, 45*(4), 513–520.

Markus, H., & Zajonc, R. B. (1985). The cognitive perspective in social psychology. In G. Lindzey & E. Aronson (Eds.), *Handbook of social psychology* (Vol. 1, pp. 137–230). New York: Random House.

Martin, M. K., & Voorhies, B. (1975). *Female of the species.* New York: Columbia University Press.

Mead, M. (1935). *Sex and temperament in three primitive societies.* New York: William Morrow.

Meyer, J. (1988). Feminist thought and social psychology. In M. M. Gergen (Ed.), *Feminist thought and the structure of knowledge* (pp. 105- 123). New York: New York University Press.

McKenna, W., & Kessler, S. J. (1977). Experimental design as a source of sex bias in social psychology. *Sex Roles, 3*(2), 117–128.

Morawski, J. G. (1985). The measurement of masculinity and femininity: Engendering categorical realities. *Journal of Personality, 53*(2), 196–223.

Natsoulas, T. (1968). On homogeneous retinal stimulation and the perception of depth. In R. N. Haber (Ed.), *Contemporary theory and research in visual perception* (pp. 452–457). New York: Holt, Rinehart, and Winston.

Ortner, S. B. (1974). Is female to male as nature is to culture? In M. Z. Rosaldo & L. Lamphere (Eds.), *Woman, culture, and society* (pp. 67–87). Stanford, CA: Stanford University Press.

Paludi, M. A., & Strayer, L. A. (1985). What's in an author's name? Differential evaluations of performance as a function of author's name. *Sex Roles, 10,* 353–361.

Riger, S. (1992). Epistemological debates, feminist voices: Science, social values, and the study of women. *American Psychologist, 47,* 730–740.

Rock, I., & Victor, J. (1968). Vision and touch: An experimentally created conflict between the two senses. In R. H. Haber (Ed.), *Contemporary theory and research in visual perception* (pp. 528–532). New York: Holt, Rinehart, & Winston.

Rubin, G. (1975). The traffic in women: Notes on the "political economy" of sex. In R. R. Reiter (Ed.), *Toward an anthropology of women* (pp. 157–210). New York: Monthly Review Press.

Rury, J. L. (1991). *Education and women's work.* Albany, NY: State University of New York Press.

Sherif, C. W. (1979). Bias in psychology. In J. A. Sherman & E. T. Beck (Eds.), *The prism of sex: Essays on the sociology of knowledge* (pp. 93–133). Madison, WI: University of Wisconsin Press.

Shields, S. A. (1975). Functionalism, Darwinism, and the psychology of women. A study in social myth. *American Psychologist, 30,* 739–754.

Shields, S. A. (1987). Women, men, and the dilemma of emotion. In P. Shaver & C. Hendrick (Eds.), *Sex and gender: Review of personality and social psychology* (pp. 229–250). Newbury Park, CA: Sage.

Shweder, R. A. (1984). Anthropology's romantic rebellion against the enlightenment, or there's more to thinking than reason and evidence. In R. A. Shweder & R. A. Levine (Eds.), *Culture theory. Essays on mind, self, and emotion* (pp. 27–66). New York: Cambridge University Press.

Shweder, R. A., & Bourne, E. J. (1984). Does the concept of the person vary cross-culturally? In R. A. Shweder & R. A. Levine (Eds.), *Culture theory. Essays on mind, self, and emotion* (pp. 158–199). New York: Cambridge University Press.

Six, B., & Eckes, T. (1991). A closer look at the complex structure of gender stereotypes. *Sex Roles, 24,* 57–71.

Smith, N. K. (1973). *Immanuel Kant's critique of pure reason.* London: Macmillan Press.

Spencer, H. (1961). *The study of sociology.* Ann Arbor, MI: University of Michigan Press.

Taylor, S. E., Fiske, S. T., Etcoff, N. L., & Ruderman, A. J. (1978). Categorical and contextual bases of person memory and stereotyping. *Journal of Personality and Social Psychology, 36*(7), 778–793.

Unger, R. K. (1979). Toward a redefinition of sex and gender. *American Psychologist, 34,* 1085–1094.

Unger, R. K., & Crawford, M. (1992). *Women and gender: A feminist psychology.* Philadelphia: Temple University Press.

Weisstein, N. (1971). Psychology constructs the female. In V. Gornick & B. K. Moran (Eds.), *Woman in sexist society* (pp. 133–146). New York: Basic Books.

White, G. L., Fishbein, S., & Rutstein, J. (1981). Passionate love and the misattribution of arousal. *Journal of Personality and Social Psychology, 41,* 56–62.

White, G. L., & Kight, T. D. (1984). Misattribution of arousal and attraction: Effects of salience of explanations for arousal. *Journal of Experimental Social Psychology, 20,* 55–64.

Woolley, H. T. (1910). Psychological literature. A review of the recent literature on the psychology of sex. *Psychological Bulletin, 7,* 335–342.

The Evolutionary Perspective

DOUGLAS T. KENRICK
MELANIE R. TROST

Bhupinder Singh the Magnificent, Seventh Maharajah of the state of Pati-ala in Northern India, had 350 wives. Among the Pahari of Northern India and the Tre-ba of Tibet, on the other hand, the tradition is for women to have more than one husband. These customs were no doubt alien to the British invaders who colonized these areas for several centuries, as it was illegal in Britain for either a man or a woman to have more than one spouse. Such cultural variations occur in other areas of behavior as well. In some cultures it is appropriate for a male to go about naked only until puberty; in others he may go naked his whole life. In some cultures women do not cover their upper body; in others they must cover their whole body, from head to toe, leaving only their eyes and hands exposed. As early anthropologists returned from the far reaches of Africa, Asia, and the South Pacific, they brought tale after tale of seemingly endless cultural diversity. Best known are Margaret Mead's descriptions of Sa-moan boys and girls who seemingly lived free of any "double standard" for virginity and sexual jealousy, and of tribes like the Tchambuli, in which American sex roles were presumably reversed, with dominant women and passive "effeminate" men (Mead, 1928, 1935).

Overwhelmed by such variation, early twentieth-century social scien-tists in the United States adopted the view that human social behavior in general and human sex roles in particular are infinitely malleable. The anthro-pological accounts complemented the then-emerging behavioral viewpoint in psychology. John B. Watson, the father of behaviorism, had adopted the empiricist assumption that human nature is a *tabula rasa*—a blank slate, subject only to the infinite serendipity of individual experience. The "cultural relativity" perspective has dominated American social science for over half a century (Freeman, 1983). Environmental explanations for gender differ-ences in behavior have often been offered without even considering any alternatives. Social scientists in the United States commonly make the default assumption that any observed differences between men and women are products of "American culture" (e.g., Cameron, Oskamp, & Sparks, 1977; Deutsch, Zalenski, & Clark, 1986; Wolfgang, 1958).

Findings that sex roles vary from one culture to the next served as a healthy antidote for ethnocentrism, and such variations that do exist indicate that human nature is not a set of fixed instincts. Beyond that, the radical environmentalist position was appealing to U.S. political values, and stood in many ways as a reaction to the racist views espoused by turn-of-the-century eugenicists (Freeman, 1983). Those who believed that society's problems were caused by "inferior genes" proposed policies to limit the proliferation of supposedly deficient non-European peoples. The doctrine of cultural relativism was thus embraced in response to an early and misinformed version of "social Darwinism." Although the relativist doctrine is more compatible with the idea that all people are "created equal," it was, from a scientific viewpoint, something of an overreaction. Of particular relevance to gender differences, some of the early claims of cultural relativity in sex roles made by anthropologists such as Margaret Mead have not held up to closer examination. The "carefree" Samoans, for instance, actually revered female virginity at marriage, and the "gentle" Tchambuli males proved to be as prone to homicidal violence as were males in other parts of the globe (Daly & Wilson, 1988; Freeman, 1983). Certainly there are cultural variations among different human groups, but cultural variations do not negate biological nature. To conclude this would be akin to a traveler to Seattle, Washington, who, after encountering snow, sunshine, rain, and sleet over a 5-day period, concludes that there is no pattern to the city's weather. There is indeed substantial variation, but a more careful analysis would reveal some underlying patterns (for instance, Seattle has more sunshine and warmer temperatures on an average day in August than on an average day in February).

Evolutionary psychologists believe that American social scientists are often like the confused Seattle traveler who jumps to a conclusion without enough information. Evolutionary theorists do not deny that there is great variation in the range of human social behavior, and that a good deal of that variation is attributable to the social environment (Kenrick, 1987). However, they believe that underneath all the variation, it is possible to discern some regularities in human behavior. They also believe that, by taking a radical environmentalist viewpoint, American social scientists have developed misleading and incomplete models of social behavior. People from different social environments are indeed unique in some ways, but they also share some behavioral patterns with all other humans. By understanding the underlying consistencies, we are better able to organize and interpret a wide array of cultural differences.

This chapter considers the contributions of evolutionary theory to our understanding of gender differences. We first describe several cross-cultural consistencies in the behaviors of men and women. Then, we explain the basics of the evolutionary perspective on human social behavior, and show how this perspective can encompass the cross-cultural findings. Finally, we consider how genetic and environmental perspectives complement one another. Gender differences result from an interaction of evolved predispositions and the cultures created by people with those predispositions.

CROSS-CULTURAL CONSISTENCIES IN MALE AND FEMALE BEHAVIOR

Social scientists have seemingly good reasons for their opposition to the notion of biologically "universal" gender differences. To begin with, men and women within a culture are more alike than they are different. On most behavioral dimensions, such as spatial abilities, verbal intelligence, and friendliness, there are more differences within a sex than between the sexes. There are women who are better than most men at solving spatial problems (such as those confronted by an architect or geographer). There are men who are friendlier than most women, and other men who have higher verbal intelligence than most women. At first glance, such overlap makes it difficult to imagine universal gender differences in behavior that compare to the universal gender differences in morphology (such as the presence or absence of testicles or a uterus). Nevertheless, even the morphological differences between men and women are not complete and nonoverlapping. Men are, on average, about 10% taller than and 30% heavier than women (Doyle, 1985). Within any culture, there are nevertheless women who are taller than most of the men. However, given a similar diet and family background, the average man is slightly taller and heavier and has somewhat more strength in the muscles of his upper body. Differences in behavior are more like these differences in height and weight than like the differences in the morphology of male and female sexual organs. Because reproductive competition is central to evolutionary theory, evolutionary theorists are particularly interested in the average differences between men and women in aggressiveness, social dominance, and mating behaviors. On average, within a culture and across different cultures, women are less aggressive, less concerned with their position in the social dominance hierarchy, less oriented toward promiscuous or polygamous sexual relationships, and more concerned with finding older males who have acquired resources and/or social status for partners. Men, on the other hand, are more aggressive and competitive, more inclined to promiscuity, and more concerned with the youth and physical attractiveness of their female partners.

Aggressiveness

According to Federal Bureau of Investigation crime statistics, 14,852 American men were arrested for murder in 1989, as compared to 1,989 women. Men thus constituted 88% of the total murderers in the United States for that year. The statistics for aggravated assault are comparable: 281,196 men arrested in 1989, compared to 43,215 women (men thus comprising 87% of the total). These differential ratios have persisted throughout this century in the United States and Canada, and a number of social scientists have attributed them to a cultural norm requiring men to be more aggressive (e.g. Chimbos, 1978; Wolfgang, 1958).

Is some feature of American culture really to blame for the sex difference in brutality? The evidence suggests a fairly clear answer: no. Daly and Wilson (1988) examined the homicide rates for a number of different societies across a number of different periods and always found that male murderers vastly outnumber the females. Among the Alur of Uganda between 1945 and 1954, of all same-sex murders, the proportion of males murdering males was .97. Among the Bhil of India between 1971 and 1975, the proportion was .99. Among the Belo Horizonte of Brazil between 1961 and 1965, 97% of same-sex murders were committed by males. Similar ratios were found for the Gros Vendre between 1850 and 1885, and for the residents of Oxford, England, between 1296 and 1398. Of the 35 cultures and periods Daly and Wilson examined, the lowest ratio was .85, among the Danish between 1933 and 1961.

Men similarly outnumber women in murdering members of the opposite sex, although this difference is somewhat less pronounced because women are more likely to kill men than they are to kill other women. Interestingly, one of the most common causes of a woman's murdering a man is self-defense—women tend to kill men who have been threatening and/or abusing them. On the other hand, a man is more likely to murder a woman who has deserted him or been sexually unfaithful (Daly & Wilson, 1988).

Behaviors related to the technology of aggressiveness show these same sex discrepancies. In a classic examination of the sex differences and similarities in division of labor, Murdock (1935) found that the sexes overlapped considerably in many tasks. For example, the manufacture of leather products was the sole province of men in 29 cultures, the usual province of men in 3 societies, acceptable for either sex in 9 societies, the usual province of women in 3 societies, and the exclusive province of women in 32 societies. However, Murdock (1935) found 121 societies in which weaponmaking was the exclusive domain of men, 1 society in which men usually made the weapons, and no societies in which women were the predominant, the usual, or the equally likely weaponmakers. In a related vein, hunting was the exclusive domain of men in 166 societies, the usual domain of men in 13 societies, and never equally or predominantly the task of women.

In sum, data on aggressive behavior indicate that men are more aggressive than women in all cultures. Men commit more murders and are more involved in producing weapons in every culture ever studied.

Dominance Competition

Although the number of women in the U.S. Senate tripled in the 1992 elections, the total is now 6 (up from 2). In 1989, the Canadian National Parliament was 13% women, whereas women constituted 6% of the British Parliament, and only 3% of the directors of major corporations in the United States (Myers, 1990). The difference in high-status attainment even prevails in occupations where men are not particularly gifted in contrast with women, such as creative writing and art. Differences in leadership attainment are found from ad hoc groups formed in the laboratory to play groups on the kindergarten playground. In one sample of juries, men were found to constitute 50% of the jury members, but were elected foremen 90% of the time (Kerr, Harmon, & Graves, 1982). Once again, such differences have been explained in terms of cultural pressures and biases in our society. Girls are presumably taught to fear success whereas boys are taught to compete. Another possibility is that sex discrimination in the United States leads to selective exclusion of women from positions of leadership.

If there is something unique about the pressures of American culture, we would again expect to find substantial variation across cultures in striving for status, and about as many cultures in which the roles are reversed. Research does not support a cultural explanation. Men are almost always the "chiefs," even in the many societies where people organize themselves around their mother's lineage. Across diverse cultures, terms related to dominance are universally considered more applicable to males (Williams & Best, 1982). As in the case of physical differences, differences in dominance behaviors are also overlapping. There are individual women in most cultures who are socially dominant over most of the men in that culture. But there are no countries in which women hold a majority of powerful posts. Margaret Thatcher was elected Prime Minister of Britain, but she was preceded and succeeded by men, and as we noted above, over 90% of the British Parliament is male. In sum, men tend to hold more positions of social dominance around the world.

Mating Behavior and Sexuality

We began this chapter by noting that some societies (such as Maharajah Bhupinder Singh's) are *polygynous* (one man marrying several women), some (such as the Tre-ba) are *polyandrous* (one woman marrying several men), and still others (like Victorian England) are *monogamous* (one man marrying one woman). This type of variation suggested to early anthropologists that there was no particular mating pattern that characterizes human nature. However, that conclusion was premature. To begin with, all societies have some form of marriage. This may not seem surprising at first, but it is worth considering that pair bonding makes humans somewhat unusual among mammals. Because of the particular physiology of mammalian reproduction, female mammals usually profit little from a permanent mate. Females can generally care for their offspring themselves, and profit more from mating with a male that has very desirable characteristics (even though other females will also want to mate with that male). An extreme example of this pattern is known as a lek, exemplified in a recent study of English fallow deer (Clutton-Brock, 1991). In this mating arrangement, all the males in a breeding population compete for a limited number of choice pieces of territory in a mating arena (called the "lek"), and females mate only with the relatively few males that have made it to the top of the territorial hierarchy. For reasons we will discuss in detail later, mammalian mating arrangements are more likely to involve this type of radical polygyny than monogamy. Do humans show any vestiges of the general mammalian tendency toward polygyny? According to Daly and Wilson (1983), the answer is yes. They analyzed data from 849 human cultures and found that the patterning of marital arrangements was far from random. Of the 849 cultures, only 4 were polyandrous, whereas 708 were polygynous and 137 were strictly monogamous. Moreover, each of the 4 societies listed as polyandrous also allowed polygyny. Among the Pahari of Northern India, for instance, brothers pool their resources to purchase a wife whom they share. If they accumulate more wealth, they will purchase additional wives. Thus, these polyandrous cultures do not constitute a complete sex-role reversal by our standards but seem, in some ways, rather "traditional" (Daly & Wilson, 1983; Hiatt, 1980; Levine, 1980).

Even in so-called monogamous cultures, men are generally more inclined toward unrestricted sexual behaviors and a desire for multiple partners. For example, 20% of American men and 10% of women in one survey reported having had extramarital intercourse, while 48% of men, but only 5% of women, reported a desire to engage in extramarital relations in the future (Johnson, 1970). Similar results were found in a survey of Germans with steady dating partners: 46% of the men, but only 6% of the women, reported a willingness to have casual sex with someone they found attractive (Sigusch & Schmidt, 1971). These findings are interesting because they were gathered at the peak of the "sexual revolution," when traditional ideas about fidelity were probably at an all-time low in popularity. More recent surveys of "post-sexual-revolution" Americans continue to reveal large discrepancies in the permissiveness of men and women (e.g., Astin, Green, Korn, & Schalit, 1987; Hendrick, Hendrick, Slapion-Foote, & Foote, 1985).

Other studies from our own research group reveal sex differences consistent with those survey findings. For example, subjects in one study were given the choice between one experiment in which they would view geometric figures or another in which they would watch an erotic film (Kenrick, Stringfield, Wagenhals, Dahl, & Ransdell, 1980). Men tended to choose the erotic film, whereas women either tended to choose the experiment on geometric figures or declined to participate in either study. In another study, men and women were asked to indicate their minimum criteria for partners at several levels of relationship involvement (Kenrick, Sadalla, Groth, & Trost, 1990). When choosing partners for a sexual liaison, men reliably indicated lower criteria than did women. For instance, men specified a minimum percentile of 51 for intelligence in a date, but only 43 for a sexual partner. Women, on the other hand, specified a minimum intelligence level of 49th percentile for a date, and a higher minimum for a sexual partner (55th percentile). In a more recent study, subjects at two universities were asked about their criteria for partners for a "one-night stand," after which they would never see the person again (Kenrick, Groth, Trost, & Sadalla, 1993). Considering all levels of relationship commitment, males and females differed most in their criteria for this explicitly low-commitment relationship: Men were very nondiscriminating, whereas women tended to be highly selective.

In sum, men across a wide variety of cultures and research methodologies indicate a greater inclination toward a multiplicity of sexual partners.

Partner Preferences

A number of studies have indicated some reliable differences between American men and women in terms of preferred characteristics in mating partners. For example, women tend to show a relative preference for wealth, social status, and seniority in a partner, whereas men show a relatively stronger preference for youth and attractiveness (Buss & Barnes, 1986; Margolin & White, 1987; Townsend, 1989). Like the differences in aggressiveness, dominance, and sexuality, these findings have typically been explained in terms of the norms of American culture (e.g., Deutsch, Zalenski, & Clark,1986; Margolin & White, 1987; Presser, 1975). As Brehm (1985) puts it, *"Traditionally, in our society* [italics added], males have been valued for their economic success, and females for their physical attractiveness" (p. 76). In a similar vein, Cameron et al. (1977) explain findings that females prefer older, taller, high-status males as due to "traditional sex-role specifications . . . frequently valued as sex appropriate *in American society* [italics added]" (p. 29) that specify that women should "look up to" their male partners.

Once again, one must support a cultural explanation by showing data from other cultures that differ. If the differences in mate preference are due to something peculiar to American culture, other cultures should sometimes show different patterns, perhaps including, for example, reversals in which women prefer youth and men prefer older women. An examination of the cross-cultural variation in these preferences does not support the cultural norms explanation, however. For instance, older men in European, Asian, African, and Southern Pacific cultures always show a tendency to marry relatively younger women, whereas younger men marry women closer to their own age (and often marry women older than themselves). Women at all ages and in all cultures tend to marry older men (Broude, 1992; Harpending, 1992; Kenrick & Keefe, 1992). Similarly, women across 37 cultures studied by Buss (1989) showed a relatively greater interest in having a partner with resources than did men, whereas men across the different cultures placed more emphasis on physical attractiveness.

Summary of Gender Differences

Compared to men, women thus tend to be: (1) less prone to homicidal violence; (2) less likely to achieve high levels of social dominance; (3) less inclined toward having multiple sexual partners; and (4) more interested in older partners who have accumulated material and social resources. Men are, on the other hand, more homicidal, more dominant, and more inclined toward polygamy and promiscuity. Younger men in all cultures mate with women their own age, whereas older men mate with women progressively more and more junior to them. Each of these gender differences has commonly been explained as due to the norms of American or Western European culture. However, each of these differences appears in a wide diversity of cultures around the world. This consistency across cultures creates problems for explanations that assume that all gender differences are under the control of gender norms arbitrarily created by different cultures (such as those controlling men's skirt-wearing in Scotland and the United States). Even more problematic is the fact that other mammalian species tend to show many of these same gender differences. Among other mammals, for instance, males tend to be generally more aggressive, more socially dominant, and less discriminating in their choice of sexual partners (Daly & Wilson, 1983). Since hamadryas baboons and Ugandan kob antelopes are unlikely to have been influenced by the social conventions displayed on American television, another explanation of these comparative similarities is called for. In the next section, we explain the general principles of evolutionary theory and how those principles have been applied to social behavior. We then address how those principles may explain gender differences in animals in general and in humans in particular.

EVOLUTION AND BEHAVIOR

Evolutionary theory consists of three assumptions, outlined by Charles Darwin (1859/1958). The first assumption is that animals are engaged in a *struggle for existence*. Even slowly reproducing animals reproduce so rapidly that any species would overrun the earth in a few centuries. This does not happen because resources are limited: When the giraffe population becomes too large, the giraffes begin to exhaust the supply of arboreal vegetation and some starve. Given the limitations of resources and the fact that other members of the same species are the main competitors for those resources most necessary to survival, animals of a given species must struggle against one another to survive. Giraffes must beat the other giraffes to the limited greenery on the tops of the trees, and lions must beat the other lions to the giraffes.

The second crucial assumption of evolutionary theory presumes *heritable variation within a species*. This assumption, quite controversial when Darwin first advanced it, is that animals within a species are not all exactly the same; they differ in many ways, and can pass some of those differences along to their offspring. Darwin (1895/1958) showed how such variations were exploited by pigeon domesticators:

> The diversity of breeds is something astonishing. The carrier, more especially the male bird, is . . . remarkable from the wonderful development of the carunculated skin about the head; and this is accompanied by greatly elongated eyelids, very large external orifices to the nostrils, and a wide gape of mouth . . . the common tumbler has the singular inherited habit of flying at a great height in a compact flock, and tumbling in the air head over heels. . . . The pouter has a much elongated body, wings, and legs; and its enormously developed crop, which it glories in inflating, may well excite astonishment and even laughter. . . . Great as are the differences between the breeds . . . all are descended from the rock pigeon. (pp. 41–42)

Later researchers found that by interbreeding the most aggressive or least aggressive rats from a litter for several generations, they could produce strains of especially gentle and especially violent rats (Lagerspetz, 1979). The same process has occurred in the best known domesticated species, dogs. All domesticated dogs come from a common ancestor, but some strains are notoriously aggressive, such as pit bulls; some are notoriously good-natured, such as golden retrievers; and some are notoriously jittery, such as Irish setters.

The third principle of evolution is that of *natural selection*, and it follows from the other two. If animals must compete with one another to survive, and if animals vary in ways that can be inherited, then animals whose variations assist in the struggle for survival will have more offspring. Those offspring will, in turn, have relatively more offspring than less well-adapted strains, and so on. Over generations, the strains that are most closely suited to their particular environments will replace those that are less well adapted. Imagine a pond that grows enough algae to support 100 catfish. Imagine that one of the catfish inherits a mutated gene that causes it to have a larger mouth than its cousins, allowing it to eat faster. This catfish will grow to maturity more quickly, reproduce sooner, and stay alive longer than the small-mouthed catfish. Its offspring will not only be more numerous but they will themselves share its physical advantage, and will outeat the next generation of small-mouthed catfishes. Keeping in mind that the pond can only support 100 catfish, the small-mouthed fish will fare less well as their large-mouthed cousins proliferate. Assuming that the large mouth does not carry some hidden cost, eventually the pond will consist entirely of large-mouthed catfish.

Most people understand how Darwin's theory applies to the physical characteristics of animals, but often misunderstand the implications of the theory for behavior. However, Darwin (1873) argued that behaviors should evolve in the same way as do physical features. A little thought reveals why this should be the case. Seals are closely related to dogs, but if a seal inherited a brain programmed to run a dog's body and tried to run down large-hoofed mammals on dry land, it would not last much longer than a dog that attempted to swim out to sea and dive for fish 50 feet below the surface. Along with a body, seals, dogs, bats, giraffes, and cobras inherit a brain programmed to do certain things with that body. Thus, evolution applies to survival-related behaviors in much the same way that it applies to physical characteristics. Those animals with behavioral variations most suited to their environment (and to their bodily equipment) will survive and outreproduce those animals with less well-adapted behavioral variations.

There is sometimes a misconception that natural selection has removed all the important differences between humans. Behavioral–genetic studies of twins and adoptees have supported the assumption that humans, like other animals, have many heritable variations that affect behavior

(Plomin, DeFries, & McClearn, 1990). Variations in personality character-istics ranging from friendliness and intelligence to depression and schizo-phrenia appear to be partially heritable. More important, males and fe-males are genetically different and are probably selected along slightly different dimensions.

Different Strategies within and between Species

Which behavioral strategy will work best in the struggle for survival? As we just indicated, it depends partly on the animal's body type and partly on the physical environment. It also depends partly on the social environ-ment. Evolutionary theorists often use the metaphor of "hawks and doves" to explicate the importance of social ecology (e.g., Dawkins, 1976). If nonaggressive doves predominate in an environment, it pays to be an aggressive hawk that preys on other birds. As the number of hawks in-creases, however, it becomes more and more dangerous to attack other birds (which may viciously counterattack). Under these circumstances, a pacifist dove (which runs from any conflict) will fare better. In fact, evolutionary theorists assume that different species of animals that share the same environment often maintain an equilibrium. If the hawk popula-tion increases, they begin to destroy the dove population, on which they prey. Hawks begin to starve and die, and the dove population increases. Of course, when the dove population increases dramatically, there are more meals for hawks, and the hawks increase again. With this type of interdependence, the populations of hawks and doves will tend to stabilize at some mutually limiting equilibrium.

Such a reciprocal equilibrium can occur *within* a species, as well. For instance, there are two types of adult male blue-gilled sunfish (Gross, 1984). One type is a large territorial male whose colorful body is highly attractive to females. A second type of male is smaller and drab in appear-ance, resembling the less resplendent female. These smaller males are known as "sneak-copulators." Rather than investing nutritional energy in developing a large flashy physique, they develop enormous sperm-producing organs. When a large territorial male is mating with a female, the smaller male will thwart his larger opponent by darting in and releasing his sperm. Obviously, the success of the smaller males' strategy depends partly on the existence of the larger males in the vicinity to attract females, and is decreased by too many other smaller sneak-copulators in the neigh-borhood. Polymorphism (or the tendency of different members of a species to have different body types) takes an even more interesting twist in another species of fish. In the cleaner wrasse, females are most numerous and congregate in harems around a large territoried male. When a large male dies, the largest female in his harem goes through a series of rapid physiological changes during which she grows larger and transforms into a male (Warner, 1984). Thus, the success of a particular combination of body type and behavior is linked to variations in the environment, and some species have evolved to change body types as the environment changes.

The most prevalent morphological and physical divisions within species are based on gender. Males and females of a given species tend to differ in size and in behavior. Some of these differences are unique: The differences between a peacock and a peahen are not the same as those between a male and a female walrus. However, some wide generalizations in sex differences can be found across a wide range of vertebrate species. Darwin noted in *The Origin of Species* (1859/1958) that males tend to be relatively larger and more showy. If one member of a fish species has more decorative fins (as in the Siamese fighting fish), if one member of a bird species has more colorful plumage (as in the peacock), or if one member of a mammalian species has larger antlers (as in the elk), it tends to be the male. There are fairly general behavioral differences as well. Males tend to be more aggressive and more inclined toward dominance competitions. Differences in mating arrangements tend to occur, as well. Polygyny is more common than polyandry among vertebrates. Two general principles are often used to explain these differences: differential parental investment and sexual selection.

Differential Parental Investment and Sexual Selection

Differential parental investment refers to the fact that males and females are inherently different in the amount of resources they invest in offspring (Trivers, 1972). Eggs are generally more costly to produce than sperm. In species that utilize internal fertilization, as do most mammals, this difference is enhanced considerably. In order to produce a single offspring, a mammalian female must carry a fetus that requires a large amniotic sac and has first priority on her nutritional intake for several months. It is generally believed that the higher ratio of body fat to muscle in the human female originally stemmed from the need to ensure survival of the costly fetus in nutritionally uncertain times (Frisch, 1988). Following birth, the female nurses the newborn, again sacrificing her own nutritional intake to provide nutrition for her progeny. Female elephant seals lose two kilograms for every kilogram gained by their pups, and the chance of a female red deer's surviving from one season to the next goes down if she bears offspring (Clutton-Brock, 1984; Trivers 1985). In some species, such as humans, the offspring must be fed and cared for even after they are weaned. Therefore, the minimum female parental investment is quite large.

Males, on the other hand, could father a child with a very low invest-ment—the amount of energy required for one act of intercourse. The record number of legitimate children recorded for one man is 899 (Daly & Wilson, 1983), and the actual number could conceivably be higher than that. On the other hand, it is biologically difficult for a woman to have more than 24 children, even if, like Maharajah Bhupinder Singh, she had 350 spouses. For example, among the Xavante, a hunter–gatherer group, the average number of offspring for males and females is 3.6 (logically, the mean has to be the same). However, the variance for women is 3.9, whereas for men it is 12.1. In other words, some Xavante men have quite a few offspring and some have very few. Only 1 of 195 Xavante women is childless at age 20, whereas 6% of men are still childless by age 40. One man in the group had 23 children, whereas the highest number of children for a woman was 8 (Daly & Wilson, 1983; Salzano, Neel, & Maybury-Lewis, 1967).

Some of the physical differences between males and females are due simply to natural selection based on this differential parental investment. Females need a different body to produce eggs, and in the case of mam-mals, to nurture the fetus and the newborn baby. However, those differ-ences are not sufficient to explain the vast differences between the sexes. Why are males larger? (One might expect that a slightly larger body would be of more use to a female mammal [who must contribute her physical resources directly to the offspring] [Ralls, 1976]). Why are males more likely to have decorative features such as antlers and peacock feathers, and to use some of those features (such as antlers) to compete with one another? Darwin used the concept of sexual selection to explain such differences. Sexual selection consists of two separable processes. Intrasex-ual selection refers to the selection pressure that one sex exerts on the other via competition. In a species in which males compete for access to females by butting their heads, those individuals with the boniest heads, the largest shoulder muscles, and the largest antlers will be more likely to win dominance competitions and survive. Epigamic selection is the other part of sexual selection. If one sex selects sexual partners on the basis of a certain feature, such as the possession of large antlers or a bright display of feathers, those features will be more characteristic of one sex than of the other. Indeed, experimental studies have verified that sexual selection does operate in the manner that Darwin suspected. For example, Andersson (1982) manipulated the lengths of tail feather displays in widow-birds. Females were more likely to mate with males whose tails were experimentally elongated and to reject males whose tails were experimen-tally shortened.

Darwin suspected that epigamic sexual selection applies more to fe-male choice of males, and female choice could explain why male vertebrates tend to be larger, showier, and more dominance oriented. The reason that females are more likely to do the picking and choosing takes us back to the concept of differential parental investment. Because females have an initially higher investment in their offspring, they are better served to be selective about their partners. An ill-chosen mating partner is, on average, less likely to be costly for a male. In a species like the fallow deer, the "arena mating" species described above, males on a lek mate with many females in the course of a day. These males appear to be completely nonselective, whereas females will only mate with the most dominant males.

Qualifying the Parental Investment Model in Application to Humans

This general mammalian model of differential parental investment and sexual selection provides a reasonable explanation for the behaviors of species like the fallow deer and the peacock, but we need to qualify it when we start talking about humans (Kenrick & Trost, 1989). Human males invest heavily in their offspring. Even Bhupinder Singh provided food, care, and shelter for his 350 wives and their offspring. In a monogamous relationship, the man may provide resources for his single wife and her offspring for all his adult life. Because human males invest heavily in their offspring, we would expect males to also be selective about choosing a mating partner. Sex differences tend to be diminished in species in which the males invest in their offspring (Lancaster, 1985). Indeed, male and female humans are relatively similar in size and decoration in contrast to peacocks and peahens, or even to our more sexually unrestricted primate cousins such as baboons.

Just because human males and females both invest in their offspring, does not mean they are both playing the same mating game, however (Kenrick & Trost, 1987, 1989). Men and women invest different resources, and so we would expect the two sexes to value different characteristics in a mate. Males invest indirect resources (e.g., food, money, protection, and security) that do not necessarily diminish as they get older. Thus, women would be expected to value men who show the ability to provide those resources. On the other hand, women directly invest their bodily resources in the offspring. Aging limits a woman's reproductive potential, and around age 50, ends it through menopause. Thus, males would be expected to place more value on signs of youth and physical health. Several authors have suggested that judgments of female physical attractiveness seem closely related to signs of youth and physical health (Alley, 1992, Cunningham, 1986; Symons, 1979).

Let us reevaluate our earlier discussion of the universal differences between men and women, considering the principles of differential parental investment and sexual selection. Differences in human mating arrangements and sexual behavior can be explained in terms of the general mammalian heritage of differential parental investment. Although both human males and human females tend to contribute resources to their offspring, it remains possible for a male, but impossible for a female, to reproduce with little investment. Thus, shopping for an impulsive sexual liaison would be less adaptive for a woman than for a man, and it makes evolutionary sense that men and women are similarly concerned about the characteristics of a marital partner, but that men are less discriminating about the characteristics of a casual sexual partner (Kenrick, et al., 1990). On the other hand, because a woman can always be certain that her offspring are her own, whereas a man cannot, males should show more extreme jealousy over sexual infidelity, as indeed the evidence suggests they do (Daly & Wilson, 1983; 1988). Because a man can be cuckolded, thereby unknowingly investing resources in offspring that are not his own, men are more likely to jealously guard the sexual activities of their mates. A female also stands to lose resources if her partner deserts her; hence jealousy is hardly the sole dominion of the male. A female, however, will lose much less if her partner is temporarily sexually unfaithful. She will lose substantial resources only if her partner leaves her for the other woman. This fact might explain why acts of violence involving spouses are more likely to be motivated by jealousy in males but by self-protection in females (Daly & Wilson, 1988).

Regarding aggression and social dominance, the evolutionary perspective offers a related explanation. Males who have obtained social dominance (like Bhupinder Singh) are, compared to low-status males, more able to provide the indirect resources that will profit their offspring. In addition, their social success may give indirect evidence of heritable characteristics that will profit their offspring. Thus, women, like female fallow deer and peahens, have tended in the past to select dominant males as sexual partners. This behavior has maintained, via sexual selection, the basic mammalian sex differences in social dominance. Higher levels of male aggressiveness persist from our mammalian ancestors not because they are likely to be attractive to females but because they may assist a male in intrasexual selection. In traditional human groups, males who are aggressive are more likely to have beaten other males for positions in the dominance hierarchy (Chagnon, 1983; Daly & Wilson, 1988). Research with primates and humans, however, suggests that it is the dominance and not the aggressiveness that appeals to females (Chagnon, 1983; Smuts, 1985; Sadalla, Kenrick, & Vershure, 1987). Females seem to prefer sexual partners who are cool and leaderlike rather than hot-headed and violent.

As we indicated earlier, the male preference for youth and physical attractiveness would be explained as due to the fact that it would have served our male ancestors to have selected partners who were physically capable of bearing children. As human females get older, they become less fertile and eventually stop reproducing when they reach menopause. Menopause probably evolved because if our female ancestors survived past age 45 or 50, it better served their genetic interests to cease reproducing and to turn their remaining energies to caring for existing children and grandchildren (Alexander, 1987). Because of the heavy investment female mammals make in their offspring, older females are progressively less able to bear viable offspring (Clutton-Brock, 1984). With increasing age, there is increasing risk of mortality to human females and their offspring (Resnik, 1986). Many mammalian females nevertheless reproduce until they die, because some chance of offspring is better than none at all. This state of affairs does not hold for humans. Since our ancestors lived in extended family groups, a woman could cease reproducing new offspring and still further her genetic interests by caring for her existing progeny. It is interesting to note that males across cultures are not simply interested in a woman 1 or 2 years younger than they are, as expected by the normative explanations of age preference (e.g. Cameron, et al., 1977). Instead, they appear to be most attracted to women who are in their peak years of fertility—the mid-20s. Men in their 20s tend to seek and marry women around their own age; older men seek progressively younger and younger women (relative to their own age). Although teenage men are not very desirable as marriage partners in any part of the world, those who do marry often marry women slightly older (Kenrick & Keefe, 1992).

Misconceptions about the Evolutionary Perspective

The evolutionary perspective suggests that the behavioral differences found between men and women across diverse cultures can be traced to evolutionary pressures that affected the two sexes somewhat differently. Our male ancestors and female ancestors co-evolved, exerting selection pressures on members of the opposite sex that still exist today. The evolutionary perspective has sometimes been accused of being "sexist" because it assumes that the differences between men and women are due to biology. However, the supposedly "enlightened," culturally based perspectives offered instead are not only inadequate to explain the existing data but actually less flattering to both sexes, and particularly to women. Those perspectives assume that women are passive pawns in cultures that omnipotent and secretive men have arbitrarily constructed to give themselves all the power and keep women in their place. The evolutionary perspective, on the other hand, offers a view of female choice as the major driving force behind gender differences in behavior. According to this view, men compete with one another not to exclude women but, ultimately, to attract the attention of women, who are simply more selective about their potential mates.

Another misconception about the evolutionary viewpoint is that it envisions behavior as under the control of genes that are oblivious to the environment. In fact, such a misconception might arise from this chapter, which has thus far argued for universal gender differences that go beyond the bounds of culture. We have focused on these generalities to argue against a radical environmentalism that excludes genetic influences on behavior and that views cultural conventions as infinitely malleable and arbitrary. Cultures are not simply arbitrarily constructed, with no regard to the genetic proclivities of the humans who inhabit them. Instead, human culture and human genes interact in several ways, which we consider next.

GENE–CULTURE INTERACTIONS

The first point to make about the relationship between genes and cultures is that cultures are in some ways constrained by the genes of the individuals making up the culture. A culture that required all 10-year-olds to try to fly off a 1,000-foot cliff would not survive long. For one thing, the inhabitants would probably rebel or run away at the first suggestion of such a custom. If not, the parents of 9-year-olds would protest after observing the results of the first year's trials. Even if its inhabitants could be completely convinced to go along with the practice, the human incapacity for flying would make it such that there would soon be no reproductive members of the society (because all the youth died before puberty).

One doubts that any culture has ever come up with such a custom. However, on the Pentecost Islands, adolescents do occasionally jump from tall towers with vines tied to their legs. The youths start with small towers and short vines, but some eventually go on to construct towers nearly 100 feet high. Because the youths study the technology of jumping and vine tying quite carefully, most do not die, although the sport is dangerous and there is an occasional fatal mishap. As one might guess from the earlier discussion, only young males engage in this dangerous behavior, and it is a form of competition for status among their peers. This "land jumping" is thus a unique and somewhat arbitrary cultural custom, but it seems to have been adopted within the genetic constraints on sex differences. Males are more likely to adopt dangerous and competitive customs than are females. One would expect that across cultures, different customs are adopted differently by males and females to fit their evolved preferences. Thus, military and athletic technologies and competitive games ought to be more appealing to males, whereas activities and technologies related to child care ought to be more appealing to females.

Cultural customs can have different relationships to genetic predispositions. They can exaggerate those predispositions, they can act against them, or they can be irrelevant. If the members of a culture set up training experiences for athletics, martial arts, and military training that exclude females, the inherent sex differences will be exaggerated. Males who are initially inclined to be pacific and sensitive, and girls who appear aggressive and competitive, might be the targets of especially strong coercive training attempts. Eventually the small average differences between two sexes could transform into two nonoverlapping distributions. It has frequently been argued by feminists that this is the state of affairs in modern American society—women and men are forced into tightly constraining roles and are not allowed to be the same. The actual evidence on this is not highly supportive. Cross-cultural studies do not reveal that American society is generally more sex-typed than other societies, and in fact, many societies are much more sex-typed (Daly & Wilson, 1988; Kenrick & Keefe, 1992). If there is role rigidity, it appears to affect males more than females (Carter & McClosky, 1984; O'Leary & Donoghue, 1978). Females in American society feel much more comfortable engaging in traditionally "masculine" activities (such as wearing pants or playing sports) than males feel engaging in traditionally "feminine" activities (such as playing with dolls or wearing dresses).

Cultural pressures can also act against biological predispositions. Many rules against violence, exploitation, and sexuality fall into this category. In fact, in an influential presidential address to the American Psychological Association, Campbell (1975) reasoned that the existence of strong social rules is often a clue to an underlying selfish genetic tendency. A society does not need as many rules to tell people to feed themselves and to take care of their children as it does to keep them from cheating or exploiting unrelated individuals. To some extent, some of the differential cultural pressures on males and females in our society may be designed to act against the unpleasant biological defaults. Boys are more likely to be disciplined for their competitiveness and aggressiveness than are girls, for instance, and the laws against rape are designed to act against hypertrophied tendencies in males, not females.

Finally, the road between genes and culture is not a one-way street. Over time, cultural pressures could be a force in natural selection. If violent males are incarcerated or killed by a society, any genetic tendencies predisposing such violence are likely to decrease in prevalence. In a related manner, cultural institutions may select individuals with particular genetic predispositions for particular roles. If the tallest males have most frequently been chosen as group leaders, and if those with the status of group leaders have access to more mating opportunities (e.g., more wives in a polygynous society), then over time, these cultural institutions could increase the preexisting sex difference in physical size. Such a scenario is not out of line with existing evidence. It is the case, for instance, that taller men win more elections in American and Canadian society (Knapp, 1978) and that high-status men in polygynous societies have more wives (Hill, 1984; Mealey, 1985). Conversely, if women are severely punished for sexual promiscuity (as in societies in which a women can be killed for infidelity, or for failing to give evidence of virginity at marriage [Daly & Wilson, 1983; Freeman, 1983]), then over time, any sex difference in sexual drive could be exaggerated by societal forces. It makes sense to assume that human cultural groups have been a force in the natural selection of human characteristics seen today.

Although it is interesting to speculate about the human evolutionary past, it is very difficult to study social customs in our ancestral cultures. Archaeological records leave hard evidence about cooking implements and weapons, and occasionally petroglyphs and art works yield clues that can be pieced together to form a plausible scenario. Anthropologists also attempt to draw inferences from existing hunter–gatherer cultures, on the assumption that our ancestors spent most of their years in such cultures. However, psychologists are more interested in studying how ongoing behavioral choices, thoughts, and emotions are influenced by observable variations in the environment that unfold over the course of a few minutes, a few days, or several years of the individual life-span. In the next section, we consider how gene–environment interactions might be related to such ongoing processes.

Gene–Environment Interactions

An important lesson of recent research on animal behavior is that genetic factors interact with the environment throughout the animal's life-span. Consider recent findings on cichlid fish from Lake Tanganyika studied by Fernald and his colleagues (Davis & Fernald, 1990). In these fish, adult males take two forms, one large and colorful, the other small and colorless. The presence of a large colorful male has been found to influence the other males' rate of maturation. When no large male is present, males mature more rapidly and there is noticeable development in the area of the hypothalamus that controls development of the gonads and the testes. However, the presence of a large male inhibits development of the crucial hypothalamic cells, and in turn, the gonads of smaller males. If the local territorial male is removed, however, smaller males compete for dominance, and the highest-ranking male goes through a series of hypothalamic and gonadal changes, as well as a sudden increase in size and coloration. The point is that there is an adaptive interplay between genetic predispositions and the social environment in these fish. Such complex interplay between physiology and the environment has been observed in other vertebrate species (e.g., Lehrman, 1966). Is there a similar interplay between genes and environment in humans? At this point, preliminary evidence indicates that the answer is, sometimes, yes. For example, Frisch (1988) has found an interplay between a woman's amount of body fat and the onset of menarche. Young girls will not enter puberty until they have reached a critical ratio of body fat to muscle, and even mature women will stop menstruating if their body fat ratio goes too low. This effect is independent of other indices of health—menstrual termination is often found in highly trained athletes. Frisch argues that a relationship between menstruation and body fat would have made sense for our ancestors, who often faced uncertain supplies of food. Infants do not survive without a reliable source of food. Without an adequate reserve of nutrition (stored as fat), the odds were that a human mother living in a hunter–gatherer ecology might have lost any offspring she produced. Thus, the fat–menstruation relationship serves as an innate insurance policy on the mother's reproductive investment.

In addition to influencing the pace of physical development and the flow of hormones in response to the environment, genetic predispositions might also influence psychological events from momentary cognitions to long-term learning. Differences in physical size provide a simple way to show how a genetically influenced difference between the sexes might lead to different life experiences. The larger size and upper-body development of males make it more likely that certain types of competition and aggressive behavior will result in rewarding outcomes. Such effects can be seen within a sex. All other things being equal, a man with the size and shape of Arnold Schwarzenegger (the former weightlifting champion and star of the movie *The Terminator*) is likely to be treated with more deference and respect by other men, and is likely to receive more amorous attention from women, than is someone the size and shape of Danny DeVito (the short, plump actor who played opposite Schwarzenegger in the movie *Twins*). Two such individuals will thus have different social learning histories and develop different self-concepts and schemas for interpreting social situations. Physical size likewise produces different experiences across the sexes. Few women are likely to experience a stranger's crossing the street to avoid contact with them on a dark night, but men experience it all the time. On the other hand, women probably have learned to have a lower threshold for feeling fear, and taking avoidant measures, at the sight of a lone male walking down the street toward them.

In terms of ongoing cognitive processes, preliminary evidence from our own laboratories indicates that men and women may attend to and remember other people in line with evolved heuristics. In a study of spontaneous recall, if either a man or a woman recalled a member of the opposite sex, that individual tended to be attractive If a member of the subject's own sex was recalled, that individual did not tend to be especially attractive. As would be predicted from our earlier discussion of sex differences in mating strategies, men were generally more likely to remember individuals of the opposite sex, and this held even if the men were romantically attached (Kenrick, 1990; Kenrick & Dengelegi, 1992). Even attached men, it seems, have their antennae tuned for potential mating opportunities. In other research, men rated themselves as less committed to their current partners following exposure to sexually attractive women (Kenrick, Gutierres, & Goldberg, 1989; Kenrick, Neuberg, Zierk, & Krones, 1992). Women's judgments of their partners were less influenced by exposure to physically attractive men. However, consistent with the sexual selection literature discussed above, exposure to socially dominant men undermined women's rated commitment to their partners (Kenrick et al., 1992).

In another study, it was found that subjects' self-ratings were strongly related to their criteria for dating and marital partners (Kenrick et al., 1993). In rating a partner for a casual sexual liaison, the relationship between self-ratings and mate standards was also high for females. That is, the more highly a woman rated her own "social value," the more she demanded in a sexual partner. For males, however, the normal relationship between self-rating and partner criteria was reduced for sexual partners. Although men with higher self-esteem wanted more desirable characteristics in a dating or marital partner, this was not the case for casual sexual partners. Taken as a whole, these findings provide preliminary support for the idea that ongoing thoughts about oneself and members of the opposite sex are influenced by evolved heuristics in interaction with the current environment.

CONCLUSION

Many important sex differences in behavior that have previously been explained as due to the influence of culture appear, instead, to be the result of evolutionary pressures. The concepts of sexual selection and differential parental investment connect human sex differences in competition, aggressiveness, sexuality, and mate choice criteria with a vast literature on life history strategies in other animals. Our evolutionary heritage is expressed through genetic predispositions that interact with the social environment. Genetic predispositions have a direct influence on biochemical and structural differences between men and women and also indirectly influence learning experiences and cognitions. Cultural influences can oppose or exaggerate biological differences between men and women. However, those cultural influences are themselves the products of interactions between human genetic predispositions and the past conditions of human existence.

REFERENCES

Alexander, R. D. (1987). *The biology of moral systems*. New York: Aldine de Gruyter.
Alley, T. R. (1992). Perceived age, physical attractiveness, and sex differences in preferred mates' ages. *Behavioral and Brain Sciences, 15*, 92.
Andersson, M. (1982, October 28). Female choice selects for extreme tail length in a widowbird. *Nature*, pp. 818–820.
Astin, A. W., Green, K. C., Korn, W. S., & Schalit, M. (1987). *The American freshman: National norms for Fall 1987*. Los Angeles: Higher Education Research Institute.
Brehm, S. S. (1985). *Intimate relationships*. New York: Random House.
Broude, G. J. (1992). The May–September algorithm meets the 20th century actuarial table. *Behavioral and Brain Sciences, 15*, 94–95.
Buss, D. M. (1989). Sex differences in human mate preferences: Evolutionary hypotheses tested in 37 cultures. *Behavioral and Brain Sciences, 12*, 1–49.
Buss, D. M. & Barnes, M. F. (1986). Preferences in human mate selection. *Journal of Personality and Social Psychology, 50*, 559–570.
Cameron, C., Oskamp, S., & Sparks, W. (1977). Courtship American style—newspaper ads. *Family Coordinator, 26*, 27–30.
Campbell, D. T. (1975). On the conflicts between biological and social evolution and between psychology and moral tradition. *American Psychologist, 30*, 1103–1126.
Carter, B. D., & McCloskey, L. A. (1984). Peers and the maintenance of sex-typed behavior: The development of children's conceptions of cross-gender behavior in their peers. *Social Cognition, 2*; 294–314.
Chagnon, N. A. (1983). *Yanomamo: The fierce people* (3rd ed.). New York: Holt, Rinehart & Winston.
Chimbos, P. D. (1978). *Marital violence: A study of interspouse homicide*. San Francisco: R & E Research Associates.
Clutton-Brock, T.H. (1984). Reproductive effort and terminal investment in iteroparous animals. *American Naturalist, 123*, 212–229.
Clutton-Brock, T. H. (1991, October). Lords of the lek. *Natural History*, pp. 34–41.
Cunningham, M.R. (1986). Measuring the physical in physical attractiveness: Quasi-experiments on the sociobiology of female beauty. *Journal of Personality and Social Psychology, 50*, 925–935.
Daly, M., & Wilson, M. (1983). *Sex, evolution, and behavior* (2nd ed.). Belmont, CA: Wadsworth.
Daly, M., & Wilson, M. (1988). *Homicide*. New York: Aldine de Gruyter.
Darwin, C. (1873). *The expression of emotions in man and animals*. London: Murray.
Darwin, C. (1958). *The origin of species by natural selection or the preservation of favoured races in the struggle for life*. New York: Mentor. (Original work published 1859)

Davis, M. R., & Fernald, R. D. (1990). Social control of neuronal soma size. *Journal of Neurobiology, 21*, 1180–1188.

Dawkins, R. (1976). *The selfish gene.* Oxford, England: Oxford University Press.

Deutsch, F. M., Zalenski, C. M., & Clark, M. E. (1986). Is there a double standard of aging? *Journal of Applied Social Psychology, 16*: 771–775.

Doyle, J. A. (1985). *Sex and gender.* Dubuque, IA: W.C. Brown.

Freeman, D. (1983). *Margaret Mead and Samoa.* Cambridge, MA: Harvard University Press.

Frisch, R. E. (1988, March). Fatness and fertility. *Scientific American*, pp. 88–95.

Gross, M. (1984). Sunfish, salmon, and the evolution of alternative reproductive strategies and tactics in fishes. In G. Potts & R. Wootton (Eds.), *Fish reproduction: Strategies and tactics* (pp. 55–75). New York: Academic Press.

Harpending, H. (1992). Age differences between mates in southern African pastoralists. *Behavioral and Brain Sciences, 15*, 102–103.

Hendrick, S. S., Hendrick, C., Slapion-Foote, J., & Foote, F.H. (1985). Gender differences in sexual attitudes. *Journal of Personality and Social Psychology, 54*, 1630–1642.

Hiatt, L.R. (1980). Polyandry in Sri Lanka: A test case for parental investment theory. *Man, 15*, 583–602.

Hill, J. (1884). Prestige and reproductive success in man. *Ethology and Sociobiology, 5*, 77–95.

Johnson, R. E. (1970). Some correlates of extramarital coitus. *Journal of Marriage and the Family, 32*, 449–456.

Kenrick, D. T. (1987). Gender, genes, and the social environment: A biosocial interactionist perspective. In P. Shaver & C. Hendrick (Eds.), *Review of personality and social psychology* (Vol. 7, pp. 14–43). Newbury Park, CA: Sage.

Kenrick, D. T. (1990). Personality and reproductive behavior: Integrating the social psychological and the evolutionary perspectives. In R.W. Bell (Ed.), *Sociobiology and the social sciences.* (Vol. 7, *Interfaces in Psychology* series). Lubbock, TX: Texas Tech Press.

Kenrick, D. T., & Dengelegi, L. (1992). *Gender differences in spontaneous recall of faces.* Unpublished manuscript, Arizona State University, Tempe.

Kenrick, D. T., Groth, G. E., Trost, M. R., & Sadalla, E. K. (1993). Integrating evolutionary and social exchange perspectives on relationships: Effects of gender, self-appraisal, and involvement level on mate selection. *Journal of Personality and Social Psychology, 64*, 951–969.

Kenrick, D. T., Gutierres, S. E., & Goldberg, L. (1989). Influence of popular erotica on judgments of strangers and mates. *Journal of Experimental Social Psychology, 38*, 131–140.

Kenrick, D. T., & Keefe, R. C. (1992). Age preferences in mates reflect sex differences in mating strategies. *Behavioral and Brain Sciences, 15*, 75–91.

Kenrick, D. T., Neuberg, S. E., Zierk, K., & Krones, J. (in press). Evolution and social cognition: Contrast effects as a function of sex, dominance, and attractiveness. *Personality and Social Psychology Bulletin.*

Kenrick, D. T., Sadalla, E. K., Groth, G., & Trost, M. R. (1990). Evolution, traits, and the stages of human courtship: Qualifying the parental investment model. *Journal of Personality, 58*, 97–116.

Kenrick, D. T., Stringfield, D. O., Wagenhals, W. L., Dahl, R. H., & Ransdell, H. J. (1980). Sex differences, androgyny, and approach responses to erotica: A new variation on the old volunteer problem. *Journal of Personality and Social Psychology, 38*, 517–524.

Kenrick, D.T., & Trost, M.R. (1987). A biosocial model of relationship formation. In K. Kelley (Ed.), *Females, males and sexuality: Theories and research* (pp. 59–100). Albany, NY: SUNY Press.

Kenrick, D. T., & Trost, M. R. (1989). A reproductive exchange model of hetero-sexual relationships: Putting proximate economics in ultimate perspective. In C. Hendrick (Ed.), *Review of personality and social psychology* (Vol. 10, pp. 92–118). Newbury Park, CA: Sage.

Kerr, N. L., Harmon, D. L., & Graves, J. K. (1982). Independence of multiple verdicts by jurors and juries. *Journal of Applied Social Psychology, 12*, 12–29.

Knapp, M. L. (1978). *Nonverbal communication in human interaction* (2nd ed.). New York: Holt, Rinehart & Winston.

Lagerspetz, K. (1979). Modification of aggressiveness in mice. In S. Feshbach & A. Fraczek (Eds.), *Aggression and behavior change: Biological and social processes* (pp. 66–82). New York: Praeger.

Lancaster, J. B. (1985). Evolutionary perspectives on sex differences in the higher primates. In A. S. Rossi (Ed.) *Gender and the life course* (pp. 3–28). New York: Aldine de Gruyter.

Lehrman, D. S. (1966). The reproductive behavior of ring-doves. In S. Coopersmith (Ed.), *Frontiers of psychological research* (pp. 81–92). San Francisco: W. H. Freeman.

Levine, N. E. (1980). Nyinba polyandry and the allocation of paternity. *Journal of Comparative Family Studies, 11*, 283–298.

Margolin, L., & White, L. (1987). The continuing role of physical attractiveness in marriage. *Journal of Marriage, 49*, 21–27.

Mead, M. (1928). *Coming of age in Samoa.* New York: William Morrow.

Mead, M. (1935). *Sex and temperament in three primitive societies.* New York: William Morrow.

Mealey, L. (1985). The relationship between social status and biological success: A case study of the Mormon religious hierarchy. *Ethology and Sociobiology, 6*, 249–257.

Murdock, G. (1935). Comparative data on the division of labor by sex. *Social Forces, 15*, 551–553.

Myers, D. G. (1990). *Social psychology* (3rd ed.). New York: McGraw-Hill.

O'Leary, V. E., & Donoghue, J. M. (1978). Latitudes of masculinity: Reactions to sex-role deviance in men. *Journal of Social Issues, 34*, 17–28.

Plomin, R., DeFries, J. C., & McClearn, G. E. (1990). *Behavioral genetics: A primer* (2nd ed.). San Francisco: W. H. Freeman.

Presser, H. B. (1975). Age differences between spouses: Trends, patterns, and social implications. *American Behavioral Scientist, 19*, 190–205.

Ralls, K. (1976). Mammals in which females are larger than males. *Quarterly Review of Biology, 51*, 245–276.

Resnik, R. (1986). Age-related changes in gestation and pregnancy outcome. In L. Mastroianni & C. A. Paulsen (Eds.) *Aging, reproduction, and the climacteric* (pp. 167–175). New York: Plenum Press.

Sadalla, E. K., Kenrick, D. T., & Vershure, B. (1987). Dominance and heterosexual attraction. *Journal of Personality and Social Psychology, 52,* 730–738.

Salzano, F.M., Neel, J.V., & Maybury-Lewis, D. (1967). Further studies on the Xavante Indians. I: Demographic data on two additional villages: Genetic structure of the tribe. *American Journal of Human Genetics, 19,* 463–489.

Sigusch, V., & Schmidt, G. (1971). Lower-class sexuality: Some emotional and social aspects in West German males and females. *Archives of Sexual Behavior, 1,* 29–44.

Smuts, B. B. (1985). *Sex and friendship in baboons.* New York: Aldine de Gruyter.

Symons, D. (1979). *The evolution of human sexuality.* Oxford, England: Oxford University Press.

Townsend, J. M. (1989). Mate selection criteria: A pilot study. *Ethology and Sociobiology, 10,* 241–253.

Trivers, R. L. (1972). Parental investment and sexual selection. In B. Campbell (Ed.), *Sexual selection and the descent of man* (pp. 136–179). Chicago: Aldine de Gruyter.

Trivers, R. L. (1985). *Social evolution,* Menlo Park, CA: Benjamin/Cummings.

Warner, R. R. (1984). Mating behavior and hermaphrodotism in coral reef fishes. *American Scientist, 72,* 128–134.

Williams, J. E. & Best, D. L. (1982). Measuring sex stereotypes. Beverly Hills, CA: Sage.

Wolfgang, M. E. (1958). *Patterns in criminal homicide.* Philadelphia: University of Pennsylvania Press.

Aspects of Early Gender Development: A Psychodynamic Perspective

IRENE FAST

In psychodynamic conceptions of gender organization, Freud's formulations remain central. They serve either as accepted frameworks for understanding developmental and clinical observations or as foci of opposition. Here I take the position that Freud's observations and his conceptions close to his clinical base have, in the main, stood the test of time and must be accounted for in any comprehensive theory of gender organization. However, the conceptual frames in which he casts these observations are in major ways untenable.

This chapter begins with an outline of Freud's theory of gender development, followed by a brief review of attempts to reconceptualize various aspects of gender development. I argue that both Freud's own observations and those made subsequently and now widely accepted require a fundamentally different theoretical model than the one Freud developed.

I propose a differentiation paradigm as a framework that might accommodate the clinical and developmental observations that gave rise to Freud's model while avoiding its conceptual difficulties. Such a framework is valuable in integrating issues of gender development with a larger body of developmental issues within psychoanalytic psychology and with differentiation perspectives outside it, in particular Piaget's work.

The body of the chapter addresses three phases in early gender development that are central to Freud's theory: the period prior to children's becoming aware of the differences between the sexes, the period (around age 18–24 months) when that recognition becomes focal, and the subsequent oedipal period. In differentiation terms these phases reflect an early undifferentiated period, a period in which sexual differences first become a focus of interest, and a period of differentiation proper. Each section addresses relevant issues in terms of established psychoanalytic theory, a possible reconceptualization in differentiation terms, and the integration of the proposed perspective with psychoanalytic conceptions of children's emergence from narcissistic experience (experience in which the child does not take into account the independence of the nonself world) and Piaget's developmental model.

FREUD'S CONCEPTIONS OF GENDER DEVELOPMENT

At the heart of Freud's theories of gender organization lies his profoundly phallocentric conception of libido. Libido is a biologically based sexual energy that, in the course of development, patterns adult sex and gender experience. Freud defines libido as fundamentally male, or as itself neutral but most forcefully expressed in a male context.

In the first of Freud's three phases, beginning at birth, boys' and girls' sex and gender experiences are identical. Boys begin life male in anatomy, male in the libidinal influences associated with their male genitals, and masculine in their libidinally based, cross-sex relation to their mother. Girls are anatomically bisexual, the clitoris a male organ and the vagina a female one. In early life only the clitoris is within girls' experience. The libidinal influences associated with it are male. Girls' relations to their mothers are, like boys', cross-sex. That is, both girls' and boys' early sex and gender experiences are fundamentally male and masculine.

In the second stage, beginning at about 18 to 24 months, children become aware of the differences between the sexes. In Freud's conception, maleness is central here too: Children at this age know only one sex, the male one; in their understanding, sex difference is a matter of having, or not having, a penis. Freud suggests that boys' reactions are relatively straightforward: They become aware that girls do not have genitals like their own and become afraid that they too might lose theirs.

His conception of girls' development is more complex. He attempts to account for the emergence of femininity from the early maleness and masculinity he ascribes to girls. He proposes that girls respond to the recognition of sexual differences with feelings that, having no penis, they have no genitals at all, or only inferior ones (the clitoris). They react with feelings of loss and envy, demands for restitution, and secret hopes that they might have a penis after all (perhaps one is inside, or will grow). They turn away from their mothers toward their fathers in disappointment and anger because the mother did not give them what she gave boys, or because she, too, is incomplete. This turn away from the mother toward the father starts them on the path to femininity, toward heterosexual relatedness.

These developments usher in the third phase, the oedipal period. Now boys, in masculine competition with their fathers for their mothers, give up their determination to best their fathers and take their appropriate places as male and masculine in the wider social world. Girls, in their new relationships to their fathers, initially hope that he will give them the penis they want. Gradually, however, they give up that wish and with it the activity and aggression associated with maleness in favor of a passive, feminine relationship to the father and the wish for a baby from him.

Freud's clinical observations of men's hidden wishes to bear a child, to be impregnated by another man, and to take the female role in sexual intercourse could not be accommodated in this fully phallocentric account. These observations led him to add another dimension to his theory. He posited a biologically based masculine and feminine theme in all persons, present from birth and influential throughout life.[1] In males, the feminine aspect of this bisexuality is expressed in wishes to take a female role with the father. It seemed to Freud that this theme was associated in his patients with issues of sex difference and of the early oedipal period. When boys become focally aware that they are male, the feminine theme becomes prominent because, being male, they must renounce the possibilities of femaleness; when the boy–father relationship of the oedipal period becomes central, boys first attempt a relationship to him as female to male, before engaging in the masculine competition of the Oedipus complex. It is the incomplete resolution of conflicts at these two developmental transitions that Freud believed were represented in his clinical observations of his male patients.

TOWARD AN ALTERNATE CONCEPTION OF EARLY GENDER DEVELOPMENT

From the time Freud (1925/1961, 1931/1961) first proposed it, his conception of gender development in women met with strong opposition. Among its earliest critics were Horney (1926), Jacobson (1968), Thompson (1943),

---

[1] Freud ascribed this bisexuality to women as well as to men. However, probably because bisexuality in women is already implied in the conception that women develop from masculinity to femininity, the bisexuality theory has been used primarily in its application to men.

and Zilboorg (1944). Recently, stimulated at least in part by renewed interest in the place of women in Western society, questions about their gender development are being raised with new vigor. These questions are leading to detailed explorations of various aspects of Freud's conceptions: examinations of Freud's hypothesis that girls' entry into the oedipal phase is stimulated by penis envy and castration anxiety (Parens, Pollock, Stern, & Kramer, 1977); unexpected observations that in girls, a developmental spurt follows their recognition of sex differences and its associated anxiety (Galenson & Roiphe, 1977); investigations of girls' reactions to boys' not having a vagina (Mayer, 1985); conceptions of girls' relations to their fathers as influential in patterning their wishes to be like him in having a penis (Benjamin, 1991); the superego structures of women as different than men's, rather than inferior to theirs (Gilligan, 1982); and sociological investigations of the place of mothering in women's lives (Chodorow, 1978).

Freud's theory of male development has stimulated no such widespread opposition and investigation. It has been generally accepted as valid in psychoanalytic thinking. However, beginning with a few early voices and increasing in volume more recently, explorations are being made that are likely to result in major theory revision. Among them are Bettelheim's (1954) theory of womb envy in boys reciprocal to penis envy in girls, Stoller's (1968) explorations of the relative importance of internal (libido) forces and environmental factors in the developmental sequence Freud proposed, Kleeman's (1966) study of genital self-discovery in a small boy, Kaftal's (1991) elaboration of boys' affectionate and cooperative ties to their fathers in relation to the competitive ties of Freud's theory, and the seminal studies of severe gender disorders in young boys by Coates and her colleagues (Coates, Friedman, & Wolfe, 1991).

My own interests have drawn me to more general considerations of Freud's theory and toward an alternative framework for accommodating psychoanalytic observations of gender development and organization. Such an approach has the advantage of greater comprehensiveness than studies of various components of Freud's theory but must, of course, fall short of the valuable attention to detail made possible by more narrowly focused approaches.

My interests arose, like those of others, out of dissatisfactions with Freud's conception of gender development in girls. On the one hand, Freud's observations seemed to be generally accepted. It appeared to be reliably observed that girls begin a major developmental advance toward a feminine gender identity at about 18 to 24 months of age. This advance is triggered by their becoming focally aware of the differences between the sexes. That awareness is associated with feelings of loss or damage. These feelings focus on maleness, specifically on male genital organs. The recognition of sex difference is followed by complex changes in girls' relations to their mothers and fathers. The wish to have a baby with the father tends to signal the successful negotiation of these developments.

On the other hand, Freud's theoretical model was altogether unacceptable. All the major propositions that shaped his phallocentric account of girls' sex and gender organizations have been found to be untenable. It is now well-known that the clitoris is not a male organ. Girls' early libidinal aims cannot be considered to be male on this basis. It is generally accepted that girls are not oblivious to their vaginas in early life (Galenson & Roiphe, 1977; Greenacre, 1950; Kestenberg, 1968; Mayer, 1985; Parens, et al., 1977; Torok, 1970). The mother is recognized as an object of identification for girls, not (or not only) one of cross-sex interest. Freud's hypothesis that girls are male and masculine in their earliest gender organization is thus left without support. His attempt to frame his observations of girls' gender development in a scheme that traces it from masculinity to femininity has lost its center.

A new formulation is needed, one that must accommodate widely accepted observations of girls' gender development on a base that does not have the conceptual problems of Freud's model.

It seems clear that a formulation of gender development in girls must also take into account its development in boys. Here new difficulties arise. Although critical attention has focused almost exclusively on Freud's conceptions of femininity, the theoretical problems of his theories of male gender development appear to be no less severe. They seem to be created by the same phallocentrism that colored his views of women. Freud's altogether male-centered conception of boys' gender development did not allow for his clinical observations of feminine themes in men. However, the bisexuality theory he proposed to account for these observations was incompatible with the developmental theory in fundamental ways.

In Freud's bisexuality theory, biological influences do not predispose the boy only to masculinity, as in the developmental framework, but also to feminine orientations. The boy does not assume that everyone is male like himself; he also has within himself a constitutionally based femininity. The recognition of sex difference not only signifies the possession or lack of a penis but includes the renunciation of feminine wishes. The boy's sex-difference-related castration anxiety stems not only from the possibility that he will lose his penis, as the girl has done, but also from an incomplete renunciation of his female wishes.

Freud recognized the incompatibility of the two accounts but was unable to resolve it. Toward the end of his career, Freud (1937/1964) spoke with regret about his inability to reconcile these two perspectives in a developmental framework despite his efforts throughout his working life.

It seems now that to be acceptable, a new formulation must apply to both male and female gender development. Moreover, this new formulation must show promise of accommodating observations of male gender development subsumed under both the developmental and the bisexuality theories.

Finally, it is clear that Freud's phallocentric emphasis extended to his views of parental influences on children's gender development. In his conception, the mother has *no* positive place. In girls' development, Freud finds no identifications with the mother that encourage feminine development. Only as girls turn away from the mother in disappointment and contempt for her lack of a penis do they move toward femininity. Their wishes for a baby occur not at all in identification with the mother. They are directed to the father and are replacements of their wishes for a penis from him.

Similarly, boys' earliest relationships to their mothers do not include identifications. The feminine wishes they renounce on recognition of sex differences (bisexuality theory) have nothing to do with the mother. They are biologically based and patterned feminine themes. Boys' wishes to bear a child are unrelated to identifications with or relationships to their mothers. They are constitutionally patterned feminine wishes to give the father a child. In oedipal conflicts, the determinative factors concern boys' relations to their fathers. These conflicts with the father are about the mother, but, Freud argued, the relationship to the mother itself has been heterosexual from birth and exerts no new influences during this period.

The importance of both mothers and fathers in children's gender development is now well established. A reformulation, therefore, must take into account the place of the mother in the gender development of both boys and girls. Moreover, it seems to me that it must do so without slighting the importance of the father.

A DIFFERENTIATION PERSPECTIVE

A differentiation paradigm seems to offer possibilities for the needed reformulation. It lends itself comfortably to the identification of three stages in early gender development congruent with those Freud proposed: an early undifferentiated period, a period in which children begin to differentiate those sex and gender characteristics appropriately ascribed to themselves and those that must be seen to be exclusively the prerogatives of other-sex persons, and a subsequent period in which they work out the implications of sex differences in their relations to the males and females in their lives.

This differentiation perspective also has broader implications, both within psychoanalytic psychology and outside it. Within psychoanalytic theory the differentiation perspective is congruent with conceptions of narcissism and developments out of narcissistic forms of experience. In narcissistic experience, all possibilities are included within the as yet inchoate self. Transitions beyond narcissistic constructions of experience become focal at about 18 to 24 months, the time when children appear also to become aware of the differences between the sexes. Each transition includes a recognition of limit. It requires children to recognize which of the attributes or capacities that they have uncritically assumed to be their own may be included in the self and which are in fact independent of it.

Among the transitions most actively investigated clinically are those from illusions of omnipotence to a differentiated recognition of intention (self) and causality (independent of self), from illusions of primary creativity to a recognition of thought (self) and what is thought about (nonself), and from illusions of an undifferentiated self-other unity to a recognition of one's own individuated self and of others independent of self (Fast, 1984). In this context, gender differentiation could be one among several major differentiations in narcissistic organizations of experience: an increasingly accurate recognition of what may be included as part of one's gender-specific self and what must be recognized as belonging to persons of the other gender.

In this form, a differentiation model of gender development might also link psychoanalytic observations and conceptions with a broader range of psychological theory through Piaget's conceptions. Throughout Piaget's working life, his fundamental interest was "examining the boundary the child draws between the self and the external world" (Piaget, 1929, p. 34) or the capacity accurately to distinguish the subjective and the objective (Piaget, 1970). Piaget elaborated the development of this boundary in his early studies of language and thought in children, their conceptions of causality, and their understanding of the world. It underlies his later studies of infancy and the development of his stage theory. Each boundary establishment is a development out of egocentrism, in which individuals uncritically assume that everything is a function of their own actions, toward a capacity accurately to recognize what must be seen to be independent of themselves.

In Piaget's model, as in psychoanalytic conceptions of narcissism, a developmental stage beginning at about 18 to 24 months takes on a particular importance: The preoperational period replaces the sensorimotor stage. Now, the child's new capacities for thought make possible major developments from autocentrism to allocentrism. From this perspective, gender differentiation falls in the context of developments beyond egocentrism, with particular focus on the period from 18 to 24 months, when the child, in the context of achieving the capacity for preoperational thought, becomes focally aware of the differences between the sexes.

DIFFERENTIATION PARAMETERS
IN GENDER DEVELOPMENT

The Early Undifferentiated Period

Freud's conceptions of an early anatomical and physiological maleness and masculinity in boys, of a bisexuality in girls of which only the male–masculine aspect is experientially available to them, and of biologically based masculine and feminine themes in all individuals are largely discounted now in psychodynamic thought. Current perspectives agree that at birth, boys and girls are anatomically male and female, respectively. The contribution of physiological influences to gender organization is the subject of energetic exploration and debate, but the kinds and degrees of such influences remain unclear. As Stoller (1968) elaborates, however, it is generally accepted that social influences override physiological ones in human gender organization. They permeate the child's experience from the time of sex ascription at birth in caregivers' pervasive encouragement of the child's development in directions the caregivers find appropriate to the child's sex.

These anatomical, physiological, and social factors are hypothesized here to constitute the earliest matrix for gender development. In the course of the next 18 to 24 months, children establish mental contents that provide the base for later gender differentiation. From the beginning of life, the infant's biological structures and functions (especially its genitals) are central to caregivers' identification of the infant as a girl or boy. Although the infant does not yet experience its genitals in gender terms, they probably color patterns of child care in subtle but pervasive ways. The infant's activities—vigorous, languid, alert, tender, assertive, curious, or angry— may be variously encouraged or discouraged by caregivers as sex appropriate. Mental registrations of the infant's interactions with females and males in the intimacies of everyday life provide further materials that will, at the point of gender differentiation, help to structure the child's personal meanings of "girl" and "boy"/"man" and "woman."

These mental contents are largely gender appropriate. Children's experiences of their own body and the encouragement of their social surrounds typically lay a solid foundation for a culture-congruent sense of a sex-specific self that will emerge in the differentiation processes. However, the available mental contents are also overinclusive. Children's registrations of their experience are narcissistic (psychoanalysis) or egocentric (Piaget). In their interactions with the males and females in their lives they do not differentiate the sex and gender aspects attributable to themselves and those that belong exclusively to other-sex persons. Therefore, they include in their inchoate selves representations of both male and female aspects of the persons in their lives.

This model postulates an early gender-undifferentiated period of a particular sort. It does not suggest that the child's early experience is not gender relevant. On the contrary. From the time of birth the infant's experience of its own body is sex specific, and the infant's interactions with others are colored by others' orientations to its sex. In this early period, however, children *themselves* do not categorize these bodily and social experiences in gender terms. It is in this sense that their experience is undifferentiated. Children exclude no aspect of experience as inappropriate or impossible for themselves on the basis of their being a girl or a boy. In adultomorphic terms, a girl or boy might, without contradiction, imagine *being* (or becoming) Mom, Grandma, Dad, Brother Billy, or Aunt Maude.

Such a view of children's early nondifferentiation in gender experience shows promise of meeting the theoretical requirements outlined previously. It applies equally to girls and to boys. Relationships to both parents are important, not, as Freud's theory suggests, only those to the father. And, perhaps most important, such a view allows for both a fundamentally gender-appropriate early gender organization *and* the occurrence of bisexual themes within the same formulation: On the one hand, it suggests that boys and girls are not exclusively male in the anatomy and physiology available to their experience but are male and female, respectively, and that the social environment encourages gender-appropriate development. On the other hand, such a view suggests that their narcissistic mental organizations are overinclusive, containing both gender-appropriate representations and ones that they will later have to exclude as impossible or inappropriate to themselves because of their sex and gender.

No direct quantitative evaluation of this conception of early nondifferentiation in gender experience is available at this time. However, ideas that persons include within themselves both femaleness and maleness might suggest residues of a time in development when both were included in the self. From a developmental perspective (to be discussed more fully later), these ideas must reflect some growth beyond fully undifferentiated experience: Complete nondifferentiation could hardly be observed; the inclusion of the male and female within one individual suggests that the two categories are being formed but that they are not yet accurately attributed to male and female persons.

Ideas that both sexes can exist together in one person can readily be found in artistic and cultural artifacts and reports of disturbed development. New Ireland sculptures of humans show both breasts and penises on the same figure (private collection). Moravia (1974) reports that among the Dogoni, an African group, village plans are laid out in the form of a hermaphrodite with maleness on one side and femaleness on the other. Among the Bambara of the Niger delta, a major god, Faro, is androgynous.

Puberty rites, studied anthropologically, have also been interpreted as focusing on issues of bisexuality. Among the Bambara, Moravia (1974) reports, boys are considered androgynous until they reach puberty. Circumcision, occurring at that time, is believed to point the boy toward a definitive maleness. And Bettelheim (1954) traces similar implications of puberty rites across a larger array of cultures. He suggests that these rites are ceremonial ways of taking the roles and functions of one's own and of the opposite sex in order to come to terms with the duality of the sexes. They help boys and girls to give up the notion that they can be bisexually complete and to commit themselves firmly to their appropriate sex roles.

In Western civilization, too, the notion of bisexual completeness is not foreign to cultural expression. The Greek myths speak of Hermaphroditus, in whom a man and woman are united, and of the thoroughly male Zeus giving birth to Athena. In a charming thirteenth-century miniature, Adam and Eve are portrayed in paradise, each, in this edenic perfection, with both male and female genitals (Rudolfski, 1984). And within present memory, a cover of a *New Yorker* (1980) magazine portrays a stylized playing card which, seen one way up, is the queen and the other way, the king.

Freud's own clinical observations, although not his interpretations of them, suggest the persistence of such ideas in the course of development. In a familiar footnote, Freud (1923/1961, p. 31, n. 1) describes a young woman who, long after she had given up the idea that she might have a penis, still believed that her mother's friends did. Freud uses the example to show the universality of the wish to have a penis. But this young woman did not attribute maleness to her mother's friends. They were, in her fantasy, women who *also* had penises. They were bisexually complete. Similarly, when Freud's (1909/1955) patient, familiarly called Little Hans, asserts that his father could *so* have a baby, he was in no say denying his father's essential masculinity. It was his solidly male father who could also bear a child. And the Wolf Man, the patient in Freud's (1918/1955) most extensive study, preoccupied with the possibility that males too could give birth, did not wish to have female capacities *instead of* male ones but *in addition to* them (Fast, 1984, Ch. 7).

In my clinical experience too, such ideas are not foreign. For one young male patient, unusually persistent, though initially hidden, ideas of bisexual wholeness underlay conscious fears of homosexuality. Clinical exploration suggested that they were related to a long-standing sense that he lived for both himself and his sister who had died in infancy. In the therapy of a woman, transitory but frightening feelings of physical merger with her husband arose when she became aware of fantasies that he was no more than her male appendage and that a much desired pregnancy would utterly fulfill her desires: Then she would have the unmistakable insignia of both maleness and femaleness. For a male visual artist, a sudden acute awareness of his female sexual partner's lack of a penis subsumed a sense of his own sexual limits: It led to explorations of work difficulties focused on his sense that without the ability to bear children, his creativity was altogether second rate.

THE RECOGNITION OF SEXUAL DIFFERENCES

Freud's conception of an early developmental period in which children become aware of the differences between the sexes is arguably one of his most seminal contributions to our understanding of gender development. Although Freud assigned major developments beyond narcissism to this same period, he did not frame his observations and ideas about gender development in these terms. Instead, he carried forward the strongly phallocentric themes of his libido theory. Freud argued that based on their clitoral and phallic experience, respectively, girls and boys initially know only one sex, the male one. Therefore, children understand sex differences only as the possession or lack of a penis.

It follows that when children begin to recognize sex differences, only girls must come to terms with sex and gender limits: They must recognize that boys have something valuable that they do not. They react with feelings of loss and inadequacy, envy of the male, complex denial of the fact that they are lacking a phallus, and demands for restitution. Boys experience no sex and gender limitation. They become aware only that girls have no penis and become fearful that they might lose theirs. Issues of inadequacy or incompleteness, envy, denial, and demands for restitution do not arise.

However, the notion that boys too must come to terms with sex and gender limits and that their reactions are complementary to those of girls in intensity and form was raised again and again by Freud's clinical observations. It is represented most clearly in two persistent themes in Freud's thinking about gender issues. Both have to do with male orientations to women's capacity to bear a child.

The first concerns children's interest in where babies come from. Freud's observations suggested to him that this was children's first sexual question and that failure to resolve it satisfactorily could have profound effects on later life. Freud spoke of this as an issue for "children," but in several ways he seems implicitly to have seen it as central only to boys' concerns. He uses the impersonal "he" to refer to the "child." However, Freud continues, in reference to children, to speak of "their" penises—an evidently unintended narrowing of the issue to one for boys (Freud, 1908/1959, p. 218). Moreover, in Freud's published case histories, the issue arises focally for male patients in three of his four major cases but for none of the female patients he discusses. And in a later footnote, Freud (1925/1961, p. 252, n. 2) comes to the conclusion that although the origin of babies may be the first sex and gender issue for boys, it is not so for girls.

However, Freud could not accommodate these clinical observations and their implications for boys' recognition of sex and gender limits in his developmental theory. More than once (e.g., Freud, 1907/1953, 1908/1959, 1910/1957) he explicitly raised the possibility that the question of where babies come from might be a sex-difference issue. If it were, it must be one for boys, who, if they recognize that babies grow in female bodies, must give up the possibility of bearing a child themselves. It would be a sexual limit reciprocal to girls' having to recognize that male genitals cannot be theirs. However, each time Freud raised the possibility, he rejected it. He argued that children know nothing about female genital organization, and that, furthermore, because they believe that babies emerge from the anus, children assume that boys and girls are equally able to give birth.

The second theme in Freud's observations that seemed to suggest that boys do experience the female ability to give birth as a sex and gender limit for themselves was the one that led to his postulating a biologically based bisexuality. It was the pervasive wish he observed in his male patients to be able to bear a child.

However, not only can the notion of a biologically based bisexuality not be integrated with Freud's developmental framework, but the characteristics it ascribes to the feminine theme of that bisexuality are contrary to those Freud actually observed clinically in his male patients. In his conception, the boy's feminine theme is a passive and masochistic one. It is directed to the father in a wish to be penetrated by him and to bear him a child. However, in his published case studies, most fully elaborated in those of Little Hans (Freud, 1909/1955) and the Wolf Man (Freud, 1918/1955), the ability to bear a child is not at all passive and masochistic. It is a desirable capacity, one that the boy wishes he had. It is oriented to the mother, not to the father. It is not a wish to be female but a wish that a boy or man might also be able to carry a child in his own body. In both patients this wish carries with it the conviction that not to be able to bear a child is a major loss, envy of women, and denials in the form of beliefs (conscious or unconscious) that boys too have the capacity to bear a child. (These issues are more fully elaborated elsewhere, specifically as they are expressed in the Wolf Man case [Fast, 1984].)

In sum, Freud's clinically based hypothesis, that in the second and third years of children's lives they become focally involved in ideas about the differences between the sexes, is widely accepted. However, his conception of the primacy of maleness can only partially account for his observations. It deals intensively with girls' recognition of the masculinity that cannot be theirs and the feelings of loss, envy, and denial that may ensue. However, it cannot accommodate Freud's own observations that boys experience the female capacity to give birth as setting sex and gender limits for themselves.

Those observations can find a place in a differentiation model. The view that children's reactions to the recognition of sex differences originate in narcissistic (Freud) or egocentric (Piaget) experience offers possibilities of including the reactions of both girls and boys. In such perspectives, children are not viewed as altogether male and masculine in their early experience. Nor are they conceived of as fundamentally bisexual. They are seen, instead, as not having differentiated the mass of their gender-relevant mental representations into those that may be included as possibilities for themselves and those that must be relinquished as possible only for other-sex persons.

Becoming aware of the differences between the sexes, then, means recognizing that there are two sexual categories among people, and working out the implications of belonging to one of the categories. Every development beyond narcissism or egocentrism requires children to become aware of the limits of what can be included as part of themselves. Both girls and boys, not only girls, must become aware of sex and gender limits. Both must accept the fact that characteristics that they have uncritically accepted as their own belong exclusively to other-sex persons.

The bodily focus of children's ideas about sex differences is not exclusively the penis. Rather, both boys and girls are seen to focus their sex-difference preoccupations on bodily aspects of other-sex persons that do, in fact, distinguish the sexes—girls on the penis, boys on the woman's capacity to give birth. Having, or not having, a penis, then, is a central early issue for girls, not for boys, as they struggle with establishing a gendered self. Reciprocally, where babies come from is a first sexual question, as Freud hypothesized—not for children, however, but for boys. Men's wishes to bear a child do not require postulating an inborn bisexuality. They can be understood developmentally as originating in boys' focus on the female capacity to give birth as the insignia of all that they believe they must give up as possibilities for themselves because they are male.

This differentiation model does not follow Freud (1925/1961) in suggesting that the meanings children ascribe to the maleness or femaleness that cannot be theirs are biologically defined—the male as active and sadistic; the female as passive and masochistic. It suggests, rather that the meanings include whatever children ascribe to maleness or femaleness as a result of their experience and capacity for understanding. For example, a girl may *believe* that without a penis she has nothing, no worthwhile genital organ. She may give up activity, adventurousness, and independence for passivity and masochism, but these are not biological givens determined by an actual physical lack. Similarly, a boy may *believe* that without the powerful creativity with which he invests childbearing he is without creative power, doomed to an empty and impersonal life. These are not, however, biological givens determined by his maleness. Rather, they are meanings with which he has invested femaleness.

The reactions of *both* boys and girls to the recognition of limit are likely to include feelings of loss, envy, denial, and demands for restitution. The denial of sex difference in this model does not result in children's believing that everyone is male like themselves, as Freud thought, but that everyone has *all* sex and gender possibilities: A father can give birth although altogether masculine; the women friends of one's mother, although fully female, also have penises; a man can live for both himself and his sister; a woman can have a male appendage and also be pregnant. Envy of the other sex and demands for restitution occur in both boys and girls. Both assume that other-sex persons, having what they themselves lack, are bisexually complete. Demands for restitution are not limited to girls' wishes for a penis. They are wishes in both boys and girls to have the possibilities of other-sex persons in addition to their own.

Although Freud's conceptions of girls' reactions to their recognition of sexual differences have been the focus of elaboration and controversy from the time they were first proposed, no theory-directed attention has been paid to complementary reactions in boys. A potentially fruitful area of inquiry might be explorations of men's reactions to their wives' pregnancies. If boys' early reactions to the recognition of sex differences do focus on women's capacity to bear children, residues of ideas and concerns relevant to that time might be reevoked in that context.

That literature is not extensive. Relevant studies number fewer than 15. They include observations of men whose disturbances in the context of their wife's pregnancies have required hospitalization (Lacoursiere, 1972; Towne, 1955; Wainwright, 1966), men whose reactions could be examined in the context of extended psychoanalytic explorations (Gerwitt, 1976; Herzog, 1982; Osofsky, 1982), and attempts at quantitative examinations of related factors. In no case were they guided by the hypothesis that these reactions reflect unresolved issues of sex difference, and the results were not interpreted in those terms.

Nevertheless, to the extent that the data allow, they do support the differentiation perspective. The nonquantitative studies report, among the most prominent reactions observed in men, feelings of loss, of having been deprived of something of utmost value to them, intense feelings of envy of their wives' capacity to give birth, and in various forms, denials that their wives could do anything that they could not.

Of the two quantitative studies, one appears to address a form of such denial (Trethowan & Conlon, 1965). Health questionnaires for the previous 9 months were administered to 327 men whose wives were in hospital to give birth, and 221 whose wives were hospitalized for other reasons. The first group reported significantly more symptoms typical of pregnancy, among them nausea, lower back pain, appetite gain or loss, and constipation. The investigators interpreted these pregnancy-like symptoms in terms of the *couvade* observed by anthropologists. The differentiation perspective invites the speculation that in this society, and perhaps in cultures studied by anthropologists, these symptoms are residues of these men's incomplete dealings with issues of sex difference. They are assertions in bodily terms of men's denial that they must recognize sex and gender limits.

The results of the other quantitative study (Hartmann & Nicolay, 1966) seem to speak in a more general way to the reemergence of sex-difference issues in men when their wives are pregnant. The investigators compared crimes committed by 91 men whose wives were pregnant with those committed by 91 men whose wives were not. Significantly, more of the former group had been arrested for sexual behavior conceptualized in psychoanalytic psychology as reflecting unresolved issues of sex difference (i.e., pedophilia, exhibitionism, rape, and lewd phone calls). The differentiation framework raises the possibility that if boys' recognition of sex and gender limits focuses on women's capacity to give birth, unresolved matters related to this recognition might be reevoked in men when their wife is pregnant. In some men, when their conflicts about sex-difference issues are particularly powerful, the conflicts may lead to the sex-difference-related sexual activity reported in this study.

DIFFERENTIATION PROPER: THE OEDIPAL PERIOD

Clinical observations first made by Freud and substantiated in subsequent clinical investigation suggest that a particular group of developments typically follows children's initial responses to the recognition of sex differences. It appears that for a time, girls tend to define the clitoris as a male organ and the vagina as a female one. In their social behavior, girls may vigorously express masculine themes. Boys, on the other hand, tend to define their penises as male and their anuses as female. They may act toward their father as though in a feminine relationship to him.

Freud did not bring these observations together in the form presented here. In his conceptions, and those of later observers, they fall into various theoretical contexts. Girls' beliefs emerging at this time, that the clitoris is a male organ, are viewed as an accurate reflection of reality, not a fantasy specific to a particular developmental period. Girls' expression of masculine themes in their behavior is seen to be an expression of clitoris-related masculine libido in a "phallic phase." Boys' belief that the anus is a female orifice and their feminine orientation to their father are viewed as expressions of the female theme of a biological bisexuality.

The differentiation perspective brings these observations together in a single conception. It suggests that in the process of gender differentiation, children initially elaborate both differentiation products within themselves. Objectively, children's genitals have been male or female from birth. However, children only now begin to define them subjectively in gender terms. At first, it seems, when children form the two categories, male and female, they ascribe both to themselves. It is in this context that little girls identify the clitoris as male and the vagina as female, and boys the penis as male and the anus as female.

Similarly, in their social orientations children appear to work out both masculine and feminine gender possibilities within themselves before making a firm gender differentiation between themselves and other-sex persons. Observably their social behaviors have been largely gender appropriate for some time. Only now, however, do the children themselves begin to categorize their behavior in masculine and feminine terms. Now, for a time, it appears that children assert both for themselves in their interactions with others. It is this phase of the differentiation process that may be being expressed in the notions cited earlier of physical and social bisexuality in clinical disorder, art, cultural artifacts, and rituals.

The attribution of other-sex characteristics to other-sex persons requires that children relinquish the possibility that the characteristics they define as exclusively other-sex can ever be their own. The proposed conception does not suggest that boys now express the feminine themes of their constitutional bisexuality and that girls behave in masculine ways as part of a drive-determined phallic phase. It suggests, rather, that for both boys and girls, other-sex characteristics now become the focus of conflict. In successful conflict resolution, children increasingly ascribe the attributes they define as belonging to the other sex firmly to other-sex persons and those appropriate to their own sex securely to themselves.

In Freud's view, only the father plays a positive role in this establishment of a gendered self. Girls move toward femininity only as they turn away from the mother toward the father. For boys, their cross-sex interest in the mother does not change; the consolidation of their masculinity triggers oedipal rivalry with the father.

In the differentiation perspective, both mothers and fathers play a major part in children's establishment of their gendered selves. Children now newly define their parents in gender terms. One's mother is now subjectively *female* in relation to one's burgeoning ideas of one's own femaleness or maleness. One's father, likewise, is *male* in relation to oneself as male or to one's female self.

The newly gendered parents become the central reality figures against whom children test their developing notions of what it is to be a boy or a girl. It is in relation to their parents that children make major progress in consolidating their ideas about whether being a boy or a girl means that one has nothing worthwhile, has all sex and gender capabilities, has been deprived, must give up possibilities of being nurturant, cannot be mentally aggressive, and so forth.

Moreover, for boys and for girls, both parents are a source of encouragement and support in the differentiation processes. For the girl, the mother is an independent source of support for her femininity as she elaborates her cross-sex relations to her father. The father provides a needed separation from the mother as the girl elaborates identifications and same-sex relations with her. For the boy, the father is of particular importance, not only as a competitive rival for the mother, but as a model for identification and a bulwark against the boy's wishes to reestablish his old intimacies with his mother as he attempts to establish a more differentiated cross-sex relation to her.

For both boys and girls, however, establishing a positive cross-sex relation to the other-sex parent also presents difficulties. Boys ascribe to their mothers their initially volatile and contradictory ideas of femaleness complementary to their ideas about their own maleness: girls newly perceive their fathers as male in relation to their realistic and unrealistic ideas of their own femaleness. Moreover, both boys and girls must now work out *positive* relationships with the other-sex parent who has been the focus of envy, feelings of deprivation, and demands for restitution. It may be that some frequently observed problems in later love relations have their origins here: feelings that the partner takes from oneself or deprives one, and corresponding demands from the lover for recompense, or wishes for retaliation.

This account has emphasized commonalities in boys' and girls' early gender development. Regularly observed differences in outcome have been left out of the discussion. In Freud's theory they are central. They are biologically rooted in the possession or lack of a penis. The differentiation perspective suggests that they may be secondary, functions of traditional family structure in this society.

The place of the mother in the rearing of children is a major aspect of family structure. Typically she is the primary caregiver for both girls and boys. This superficial sameness, however, may have complex and different implications for gender development in the two sexes. One example may suffice to suggest directions for further exploration.

As the central figure in a child's early life, the mother plays a central role in the processes of self–other differentiation for both girls and boys. By 18 to 24 months of age, when they become focally aware of the differences between the sexes, children have normally made some progress toward recognizing themselves as distinct from their mother (Mahler, Pine, & Bergmann, 1975). Now, however, in the recognition of sexual differences, mothers do not play the same roles for boys and girls. Boys must recognize themselves to be sexually different from their mothers, their primary caregiver and the focus of their separation–individuation efforts. Girls, at this early stage of gender differentiation, appear to have an easier time. They must recognize themselves as different from their fathers, who is typically neither their primary caregiver nor a major focus of differentiation and individuation struggles.

In this developmental context, boys may easily fuse issues of sex difference and separation–individuation. On the one hand, the boy's sexual difference from his mother may seem to him to be a new and further separation from her. On the other hand, the wish to merge with her in the progressive–regressive alternation of normal individuation may carry new dangers: To be one with her threatens the boy's gender identity. The outcome, then, may be an insecure sense of his masculinity, undermined by his wish–fear of merger and/or a sharply delimited and impersonal masculinity rigidly set off from the femininity he equates with both desired closeness and feared loss of identity.[2]

Girls' situations are quite different. They must work out separation–individuation issues with their mothers but recognize their sexual differences from their fathers. The two issues are not so thoroughly fused for girls in the first differentiation period. In the differentiation period proper, however, girls must form gender identifications with their mothers as female, the very person from whom they have been establishing their separate identity. The danger, then, is not that by merging with her mother a girl might lose her identity as female. Rather, by such a merger she may fail to establish herself as an *independent* female. Her sense of herself as female may occur in the two-person unity of incomplete separation. The resulting difficulties are not as immediately obvious as the boy's. However, they may become evident in later mother–daughter separation problems, when the girl becomes involved in heterosexual relationships, career choices, or the processes of pregnancy and motherhood.

SUMMARY

It is widely accepted that Freud's observations of gender development and organization are compelling but that the conceptual forms in which he

---

[2] The proposition that the initial stages of gender differentiation are more difficult for boys than for girls invites the hypothesis that notions of bisexual completeness will persist more strongly in men than in women. This hypothesis is supported in a quantitative empirical study of men's and women's Rorschach imagery (Fast, 1984, pp. 146–159).

casts his views of women's development are profoundly compromised by his phallocentric orientations. I argue here that this phallocentrism results in equally severe problems in his conceptions of male gender development. Both are skewed, moreover, by the phallocentrism that also permeates his views of mothers' and fathers' roles in their children's establishment of their gendered self. Therefore, a satisfying reformulation of Freud's gender theory of female development must speak to gender developments in men as well, and it must account for the influence of both parents in those processes.

I propose a differentiation framework for gender development that is congruent with Freud's conception of narcissism and developments beyond that experience form, and with Piaget's of egocentrism and growth from autocentrism to allocentrism. This differentiation framework is outlined as it applies to the three major phases of early gender development that Freud identified: the period before children become aware of sex differences, the events surrounding their recognition of those differences, and the subsequent oedipal period, in which children consolidate their gendered identities.

The discussion of each phase suggests how the differentiation model accounts for similarities and differences in girls' and boys' development. This chapter speaks to the observations that led Freud to propose two fundamentally contradictory theories to account for male gender development. It specifies major roles for both mothers and fathers in the developmental tasks of each stage. Finally, for each phase this chapter delineates significant differences between the implications of Freud's theory and those of a differentiation perspective.

REFERENCES

Benjamin, J. (1991). Father and daughter: Identification with a difference—A contribution to gender heterodoxy. *Psychoanalytic Dialogues*, *1*, 277–300.

Bettelheim, B. (1954). *Symbolic wounds*. Glencoe, IL: Free Press.

Chodorow, N. (1978). *The reproduction of mothering*. Berkley, CA: University of California Press.

Coates, S., Friedman, R. C., & Wolfe, S. (1991). The etiology of boyhood gender identity disorder: A model for integrating temperament, development, and psychodynamics. *Psychoanalytic Dialogues*, *1*, 481–523.

Fast, I. (1984). *Gender identity: A differentiation model*. Hillsdale, NJ: Erlbaum.

Freud, S. (1953). The sexual enlightenment of children. In J. Strachey (Ed. and Trans.), *The standard edition of the complete psychological works of Sigmund Freud* (Vol. 7, pp. 135–243). London: Hogarth Press. (Original work published 1907)

Freud, S. (1955). Analysis of a phobia in a five-year-old boy. In J. Strachey (Ed. and Trans.), *The standard edition of the complete psychological works of Sigmund*

Freud (Vol. 10, pp. 5–147). London: Hogarth Press. (Original work published 1909)

Freud, S. (1955). From the history of an infantile neurosis. In J. Strachey (Ed. and Trans.), *The standard edition of the complete psychological works of Sigmund Freud* (Vol. 17, pp. 1–122). London: Hogarth Press. (Original work published 1918)

Freud, S. (1957). Leonardo da Vinci and a memory of his childhood. In J. Strachey (Ed. and Trans.), *The standard edition of the complete psychological works of Sigmund Freud* (Vol. 11, pp. 63–71). London: Hogarth Press. (Original work published 1910)

Freud, S. (1959). On the sexual theories of children. In J. Strachey (Ed. and Trans.), *The standard edition of the complete psychological works of Sigmund Freud* (Vol. 9, pp. 205–226). London: Hogarth Press. (Original work published 1908)

Freud, S. (1961). The ego and the id. In J. Strachey (Ed. and Trans.), *The standard edition of the complete psychological works of Sigmund Freud* (Vol. 19, pp. 1–66). London: Hogarth Press. (Original work published 1923)

Freud, S. (1961). Female sexuality. In J. Strachey (Ed. and Trans.), *The standard edition of the complete psychological works of Sigmund Freud* (Vol. 21, pp. 223–243). London: Hogarth Press. (Original work published 1931)

Freud, S. (1961). Some psychical consequences of the anatomical distinction between the sexes. In J. Strachey (Ed. and Trans.), *The standard edition of the complete psychological works of Sigmund Freud* (Vol. 19, pp. 248–258). London: Hogarth Press. (Original work published 1925)

Freud, S. (1964). Analysis terminable and interminable. In J. Strachey (Ed. and Trans.), *The standard edition of the complete psychological works of Sigmund Freud* (Vol. 23, pp. 216–253). London: Hogarth Press. (Original work published 1937)

Galenson, E., & Roiphe, H. (1977). Some suggested revisions concerning early female development. In H. P. Blum (Ed.), *Female psychology* (pp. 29–58). New York: International Universities Press.

Gerwitt, A. R. (1976). Aspects of prospective fatherhood. *Psychoanalytic Study of the Child, 31*, 237–271.

Gilligan, C. (1982). *In a different voice: Psychological theory and women's development.* Cambridge, MA: Harvard University Press.

Greenacre, P. (1950). Special problems of early female sexual development. *Psychoanalytic Study of the Child, 5*, 122–138.

Hartmann, A. A., & Nicolay, R. (1966). Sexually deviant behavior in expectant fathers. *Journal of Abnormal Psychology, 71*, 232–234.

Herzog, J. M. (1982). Patterns of expectant fatherhood: A study of the fathers of a group of premature infants. In S. H. Cath, et al. (Eds.), *Father and child.* Boston: Little, Brown.

Horney, K. (1926). The flight from womanhood. *International Journal of Psycho-Analysis, 7*, 324–339.

Jacobson, E. (1968). On the development of the girl's wish for a child. *Psychoanalytic Quarterly, 37*, 523–538.

Kaftal, E. (1991). On intimacy between men. *Psychoanalytic Dialogues, 1*, 305–328.

Kestenberg, J. S. (1968). Outside and inside, male and female. *Journal of American Psychoanalytic Association, 16*, 457–520.

Kleeman, J. A. (1966). Genital self-discovery during a boy's second year. *Psychoanalytic Study of the Child, 21*, 358–392.

Lacoursiere, A. B. (1972). Fatherhood and mental illness: A review and new material. *Psychiatric Quarterly, 46*, 190–124.

Mahler, M. S., Pine, F., & Gergmann, A. (1975). *The psychological birth of the infant*. New York: Basic Books.

Mayer, E. L. (1985). "Everybody must be just like me": Observations on female castration anxiety. *International Journal of Psycho-Analysis, 66*, 331–347.

Moravia, A. (1974). *Which tribe do you belong to?* New York: Farrar, Strauss Geroux.

New Yorker. (1980, February 18). Cover illustration.

Osofsky, H. (1982). Expectant and new fatherhood as a developmental crisis. *Bulletin of the Menninger Clinic, 46*, 109–124.

Parens, H., Pollack, L., Stern, J., & Kramer, S. (1977). On the girl's entry into the Oedipus complex. In H. P. Blum (Ed.), *Female psychology* (pp. 79–108). New York: International Universities Press.

Piaget, J. (1929). *The child's conception of the world*. Totawa, NJ: Littlefield, Adams.

Piaget, J. (1970). Piaget's theory. In P. Mussen (Ed.), *Carmichael's manual of child psychology* (3rd ed.) (Vol. 1, pp. 703–722). New York: Wiley.

Rudolfski, B. (1984). *The unfashionable body*. New York: Van Nostrand Reinhold.

Stoller, R. J. (1968). *Sex and gender*. New York: Science House.

Thompson, C. (1943). "Penis envy" in women. *Psychiatry, 6*, 123–125.

Torok, M. (1970). The significance of penis envy in women. In J. Chasseguet-Smirgel (Ed.), *Female sexuality* (pp. 135–170). Ann Arbor, MI: University of Michigan Press.

Towne, R. D. (1955). Psychosis in males related to parenthood. *Bulletin of the Menninger Clinic*, 19–26.

Trethowan, W. H., & Conlon, M. F. (1965). The couvade syndrome. *British Journal of Psychiatry, 111*, 57–66.

Wainwright, W. H. (1966). Fatherhood as a precipitant of mental illness. *American Journal of Psychiatry, 123*, 40–44.

Zilboorg, C. (1944). Masculine and feminine: Some biological and cultural aspects. *Psychiatry, 7*, 257–296.

GENDER ACROSS THE LIFE-SPAN AND ACROSS CULTURES

Gender and Childhood Socialization

CAROL NAGY JACKLIN
CHANDRA REYNOLDS

What happens in childhood that ensures that women and men have learned that culture's expectations concerning gender-specific behavior? How do little girls acquire girl-like behavior and little boys acquire boy-like behavior? Or do they acquire these expectations by learning at all? Can genetic explanations account for what seems to be a cultural phenomenon? Developmental psychologists have historically viewed the childhood gender socialization process as one in which parents teach, or somehow transmit to their children, the rules and expectations of their culture. The mechanics of transmission have been the basis of several theoretical viewpoints. It is the contemporary incarnations of these viewpoints that we wish to examine.

For the last several decades there have been three dominant theories of gender-role socialization or transmission within developmental psychology (for a review, see Maccoby & Jacklin, 1974). These classic theories of how the process of transmitting expectations of gender is believed to work—psychoanalytic theory; social learning theory; cognitive theory—are covered as different viewpoints in other chapters of this volume. In this chapter, our discussion is limited to the childhood socialization aspects of these theoretical viewpoints and related viewpoints.

Very little empirical work has been done on Freudian theory, from a childhood socialization viewpoint, since the classic work of the 1950s did not find evidence for Freudian claims (Sears, Maccoby, & Levine, 1957). We do not consider the Freudian viewpoint in this chapter. Social learning theory has contemporary advocates and work continues with this theoretical approach. We describe some of this current work. Cognitive developmental theory, which evolved from and has kept many of the elements of social learning theory, has evolved into gender schema theory. This new theory was developed in the early 1980s, growing out of both cognitive–developmental theory and the schema work being done at the time in memory research. (For the background of this theory in memory research, and its current use in gender socialization, see Archer & Lloyd, 1982.)

Parallel in time, but completely separate in viewpoint and methodology, another body of research concerning childhood gender socialization has emerged. This viewpoint and methodology—behavioral genetics—attempts to assess the impact of heredity and environment on many aspects of childhood socialization, including gender. For many years, little or no dialogue existed between behavioral genetic viewpoints and developmental psychology viewpoints. Only recently have attempts been made to bridge the gap between the childhood socialization viewpoints of developmental psychologists and behavioral geneticists (e.g., Hoffman, 1991).

In this chapter, we consider several viewpoints of the childhood socialization of gender:

1. Contemporary social learning theory;
2. Gender schema theory; and
3. Behavioral genetics.

We also discuss central problems of the contemporary viewpoints, including (1) the asymmetry of gender roles, (2) race, class, and ethnicity, and (3) the measure and meaning of the influences of biology and the environment, as well as the implications of these contemporary viewpoints.

CONTEMPORARY SOCIAL LEARNING THEORY

Social learning theory has been a leading theory of childhood socialization. In the 1960s, social learning theory was used to describe the learning of gender-related behavior (Mischel, 1966). In its simplest form, social learning theory is the view that gender roles are learned because they are taught by social agents. It is an extension of the learning theories that were central to psychology at the time.

Parents and other caretakers are believed to treat girls and boys differently from the very beginning of life. This process has been called differential socialization. Girls are assumed to be rewarded for certain behaviors and punished for other behaviors. And these are not the same sets of behaviors for which boys are assumed to be rewarded or punished. The child is seen as relatively passive, if not actually a blank slate on which different experiences are written. Many studies have been done to try to document the reward and punishment of girls and boys for different behaviors. However, Maccoby and Jacklin's (1974) review of the socialization literature, suggest little empirical evidence for differential socialization by parents in the database that was available at that time.

Two recent reviews of the empirical literature of differential socialization come to opposite conclusions. Hoffman (1991) concludes that "there is abundant data demonstrating that parents do treat boys and girls differently" (p. 195). On the other hand, in a recent meta-analysis of the present literature, Lytton and Romney (1991) conclude that there is only very small evidence of parents' differential socialization. We will survey the data of each position.

Lytton and Romney examined 1,250 studies, 172 of which they could use in their meta-analysis. They divided these studies into 19 areas of socialization (e.g., achievement encouragement, verbal interaction, restrictiveness, encouragement of dependency). In 18 of these areas, they found no evidence of differential socialization. In studies on populations in North America, in only one area (direct encouragement of gender-typed activities), did they find significant differences. Direct encouragement of gender-typed activities is also the area in which Huston (1983, 1985) documented differential treatment. In studies in other Western countries, Lytton and Romney (1991) found that physical punishment is used more often with boys than with girls.

The popular view is that parents do in fact differentially socialize gender (although people tend to believe this about others and not about themselves *(although they often won't admit it)*). Why, then, is it so difficult to document? Several possibilities come to mind: (1) parents may actually treat young girls and boys similarly, (2) researchers may have looked at the wrong kinds of situations, or (3) parents may be unwilling to engage in differential socialization when researchers are present. Parents may believe they should be acting in a nonsexist manner for the benefit of the researchers. These effects of the researcher on the results of a study are called demand characteristics. The experimenter may seem to be "demanding" that the parents *not* treat the girls and boys differently.

As with any null results, these possibilities are difficult to address. However, some analyses of the Lytton and Romney (1991) work provide clues. Their meta-analysis found no changes in amount of differential socialization with time. That is, studies done with subjects born in the 1940s showed no more (or less) differential socialization than studies done with subjects born in the 1980s. Over those decades there has been a large change in what could be viewed as the demand characteristics of the studies, but no change in the results of the studies. It seems likely that at least the demand characteristics do not drive the parents' behaviors.

Perhaps the encouragement of gender-typed activities by parents, although not a large difference (in terms of size of effects or in terms of other possible parental treatments), has long-reaching effects. Or perhaps developmental psychologists have looked too exclusively at parents as socializing agents.

Peers as gender socializers have entered the literature (e.g., Thorne, 1993), but almost no work has been done on nonfamily adults. The less we know individuals, the more stereotyping we do. Parents know their children best. Aunts, uncles, and grandparents all can be cultural transmitters of stereotypes. What makes work on nonparental adults the most difficult for psychologists is that different children are likely to have different relatives (or different nonrelatives) who are important to them. It is precisely these nonnormative agents that most need to be studied (Bandura, 1982).

A central criticism of the social learning theory viewpoint is that no matter who the socializing agent is, the theory depicts the child as a largely passive recipient of culturally transmitted information. Although this viewpoint was acceptable to developmental psychology when the social learning viewpoint was first espoused, it is not acceptable now. The current theoretical viewpoint of the developing child, the parent–child relationship, and the family is that these are dynamic, interactional units (e.g., Clarke-Stewart & Friedman, 1987; Scarr & McCartney, 1983).

The contemporary social learning viewpoint concentrates on other ways in which children learn from their social worlds beside the direct reward and punishment of their behavior. Imitation has become an important part of social learning theory (Bandura, 1969). It is believed that children choose to imitate models of the same sex (their parents, other children, other adults, and even characters from print or visual media). Observing models is seen as a powerful force impelling children to adopt gendered behaviors.

Recent work on the effects of modeling shows that children are certainly not passive imitators. Children pick and choose when they do and do not imitate behavior. If a same-gender adult is doing something different from other adults, children are unlikely to imitate the behavior, even if their parent is the "odd person out." Selective cognition and probability assessment by the child go along with imitation (Bussey & Bandura, 1984).

There is other evidence of children's active participation in the learning process. Parents' positive reinforcement is not effective in changing children's toy choices, but parents' own toy choice does influence their children's choices (Eisenberg, Wolchik, Hernandez, & Pasternack, 1985). Fagot (1985) has demonstrated that the person who does the reinforcement makes all the difference. Reinforcement only works when it is administrated by certain people. Girls respond to reinforcement when it is given by teachers (either female or male teachers) but not when it is given by boys. On the other hand, boys respond to reinforcement when it is given by other boys but not when it is given by teachers or by girls. The process of selective cognition brings us to the second general childhood socialization viewpoint—gender schema theory.

GENDER SCHEMA THEORY

Classic cognitive developmental theory, as it describes the learning of gender-related behavior, was postulated by Kohlberg (1966). Kohlberg believed gender development was analogous to the Piagetian theory of physical constancy (Piaget, 1954). Kohlberg hypothesized that children cannot understand generalized concepts such as their own sex and its accompanying gender-role expectations until their cognitive abilities are sufficiently developed to a stage or level at which they can understand the constancy of gender. Although many have found some support for the traditional Kohlberg theory, others have criticized it. One problem, for example, is that children do learn gender roles very early, and much earlier than gender constancy can be demonstrated.

A more sophisticated variant of cognitive developmental theory and social learning theory is gender schema theory (Bem, 1981, 1983, 1985; Liben & Signorella, 1980, 1987; Martin & Halverson, 1981, 1983). A schema is a set of ideas that helps an individual organize information. Schemas are changing and evolving networks or patterns of associations used to organize new information and to filter information when deciding what they will and will not process. The schema one uses is never the only possible way of organizing information.

Gender schemas develop from all the diverse information a child acquires that has anything to do with gender. Included in this information can be modes of behavior, properties of objects, attitudes, and even feeling states. There is a considerable body of research findings documenting gender schemas (e.g., Bem, 1985).

Gender schemas are primary for young children in this culture. That is, young children in this culture make myriad associations with gender. With age, gender often becomes less of a salient category. However, there are wide individual differences in the degree to which gender schemas are primary. Children (and adults) vary from the "gender schematic"—those who are very reliant on gender-role associations—to the "gender aschematic"—those who are nonreliant on gender-role associations (Bem, 1985). Gender schema theory sees children as learning to sort people, behavior, and attributes into the culture's definitions of feminine and masculine.

A recent study on gender saliency was conducted by Hort, Leinbach, and Fagot (1991). They tested 108 children between 18 months and 4 years of age on (1) ability to label correctly categories of gender, (2) the extent the children demonstrated gender to be a salient aspect to sort items, (3) the extent the children expressed preferences for typical gender-stereotyped items, (4) how much gender-relevant knowledge the children evidenced, and (5) memory for gender-relevant information. Results indicated a significant positive correlation between amount of knowledge of gender and the extent of gender as a salient feature on which to categorize.

However, many aspects associated with these two cultural categories (female–male) make them problematic. Having "lenses" that force one to perceive the world in female and male categories limits both girls and boys. It disregards the enormous differences within the female and male categories and the enormous differences within girls and within boys. But besides the limitations forced by any categories, these particular categories are asymmetrical. The male category has more power and prestige associated with it. Thus young children learn more than the particular roles attached to the female and male categories; they also learn about patriarchy (Bem, 1993).

Other gender schema studies have focused on parental and nonparental influences on children's formation of schemas. For example, Nihlen and Bailey (1988) studied the effect of interactions with adults in nontraditional occupations on children's gender schemas. Analyses were conducted on the types of questions children asked. Results indicated some encodement of gender-related information regarding "cultural definitions of maleness and femaleness" as well as the formation of gender-relevant schemas about the work field. Most questions posed were relevant to occupation itself rather than to gender.

Other gender schemas related to occupation have been studied, examining, for example, whether parents' gender stereotypes, mother's employment status, and the extent to which parents' occupations were traditional were related to their pre-school-aged children's occupational interests (Barak, Feldman, & Noy, 1991). Parents filled out the Attitudes toward Women Scale (AWS) (Spence & Helmreich, 1972; Spence, Helmreich, & Stapp, 1973) and parents' occupations were rated as to conventionality for given gender. Children's vocational interests were also rated as to traditionality. Results indicated that the mother's occupation (whether traditional or nontraditional) was significantly related to the types of occupational interests of their children (traditional vs. nontraditional) for both girls and boys.

Gender-role knowledge, flexibility, and gender schematization in 60 children ages 33 months to 60 months were examined by Levy (1989). Information on these dimensions was gathered from parents' reports of their child's social environment, including time spent with their child, occupational status, number and gender of siblings in the family, and the target's preferred television programs and toy. Children completed the sex-role discrimination task (Edelbrock & Sugawara, 1978) and a schematic processing task where they were asked to indicate preferences for one of two toys pictured in black and white drawings. Results indicated some differential relationships between cognitive and social variables among boys and girls. The more that boys interacted with their father, the greater their gender schematization. For girls this was true for greater interaction with both parents. The more interaction with both parents, the less gender-role flexibility was displayed for both girls and boys. Maternal employment outside the home for girls in the study was related to higher gender-role flexibility. Boys in a family with many siblings evidenced greater gender-role knowledge. Children with fewer siblings evidenced more gender-role flexibility. Boys who preferred "entertainment television" had higher gender-role knowledge. Girls who preferred educational programs demonstrated more gender-role flexibility.

The relation of gender labeling and stereotypical gender behavior has been investigated by Fagot and Leinbach (1989), who conducted a longitudinal study using home observations in order to examine application of gender labels, stereotypical gender behavior, and parental attitudes toward these stereotypical behaviors. At 18 months, the children were unable to pass the gender-labeling task. By 27 months, half of the children passed this task. At 18 months, no differences were found between boys' and girls' gender-stereotyped behavior. However, at 18 months, parents of those who later passed the labeling task (at 27 months) provided more positive and negative reactions to gender-stereotyped toy play. Indeed, at 27 months, early labelers showed more gender-stereotypical behaviors than did late labelers, although parents of early versus late labelers did not differ in their reactions to gender-stereotypical behaviors. Results indicated higher "sex-role discrimination" among early labelers and no difference for "sex-role preference" at 4 years of age.

Gender schema theory is very broad in scope. Socialization of gender involves active creation of schemas from information that comes from several sources including the family. More research on the engenderment of children should clarify the relative importance of people and events that are influential on schema formation. While gender schema theory appears broad in scope, genetic influences are not specifically considered. For example, is it possible that the extent to which gender is salient to a child in forming schemas may be influenced by both genes and environment?

BEHAVIORAL GENETICS

The behavioral genetic viewpoint is that the influences on behavior can be classified as genetic or environmental in nature. Simply stated, there are two influences that make family members (e.g., twins or siblings) similar: genes they share and the environment they share. Two influences make family members different from each other: genes they do not share and the environment they do not share. Thus, the behavioral geneticist studies some relatives who are more alike and less alike based on how many genes or how much environment they share and determines how important genetic influences are and how important environmental influences are (both shared and nonshared) on any characteristic on which people differ (see Plomin, DeFries, & McClearn, 1990).

For example, adoption studies are used in behavioral genetics. Biological parents are similar to their adopted-away offspring in that they share 50% of their genes. Adoptive parents are similar to their adopted child only in that they share an environment (provided that the adoption agency did not seek adoptive parents who were similar to the biological parent with respect to the traits or behaviors being studied, a phenomenon known as selective placement).

Studies of gender socialization that use the behavioral genetic methodology focus on different problems and use different measures than those of the social learning and gender schema viewpoints described above. For example, behavioral genetic studies in gender socialization have largely focused on the masculinity–femininity (MF) scales of the Minnesota Multiphasic Personality Inventory (MMPI), California Psychological Inventory (CPI), and Personal Attitudes Questionnaire (PAQ), as outcome measures. We will consider studies using these instruments in turn.

Some tentative evidence was found for heritability of the MF scale of the MMPI in a small adolescent twin study (Dworkin, Burke, Maher, & Gottsman, 1976). Using the CPI, Loehlin (1985) reported results of reanalyzed data from two twin studies (Horn, Plomin, & Rosenman, 1976; Loehlin & Nichols, 1976) and one adoption study (Loehlin, Willerman, & Horn, 1982) where 32% of the observed variance for the femininity scale scores was explained by genetic influences and only 1% of the observed variance was accounted for by common environment.

What about multidimensional studies of masculinity and femininity? In one study using the PAQ, genetic influences accounted for twin similarity for the masculinity scores but not for femininity scores (Rowe, 1982). In another study, although heritabilities for masculinity scores accounted for more variance (46–48), significant heritabilities for femininity scores in prepubertal and postpubertal twins were found on both the Children's Personality Attributes Questionnaire and the Adolescent Self-Perception Inventory in child and adolescent twins (20% and 30%, respectively) (Mitchell, Baker, & Jacklin, 1989).

One twin study examined whether same-sex twins differ from opposite-sex twins in terms of similarity of gender role (Elizabeth & Green, 1984). Results indicated that male monozygotic twins were significantly more similar than any other twin group. Opposite-sex twins were least similar to any other twin group. This provides some tentative evidence that gender-role development may be more heritable for males. However, neither estimates of heritability nor estimates of shared environment were obtained. It is not clear from this study, therefore, whether male twin similarity is due to genetic or shared environmental influences or both.

Family studies, incorporating unidimensional indices of masculinity–femininity, have suggested that same-sex relatives show moderate resemblance whereas opposite-sex relatives show little resemblance (e.g., Ahern, Johnson, Wilson, McClearn, & Vandenberg, 1972; Munsinger & Rabin, 1978). However, family studies cannot distinguish between common environmental influence and genetic influences but suggest that genetic and/or environmental influences are important to familial similarity for masculinity and femininity.

Twin perceptions of *differential* parental treatment does not have an impact on twin *dissimilarity*. In a retrospective study of twin dissimilarity when growing up (Baker & Daniels, 1990), masculinity and femininity scores as measured by the Bem Sex Role Inventory (1974) were not affected by twin interaction. However, twin interaction has an impact on twin differences for masculinity scores. The twin who was more "antagonistic" and acted as the "caretaker" of the twin pair had higher scores on the masculinity scale, reflecting more leadership and assertiveness than the co-twin.

From the studies reviewed above, it appears that familial or shared environment does not contribute significantly to individual variation in masculinity or femininity. It also appears that twin perceptions of differential parental treatment do not account for differences in masculinity or femininity scores. This is in accord with the general behavioral genetic conclusions of the personality literature. That is, using these methods and measures, behavioral geneticists have concluded that environment *shared* by family members, such as the effect of parental rearing styles or socioeconomic status, does *not* influence the similarity found among family members for many personality characteristics (for reviews, see Henderson, 1982; Plomin, 1989). Instead, they conclude that familial similarity for personality by and large is due to genetic influences.

Behavioral genetic studies of femininity and masculinity as traits have found a lack of shared environmental influences, but research on attitudes has shown evidence of both shared environmental and genetic influences. Specifically, twin studies have shown significant effects of shared environment for attitudes related to religious, political, and sexual conservatism as well as for racial prejudice (see Eaves, Eysenck, & Martin, 1989; Truett, Eaves, Meyer, Heath, & Martin, 1992). In addition, the amount of genetic and shared environmental influences differs for females and males for some attitudes. While prior work suggested that the shared environmental influences might be explained by assortative mating (where men and women choose partners based on certain characteristics), recent research by Truett et al. (1992) suggests that not all of the shared environmental influences can be explained by assortative mating effects. For example, a characteristic that is almost entirely environmentally influenced, church attendance, is related to measures of conservative attitudes. These attitude measures did not contain many items in regard to women's roles. However, future research on mechanisms of cultural and genetic inheritance on attitudes should examine these variables.

Behavioral genetic results are hard to reconcile with non-behavioral genetic research where the familial environment has been the primary area of investigation of gender socialization. How can we resolve this apparent inconsistency? A critique of these studies is provided by Hoffman (1991). She details the methodological problems of this theoretical viewpoint. Moreover, she tries to show how aspects of this viewpoint can be reconciled with aspects of traditional developmental psychology.

Most non-behavioral-genetic studies examine gender socialization by looking at the effect of gender socialization on only one child within a family (e.g., Bradley & Gobbart, 1989; Fagot & Hagan, 1991). Thus, although parents may be influential in gender socialization, the effects or type of gender socialization may vary across family members. In this regard, Hoffman (1991) has made similar comments regarding the lack of common environmental influences on personality and other characteristics.

A central problem of twin studies is that differences in parental treatment of monozygotic versus dizygotic twins exist. Parents of monozygotic twins treat their twins more similarly than do parents of dizygotic twins (see Lytton, 1977; Scarr & Carter-Salzman, 1979). Hoffman (1991) posits that this differential treatment leads to more similar (i.e., common) environments for monozygotic than for dizygotic twins, artificially leading to findings that common environment has little influence on a variety of behaviors. Indeed, differential treatment may be influenced by the fact that identical twins invite more similar treatment given that they are genetically identical (Lytton, 1977).

Although differential treatment has been observed, the important question is: Does the different parental treatment of twin types influence differences between twin types? In one study, the greater similarity of treatment among monozygotic twins versus dizygotic twins of high school age could account for very little in terms of similarity on cognitive ability and personality measures (Loehlin & Nichols, 1976). That is, the median correlation among twin differences on ability and personality measures and similarity of treatment was .06. In fact, very few of the hundreds of correlations exceeded .2, and only in the dizygotic twin group. In a second study, perceived zygosity was found to relate to similarity of personality (Scarr & Carter-Salzman, 1979). However, those dizygotic twins who believed themselves to be monozygotic were in fact more genetically similar.

There is little evidence to suggest that the differential parental treatment of monozygotic versus dizygotic twins impacts twin similarity on cognitive ability or personality measures in any great manner, at least during adolescence. On the other hand, as we have noted earlier, primary caregivers may not be as influential on gender socialization as secondary caregivers, peers, or other socializing agents.

Finally, the effects of twins on family relationships may differ from the effects of singletons on families. Some evidence that the types of birth variables affect twin types differently is provided by Sandbank (1988). Sandbank (1988) reported that birth order, birth weight, sex, and zygosity (monozygotic or dizygotic) were influential in terms of personality as well as family relationships in a small study on twins.

We cannot resolve the conflictual findings of the behavioral genetic viewpoint of gender socialization and the social learning and gender schema viewpoints. Until studies use similar measures and specifically address questions of these differing viewpoints, little progress is likely to be made.

CENTRAL PROBLEMS
OF CONTEMPORARY VIEWPOINTS

Asymmetry of Gender Roles

An underlying assumption of all the viewpoints of childhood gender socialization is that there are two sets of behaviors for children to learn. The viewpoints differ as to the system of learning, and we have previously discussed differential reinforcements, role modeling, cognitive processing, and matching. However, a central problem of all these viewpoints is that there are really more than two sets of behaviors to be learned. That is, there is a complex patriarchal system in which the two sets of gendered behaviors are not equal. The child has to and does process more than appropriate behaviors; the child processes the presence or absence of power, high or low self-esteem, and all the residue of the patriarchal system (Bem, 1993).

In the last decade, scholarship has emphasized the value of the female in the asymmetry of gender roles (e.g., Gilligan, 1982; Harding, 1986). The work has celebrated female differences. Feminist psychologists are now grappling with the similarities versus differences viewpoints (e.g., Jacklin, 1991). We will return to this point later.

Race, Class, and Ethnicity

A second central problem of the childhood socialization viewpoint is the limited populations on which the research has been conducted. That is, the samples of children on which the research has been conducted are a small and selected sample of the universe of available children. Race, class, and ethnicity have been largely left out of our understandings of gender socialization. The vast majority of the studies cited in this chapter, and, we suspect, in this volume, have samples of Euro-American middle-class children and adults. This problem is not limited to the socialization-of-gender literature. It is equally true of much of the developmental literature and indeed the psychological literature as a whole. Gender research grew out of a reaction to the conclusions and theory drawn on such limited samples as Euro-American males. Yet this research area, in an effort to clarify misconceptions about gender differences and similarities, has also worked with limited samples.

We have evidence that race, class, and ethnicity variables make a difference in the study of gender (Bardwell, Cochran, & Walker, 1986; Binion, 1990; Price-Bonham & Skeen, 1982), although the nature of these differences is not yet clear. There are clues in recent work of differences in girls in Afro-American culture or Latino or Euro-American culture (Bell, 1989; Grant, 1984; Reid, Trotter, & Tate, 1991). There are other clues that family variables are different in these three cultures and different still in Asian-American cultures (McGoldrick, Garcia-Preto, Hines, & Lee, 1989; Gold & St. Ange, 1974; Harrison, Wilson, Pine, Chan, & Buriel, 1990). Because theoretical viewpoints have been based on limited samples, our viewpoints are also limited. Recognizing this fact, as well as recognizing that gendered issues are not the same in different cultures (Munroe, Shimmin, & Munroe, 1984; Whiting & Edwards, 1988), should help to broaden our thinking about the theoretical viewpoints that we do have.

The Measure and Meaning of Influences of Biology

We have discussed one of the theoretical viewpoints that includes the (inherited) biological aspects of gender—the behavioral genetics viewpoint. As we indicated earlier, and others have elaborated (Hoffman, 1991), it is impossible currently to compare the explanatory value of one viewpoint with that of the other viewpoints because the studies use non-overlapping measures. However, here we wish to comment on common uses of biological explanations.

We are biological organisms. We are clearly limited by our body in important and basic ways. Yet biological explanations are often used as arguments for the status quo; as arguments of those in power to keep others from sharing power. These arguments have been used by the patriarchy to keep women in "their place" and by whites to keep blacks in "their place" (Sayers, 1982). Certainly, even given the existence of genetic influences, there is no implication that these effects are immutable. Indeed, there are examples of the positive effects of environment on the potentially damaging effects of genetic disorders (see Plomin, De Fries, & McClearn, 1990). Although biological explanations can be misused, there is no reason to ignore the research or not to do the research. Knowledge can be power, but we must ensure that people are educated about what the knowledge really means, so it is less likely to be misused. It is this use of the behavioral genetic viewpoint, and not the theoretical viewpoint itself, that we wish to criticize.

IMPLICATIONS OF CONTEMPORARY VIEWPOINTS

We have reviewed very different theoretical viewpoints of the childhood socialization of gender: social learning; gender schema; behavioral genetic. These viewpoints have emphasized different aspects of how an individual becomes gendered. Each of the three approaches is very broad in its approach to the transmission of gender.

Social learning theory focuses on the "environment" as it influences or shapes children's behavior to the exclusion of genetic influences. Also excluded in social learning theory is the notion of the child as an agent in forming its own behaviors. Gender schema theory too, while broad in its consideration of social influences, does not take into account the role of biology in the formation of gender schemas. That is, heritable factors could be studied as to how they play a role in terms of saliency of gender, and/or the acquisition of information from the environment and how it is used in forming gender schemas. It may be, for example, that flexibility and rigidity as traits are heritable and thus play a role in schema formation.

Behavioral genetic approaches, on the other hand, take into account both genes and environment, but the specificity of the nonshared environmental influences has not been identified. Most biometrical approaches have modeled passive environmental transmission rather than allowing the modeling of an interactive role of the child in shaping his/her environment.

But the implications of all these viewpoints is the same: If one could understand the childhood socialization of gender, one could change the gendered aspects of individuals and thus change the gendered aspects of society. It might be harder to change some aspects of behavior than others. To understand which aspects would be hardest to change, we would use information from the behavioral genetic studies. Childhood is not the only point in the life-span when the gendered aspects of individuals can be changed; it is simply the one we are discussing here. But if we could change the gendered aspects of individuals, in what way would we change them?

Would our goal be to make girls and boys similar or different? In the 1970s, the answer of feminist psychologists would have been to try to raise children without the limitations of gender roles (Jacklin, 1991). The goal would have been to try to raise a "gender-aschematic child in a gender-schematic society" (Bem, 1983, p. 598). However, now the answer is less clear. In the last decade there has been a rise in the research and writing celebrating gender differences, from both a feminist point of view (e.g., Gilligan, 1982) and a patriarchal point of view (e.g., Bly, 1990). Is the goal to emphasize differences or similarities? Entire symposia have recently debated the nuances of just these choices (e.g., Kimball, 1991).

As we have noted above, gender roles are asymmetrical. In childhood these roles do limit boys, but they particularly limit girls. Men are limited by gender roles, but the limitations on women are even greater (Unger & Crawford, 1992). Because of the asymmetry of power of these roles, we are similarity advocates between gender groups and difference advocates within gender (and other) groupings. Knowing how gender socialization works would help all socializing agents to raise children without the limitations of these roles. And without the limitations of gender roles there will be greater differences between individuals, and thus within groups of girls and groups of boys.

ACKNOWLEDGMENTS

The authors would like to thank Laura A. Baker for her careful reading of the manuscript.

REFERENCES

Ahern, F. M., Johnson, R. C., Wilson, J. R., McClearn, G. E., & Vandenberg, S. G. (1972). Family resemblances in personality. *Behavior Genetics, 12,* 261–280.

Archer, J., & Lloyd, B. (1982). *Sex and gender.* London: Cambridge University Press.

Baker, L. A., & Daniels, D. (1990). Nonshared environmental influences and personality differences in adult twins. *Journal of Personality and Social Psychology, 58,* 103–110.

Bandura, A. (1969). Social-learning theory of identificatory processes. In D. A. Goslin (Ed.), *Handbook of socialization theory and research* (pp. 213–262). Chicago: Rand McNally.

Bandura, A. (1982). The psychology of chance encounters and life paths. *American Psychologist, 37*(7), 747–755.

Barak, A., Feldman, S., & Noy, A. (1991). Traditionality of children's interests as related to their parent's gender stereotypes and traditionality of occupations. *Sex Roles, 24,* 511–524.

Bardwell, J. R., Cochran, S. W., & Walker, S. (1986). Relationship of parental education, race and gender to sex role stereotyping in five-year-old kindergartners. *Sex Roles, 15,* 275–281.

Bell, L. A. (1989). Something's wrong here and it's not me: Challenging the dilemmas that block girls' success. *Journal for the Education of the Gifted, 12,* 118–130.

Bem, S. L. (1974). The measurement of psychological androgyny. *Journal of Consulting and Clinical Psychology, 42,* 155–162.

Bem, S. L. (1981). Gender schema theory: A cognitive account of sex-typing. *Psychological Review, 88,* 354–364.

Bem, S. L. (1983). Gender schema theory and its implications for child development: Raising gender-aschematic children in a gender-schematic society. *Signs, 8,* 598–616.

Bem, S. L. (1985). Androgyny and gender schema theory: A conceptual and empirical integration. In T. B. Sonderegger (Ed.), *Nebraska symposium on motivation: Psychology of gender.* Lincoln, NB: University of Nebraska Press.

Bem, S. L. (1993). *The lenses of gender: An essay on the social reproduction of male power.* New Haven, CT: Yale University Press.

Binion, V. J. (1990). Psychological androgyny: A black female perspective. *Sex Roles, 22* (7/8), 487–507.

Bly, R. (1990). *Iron John.* Reading, MA: Addison-Wesley.

Bradley, B. S., & Gobbart, S. K. (1989). Determinants of gender-typed play in toddlers. *Journal of Genetic Psychology, 150,* 453–455.

Bussey, K., & Bandura, A. (1984). Influence of gender constancy and social power on sex-linked modeling. *Journal of Personality and Social Psychology, 47,* 1292–1302.

Clarke-Stewart, A., & Friedman, S. (1987). *Child development: Infancy through adolescence.* New York: Wiley.

Dworkin, R. H., Burke, B. W., Maher, B. A., & Gottsman, I. I. (1976). A longitudinal study of the genetics of personality. *Journal of Personality and Social Psychology, 34,* 510–518.

Eaves, L. J., Eysenck, H. J., & Martin, N. G. (1989). *Genes, culture and personality: An empirical approach.* London: Academic Press.

Edelbrock, C., & Sugawara, A. I. (1978). Acquisition of sex-typed preferences in preschool aged children. *Developmental Psychology, 14,* 614–623.

Eisenberg, N., Wolchik, S. A., Hernandez, R., & Pasternack, J. A. (1985). Parental socialization of young children's play: A short-term longitudinal study. *Child Development, 56,* 1506–1513.

Elizabeth, P. H., & Green, R. (1984). Childhood sex-role behaviors: Similarities and differences in twins. *Acta Geneticae Medicae et Gemellogiae, 33,* 173–179.

Fagot, B. I. (1985). Beyond the reinforcement principle: Another step toward understanding sex role development. *Developmental Psychology, 2,* 1097–1104.

Fagot, B. I., & Hagan, R. (1991). Observations of parent reactions to sex-stereotyped behaviors: Age and sex effects. *Child Development, 62*, 617–628.

Fagot, B. I., & Leinbach, M. D. (1989). The young child's gender schema: Environmental input, internal organization. *Child Development, 60*, 663–672.

Gilligan, C. (1982). *In a different voice: Psychological theory and women's development.* Cambridge, MA: Harvard University Press.

Gold, A. R., & St. Ange, M. C. (1974). Development of sex role stereotypes in black and white elementary school girls. *Developmental Psychology, 10*, 461.

Grant, L. (1984). Black females "place" in desegregated classrooms. *Sociology of Education, 57*, 98–111.

Harding, S. (1986). *The science question in feminism.* Ithaca, NY: Cornell University Press.

Harrison, A. O., Wilson, M. N., Pine, C. J., Chan, S. Q., & Buriel, R. (1990). Family ecologies of ethnic minority children. *Child Development, 61*, 347–362.

Henderson, N. D. (1982). Human behavior genetics. *Annual Review of Psychology, 33*, 403–440.

Hoffman, L. W. (1991). The influence of the family environment on personality: Accounting for sibling differences. *Psychological Bulletin, 110*, 187–203.

Horn, J. M., Plomin, R., & Rosenman, R. (1976). Heritability of personality traits in adult male twins. *Behavior Genetics, 6*, 17–30.

Hort, B. E., Leinbach, M. D., & Fagot, B. I. (1991). Is there coherence among the cognitive components of gender acquisition? *Sex Roles, 24*, 195–207.

Huston, A. C. (1983). Sex-typing. In P. H. Mussen (Ed.), *Handbook of child psychology* (4th ed.) (Vol. 4, pp. 387–467). New York: Wiley.

Huston, A. C. (1985). The development of sex-typing. *Developmental Review, 5*, 1–17.

Jacklin, C. N. (1991, March). *Research on gender similarities and differences.* Paper presented at the meeting of the Association for Women in Psychology, Hartford, CT.

Kimball, (1991, March). *Thinking about gender similarities and differences.* Symposium at the meeting of the Association for Women in Psychology, Hartford, CT.

Kohlberg, L. (1966). A cognitive-developmental analysis of children's sex-role concepts and attitudes. In E. E. Maccoby (Ed.), *The development of sex differences* (pp. 82–173). Stanford, CA: Stanford University Press.

Levy, G. D. (1989). Relations among aspects of children's social environments, gender schematization, gender- role knowledge, and flexibility. *Sex Roles, 21*, 803–823.

Liben, L. S., & Signorella, M. L. (1980). Gender-related schemata and constructive memory in children. *Child Development, 51*, 11–18.

Liben, L. S., & Signorella, M. L. (Eds.). (1987). *Children's gender schemata.* San Francisco: Jossey-Bass.

Loehlin, J. C. (1985). Fitting heredity–environment models jointly to twin and adoption data from the California Psychological Inventory. *Behavior Genetics, 15*, 199–221.

Loehlin, J. C., & Nichols, R. C. (1976). *Heredity, environment, and personality.* Austin, TX: University of Texas Press.

Loehlin, J. C., Willerman, L., & Horn, J. M. (1982). Personality resemblances in adoptive families when the children are late adolescent or adult. *Journal of Personality and Social Psychology, 48,* 376–392.

Lytton, H. (1977). Do parents create, or respond to, differences in twins? *Developmental Psychology, 13,* 456–459.

Lytton, H., & Romney, D. M. (1991). Parents' differential socialization of boys and girls: A meta-analysis. *Psychological Bulletin, 109*(2), 267–296.

Maccoby, E. E., & Jacklin, C. N. (1974). *The psychology of sex differences.* Stanford, CA: Stanford University Press.

Martin, C. L., & Halverson, C. F. (1981). A schematic processing model of sex-typing and stereotyping in young children. *Child Development, 52,* 1119–1134.

Martin, C. L., & Halverson, C. F. (1983). The effects of sex-typing schemas on young children's memory. *Child Development, 54,* 563–574.

McGoldrick, M., Garcia-Preto, N., Hines, P. M., & Lee, E. (1989). Ethnicity and women. In M. McGoldrick, C. M. Anderson, & F. Walsh (Eds.), *Women in families: A framework for feminist therapy* (pp. 169–199). New York: W. W. Norton.

Mischel, W. (1966). A social-learning view of sex differences in behavior. In E. E. Maccoby (Ed.), *The development of sex differences* (pp. 56–81). Stanford, CA: Stanford University Press.

Mitchell, J. E., Baker, L. A., & Jacklin, C. N. (1989). Masculinity and femininity in twin children: Genetic and environmental factors. *Child Development, 60,* 1475–1485.

Munroe, R. H., Shimmin, H. S., & Munroe, R. L. (1984). Gender understanding and sex-role performance in four cultures. *Developmental Psychology, 20,* 673–682.

Munsinger, H., & Rabin, A. (1978). A family study of gender identification. *Child Development, 49,* 537–539.

Nihlen, A. S., & Bailey, B. A. (1988). Children's display of gender schemas throu interaction with notraditional workers. *Anthropology and Education Quarterly, 19,* 155–162.

Piaget, J. (1954). *The construction of reality in the child.* New York: Basic Books.

Plomin, R. (1989). Environment and genes: Determinants of behavior. *American Psychologist, 44,* 105–111.

Plomin, R., DeFries, J. C., & McClearn, G. E. (1990). *Behavioral genetics: A primer.* New York: W. H. Freeman

Price-Bonham, S., & Skeen, P. (1982). Black and white fathers' attitudes towards children's sex roles. *Psychological Reports, 50,* 1187–1190.

Reid, P. T., Trotter, K. H., & Tate, C. S. (1991, March). *Children's self-presentations with infants: Age, gender, and race comparisons.* Paper presented at the conference of the Society for Research in Child Development, Seattle, WA.

Rowe, D. C. (1982). Sources of variability in sex-linked personality attributes: A twin study. *Developmental Psychology, 18,* 431–434.

Sandbank, A. C. (1988). The effect of twins on family relationships. *Acta Geneticae Medicae et Gemellogiae, 37,* 161–171.

Sayers, J. (1982). *Biological politics: Feminist and anti-feminist perspectives.* London: Tavistock.

Scarr, S., & Carter-Salzman, L. (1979). Twin method: Defense of a critical assumption. *Behavior Genetics*, *9*, 527–542.

Scarr, S., & McCartney, K. (1983). How people make their own environments: A theory of genotype environment effects. *Child Development*, *54*, 424–435.

Sears, R. R., Maccoby, E. E., & Levine, H. (1957). *Patterns of child rearing*. Evanston, IL: Row, Peterson.

Spence, J. T., & Helmreich, R. L. (1972). The Attitudes toward Women Scale: An objective instrument to measure attitudes toward the right and roles of women in contemporary society. *JSAS Catalog of Selected Documents*, *2*, 66–67.

Spence, J. T., Helmreich, R. L., & Stapp, J. (1973). A short version of the Attitudes toward Women Scale (AWS). *Bulletin of the Psychonomic Society*, *2*, 210–220.

Thorne, B. (1993). *Gender play: Girls and boys in school*. New Brunswick, NJ: Rutgers University Press.

Truett, K. R., Eaves, L. J., Meyer, J. M., Heath, A. C., Martin, N. G. (1992). Religion and education as mediators of attitudes: A multivariate analysis. *Behavior Genetics*, *22*, 43–62.

Unger, R. & Crawford, M. (1992). *Women and gender: A feminist psychology*. New York: McGraw-Hill.

Whiting, B. B., & Edwards, C. P. (1988). *Children of different worlds: The formation of social behavior*. Cambridge, MA: Harvard University Press.

A Cross-Cultural Viewpoint

DEBORAH L. BEST
JOHN E. WILLIAMS

When examining the multifaceted topic of gender, it may be useful to remember that human males and females are, after all, only slightly variant forms of the same animal species. By this we mean that anatomically and physiologically, males and females are much more similar than they are different, and as a result, they are for the most part interchangeable with regard to social behaviors and roles—childbearing being the major exception. On the other hand, in many societies there seems to be a preoccupation with emphasizing the differences between females and males, with the result that the two gender groups are often referred to as "opposite" sexes instead of the more appropriate "other" sexes. This attention to differences and emphasis on oppositeness lead to an expectation that gender must always be a highly important factor in the determination of human behavior. As we review some recent cross-cultural research related to gender, the reader may be surprised at times at how little difference gender seems to make when viewed against the broad background of variability in psychological characteristics across cultural groups.

In this chapter we review some recent gender-related, cross-cultural research conducted with young adult subjects, followed by a review of the child research. We discuss adult studies before the child studies because it is easier to understand what children are learning about gender when one is aware of the adult attitudes and belief systems within which the children's development occurs. Before reviewing the research, we consider the cross-cultural perspective in a more systematic manner in order to point out some of the complexities involved in doing cross-cultural research.

CROSS-CULTURAL PSYCHOLOGY

Cross-cultural psychology is concerned with the degree to which psychological processes and behaviors are relatively invariant across cultures or tend to vary systematically with cultural influences. Generally speaking, cross-cultural psychologists accept firm evidence leading to either conclusion, although it is also clear that some cross-cultural psychologists are more interested in pancultural generalities while others search for significant cultural effects. Often, the cross-cultural question arises when someone wonders whether a psychological theory and its supporting empirical data developed in one cultural setting will work in other cultural settings, which is often found to be the case. The findings of cross-cultural psychology to date have demonstrated that persons from various cultural settings around the world are much more similar than they are different with regard to psychological processes, including those related to gender.

Under the best of circumstances, cross-cultural research may be considered quasi-experimental in nature. Viewed in this manner, persons in naturally occurring cultural groups are assumed to have experienced different cultural influences or contexts (Rogoff, Gauvain, & Ellis, 1984) that are conceptualized as differences in "experimental treatments." If one were to conduct a study and find reliable differences in the behavior of persons from different groups, one would be inclined to conclude that different cultural influences may have been responsible for the behavioral differences observed. However, the problem with all quasi-experimental studies is the difficulty in assuring oneself that the groups are equivalent in all respects other than the naturally occurring "treatment." Concern with equivalence becomes critical when one is dealing with different cultural groups because of the large number of differences that may exist among them.

One might assume that psychologists doing cross-cultural research must cope with problems that are qualitatively different from those that other psychologists encounter. Yet, as one becomes more knowledgeable about cross-cultural research, one realizes that the differences in the problems are not a matter of kind but of degree. Consider, for example, a psychologist who wishes to compare sex stereotypes in Great Britain and France. It is obvious that this researcher will face the problem of language equivalence in the English and French versions of the research questionnaire. Similarly, an American psychologist who wishes to compare sex stereotypes among various ethnic groups in the United States will face, in principle, the same question of language appropriateness. However, all the American subjects "speak English," therefore the researcher may simply ignore the question of language appropriateness for his/her subjects. Thus, cross-cultural psychologists do not face problems that are qualitatively different from other psychologists, but they must address certain problems more directly than do persons working within a single culture.

Cross-cultural psychologists attempt to conceptualize some of their methodological problems or their degree of sensitivity to culture using the *emic–etic* distinction. Generally speaking, emic concerns are related to intracultural validity, whereas etic concerns focus on intercultural validity. Logically speaking, emic concerns always precede etic concerns. By this we mean that researchers should first ensure that their procedures are appropriate in the context of each of the cultures they are studying. Only after one is satisfied that the procedures are appropriate to address the questions within each of the cultures can one move to etic concerns and ask whether the methods employed will permit legitimate and valid comparisons across cultural groups. When one develops an etic method that is sensitive to or adapted to appropriate emic matters, it is referred to, approvingly, as a derived etic. On the other hand, the multicultural application of a method originally developed in one cultural setting without consideration for appropriateness in the other cultural settings is described, disapprovingly, as a pseudo-etic or an imposed etic.

To illustrate the emic–etic issue we note the experience of researchers who have translated masculinity–femininity scales developed in the United States into other languages and administered and scored them using the standard American scoring system (e.g., Basow, 1984; Spence & Helmreich, 1978). Sometimes the outcomes of such research have provided evidence of a substantial degree of cross-cultural generality in the meaning of masculinity–femininity. Thus, studies employing the Fe (now F/M) scale of the California Personality Inventory in other countries have demonstrated that the mean scores obtained from the self-descriptions of men are regularly more masculine, while those obtained from women are regularly more feminine, as judged by the American scoring system (e.g., Gough, 1966; Gough, Chun, & Chung, 1968; Levin & Karni, 1971; Nishiyama, 1975; Pitariu, 1981; Torki, 1988). On the other hand, a dramatic case of the failure of translated items to work in another culture is reported by Kaschak and Sharratt (1983), who were interested in developing a Spanish-language Latin American Sex-Role Inventory based on the responses of university students in Costa Rica. Included in the preliminary pool of 200 items were Spanish translations of the items from the Spence and Helmreich (1978) Personal Attitudes Questionnaire (PAQ) and the Bem Sex Role Inventory (BSRI) (1974). It is reported that only two of the PAQ items were found to discriminate between men and women. The BSRI items fared better, with approximately half of the items found to be discriminating. From these findings it is clear that many items that represent masculinity and femininity in the United States did not do so in Costa Rica. Similar conclusions were reached by Ward and Sethi (1986) from BSRI studies conducted in South India and Malaysia and by Lara-Cantu and Navarro-Arias (1987) from a BSRI study conducted in Mexico. Taken as a whole, these studies indicate that the careful evaluation of masculinity–femininity across cultures requires that proper attention be paid to certain culture-specific (emic) considerations in the definition of masculinity–femininity.

As noted earlier, cross-cultural psychologists are interested in both similarities and differences in behavior across cultural groups, and we will comment on the relative ease of interpreting similarity and difference data. Many of the methodological problems encountered by cross-cultural psychologists are such that they are likely to produce spurious evidence of differences in behavior rather than spurious evidence of similarities. As examples, poor subject selection or poor translations of materials are likely to lead to differences, not similarities, in the responses of subjects from different cultural groups. As a result, when cross-cultural psychologists obtain similarity in behaviors across cultures, they consider the similarity to have occurred despite whatever methodological problems might exist, and thus, similarity tends to be taken at face value. This is particularly true when dealing with similarities in *patterns* of findings across cultural groups rather than similarity in a single score measure. In contrast, the observation of differences in the behavior of various cultural groups is examined much more cautiously, with the conservative view being that observed differences are not considered cultural differences unless they are systematically related to independently established cultural variables. As a consequence, the ideal cross-cultural study tends to involve a large sample of groups, perhaps 10 or more, so that the observed differences can be correlated with cultural comparison variables, such as socioeconomic development. If the differences are related significantly to cultural comparison variables, they may be considered to reflect cultural differences; otherwise, the observed differences are assumed to be due to chance factors.

Although having a large number of countries in a cross-cultural study is meritorious, it does not follow that studies involving only two or three countries have no value. Their value depends on the manner in which the countries were selected. First, consider the situation in which subjects from three countries are chosen because they are known to differ with regard to some theoretically relevant cultural variable that leads to the prediction of a particular pattern of differences in the behavior of the three subject groups. If the observed differences conform to the predicted pattern, the theory is supported. On the other hand, if the three countries are chosen purely by happenstance or convenience with no theoretically predicted pattern of differences, the observed differences are, conservatively, most reasonably attributable to "chance factors," including whatever methodological problems may exist in the study.

With the foregoing considerations in mind, we now examine several representative projects in which questions related to gender have been studied cross-culturally.

GENDER RESEARCH AT THE ADULT LEVEL

Space limitations preclude a comprehensive review of all cross-cultural adult research related to gender, so we focus on a discussion of findings from five recent studies involving large numbers of cultural groups: Hofstede's (1980) study of work-related values; Buss, et al.'s (1990) study of preferences in mate selection; and our own studies of sex-role ideology, gender stereotypes, and self-concepts of men and women (Williams & Best, 1982, 1990a, 1990b).

Masculine Work-Related Values

Hofstede (1980) compared work-related values in 40 countries by obtaining access to attitude survey data collected from thousands of employees of subsidiaries of IBM, a large multinational business organization, that manufactures and sells high-technology products. IBM had surveyed its employees to gain information about a variety of topics, and within the 150-item questionnaire were a number of items concerning work-related values. Hofstede extracted and used these items in his investigation.

Employing factor-analytic techniques, Hofstede derived four scales of work-related values. The first three scales were Power Distance, Uncertainty Avoidance, and Individualism. The final scale expressed the extent to which values of assertiveness, money, and things prevail in a society rather than the values of nurturance, quality of life, and people. Hofstede named this scale Masculinity (MAS) because research indicates that male employees usually assign greater weight to the first set of values whereas females assign greater weight to the second set.

Based on his data, Hofstede computed a masculinity (MAS) index for each of the 40 countries in his study. This index measured the degree to which the respondents of both sexes within a country tend to endorse goals usually more popular among men, high MAS, or among women, low MAS. The five countries with the highest MAS indices were Japan, Austria, Venezuela, Italy, and Switzerland; the five countries with the lowest MAS indices were Sweden, Norway, Netherlands, Denmark, and Finland.

Hofstede made an extensive set of comparisons between the country MAS scores and the findings from a wide variety of studies conducted by other researchers. His summary of the associations discovered is presented as Table 9.1, which shows that the MAS scores of the countries were related to a large number of attitudes, beliefs, and social roles. It appears that the type of work-related values held in a country are related to a much broader range of variables than one might expect.

From the methodological point of view, we note that Hofstede was able to use previously collected data for his analyses, thus avoiding the difficult and time-consuming task of arranging for data samples to be

TABLE 9.1. Summary of Connotations of Masculinity Index Differences Found in Survey and Related Research

Low MAS countries	High MAS countries
Managers relatively less interested in leadership, independence, and self-realization.	Managers have leadership, independence, and self-realization ideal.
Belief in group decisions.	Belief in the independent decision maker.
Weaker achievement motivation.	Stronger achievement motivation.
Achievement defined in terms of human contacts and living environment.	Achievement defined in terms of recognition and wealth.
Work less central in people's lives.	Greater work centrality.
People prefer shorter working hours to more salary.	People prefer more salary to shorter working hours.
Company's interferences in private life rejected.	Company's interference in private life accepted.
Greater social role attributed to other institutions than corporation.	Greater social role attributed to corporation.
Lower job stress.	Higher job stress.
Less skepticism as to factors leading to getting ahead.	Skepticism as to factors leading to getting ahead.
Managers have more of a service ideal.	Managers relatively less attracted by service role.
Smaller or no value differences between men and women in the same jobs.	Greater value differences between men and women in the same jobs.
Sex-role equality in children's books.	More sex-role differentiation in children's books.

Note. Adapted from Hofstede (1980, pp. 228–289). Copyright 1980 by Sage Publications. Adapted by permission.

obtained. Furthermore, the comparability of subjects across country samples was more certain since employees from a single large, homogeneous company were used. Such an approach to cross-cultural psychology has much to recommend it when it is possible—which is not very often.

Preferences in Mate Selection

Turning to an area of research in which gender would be assumed to be critical, Buss, et al. (1990) examined the effects of culture and sex on mate preferences in 37 samples of respondents ($N = 9,474$) from 33 countries located on six continents and five islands.

The principal data were obtained from two similar lists of potential mate characteristics (dependable character, chastity, good health, etc.). For one list, the subjects indicated their preferences by rating the 18 items on a four-part scale, and on the other list the same subjects indicated their preferences by ranking the 13 items.

The most striking finding from the Buss study (Buss, et al., 1990) was the remarkable degree of agreement in preferences for mate characteristics among men and women. Comparing all women and all men in the study, both genders agreed in ranking "kind and understanding" first; "intelligent" second; "exciting personality" third; "healthy" fourth; and "religious" last. The Spearman rho correlation between male and female ranks was $+.92$. Despite the overall gender similarity, the authors did find, as hypothesized, that women generally valued good earning capacity in a potential mate more than men did, whereas men generally valued physical appearance more than women did.

On the other hand, Buss, et al. (1990) report that culture was found to have a powerful influence, with cultural effects being found on virtually every item and great variation being found in the magnitude of the cultural effects.[1] For example, the largest effect of culture occurred for the variable of chastity, with groups from East and Southeast Asia placing great importance on this factor and groups from Northern Europe viewing chastity as irrelevant or unimportant.

Buss, et al. (1990) conclude that there were substantial commonalities among all samples, suggesting that there is some unity to human mate preferences that may be regarded as "species typical." On the other hand, no sample was exactly like any other sample—each displayed unique mate preference orderings.

---

[1] Buss, et al. (1990) seem to assume that all their group differences are "cultural" differences when, as noted earlier, some apparent group differences may be produced by a variety of methodological flaws.

Sex Role Ideology

Now we will turn to our own cross-cultural research conducted over the past 15 years concerning sex-role ideology, gender stereotypes, and self-concepts of men and women. All human societies consist of men and women who must interact with one another, usually on a daily basis, and who have developed customs embracing prescriptive beliefs about the manner in which men and women are to relate to one another. Sex-role ideology refers to an individual's beliefs about proper role relationships between women and men.

Although there are a number of ways in which sex-role ideologies might be classified across cultures, in our research (Williams & Best, 1990b) we have chosen to classify them along a continuum ranging from traditional to modern. Traditional ideologies hold that men are more "important" than women and that it is proper for men to exercise control and dominance over women. On the other hand, modern ideologies represent a more egalitarian viewpoint in which women and men are viewed as equally important, and dominance of one gender over the other is rejected. The egalitarian viewpoint is sometimes labeled a feminist position since it is often advocated by proponents of the women's liberation movement.

The findings summarized here have been reported in detail elsewhere (Williams & Best, 1990b). Approximately 100 university students, evenly divided by gender, from each of 14 countries in North and South America, Europe, and Asia, were administered the Kalin Sex Role Ideology (SRI) measure (Kalin & Tilby, 1978), a 30-item scale concerning role relationships between men and women. Sample items included, "The husband should be regarded as the legal representative of the family group in all matters of law" and "A woman should have exactly the same freedom of action as a man." Half of the items were phrased in a traditional direction, as in the first example, and the other half of the items were phrased in a modern direction, as in the second example.

Before using the items in a particular culture, the cooperating researcher in that country was asked to evaluate the appropriateness of the item pool in that culture and to consider adding or deleting items from the standard measure. In no case did the cooperating researcher suggest additional items, but there were two instances in which particular items were considered inappropriate and were deleted. In this way we attempted to ensure that our items were generally appropriate before using them for comparative cross-cultural analyses.

Subjects expressed their degree of agreement or disagreement with each item along a 7-point rating scale. In scoring, subjects' responses to the traditional items were reversed so that high scores were indicative of relatively modern views and low scores were indicative of relatively traditional views.

The mean SRI scores obtained from the men and women subjects in each of the 14 countries are displayed in Figure 9.1. The countries are rank-ordered such that those with more modern ideologies are on the left and countries with more traditional ideologies are on the right.

Analysis of these scores revealed significant differences between countries which is reflected in the rank order shown in Figure 9.1. Also, there was an overall tendency for women to have slightly more modern views than did men, but this was not true in all countries (e.g., Malaysia and Pakistan).

As can be seen in Figure 9.1, there was a relatively high degree of correspondence between the mean scores for men and women in given countries; the product–moment correlation between the mean scores for men and women across the 14 countries was .95, indicating a high degree of agreement. Viewed broadly, the results summarized in Figure 9.1 suggest that the effect of culture was greater than the effect of gender. Indeed, there is more agreement among men and women within the same cultural group than there is among persons of a given gender across all cultural groups.

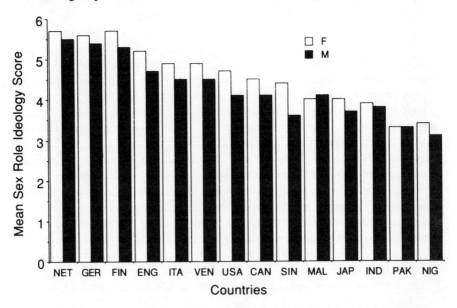

FIGURE 9.1. Mean Sex-Role Ideology scores for female (F) and male (M) subjects in 14 countries (Netherlands, Germany, Finland, England, Italy, Venezuela, United States, Canada, Singapore, Malaysia, Japan, India, Pakistan, Nigeria). From Williams and Best (1990b, p. 91). Copyright 1990 by Sage Publications. Reprinted by permission.

As noted earlier, before one can conclude that observed variations between countries are due to cultural factors, the variations must be demonstrated to be related to some cultural comparison variables. For the SRI scores, a substantial relationship was found between the pooled scores of men and women and economic–social development. That is, sex-role ideology tended to be more modern in more developed countries. Sex-role ideology also appeared to be more modern in more heavily Christian countries, in more urbanized countries, and in countries in the high latitudes (i.e., relatively far from the equator).[2]

Sex Stereotypes

Having just seen evidence of substantial cross-cultural variation in sex-role ideology, one might expect these differences to be paralleled by substantial cross-cultural variation in the manner in which men and women are viewed. These views concern the psychological characteristics or traits that are believed to be differentially associated with women and men (i.e., female and male sex-trait stereotypes). In this section we examine the evidence of pancultural similarities and possible cultural differences in the traits differentially ascribed to men and women. The data we will summarize are our own (Williams & Best, 1982, 1990a).

In this study, subjects were presented with a list of 300 adjectives and were asked to indicate whether, in their culture, each adjective was more frequently associated with men, more frequently associated with women or not differentially associated by gender. The adjectives employed were from the item pool of the Adjective Check List (ACL) (Gough & Heilbrun, 1980) which included absent-minded, active, adaptable, adventurous, affected, affectionate, aggressive, alert, aloof, ambitious, and so on. Subjects were approximately 100 university students evenly divided by gender in each of 25 countries. The items were presented in English when appropriate and in one of 12 other languages when necessary.

In each country, the data were tallied separately for men and women subjects to determine the frequency with which each adjective was associated with men and with women. After determining that the responses of men and women subjects were highly similar, the data in a given country were pooled for all subjects to determine the number of subjects associating each adjective with women and the number associating each with men. These frequencies were then converted to an $M\%$ score, with high values

---

[2] The correlation of psychological variables with latitude, at first surprising, will be seen to recur later in this chapter, as well as being a robust finding in other cross-cultural psychological studies (e.g., Hofstede, 1980).

indicating items that were highly associated with men, low values indicating items that were highly associated with women, and scores in the mid-range indicating items that were associated equally with men and women. In this manner, an array of 300 $M\%$ scores were obtained in each country, indicating the relative degree to which each of the adjectives was associated with men and with women.

These data were first analyzed at the item level by computing a correlation coefficient between each pair of the 25 countries across all 300 items. The correlation coefficients resulting from this analysis were all positive in sign, ranging from .35 for Pakistan versus Venezuela to .94 for Australia versus England. Thus, across all comparisons this analysis indicated varying degrees of similarity in the gender stereotypes in the different pairs of countries. When the correlation coefficients were squared in order to obtain an index of common variance (r^2), the mean common variance across all 25 countries was 42%, indicating a substantial degree of agreement concerning the psychological characteristics differentially associated with men and with women.

Another interesting finding at the item level of analyses was the rather dramatic difference in the variances of the $M\%$ scores in the different cultural groups. A high variance score would be obtained in a country where there were rather large numbers of extremely high and extremely low $M\%$ items, whereas a relatively low variance score would indicate that there were few such extreme values. Viewed in this manner, the variance score can be used as an index of the degree to which subjects in a given country considered men and women to be psychologically different. Using this index, the two genders were seen to be most different in the Netherlands, Finland, Norway, and Germany and viewed as least different in Scotland, Bolivia, and Venezuela.

Keeping in mind the dictum that observed variations between cultural groups are not necessarily cultural differences, we can ask whether or not cultural factors may be implicated in the differences in variances. The answer is in the affirmative; the variances tended to be higher (i.e., men and women are seen as relatively more different) in Protestant than in Catholic countries, in more developed countries, and in countries where Hofstede's male work-related values reflected less emphasis on power, assertiveness, money, and things (MAS) and more emphasis on individualism (Williams & Best, 1982, Appendix D).

The correlational and variance analyses just presented provide no sense of the varying qualities that are differentially associated with the male and female sex stereotypes. Also, given the rather large number of items involved, it was considered desirable to summarize them for cross-cultural comparison. In order to address this, we applied three theoretically derived scoring systems to the cross-cultural sex-stereotype data.

The first step in this process was to identify in each country items with
M%s of 67 and higher and items with M%s of 33 and lower which were
referred to, respectively, as the focused male-stereotype items and the
focused female-stereotype items.

In each country, the two item sets were first scored using an affective
meaning scoring system (Best, Williams, & Briggs, 1980; Williams & Best,
1977). This system, patterned after Osgood's three factors of affective
meaning which have been shown to have cross-cultural generality (Osgood, May, & Miron, 1975; Osgood, Suci, & Tannenbaum, 1957), scores
adjective sets with regard to their mean favorability, strength, and activity.
This analysis led to the findings noted at the top of Table 9.2, where it
can be seen that in all countries the male-stereotype items were more
active and stronger and the female-stereotype items were more passive
and weaker. Interestingly, there was no pancultural effect for favorability
which tended to favor the male stereotype in certain countries (e.g., Japan,
South Africa, Nigeria) and the female stereotype in others (e.g., Italy,
Peru, Australia), with approximately equal numbers of countries in
each group.

The second scoring system applied to the focused sex stereotypes
in the 25 countries was based on the five functional ego states of Transactional Analysis Theory (Berne, 1961, 1966; Woolams & Brown, 1978).
This system (Williams & Williams, 1980) scores a given set of adjectives

**TABLE 9.2. Summary of Pancultural Similarities
in Sex-Trait Stereotypes**

More characteristic of men	More characteristic of women	Not differentially characteristic
Affective Meanings		
Active	Passive	Favorability
Strong	Weak	
Ego States		
Critical Parent	Nurturing Parent	Free Child
Adult	Adapted Child	
Psychological Needs		
Dominance	Abasement	Order
Autonomy	Deference	Intraception
Aggression	Succorance	Change
Exhibition	Nurturance	
Achievement	Affiliation	
Endurance	Heterosexuality	

Note. From Williams and Best (1990a, p. 229). Copyright 1990 by Sage Publications. Reprinted by permission.

in terms of its relative loading on Critical Parent, Nurturing Parent, Adult, Free Child, and Adapted Child ego states. Although there is no research to support the importance of these concepts cross-culturally, impressionistically they seem to be meaningful and understandable in most cultural settings. Moreover, ego state scores are provided as one of the alternate scoring profiles for the ACL when it is used to assess self-descriptive personality. As can be seen in the center portion of Table 9.2, this analysis indicated that across all countries the Critical Parent and Adult ego states tended to be more characteristic of men while the Nurturing Parent and Adapted Child ego states were more characteristic of women, with the Free Child ego state not being differentially associated.

The third scoring system enabled us to score item sets in terms of their relative loading on 15 psychological needs, which are derived from Murray's theory of human behavior and are used for the standard self-descriptive ACL personality assessment (Gough & Heilbrun, 1980). At the bottom of Table 9.2 are listed the psychological needs that were found to be more characteristic of men (e.g., dominance) and those more characteristic of women (e.g., nurturance). Note that out of the 15 psychological needs, 12 were clearly associated with one gender group or the other. In summary, the findings shown in Table 9.2 suggest the utility of a pancultural model of sex stereotypes, with strong evidence for it demonstrated in each of the 25 countries in the study.

The rather overwhelming evidence in support of a general pancultural sex-stereotype model obviously requires rather powerful pancultural influences as explanations. The reader interested in these influences is referred to our theoretical discussions elsewhere (Williams & Best, 1982, 1990b). In brief, we argue that a similarity in sex stereotypes across cultures arises from commonalities in the biological and sociological factors with which all human groups must contend if they are to survive.

Although the general differences between the male and female stereotypes just discussed were clearly present in the data from all countries, there were also some variations between countries in terms of the *degree* to which a particular effect was observed. Moreover, some of these effects were found to be related to cultural comparison variables. For example, the strength and activity differences between the male and female stereotypes were greater in socioeconomically less developed countries than in more developed countries. Strength and activity differences also tended to be greater in countries where literacy was low and the percentage of women attending the university was low. These findings suggest that economic and educational advancement may be accompanied by a reduction in the tendency to view men as stronger and more active than women. We note, however, that the effect was merely reduced—not eliminated.

In sum, in the area of adult gender stereotypes the evidence for pancultural similarities greatly outweighs the evidence of cultural differences, but there is, nevertheless, some variation in the sex stereotypes from country to country that can be attributed to cultural variables.

Self Concepts

Having reviewed the evidence for a general pancultural model of sex stereotypes which proposes that men and women differ substantially, if not dramatically, in their psychological makeup, we can now inquire as to the self-concepts of men and women and the degree to which these self-perceptions incorporate the characteristics contained in the sex stereotypes. The subjects for the self-concept study were the same as those who provided the sex-role ideology data discussed above (Williams & Best, 1990b). In each of the 14 countries, approximately 100 university students, evenly divided between women and men, described first their actual self ("descriptive of you as you really are") and then their ideal self ("descriptive of the person you would like to be") using the 300 ACL adjectives employed previously in the sex-stereotype study. The set of items that the individual chose as descriptive of actual self was scored using the affective meaning system to obtain mean scores for favorability, strength, and activity; items selected as being descriptive of ideal self were scored in a similar manner. The actual and ideal self-descriptive item sets were also scored to obtain a culture-specific mean $M\%$ score for each description, employing the $M\%$ values for that particular country as determined in the earlier study of sex stereotypes. These mean $M\%$ scores might be considered as rough indices of "masculinity–femininity," with self-descriptions having relatively high mean $M\%$s being considered relatively masculine and self-descriptions having relatively low $M\%$s being relatively feminine.

Analyses of the mean $M\%$ scores in each country provided evidence of the effects of both gender and type of concept, self or ideal self. Regarding gender, men in all countries scored higher than did women, providing evidence of greater masculinity among the male subjects than among the female subjects which was hardly surprising. On the other hand, the effect of type of self-concept indicated that, for both men and women, the mean $M\%$ for ideal self was higher than for self, demonstrating that both gender groups wished to be "more masculine" than they thought they were. The latter effect may be related to the fact that, as noted earlier, the male stereotype is both stronger and more active than the female stereotype.

It may be these qualities that people are seeking rather than a greater degree of "masculinity" per se.

Our study was, to the best of our knowledge, the first large-scale cross-cultural study of masculinity–femininity in which these concepts were defined in local, culture-specific terms. We were hopeful that this methodologically superior derived etic approach might lead to some interesting findings about cultural variations in masculinity–femininity. However, this expectation was largely unrealized. While observed differences in mean $M\%$s of self-concepts were found, we were unable to find substantial associations between this variation and variation in our cultural comparison variables, such as economic–social development. Across cultural groups, we have no evidence that, relative to their own culture's definition of femininity and masculinity, women in some societies are more feminine than women in other societies or that men in some societies are more masculine than men in others.

On the other hand, more interesting findings concerning cultural influences were obtained when the affective meaning scoring system was applied to the self and ideal self concepts of the men and women in the 14 different countries. Overall, there was a tendency for the male and female self-descriptions to "echo" faintly some of the characteristics of the sex stereotypes. That is, in most countries the men's self-concepts were both stronger and more active than the women's self-concepts. On the other hand, there were groups where the expected activity and strength differences did not appear. From this we conclude that simply because the sex stereotypes propose that men and women differ in certain psychological characteristics, these differences in characteristics are not necessarily incorporated into the self-concepts of the men and women in a given country.

Looking at our scoring systems, there were the usual interesting differences observed in affective meaning scores across countries. As a means of examining the possible relationship between these scores and cultural comparison variables, we computed an overall differentiation score based on the degree to which the men's and women's self-concepts in a given country were differentiated across the affective meaning dimensions. When these composite affective meaning difference scores were correlated with the usual set of cultural comparison variables, some interesting relationships were observed. For example, the differences between men's and women's self-concepts were greater in less developed countries than in more developed countries; the differences in the self-concepts of men and women were less when women were employed outside the home or when they constituted a large percentage of the university population; the difference between the self-concepts of men and women were less in the higher latitudes ($r = -.76$); and differences in the self-concepts of men and women were less in countries with a relatively modern sex-role ideology.[3]

Thus, we are presented with something of a paradox. When we use our masculinity–femininity scoring system, which seems methodologically superior because of its reliance on culture-specific definitions, we obtain scant evidence of true cross-cultural variation and greater evidence of pancultural definitions of masculinity–femininity. On the other hand, when we use our affective meaning scoring system, which may be culturally biased since it is based on scores from English-speaking persons in the United States, we find a number of robust relationships with cultural comparison variables. We are not able to resolve this paradox to our own satisfaction. It may be that the use of 14 different culture-specific scoring systems for masculinity–femininity actually introduces substantial error variance into the analysis, whereas the affective meaning scoring system, whatever its possible bias, has the advantage of using a standard "measuring stick" for evaluating the responses of persons from all of the different samples.

GENDER RESEARCH INVOLVING YOUNG CHILDREN

Sex-Stereotype Measure

Having found consistent, well-established beliefs among adults about the characteristics associated with men and women, we naturally wondered how early these stereotypes developed. In order to devise a measure for assessing children's knowledge of adult-defined stereotypes, we began with the focused male and female stereotypes. By combining synonymous adjectives, we constructed a set of 24 stories based on these adjectives, the Sex Stereotype Measure (SSM) (Williams, Bennett, & Best, 1975). The SSM II (Best, et al., 1977) was developed later by revising and extending the procedure to 32 stories, 16 representing female traits (affectionate—"hugs and kisses") and 16 representing male traits (aggres-

---

[3] Somewhat contrary to these findings of self-concept, in a recent study of international adolescents in the Netherlands, using the affective meaning stereotype differentiation scores for the 18 nationalities represented in their study and ours (Williams & Best, 1982), Gibbons, Stiles, and Shkodriani (1991) found that in countries that are more traditional with regard to men's and women's roles, men and women are stereotyped less with regard to their psychological traits.

sive—"gets into fights"). An example of a female stereotype story is as follows: "One of these people is emotional. They cry when something good happens as well as when everything goes wrong. Which is the emotional person?" (Williams & Best, 1990a, p. 345). An example of a male story is, "One of these people is adventurous. They went on a safari to explore Africa. They saw lots of lions, elephants, and monkeys. Which person is adventurous?" (Williams & Best, 1990a, p. 345). Each story is presented with silhouette figures of a male and a female, and the child is asked to select the person described in the story.

Three scores are derived from the measure, a female-stereotype score, a male-stereotype score, and a total score. Each of the subscores has a range of 0–16, with high scores indicating greater stereotype knowledge, low scores a reversal of conventional stereotypes, and scores around 8 indicating no consistent association of stereotypes with either gender. Total scores have a range of 0–32 and a chance midpoint of 16.

Findings in the United States

Our initial research was conducted in the United States with children ranging from kindergarten through high school age (Best, et al., 1977; Williams & Best, 1982, 1990a). An overview of our findings, shown in Figure 9.2, indicates a consistent pattern of regularly increasing stereotype knowledge across the age range, similar to a typical learning curve pattern. At the younger ages, the male-stereotype items were known somewhat better than the female-stereotype items, but this difference in knowledge decreased and virtually disappeared at the older age levels. The most dramatic increases in stereotype knowledge occurred in the early elementary school years, with scores reaching a plateau in the junior high years.

Examination of individual item responses indicated that at the kindergarten level, 57% of the female item responses were stereotyped and 65% of the male items, whereas at age 15, stereotyped responses increased to 90% for the female items and 88% for the male items. Certain items, such as affectionate, gentle, strong, and aggressive, were learned quite early, while items such as frivolous and steady were learned somewhat later.

Stereotype Traits in Self and Peer Descriptions

Although our research has demonstrated that children's knowledge of sex-trait stereotypes is well established by 8 years of age, we have conducted only one study to see whether these belief systems are related to children's perceptions of themselves and their peers. Using modified stories from the SSM II with 9-year-olds in the United States (Davis, Williams, &

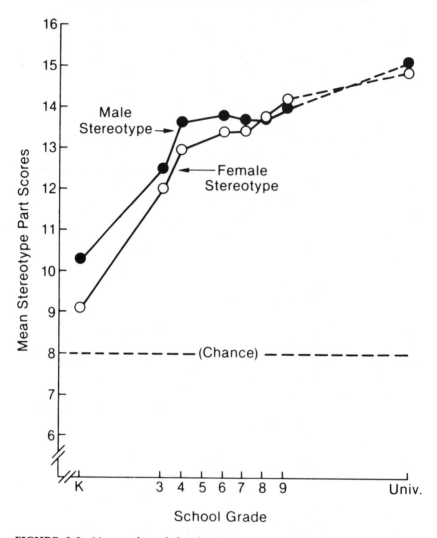

FIGURE 9.2. Mean male and female SSM II scores for subjects in the United States. From Williams and Best (1990a, p. 168). Copyright 1990 by Sage Publications. Reprinted by permission.

Best, 1982), we found that the characteristics that children attribute to the boys and girls with whom they interact are highly similar to those they associate with adult men and women.

Although the level of stereotyping was not dramatic in children's self-descriptions, an interesting asymmetry did result. Girls used female traits to describe themselves to a greater extent than they used male traits, but boys used male and female traits equally. This difference may occur because the natural characteristics of young children are more congruent with the female stereotype than with the male. Indeed, the Transactional Analysis scores for the adult-defined male and female stereotypes, discussed earlier, are consistent with this interpretation. Thus, it appears that stereotypes are incorporated into children's views of themselves and others, but additional cross-cultural investigation is needed to show the generality of these findings.

Development of Sex-Trait Stereotypes Viewed Cross-Culturally

As a consequence of our research in the United States, we were able to determine the appropriate age groups for the study of cross-cultural patterns in the development of stereotypes. We identified cooperating researchers and asked them to administer the SSM II to a group of 5–6-year-olds, 8–9-year-olds, and, if available, 11-year-olds in their respective countries. The children were generally comparable, being largely middle class and from urban areas, with approximately half of the group in each country being male and the other half female.

Although it may have been desirable to derive a separate version of the SSM II to reflect the adult-defined stereotypes in each country, the general similarity of the adult stereotypes in the United States to those in other countries led us to believe that the American SSM II items would be appropriate for cross-cultural use. Hence, we employed the same SSM II items with all subjects and presented them in translated form when necessary. Responses to individual traits were examined, as well as the male- and female-stereotype item groups. Including the United States data, our cross-cultural project incorporated SSM II data from 5- and 8-year-old children in 25 countries and from 11-year-olds in 5 countries.

Knowledge of Stereotype Items

In each country the percentage of children who selected the male or female figure in response to each story was calculated. The cross-cultural similarity in the traits associated with men and women can be seen in Table 9.3, which presents the stereotyped responses to each SSM II item by children in all countries.

Looking at the male items, 11 of the 16 traits had a mean percentage of 60 or greater at the 5-year level, and the overall percentage of stereotyped responses rose from 61 at the 5-year level to 71 at the 8-year level. Examination of the female items indicates that 8 of the 16 items were associated with the female figure at least 60% of the time. These data suggest that

TABLE 9.3. Mean Percentages of Stereotyped Responses to SSM II Items by 5- and 8-Year-Old Children in All Countries

	Male items			Female items		
Item	5 years	8 years	Item	5 years	8 years	
Strong	81 (23)	94 (25)	Weak	66 (16)	85 (25)	
Aggressive	76 (20)	90 (25)	Appreciative	63 (13)	84 (24)	
Cruel	72 (20)	87 (25)	Softhearted	67 (20)	80 (24)	
Coarse	64 (14)	84 (25)	Affected	66 (18)	79 (23)	
Adventurous	60 (12)	77 (21)	Gentle	63 (14)	81 (24)	
Disorderly	60 (13)	74 (21)	Meek	64 (17)	80 (24)	
Loud	63 (14)	77 (25)	Excitable	60 (9)	76 (22)	
Independent	60 (14)	76 (22)	Emotional	68 (20)	79 (23)	
Boastful	64 (15)	70 (22)	Affectionate	63 (18)	72 (20)	
Severe	61 (13)	68 (22)	Dependent	54 (8)	66 (17)	
Enterprising	61 (14)	65 (14)	Flirtatious	54 (7)	63 (14)	
Dominant	61 (11)	68 (19)	Complaining	50 (4)	61 (15)	
Confident	51 (5)	56 (11)	Fussy	47 (5)	52 (8)	
Logical	51 (9)	52 (7)	Talkative	48 (2)	52 (7)	
Jolly	46 (1)	50 (8)	Changeable	52 (5)	51 (5)	
Steady	44 (3)	43 (6)	Frivolous	47 (4)	35 (3)	
Overall *M*	61	71		58	69	

Notes. Figures in parentheses are the number of countries in which the percentages of stereotyped responses were 60+. Total number of countries is 24 for 5-year-olds and 25 for 8-year-olds.
From Williams and Best (1990a, p. 198). Copyright 1990 by Sage Publications. Reprinted by permission.

there was a tendency for children to know slightly more of the male items than the female items. Overall, mean percentages across all items and across all countries was 58 at the 5-year level and rose to 68 at the 8-year level, demonstrating a pattern of increasing knowledge.

Looking at the 8-year-olds' data, there were only four female and four male items that were not yet associated with the expected sex, perhaps reflecting the fact that some traits are learned earlier than are others. Moreover, there was substantial cross-cultural similarity in the characteristics young children associated with men and women. By 5 years of age, considerable sex-trait stereotype learning has taken place, and further increases occur up to age 8. While there are only limited data available for 11-year-olds, their scores follow the same pattern of continued learning found in the United States.

Female and Male Stereotype Scores

Cross-cultural differences can be seen more clearly in the composite male- and female-stereotype subscores which are shown in descending order in

Table 9.4. Across all countries, the mean male-stereotype score for 5-year-olds was 9.8 and the female-stereotype score was slightly lower, 9.3. These scores suggest that 5-year-old children have already acquired knowledge of many of the traits that adults associate with males and females. Relative to the other countries, both male and female scores were unusually high in Pakistan and relatively high in New Zealand and England. Scores were atypically low in Brazil, Taiwan, Germany, and France.

An interesting pattern to examine is the difference between children's knowledge of the male- and female-stereotype items in the various countries. In 17 of the 24 countries studied, the male-stereotype items were better known than the female items. In countries such as Taiwan, France, Pakistan, and Ireland, the male items apparently are more salient for children and are consequently better known. Germany is the only country in which there was a clear tendency for the female stereotype to be better

TABLE 9.4. 5-Year-Olds: Descending Order of Summary Scores for Male and Female Stereotypes (24 countries)

Male stereotype		Female stereotype		Male–Female	
Pakistan	13.5	Pakistan	11.4	Taiwan	+ 2.8
England	10.8	New Zealand	11.2	France	+ 2.4
Taiwan	10.6	Germany	10.6	Pakistan	+ 2.1
New Zealand	10.6	Portugal	10.5	Ireland	+ 1.6
Canada	10.5	England	10.0	United States	+ 1.2
United States	10.3	Malaysia	9.9	Netherlands	+ 1.2
Japan	10.3	Canada	9.5	Canada	+ 1.0
Finland	10.2	Finland	9.5	Japan	+ 0.9
Malaysia	10.2	Nigeria	9.5	Norway	+ 0.8
Netherlands	10.2	Peru	9.5	India	+ 0.8
Peru	10.2	Chile	9.5	England	+ 0.8
Ireland	10.0	Japan	9.4	Finland	+ 0.7
Nigeria	9.9	Italy	9.2	Peru	+ 0.7
France	9.7	United States	9.1	Venezuela	+ 0.7
Norway	9.6	Netherlands	9.0	Thailand	+ 0.4
India	9.4	Spain	9.0	Nigeria	+ 0.4
Thailand	9.3	Brazil	9.0	Malaysia	+ 0.3
Venezuela	8.9	Thailand	8.9	Italy	− 0.3
Italy	8.9	Norway	8.8	Spain	− 0.6
Chile	8.8	India	8.8	New Zealand	− 0.6
Portugal	8.7	Ireland	8.4	Chile	− 0.7
Spain	8.4	Venezuela	8.2	Brazil	− 1.0
Brazil	8.0	Taiwan	7.8	Portugal	− 1.8
Germany	7.6	France	7.3	Germany	− 3.0

Note. From Williams and Best (1990a, p. 215). Copyright 1990 by Sage Publications. Reprinted by permission.

known than the male stereotype. Note the intriguing contrast between
the patterns of stereotype knowledge for Germany and France, two neigh-
boring European countries.

An important point concerning the value of cross-cultural research
is clearly illustrated by the data just discussed and shown in Table 9.4.
Note that the United States was among those countries in which the male
items were better known than the female items. Had we not extended our
study of sex stereotypes cross-culturally, our assumptions concerning their
development would have been based on data that were not really representative of the variability around the world. From our United States data
we would have concluded that characteristics stereotypically associated
with men were in some way more salient for all children, and hence were
learned earlier, than characteristics associated with women. However, our
cross-cultural research indicates that such a conclusion is not warranted.
Indeed, some dimension other than gender association of characteristics,
perhaps style of interaction with parents or other adults, may be responsible for the differential rate of learning observed between the stereotypically masculine and feminine traits.

Returning to our cross-cultural findings, with an increase of one or
two items, the country differences found with the scores of the 8-year-
olds are very similar to those of the 5-year-olds shown in Table 9.4, so
they will not be presented here. However, to illustrate the cross-cultural
variation in the development of sex stereotypes, the mean total stereotype
scores for both 5- and 8-year-olds is shown in Figure 9.3. In each country
the lower edge of the bar represents the total stereotype score of the 5-
year-olds and the upper edge represents the score for the 8-year-olds.
Differences in the general level of stereotype knowledge are evident in
Figure 9.3, as are the differential rates of increase in knowledge from 5
to 8 years of age. At both the 5- and 8-year-old level, Pakistani children
know more of the stereotype items than do children in other countries.
Furthermore, compared with children in the other countries, Pakistani
children show the smallest gain in knowledge from 5 to 8 years of age.
Greater increases from age 5 to age 8 are seen in the United States, Brazil,
and Spain.

In trying to interpret these cross-cultural findings, we first looked
at the similarities between countries. Recall that we found considerable
pancultural generality in the characteristics differentially associated with
men and women. Although there were variations between countries in
the rate of learning, there was a general developmental pattern in which
the acquisition of stereotypes begins prior to age 5, accelerates during the
early school years, and is completed during the adolescent years. Boys
and girls seem to learn the stereotypes at the same rate, and there is some
tendency for the male-stereotype traits to be learned somewhat earlier

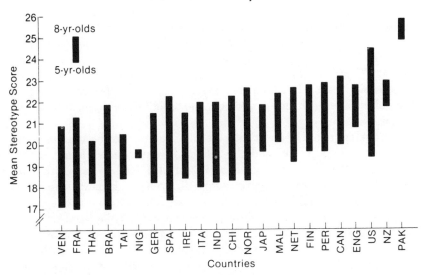

FIGURE 9.3. Mean total Sex Stereotype Measure II scores in 23 countries (Venezuela, France, Thailand, Brazil, Taiwan, Nigeria, Germany, Spain, Ireland, Italy, India, Chile, Norway, Japan, Malaysia, Netherlands, Finland, Peru, Canada, England, United States, New Zealand, Pakistan). From Williams and Best (1990a, p. 220). Copyright 1990 by Sage Publications. Reprinted by permission.

than the female-stereotype traits. The stereotypes we found seem to be universal models that are modified to some degree by specific cultural influences.

Cultural Comparison Variables

Given the possibility of methodological flaws, such as imperfect translations and nonequivalent subject groups, as with the adult studies, we again took a conservative approach to examining cross-cultural differences. We considered only those country differences that were compelling theoretically or statistically and were related to important cultural comparison variables, such as national or demographic values (e.g., educational, religious, or economic variables).

We found three demographic indices positively correlated with the amount of common variance shared by the children's scores at the 8-year-old level: the percentage of Christians in a country, the percentage of the population that is urban, and the percentage of the school-age population attending school. The size of the population was negatively correlated with the shared variance in the children's stereotype scores. Interestingly, these variables were not related to the stereotypes at the adult level, suggesting that these demographic factors may be associated with the learning process rather than with the adult perceptions of men and women. In the more urbanized countries where education is emphasized, children appear to learn stereotypes that are perhaps more similar to those in other countries. By the adult level, however, these stereotypes are refined by the culture such that urban and educational influences seem to have less importance.

Looking more closely at the pattern of correlations between the children's stereotype scores and the religious measures, we found that in predominantly Muslim countries, 5-year-olds tend to associate traits with the two sexes in a more highly differentiated manner and they learn the stereotypes, particularly the male items, at an earlier age than in non-Muslim countries. For the percentage of Christians and Catholics in the various countries, the correlational pattern was just the opposite of that found with the percentage of Muslims index. Children in predominantly Catholic countries are somewhat slower in their initial learning of the stereotypes, and they show a greater increase in knowledge during the 5-to 8-year interval. This slower initial learning may be related to the fact that the adult-defined stereotypes are somewhat less differentiated in Catholic countries. Similar to the findings with the percentage of Catholics, the relationships between stereotype scores and the percentage of Christians index indicated that in countries with large concentrations of Christians, children show greater increases in knowledge from 5 to 8 years of age and the difference in knowledge of the male and female stereotypes is minimal. These correlational data indicate that culture does indeed have an impact upon gender-stereotype learning.

Nature–Nurture Questions and Cross-Cultural Research

Although cultural factors seem to alter the content of gender stereotypes and the rate at which children learn them, there is a striking similarity across cultures in the traits that are differentially ascribed to men and women. Researchers interested in gender differences in any domain of personality or behavior often point to cross-cultural similarities as evidence for biological bases for such differences. For example, if men are more aggressive than women across a number of cultures under study, it is assumed that gender difference in aggression must be caused by genes and hormones, an assumption that implies complete biological determinism. However, biology alone cannot cause behavior. The long-standing nature–nurture controversy in developmental psychology has clearly shown the naiveté of such an assumption. Nature and nurture are not dichotomous (Johnston, 1987); they interact in such a way that it is impossible to separate their effects, and often the individual contributions of each cannot be determined.

In contrast to biological explanations, similarities in socialization practices have also been invoked as explanations for cultural universals in gender differences. Barry, Bacon, and Child (1957) examined socialization practices in over 100 societies and found that while boys are generally raised to achieve and to be self-reliant and girls are generally raised to be nurturant and responsible, societies differed in their emphases on these behaviors. Variations in socialization practices among societies were related to variations in the behaviors displayed by boys and girls. Even when the direction of a gender difference is constant, the magnitude of the difference may vary across cultures.

Cultural variation in some gender-related behaviors may be so extreme that by comparison gender differences appear minor. Perhaps the best example of such extreme cultural diversity is seen in Margaret Mead's classic study of three primitive tribes in New Guinea (Mead, 1935). Mead found that among the Mundugamor both men and women act aggressively and have little parental orientation. The opposite was true for the Arapesh; both men and women were gentle and nurturant. Among the Tchambuli, stereotypical roles were reversed, with men being more nurturant and women more aggressive. From a Western viewpoint, these societies created men and women who are both masculine and feminine, and who reversed the usual gender roles. Although' such extreme differences do exist, pancultural generalities in gender differences, particularly in the areas of aggression and parenting, are often interpreted as evidence for biological influence operating either directly or in concert with socialization practices (Ruble, 1988).

Cross-Cultural Views of Gender-Related Learning Theories

Even though there is theoretical disagreement about the sources of influence and the course of sex-role development, most theories, whether more biological or learning oriented, do emphasize the gender information readily available in the child's culture. The value of the cross-cultural approach is that because it is not itself a theory but an amalgam of comparative orientations and methodologies that stress the formative role of the sociocultural context, virtually no theory or model of gender is inconsistent with it. Moreover, aspects of a particular theory that are not readily testable in a single, homogeneous culture may be easily evaluated through comparison of more diverse cultural groups. Since social learning and cognitive developmental theories are perhaps the best known of the theories concerned with the development of gender knowledge, these two will be used to illustrate the contributions of the cross-cultural viewpoint to theory testing and development.

Social Learning

Social learning theories (Bandura, 1969; Bussey & Bandura, 1984; Mischel, 1970) consider sex-role development to be the result of cumulative experience. Parents, teachers, peers, and other socialization agents shape children's gender-related behaviors through modeling, expectations, toy choices, reinforcement and punishment of gender-appropriate and -inappropriate behaviors, and other differential treatment of boys and girls.

Research conducted in the United States has shown that same-sex and opposite-sex parents react differently to their children, with fathers showing more differential behavior. Boys receive more physical stimulation than do girls (Lamb, 1976, 1977), they are given more freedom and independence than are girls (Maccoby & Jacklin, 1974), and they are expected to achieve in different areas than are girls (Hess & Shipman, 1967). Interestingly, the few studies conducted in other countries concerning differential treatment of boys and girls (e.g., Bronstein, 1984; Russell & Russell, 1987) do not show the same patterns as those found in the United States. For example, Lamb and his colleagues (Lamb, 1976, 1977; Lamb, Frodi, Hwang, Frodi, & Steinberg, 1982; Sagi, Lamb, Shoham, Dvir, & Lewkowicz, 1985) have shown that in contrast to data collected in the United States, observations of Swedish and Israeli kibbutzim parents and children revealed no gender differences for parental play style with infants and toddlers.

A recent study (Best, House, Barnard, & Spicker, 1991) looking at playground interactions between preschool children and their parents further illustrates the value of cross-cultural research for examining concepts derived from social learning theory. The study does not purport to be a test of social learning theory per se. However, the study examined cross-cultural differences in parent–child interactions which according to social learning theory are one important contributor to children's learning of gender-related behaviors and traits. Parents and children were observed while interacting in public parks and playgrounds in France, Germany, and Italy, and both gender and country differences were found. Specifically, French and Italian parents and children displayed more interactive behaviors than did German parent–child dyads. French and Italian children showed objects and shared them more with their father than with their mother, but the pattern was reversed for the German children. These differences in interactional patterns may be related to differences found in sexstereotype learning discussed earlier. Recall that unlike the French and Italian children, German children demonstrated greater knowledge of the female-stereotype traits than of the male traits. Perhaps the female characteristics are learned earlier by German children as a result of greater interaction with their mother than with their father, a pattern that was not found in France and Italy, where the male stereotype items were somewhat better known.

Although there is substantial evidence in the United States and cross-culturally to indicate that social learning plays a part in gender-role learning, it is clear that social learning by itself is not a sufficient explanation. The patterns of differential treatment of boys and girls found cross-culturally demonstrate great variation and are not consistently tied to differential behavior (Bronstein, 1984; Lamb, et al., 1982; Russell & Russell, 1987). Tasks assigned to children as well as the models available in the larger culture provide opportunities for them to learn differential roles and encourage distinct behaviors. Additional cross-cultural research is needed to identify the salient aspects of culture that contribute to children's gender-role learning and behavior. Cross-cultural research provides an excellent source of data for testing hypotheses extrapolated from social learning theories. Moreover, the cross-cultural viewpoint is not inconsistent with the general notions of social learning theories, which emphasize children's experiences.

Cognitive Developmental

Turning to the other most prominent theory of gender-role learning, cognitive–developmental theory (Kohlberg, 1966; Kohlberg & Ullman, 1974; Ruble, 1987), again we see an emphasis on the role of external forces in shaping children's gender-role orientation. The impact of these factors, however, is governed by the emerging cognitive structures of the child. According to cognitive developmental theories, children progress through stages of understanding in acquiring gender knowledge and the degree of understanding structures their experiences.

Slaby and Frey (1975) identified four stages in the development of gender understanding. In Stage 1 children do not correctly distinguish between the sexes. However, by age 2 to 3 they begin to use gender labels for themselves and others and soon achieve Stage 2, gender identity. Stage 3, gender stability, is attained when children understand that gender remains constant across time ("When you grow up, will you be a mommy or daddy?"). In the final stage, Stage 4, gender consistency, children understand that gender is unaffected by motives or changes in clothing and activity ("If you played with dolls/trucks (the opposite-sex toy), would you be a boy or girl?"). These latter two stages, which are achieved by age 4½ to 5, are functionally unrelated to Stage 2 and involve the conservation of gender identity, similar to other conservational thinking acquired during the development of operational thought (Marcus & Overton, 1978; Piaget & Inhelder, 1966).

The value of the cross-cultural approach for clarifying and elaborating gender concepts from cognitive–developmental theory is clearly illustrated by a four-culture study of gender understanding conducted by Munroe, Shimmin, and Munroe (1984). These researchers assumed that since all societies are organized to some extent according to sex-based principles, Stage 2 gender-identity classification skills would develop under almost any cultural conditions. The latter two stages of stability and consistency might also be expected to exist in all cultures since their development depends on cognitive structures of operational thought that are presumably universal as well (Cole & Scribner, 1974; Jahoda, 1980). In addition, the sequence of development should follow that found with children in the United States.

Given this framework of similarities in the stages and the sequence of development, Munroe, et al. (1984) reasoned that the effect of culture would be seen in differential rates of development based on the degree to which the various societies emphasize the distinctions between males and females. The researchers selected four societies in which to examine cultural effects: two, the Logoli of Kenya and the Newars of Nepal, where childhood experiences are sharply differentiated, and two, the Garifuna of Belize and the Samoans of American Samoa, where girls and boys are treated almost equally. They hypothesized that because of sex distinction in socialization practices, gender classification should be more salient and achieved earlier for the Kenyan and Nepalese children. However, since the stability and consistency stages are dependent on structural factors for their emergence, they would be less influenced by sociocultural factors and should appear at essentially the same time in the four cultures.

Across cultures, Munroe, et al. (1984) found that children's understanding of gender conformed to the orderly progression through stages discovered for children in the United States. In contrast, the culture-specific predictions were not supported. Children in the two sex-differentiating cultures, Kenya and Nepal, did not attain Stage 2 at an earlier age than did children in Belize and Samoa. In fact, the Kenyan children reached Stage 2 at an older age than did the Samoan children, and the Nepalese children did not differ from the other groups. Attainment of Stages 3 and 4 showed little variation across cultures. Taken as a whole, these findings indicate the dominant contribution of cognitive developmental factors and the concomitantly small contribution of culture-specific factors in the development of gender concepts. Although the researchers urge cautious interpretation until other more culturally distinct groups are studied, they suggest that their findings support Kohlberg's notion of some relatively invariant developmental trends in sex-role concepts and attitudes based on culturally universal modes of conceptualization.

Examination of the social learning and cognitive–developmental theories of gender development clearly illustrate the value of the cross-cultural examination of gender. While biological, social, cognitive, and other factors are certainly involved in the development of gender knowledge and roles, the complexity of their interactions cannot be appreciated without evidence of consistencies and variations across different cultural contexts.

The Value of Cross-Cultural Research

Research on the development of gender concepts has sometimes been inaccurate because of the failure to include an integrated cross-cultural perspective. Edwards and Whiting (1980) suggest that such a perspective is important for two reasons. First, it broadens the foundation of empirical information, providing a greater range of variation than do single-culture studies. This, in turn, offers greater opportunity for examination of antecedent variables. Second, a cross-cultural perspective provides a more complete analysis of the learning environments of children, which yields a better understanding of how cultural processes affect children's development.

These points are clearly shown in the Six-Culture study (Edwards & Whiting, 1974; Whiting & Edwards, 1973, 1988; Whiting & Whiting, 1975) that examined aggression, nurturance, responsibility, and help- and attention-seeking behaviors of children ages 3 to 11 in Okinawa, Mexico, the Philippines, India, Kenya, and the United States. Relevant to the first point concerning the range of cultural variation, fewer gender differences were found in the three samples (the United States, the Philippines, and Kenya) where both boys and girls were assigned care for their younger siblings and were asked to perform household chores. In contrast, more differences were found in the samples (India, Mexico, Okinawa) where boys and girls were treated dissimiliarly and girls were asked to assume more responsibility for siblings and household tasks. In fact, the fewest gender differences were found in the American sample, in which neither girls nor boys were assigned many child-care or household tasks. By using other comparative samples, the extent and variability in gender differences was much greater than would have been seen if only an American sample had been examined. Indeed, the relationship of gender differences and the antecedent variable of task assignment would not have been explored if only an American sample had been studied.

Cross-cultural findings concerning the development of nurturance illustrate the second point regarding conceptualizations of the learning environment of children. Maccoby and Jacklin (1974) suggest that the reason American research has failed to demonstrate the learning of nurturant behavior is because a child's offering of nurturance to an infant or younger child has generally been ignored. Instead, most American studies have focused on the mother–child and same-age peer observations rather than looking at cross-age interactions. By limiting study to only a few interactions, the richness of the learning environment has been neglected.

Extensive examination of the learning environment is shown in the Six-Culture study. Edwards and Whiting (1980) found that gender differences in nurturance were most consistent in behavior directed toward infants and toddlers rather than in behavior directed toward mothers and older children. With further analyses they found that this gender difference was not necessarily due to mothers assigning more childcare chores to girls but that girls were more willing to comply with such requests. Further, since infants seem to elicit more nurturant behavior than do older children, regardless of the gender of the caregiver, girls who spent more time with infants demonstrated more nurturance than boys who were not engaged in as much infant interaction. These findings suggest that culture shapes nurturance, and perhaps other social behaviors, by selecting the company that children keep and the activities that engage their time (Edwards & Whiting, 1980; Munroe, Munroe, & Shimmin, 1984). The cultural learning environment can maximize, minimize, or possibly eliminate gender differences in certain social behaviors, and if we limit our research to only a few social contexts or activities, we may miss much of the action where gender-role learning takes place.

CONCLUSION

Although biological factors may establish predispositions and restrictions on the development of gender roles and behaviors, most researchers would agree that sociocultural factors are the primary determinants of an individual's gender orientation (Ruble, 1988). Culture can have profound effects on behavior, dictating how babies are delivered, how children are socialized, how one dresses, and what adult roles men and women will assume. While such culturally prescribed rules are well-known by social scientists, their impact on the development of gender identity and roles is often overlooked or disputed.

Variations between cultural groups are certainly greater than variations within a single, homogeneous culture, and as a consequence, cross-cultural studies provide an excellent "testing ground" for theoretical concepts and predictions. Predictions that are supported and replicated across very different populations are certainly robust and are likely to result in richer, more complete explanations of gender-related behavior. Indeed, the cross-cultural approach is not inconsistent with any of the views of gender described in this volume and it may serve as a valuable addition to understanding these other viewpoints.

REFERENCES

Bandura, A. (1969). Social learning theory of identificatory process. In D. A. Goslin (Ed.), *Handbook of socialization theory and research* (pp. 213–262). Chicago: Rand McNally.

Barry, H., III, Bacon, M. K., & Child, I. L. (1957). A cross-cultural survey of some sex differences in socialization. *Journal of Abnormal and Social Psychology*, *55*, 327–332.

Basow, S. A. (1984). Cultural variations in sex typing. *Sex Roles, 10*, 577–585.

Bem, S. L. (1974). The measurement of psychological androgyny. *Journal of Consulting and Clinical Psychology*, *42*, 155–162.

Berne, E. (1961). *Transactional analysis in psychotherapy*. New York: Grove.

Berne, E. (1966). *Principles of group treatment*. New York: Oxford University Press.

Best, D. L., House, A. S., Barnard, A. E., & Spicker, B. S. (1991, July). *Parent–child interactions in France, Germany, and Italy: The effects of gender and culture*. Paper presented at IACCP Regional Conference, Debrecen, Hungary.

Best, D. L., Williams, J. E., & Briggs, S. R. (1980). A further analysis of the affective meanings associated with male and female sex-trait stereotypes. *Sex Roles, 6*, 735–746.

Best, D. L., Williams, J. E., Cloud, J. M., Davis, S. W., Robertson, L. S., Edwards, J. R., Giles, H., & Fowles, J. (1977). Development of sex-trait stereotypes among young children the United States, England, and Ireland. *Child Development, 48*, 1375–1384.

Bronstein, P. (1984). Differences in mothers' and fathers' behaviors toward children: A cross-cultural comparison. *Developmental Psychology, 20*, 995–1003.

Buss, D. M., et al. (1990). International preferences in selecting mates: A study of 37 cultures. *Journal Cross-Cultural Psychology, 21*, 5–47.

Bussey, K., & Bandura, A. (1984). Influence of gender constancy and social power on sex-linked modeling. *Journal of Personality and Social Psychology*, *47*, 1292–1302.

Cole, M., & Scribner, S. (1974). *Culture and thought: A psychological introduction*. New York: Wiley.

Davis, S. W., Williams, J. E., & Best, D. L. (1982). Sex-trait stereotypes in the self and peer descriptions of third grade children. *Sex Roles, 8*, 315–331.

Edwards, C. P., & Whiting, B. B. (1974). Women and dependency. *Politics and Society, 4*, 343–355.

Edwards, C. P., & Whiting, B. B. (1980). Differential socialization of girls and boys in light of cross-cultural research. *New Directions for Child Development, 8*, 45–57.

Gibbons, J. L., Stiles, D. A., & Shkodriani, G. M. (1991). Adolescents' attitudes toward family and gender roles: An international comparison. *Sex Roles, 25*, 625–643.

Gough, H. G. (1966). A cross-cultural analysis of the CPI femininity scale. *Journal of Consulting Psychology, 30*, 136–141.

Gough, H. G., Chun, K., & Chung, Y. E. (1968). Validation of the CPI femininity scale in Korea. *Psychological Reports, 22*, 155–160.

Gough, H. G., & Heilbrun, A. B., Jr. (1980). *The Adjective Check List manual.* Palo Alto, CA: Consulting Psychologists Press.

Hess, R. D., & Shipman, V. C. (1967). Cognitive elements in maternal behavior. In J. P. Hell (Ed.), *Minnesota symposia on child psychology* (pp. 57–81). Minneapolis, MN: University of Minnesota Press.

Hofstede, G. (1980). *Culture's consequences: International differences in work-related values.* Beverly Hills, CA: Sage.

Jahoda, G. (1980). Cross-cultural comparisons. In M. H. Bornstein (Ed.), *Comparative methods in psychology* (pp. 105–148). Hillsdale, NJ: Erlbaum.

Johnston, T. D. (1987). The persistence of dichotomies in the study of behavioral development. *Developmental Review, 7,* 149–182.

Kalin, R., & Tilby, P. (1978). Development and validation of a sex-role ideology scale. *Psychological Reports, 42,* 731–738.

Kaschak, E., & Sharratt, S. (1983). A Latin American sex role inventory. *Cross-Cultural Psychology Bulletin 18,* 3–6.

Kohlberg, L. (1966). A cognitive–developmental analysis of children's sex role concepts and attitudes. In E. E. Maccoby (Ed.), *The development of sex differences* (pp. 82–173). Stanford, CA: Stanford University Press.

Kohlberg, L., & Ullman, D. Z. (1974). Stages in the development of psychosexual concepts and attitudes. In R. C. Friedman, R. M. Richart, & R. L. Vande Wiele (Eds.), *Sex differences in behavior* (pp. 209–223). New York: Wiley.

Lamb, M. E. (1976). Twelve-month-olds and their parents: Interactions in a laboratory playroom. *Developmental Psychology, 12,* 435–443.

Lamb, M. E. (1977). Father–infant and mother–infant interaction in the first year of life. *Child Development, 48,* 167–181.

Lamb, M. E., Frodi, A. M., Hwang, C. P., Frodi, M., & Steinberg, J. (1982). Mother– and father–infant interaction involving play and holding in traditional and nontraditional Swedish families. *Developmental Psychology, 18,* 215–221.

Lara-Cantu, M. A., & Navarro-Arias, R. (1987). Self-descriptions of Mexican college students in response to the Bem Sex Role Inventory and other sex role items. *Journal of Cross-Cultural Psychology, 18,* 331–344.

Levin, J., & Karni, E. S. (1971). A study of the CPI femininity scale. *Journal of Cross-Cultural Psychology, 2,* 387–391.

Maccoby, E. E., & Jacklin, C. N. (1974). *The psychology of sex differences.* Stanford, CA: Stanford University Press.

Marcus, D. E., & Overton, W. F. (1978). The development of cognitive gender constancy and sex role preferences. *Child Development, 49,* 434–444.

Mead, M. (1935). *Sex and temperament in three primitive societies.* New York: Morrow.

Mischel, W. (1970). Sex-typing and socialization. In P. H. Mussen (Ed.), *Carmichael's manual of child psychology* (pp. 3–72). New York: Wiley.

Munroe, R. H., Munroe, R. L., & Shimmin, H. S. (1984). Children's work in four cultures: Determinants and consequences. *American Anthropologist, 86,* 369–379.

Munroe, R. H., Shimmin, H. S., & Munroe, R. L. (1984). Gender understanding and sex role preference in four cultures. *Developmental Psychology, 20,* 673–682.

Nishiyama, T. (1975). Validation of the CPI femininity scale in Japan. *Journal of Cross-Cultural Psychology, 6,* 482–489.

Osgood, C. E., May, W. H., & Miron, M. S. (1975). *Cross-cultural universals of affective meaning.* Urbana, IL: University of Illinois Press.

Osgood, C. E., Suci, G. J., & Tannenbaum, P. H. (1957). *The measurement of meaning*. Urbana, IL: University of Illinois Press.

Piaget, J., & Inhelder, B. (1966). *The psychology of the child* (H. Weaver, trans.). New York: Basic Books.

Pitariu, H. (1981). Validation of the CPI femininity scale in Romania. *Journal of Cross-Cultural Psychology, 12*, 111–117.

Reis, H. T., & Wright, S. (1982). Knowledge of sex-role stereotypes in children aged 3 to 5. *Sex Roles, 8*, 1049–1056.

Rogoff, B., Gauvain, M., & Ellis, S. (1984). Development viewed in its cultural context. In M. H. Bornstein & M. E. Lamb (Eds.), *Developmental psychology: An advanced textbook* (pp. 533–571). Hillsdale, NJ: Erlbaum.

Ruble, D. N. (1987). The acquisition of self-knowledge: A self-socialization perspective. In N. Eisenberg (Ed.), *Contemporary topics in developmental psychology* (pp. 243–270). New York: Wiley.

Ruble, D. N. (1988). Sex-role development. In M. H. Bornstein & M. E. Lamb (Eds.), *Developmental psychology: An advanced textbook* (2 nd ed.) (pp. 411–460). Hillsdale, NJ: Erlbaum.

Russell, G., & Russell, A. (1987). Mother–child and father–child relationships in middle childhood. *Child Development, 58*, 1573–1585.

Sagi, A., Lamb, M. E., Shoham, R., Dvir, R., & Lewkowicz, K. (1985). Parent–infant interaction in families on Israeli kibbutzim. *International Journal of Behavioral Development, 8*, 273–284.

Slaby, R. G., & Frey, K. S. (1975). Development of gender constancy and selective attention to same-sex models. *Child Development, 46*, 849–856.

Spence, J. T., & Helmreich, R. L. (1978). *Masculinity and femininity: Their psychological dimensions, correlates, and antecedents*. Austin, TX: University of Texas Press.

Torki, M. A. (1988). The CPI femininity scale in Kuwait and Egypt. *Journal of Personality Assessment, 52*, 247–253.

Ward, C., & Sethi, R. R. (1986). Cross-cultural validation of the Bem Sex Role Inventory: Malaysian and South African research. *Journal of Cross-Cultural Psychology, 17*, 300–314.

Whiting, B. B., & Edwards, C. P. (1973). A cross-cultural analysis of sex differences in the behavior of children aged three through eleven. *Journal of Social Psychology, 91*, 171–188.

Whiting, B. B., & Edwards, C. P. (1988). *Children of different worlds: The formation of social behavior*. Cambridge, MA: Harvard University Press.

Whiting, B. B., & Whiting, J. W. M. (1975). *Children of six cultures: A psychocultural analysis*. Cambridge, MA: Harvard University Press.

Williams, J. E., Bennett, S. M., & Best, D. L. (1975). Awareness and expression of sex stereotypes in young children. *Developmental Psychology, 11*, 635–642.

Williams, J. E., & Best, D. L. (1977). Sex stereotypes and trait favorability on the adjective check list. *Educational and Psychological Measurement, 37*, 101–110.

Williams, J. E., & Best, D. L. (1982). *Measuring sex stereotypes: A thirty-nation study*. Beverly Hills, CA: Sage.

Williams, J. E., & Best, D. L. (1990a). *Measuring sex stereotypes: A multination study*. Beverly Hills, CA: Sage.

Williams, J. E., & Best, D. L. (1990b). *Sex and psyche: Gender and self viewed cross-culturally*. Newbury Park, CA: Sage.

Williams, K. B., & Williams, J. E. (1980). The assessment of transactional analysis ego states via the adjective check list. *Journal of Personality Assessment*, *44*(2), 120–129.

Woolams, S., & Brown, M. (1978). *Transactional analysis*. Dexter, MI: Huron Valley Press.

INTEGRATION

The Psychology of Gender:
A Perspective on Perspectives

MAHZARIN R. BANAJI

> . . . restraint is *not* the same in a man as in a woman, nor justice
> or courage either, as Socrates thought; the one is the courage
> of a ruler, the other the courage of a servant, and likewise with
> the other virtues.
> —ARISTOTLE (circa 335 B.C./1992, p. 95)

> Gender is an imposed inequality of power first, a social status
> based on who is permitted to do what to whom, and only
> derivatively a difference.
> —CATHARINE A. MACKINNON (1990, p. 213)

In this chapter, I focus on the assumptions of theory and method that
underlie the contributions to this volume. I address (1) the problematic
and recurring question of gender difference, (2) the accomplishments of
empirically based social and cognitive accounts of gender, (3) the nature
of social constructionist, psychoanalytic, and sociobiological approaches
to gender, and (4) cross-cultural approaches to understanding the emergence and construction of gender. The perspective adopted here is jointly
informed by the century-long American tradition of viewing psychology as
a science and by the relatively more recent tradition of American feminist
thought. The intellectual forces of science and feminism share the goal of
antiauthoritarianism in the search for an accurate representation of reality
and the goal of egalitarianism as a vision of the future. Together, they
form a formidable partnership. Separated, they result in pseudo science
and an ineffectual feminism.

A MATTER OF DIFFERENCE

Psychology's short history is marked by a long-standing interest in group
differences. As the history of that research indicates, investigations of

difference have never been just a matter of difference. The record of empirical psychology's first analyses of the origin and nature of difference showcases the tragedy of belief in the purity of the scientific method and the result of theories produced by a socially homogeneous tribe of investigators. While I will not review psychology's murky past on group difference research in general, I will remind readers that psychological differences concerning gender and race have been among the most examined differences (for historical reviews and critical analyses, see Bleier, 1988; Fausto-Sterling, 1985; Genova, 1989; Gould, 1981; Haraway, 1989; Lewin, 1984; Lewontin, Rose, & Kamin, 1984). Knowledge of this history is incumbent on any contemporary scientist conducting research on social groups.

Important contributions to the sociology of knowledge in general (Merton, 1973; Fiske & Shweder, 1986) and to the question of gender in science (Eagly & Carli, 1981; Keller, 1985; Unger, 1988; Harding, 1986) have informed us that the production of normal science from hypothesis construction to data interpretation and policy implication is value-laden. We are fortunately aware that reputable investigators proposed and obtained support for theories of difference that are now known to be inaccurate or false (e.g., theories about the relationship between brain size and intelligence or the x-linked chromosome carrying intelligence) (see Gould, 1981; Fausto-Sterling, 1985). Such events in the history of the science of group differences have led some social scientists to question, in a variety of ways, the integrity of the scientific method (see Hare-Mustin & Marecek, 1990a; Hubbard, 1988; Reinharz, 1985). Although I believe that rejection of the scientific method is misguided, it is for feminist psychologists to continually address issues concerning the sociology of knowledge as they confront future understandings of gender.

Locating Gender Difference

Social versus Biological Emphases

Whatever the central concern of individual chapters in this volume, each takes a position regarding the following question: What are the origins and/or consequences of the most fundamental dichotomy of life, that is, sex and gender. Controversies have ranged from questions about whether differences exist at all, and if they do, why they emerge and how they must be treated. A fascination with difference in psychology, as in other life sciences and social sciences as well, is embodied in debates about the distinction between the (essential) innate versus the (imposed) acquired nature of gender difference. It is the same quest that drives the search for the meaning of difference through sociobiological evolution (e.g., Buss, 1989; Dickemann, 1979; for critiques, see Dupre, 1990; Hubbard, 1990; Kitcher, 1990) and in sociocultural evolution and social-situational demands (Ashmore & Del Boca, 1986; Bem, 1983; Eagly, 1983; Eagly, 1987; Epstein, 1988; Farganis, 1986; Freize, Parsons, Johnson, Ruble & Zellman, 1978; O'Leary, Unger, & Wallston, 1985; Ridgeway, 1992; Spence & Helmreich, 1978; Stewart & Lykes, 1985; Williams & Best, 1990).

Some investigations of gender begin with observations of tangible differences between men and women in the social positions they occupy within the family, in interpersonal interactions, and in professional and public life. Analyses of the causes of such differences have been traditionally problematic, because it is here that interpretations of the underlying cause of observed difference have direct material implications for the quality of life of members of these groups. The two distinct emphases have led to differences in the attributes of gender that are examined, differences in method, and differences in praxis. Those whose research leads them to biological–sociobiological explanations tend to stress the adaptiveness of difference in the successful survival of the species which is considered the reason for (among other outcomes) greater male aggression and greater emphasis on physical attractiveness in women. Others whose research leads them to interpret differences in social psychological and sociocultural terms view gender differences as a product of the treatment of males and females by culturally prescribed actions. In spite of the varied nature of social accounts of gender, social psychologists are united in the belief that if differences in treatment (opportunity and experience) are eliminated, psychological gender differences as they currently exist will also be eliminated (Bem, 1983, 1993). Linking existing psychological differences to nonpsychological, material differences between males and females (e.g., social, economic, legal, and political status) and documenting the rapid reduction or elimination of differences may well be viewed among psychology's most important contributions to advances in understanding the malleability of gender. The contributions to this volume do not assume deterministic positions one way or another, and Kenrick and Trost (Chapter 6, this volume) explicitly address the issue of the interdependence of the biological and social.

Locating Gender in the Target or Perceiver

Deaux (1984) noted three themes that characterized her discovery of evolving approaches over a decade of research on gender. The first phase, she noted, consisted of a focus on individual differences (i.e, How do men and women differ on various psychological dimensions?), whereas the second phase shifted focus from the sex of the target to the gender identity of the target (i.e., What are the psychological correlates of masculinity and femininity?) Both approaches locate gender as a property of the subject and data about difference are obtained by measuring female and male or feminine and masculine individuals. The third approach marks a more prominent departure from the traditional difference approach. Here, gender is viewed as a social category, and it is knowledge about gender differences located in a perceivers' mind that are examined to understand the assumptions, beliefs, and expectations about female and male. In particular, such differences in the mental life of the perceiver are useful when they are shown to create tangible differences in the behavior of targets.

Not surprisingly, early research on gender, like research on race and other group differences, measured men and women to identify differences in performance. The focus was on which group had how much of some hypothetical construct as measured by available, if crude, instruments. In the context of beliefs about gender differences that were not subjected to empirical test, early research on gender began by documenting comparisons of male and female. The result of careful analyses of experimental data, this research still casts some doubt on existing lay beliefs, scientific theories of female inferiority in personality, intellectual abilities, or morality (Freud, 1925/1961, 1931/1961; Kohlberg, 1981; Lehrke, 1972). The landmark volume by Maccoby and Jacklin (1974) is a case in point. Their qualitative analysis of several studies on each of several psychological dimensions, ranging from cognitive and intellectual abilities to personality and social abilities, showed that barring a few differences, females and males were more similar to than different from each other in psychological functioning.

The task of demonstrating a lack of gender difference, however, is not easy, especially for those with an allegiance to the experimental method. Individual studies showing no difference between males and females are suspect because they uphold the null hypothesis. Meta-analyses have therefore been conducted with greater frequency to make the point of difference or lack of difference more emphatically (e.g., Eagly & Carli, 1981; Hall, 1984; Hyde, 1984; Swim, Borgida, Maruyama, & Myers, 1989). Reports such as Feingold's (1988) longitudinal analysis of female and male scores on the Differential Aptitude Test from the 1940s to the 1980s, showing a substantial decrease in gender differences over time, makes an impressive argument in favor of diminishing differences as a function of changes in social circumstances. The research documenting a lack of differences holds a historically important position in psychology. In the 1970s it represented a brand of psychological research that was responsible, among other contributions, for raising questions about widespread assumptions of difference in the absence of empirical evidence. The tradition of noting a lack of gender differences continues even today, especially when intuition suggests the existence of difference as seen in research on implicit stereotypes (Banaji & Greenwald, in press; Banaji, Hardin, & Rothman, in press) on emotional expression (Brody, 1985; LaFrance & Banaji, 1992), and on some cognitive abilities that previously showed larger gender differences (Feingold, 1988).

Observations of a lack of difference represent only one part of an at least two-part story about gender-difference research. If women and men live lives that are palpably different in the knowledge they have, the work they do, the positions they occupy, and the rights they have, it should not be surprising that such differences are mirrored in psychological differences, which in turn allow the maintenance of gender differences in related spheres. Following this reasoning, research on gender has also documented an array of differences: in nonverbal behavior (Hall, 1984), in the verbal expression of emotion (Brody, 1985; LaFrance & Banaji, 1992), in attributional styles (Deaux, 1984), in influenceability (Eagly & Wood, 1982), and in aggression (Hyde, 1984). But as Hyde (1981) and Deaux (1984) have commented, many of these differences are quite small, accounting for 1 to 5% of the variance. Such figures are not much help to those who would recommend social policy changes based on gender differences observed in the laboratory.

Most scientists who document gender differences are often explicit in identifying the mechanisms that cause such differences. Among the more persuasive studies are those by Eagly and Wood (1982), in which a perceived gender difference was first demonstrated and subsequently removed by equating status. Thus, what appeared to be a difference in the perception of male and female behavior was shown to be related to some other nonpsychological difference (e.g., status/power) (see also Wood & Karten, 1986). In opposition to such research showing the malleability of gender differences, others see males and females as "fundamentally" different, and in its recent feminist incarnation this position has been referred to as a "celebration of difference" (Rhode, 1990). The aim of this latter approach is to emphasize and magnify differences in order to expose the psychological ramifications of early interactional differences such as those assumed to be inherent in the sex composition of parent–child interaction. Epitomized in the well-known argument by Gilligan (1982), the position of differences in moral development and adult morality appear to be more debated and accepted in disciplines other than psychology. The practice in much psychological research is to ignore the question of whether or not observed differences are to be valued. In this sense, research in social, cognitive, and developmental psychology has been untouched by the general intellectual debate on difference (see Rhode, 1990). In accordance, the writers of the chapters in this volume do not evaluate the nature of differences or ask evaluative questions about which end of the spectrum (female or male) must be sacrificed in favor of the other.

Research compatible with Deaux's (1984) identification of a third approach demonstrated how the grouping of humans into two classes, male and female, can produce striking differences in the manner in which they are judged and treated. For these scientists, the hypothesis that social conditions can and do create differences between social groups led to experimental demonstrations of gender difference in treatment when gender ought to have been irrelevant to the dimension of judgment. Several ingenious experiments comprise this category of evidence (see, e.g., Deaux & Emswiller, 1974; Goldberg, 1968; Hansen & O'Leary, 1985; Lott, 1987; Porter, Geis, Cooper & Newman, 1985; Skrypnek & Snyder, 1982; Snyder, Tanke, & Berscheid, 1977; Wallston & O'Leary, 1981). In many of these experiments, the protocol involved presenting information that was identical in every way except a critical association to a female–male attribute or feminine–masculine characteristic. Differences in the thoughts, judgments, and behavior of observers that resulted from differences in knowledge about gender serve as sharp reminders of the power of gender in evoking differential cognitive responses and overt behavior in perceivers and targets. Do such differences in behavior occur consciously? Although most studies have not obtained explanations from subjects for their gender-biased judgments, it is possible that their explanations may not reflect the influence of gender or judgment (for a general discussion of subject's inability to identify the causes of influence on judgment, see Nisbett & Wilson, 1977). Current research on the operation of implicit gender stereotyping seeks to identify the ways in which judgments may unconsciously be influenced by the presence of social category information (see Banaji & Greenwald, 1993; Geis, Chapter 2, this volume).

Deaux's (1984) scheme is useful even a decade later, for the literature reviewed in this volume may also be characterized as continuing in the individual-difference tradition of gender (Best & Williams, Chapter 9, this volume; Cross & Markus, Chapter 3, this volume; Fast, Chapter 7, this volume; Kenrick & Trost, Chapter 6, this volume; Lott & Maluso, Chapter 4, this volume), with less emphasis on the second approach of measuring gender identity (Best & Williams, Chapter 9, this volume; Cross & Markus, Chapter 3, this volume), and greater emphasis on research in the third tradition of viewing gender as a social category (Cross & Markus, Chapter 3, this volume; Geis, Chapter 2, this volume).

As we analyze the findings and theoretical positions presented in the chapters in this volume, we must keep in mind that the psychology of gender remains a psychology of gender difference. To relabel Deaux's categories, psychological research on gender continues to be on individual difference, gender-identity difference, or treatment differences (on the part of perceivers). While many have debated whether the focus on difference is useful (see Rhode, 1990), until gender inequalities exist, that is, until psychological and material lives reflect unwelcome covariation due to gender, a psychology of gender difference will continue to be the focus of research and debate.

Social Beliefs, Social Learning, and Social Cognition in Constructions of Gender

Self-Fulfilling Prophecies

I believe that three chapters in this book are among the most valuable contributions of psychology to contemporary analyses of gender. In her own elegant and powerful research on gender, Geis has documented for us some of the more memorable examples of the interrelationship of gender and status/power (Brown & Geis, 1984; Geis, Boston, & Hoffman, 1985; Porter & Geis, 1981; Porter, Geis, Cooper, & Newman, 1985). In her chapter (Chapter 2, this volume), Geis accomplishes the most scholarly and incisive review to date on the self-fulfilling nature of gender prophecies. In the tradition of classic social psychology, the research represents a strong case for how an initially false belief causes the very behavior that, in turn, justifies the "truth" of the initial false belief. Among the many valuable lessons to be learned from this research (lessons that sorely require greater popularizing), are that (1) unconsciously held beliefs can and do influence behavior; (2) such beliefs influence mental functions of perception, inference, and memory; and (3) such beliefs also influence the behavior that produces the ultimate confirmation of the original belief.

Other psychologists have investigated the nature of the process underlying self-fulfilling prophecies (Hirt, 1990; Miller & Turnbull, 1986; Snyder & Swann, 1978), and Geis extends such analyses by focusing on the variables that are crucial to gender: differences in role, status, power, authority models, and sexuality. For example, Geis points out how self-fulfilling prophecies can lead to the choice of men for high-status positions and women for subordinate positions. But rather than the simpler (and often true) explanation that such a choice may be made in favor of a better trained (male) individual, Geis leads to the more interesting (if cynical) conclusion that we spontaneously and unconsciously create differences in the behavior of others that confirm our gender stereotypes. The experiments she reviews are critical because the methods of most of the experiments show how discriminatory acts occur when little individuating information is available to differentiate among targets. That these acts are performed without the awareness of perceivers and targets raise important questions about new strategies for change that must be developed (see Banaji & Greenwald, 1993).

Geis's chapter (Chapter 2) shows off social psychology in its most classic form by demonstrations of the power of the immediate social situation in the production of behaviors that are not freely chosen, while maintaining the illusion of choice. Evidence about human perceivers as efficient but nevertheless flawed information processors is brought home effectively. The origin of false beliefs is clearly positioned in the social conditions of gender rather than inside the (gendered) individual target of the prophecy, and in this regard Geis's analysis is similar to the social learning account of Lott and Maluso (Chapter 4, this volume). To show the "false creation" component of belief confirmation, Geis produces evidence to show how counterstereotypical models even through brief exposure can halt the cycle of self-fulfilling prophecies (Geis, Brown, Jennings, & Porter, 1984). Earlier, I mentioned research by Eagly and Wood (Eagly & Wood, 1982; Wood & Karten, 1986) to show the malleability of some gender effects. Geis's research has a similar optimistic character: It suggests that changes in social structure will produce changes in cognitive structure (see also Banaji & Greenwald, 1993).

Social Cognition

Cross and Markus (Chapter 3, this volume) capitalize on the learning that has occurred at the intersection of social and cognitive psychology and effectively apply it to review the social cognition research on gender. They focus on how the content and process of thought are influenced by the presence of gender. Their chapter is similar to the one by Geis insofar as both are committed to the view that gender is a creation of social forces and that analyses of thoughts and beliefs are valuable in examinations of gender. There are specific junctions at which analyses of cognition have proved worthwhile, and Cross and Markus review literatures covering memory for stereotype-consistent or -inconsistent information, stereotype-based judgments, the activation of stereotypes, the influence of stereotypes on behavior, and conditions that produce changes in stereotypes ("schemas," to use their term). A focus on memory and biases in information processing allows an understanding of how knowledge about gender is kept alive and is resistant to change. This quite extensive review by Cross and Markus represents the unique advantages of social cognition approaches in social psychology: (1) specifying and testing the cognitive mechanisms by which gender emerges and is sustained and (2) identifying the interrelationship between gender and cognition, in particular, the obvious but ignored link between the reality of the social category one inherits (e.g., gender) and the acquisition of knowledge permitted by it and judgments that are produced in response to it.

In a previous review of research on self, Markus and Cross (1990) developed an argument for viewing gender (among other social categories) as an important conduit in the emergence of self, by pointing out the interpersonal nature of the development of self. Their present analysis is enhanced by a special focus on the role of self in the articulation of gender, this time attending to the intraindividual mental processes involved in the development of a gendered self. Because recent research on self has viewed it as a dimension of personality, reminding readers of the social basis of self is itself a contribution. Markus's own work is relevant here (Markus & Kitayama, 1991; Markus & Oyserman, 1988), as is research by McGuire and McGuire (1988) documenting the importance of gender in spontaneous self-description: For both boys and girls, the likelihood of mentioning their gender in a self-description was inversely related to the number of same-sex members of the family. Boys from largely female households and girls from largely male households were more likely to mention gender in their self-descriptions than those in more evenly gendered families. Such differences in the content of spontaneous self-descriptions show how dramatically social structure impinges on cognitive structure.

Social Learning

While both Geis and Cross and Markus focus largely (although not exclusively) on the behavior of perceivers of gender, Lott and Maluso (Chapter 4, this volume) view gender as a subject variable. In particular, they explicate the ways in which gender emerges through the process of learning. Their version of social learning has an obvious connection to an earlier learning theory (Miller & Dollard, 1941), although both the focus on gender and the clear advantage of including cognitive entities (such as beliefs and attitudes) produce a strong and quite appealing statement of gender as the behavioral outcome of learning.

Take the particular example discussed by Lott and Maluso to make the point that "consequences are often intertwined with opportunities for practice that typically precede, and provide the setting for, behavioral outcomes" (p. 102). For example, a doll is a toy that provokes the expression of emotion and caring (hugging, stroking), while a ball demands action (throwing, kicking). In a particular work that they cite (Stern & Karraker, 1989), adults acted equally warmly and responsively to infants labeled boys or girls, but these adults did differ in the type of (stereotyped) toy they offered the infant. An interesting sequence of events and attributions may follow: The adult might be correctly aware that no difference in warmth was shown toward male or female children. In fact, conscious effort may be made to show equivalent emotion toward both female and male infants. However, an implicit handing of a sex-stereotypical toy may well create the stereotypical behavior that, in turn, could provide confirmation that a female child demonstrated more emotion and caring in spite of neutral treatment. Banaji, LaFrance, and Beall (1992) offer a similar analysis of how emotionality in adult males and females may develop, based on the finding that females generate more symbolic (emotional) possessions of value than instrumental ones, while males generate many fewer symbolic possessions than females do and a slightly greater number of instrumental possessions than symbolic ones. Although males and females show equivalent emotion toward valued symbolic and instrumental possessions, the greater number of emotion-eliciting stimuli (symbolic possessions) in the case of females is thought to provide, in Lott and Maluso's sense, greater opportunities for the expression of emotion.

A social learning approach brings a perspective to analyses of gender that is both unique and at the same time has infiltrated so much of current thinking about human behavior that (as with aspects of behaviorism, cf. Hintzman, 1990) its influence is hard to detect and sometimes easy to dismiss. Most notably, a social learning account of gender has created a science of the environmental contingencies that produce gender differences, located the origins of gender outside the physical and psychological entities that embody it, demystified gender by identifying it as one of several stimuli to which learned responses are evoked, and linked material conditions of existence to the environment in which the psychological development of gender occurs. Many marxist and feminist theorists, perhaps because of disciplinary blinders that disallow attention to experimental treatments, have unfortunately missed this powerful psychological account of the nature and emergence of gender.

The three chapters that review the research on the social conditions that create and sustain gender provide among the sturdiest data about gender differences that are available across the disciplines engaged in examinations of gender. In comparison with alternative analyses within psychology and outside it, these approaches (without reference to faith, reason, or personal conviction) unveil gender as an indisputable fact of life, consider the social and cognitive forces that create and sustain its evolution, and identify obvious paths by which the future can be dramatically altered if gender egalitarianism is an a priori value. In so doing, such research mirrors the commitment of older sciences to the vision of a better world (Conant, 1951; Whitehead, 1925/1975). Because I find the logic of these approaches to gender compelling, and because their goal is so obviously a feminist one, it is worth questioning the response of anti-science and especially anti-experimental postmodernists in psychology and elsewhere to the methods and findings that define this approach to gender.

SOCIAL CONSTRUCTIONISM, SOCIOBIOLOGY, AND PSYCHOANALYSIS

Part II of this volume contains three chapters on the social constructionist, sociobiological, and psychoanalytic views of gender. I will have less to say about them because they represent broader theoretical statements about gender and do not provide evidence of the same depth as the chapters in the previous section. However, their strength lies in the issues they raise about the nature of difference and the message they bring about the consequences of gender differences.

Social Constructionism

Social constructionism is psychology's code word for postmodernism, and it has been accompanied of late by proposals of a uniquely feminist method (Hare-Mustin & Marecek, 1990b; Reinharz, 1992; for a discussion of perspectives on method, see Riger, 1992). That version of social construction is absent in this volume. Instead, Beall's spin (Chapter 5, this volume) on social constructionism is to view gender as a product of culture (by showing variability in notions of gender across cultures) and social practice, and to express the always needed awareness about biases in scientific practice. In this form, a social constructionist approach is congruent with the assumptions that underlie much social psychological research on gender (see Geis, Chapter 2; Cross & Markus, Chapter 3; Lott & Maluso, Chapter 4). In fact, Beall explicitly notes: "However, I do not advocate discontinuing scientific inquiry about the nature of gender and gender relations" (p. 144), and here Beall's view may not represent other social–constructionist positions. Beall's social constructionism is a view with which few psychologists would disagree and her observations provide useful points of comparison in both form and content. For example, her strategy is to look for differences across cultures, and use such differences to educate us about the importance of sociocultural patterning in creating the varied faces of gender. This form of argument is quite similar to those who look cross-culturally for evidence about the *similarity* of sex-linked behaviors across cultures (e.g., Buss, 1989; Kenrick & Trost, Chapter 6). Potentially useful discussions about the value and interpretation of cross-cultural data can occur on topics on which social constructionists and sociobiologists both claim to have evidence: By what criteria is an observation to be defined a similarity or difference? How should superficial differences between cultures be extracted from a cross-cultural examination to assure that accurate evidence of differences are being obtained? Can similarities appear in spite of differing underlying causes? For such questions to be meaningfully addressed, criteria for identifying similarities and differences must be explicitly asserted and an attempt to understand the mechanism by which two cultures are set apart must be posited at a level more specific than what is typically captured by the term "culture."

The Evolutionary Perspective

In scientific writing, it is often the case that when one says "the scientific method," one is referring to the method of experimentation generally attributed to Bacon (see Eiseley, 1973). But there is a close competitor, the differential equation, which allows stating theories in a rigorous, precise, and compact form. Since Newton and Bacon, the differential equation and the controlled experiment have been, to construct a stodgy metaphor, the wind and sail of science. Sometimes a science is able to effectively exploit only one of these methods. Social psychology, for example, is largely an experimental science with not much of a role, in its current state, for detailed systemic theories of the kind that differential equations are able to express elegantly. By contrast, fields such as plate tectonics, so-called GUTs (Grand Unified Theories) (see Carrigan & Trower, 1989) in physics or big-bang cosmology, are almost exclusively expressed in differential equations with (currently) not much of a role for experimental treatments.

In this context, sociobiological approaches are alluring because of the prospect they offer for combining the rigor of the differential equation with the power of controlled observation, if not experimentation. Since well before Darwin, the observational demands of biology have been well understood (see Eiseley, 1961; Desmond, 1989). In this century, however, biology has taken on new mathematical and computational dimensions that have greatly expanded its explanatory power. Since the publication of Lotka's groundbreaking book in 1926 (Lotka, 1956), mathematical models have become ubiquitous in biology (e.g., Hoppenstadt, 1982; Pigelou, 1969; Smith, 1971).

The primary power of these models lies in the fact that differential equations represent relative rates of change (dy/dx represents the rate of change of y wrt x, and the integral of y wrt x gives the area under the curve obtained by plotting y with respect to x). As a result, a differential equation is able to relate one or more rates of change to some absolute characteristics of the environment. For example, in elementary physics, to say that the acceleration due to gravity is 32 feet per second squared is to say that a particular rate (of change of velocity with respect to time) is a constant and is equal to the product of Newton's constant times the mass of the earth divided by the square of the earth's radius (which in turn is approximately 32 feet per second squared). Thus, differential equations provide a way of characterizing causal mechanisms that effect change in an environment, both suddenly and slowly and directly and indirectly.

It is helpful to understand the role that these equations play in socio-biological modeling. An equation that is one of the oldest in mathematical biology will serve, namely, the so-called predator–prey equation, sometimes known as the Lotka–Volterra equation after its inventors. The model is about an ecological situation that involves two species, one of which preys on the other. Let $H(t)$ be the population of the prey and $P(t)$ the population of the predator.[1] The differential equations that make up the classic predator-prey model are:

$$dH/dt = aH - \alpha HP \qquad (1)$$

$$dP/dt = -cP + \gamma HP \qquad (2)$$

where $H(t)$ and $P(t)$ are the populations of prey and predator at time t and a, c, α, and γ are simply constants that are all assumed to be positive. Solving these equations leads to some qualitative conclusions:

1. The sizes of the predator and prey oscillate.
2. The period of oscillation is independent of the initial conditions (i.e., the initial values of H and P). Rather, it is dependent on the parameters a, c, α, and γ.
3. The predator and prey populations are out of phase by one quarter cycle; that is, there is a one-quarter cycle time difference in when the predator and prey population reach a maximum or a minimum, and the prey's population reaches its maximum one-quarter cycle before that of the predator.

The qualitative conclusions are derived from careful analysis of the solutions of these equations. It is worth noting these equations in some detail, because they represent one of the first examples of theoretical models of population biology that were also compared with data about the actual population growth and reduction (in fisheries). It is worth repeating Volterra's assessment:

> Both D'Ancona and I working independently were equally satisfied in comparing results which were revealed to us separately by calculus and by observation, as these results were in accord; showing for instance that man [sic] in fisheries, by disturbing the natural condition of proportion of two species, one of which feeds upon the other, causes diminution in the quantity of the

[1] Of course, we make the usual assumptions:
(1) when the population of prey is zero the predator dies out, i.e. $dP/dt = -cP$, $c > 0$, when $H = 0$;
(2) in the absence of the predator, the prey grows without bound, i.e. $dH/dt = aH$, $a > 0$, for $P = 0$.

species that eats the other, and an increase in the species fed upon. (See Chapman, 1931, p. 410)

I have attempted this rather detailed explanation because I wish to point out an underlying commonality to the theories described by this rather simple model. First, there is a clear mechanism at work: a resource depletion mechanism and an equilibrating resource-generation mechanism, and the connection between these two is clearly expressed by the equation. Second, there is substantial empirical evidence to support the constraint that connects the two mechanisms; that is, the data support the differential equation as being a realistic if somewhat abstract characterization of the ecosystem under study.

The evolutionary efforts reported by Kenrick and Trost follow a different strategy. Like Beall, Kenrick and Trost also gather data from a variety of cultures, but in contrast, their focus is on the abundance of similarity to be observed through cross-cultural analyses. Kenrick and Trost do a fine job of gathering data about the similarity across cultures in gender-specific patterns of aggression, mate-selection, and so on. While they provide examples of quaint customs (e.g., among the Palahari of Northern India, brothers pool their resources to purchase a wife they share; if they accumulate more wealth, they will purchase additional wives), it is not always clear what theory is explicated by such behavior (e.g., the pooling of resources for a wife). What is difficult to detect is the mechanism that explains such patterns of behavior.

Kenrick and Trost's observations are not to be underestimated. Such observations can prompt hypotheses about the nature of differences between females and males. However, such observations are not easily amenable to specific tests of mechanisms that are needed if an explanation of the observed behavior is a concern. Anthropological observations are often unsatisfactory if they are not accompanied by a method for identifying an explanatory mechanism responsible for the behavior. For example, data of the sort obtained by Dickemann (1979) were challenged on this basis (among others) by Kitcher (1989). Descriptive analyses of similarity in worldwide customs, no matter what their degree of similarity, must be subjected to some test of the ecosystem under study. The absence of mechanisms to explain interesting cultural comparisons are a problem with many large-scale cross-cultural analyses, regardless of the explanation to which the theory is partial (see Williams & Best, Chapter 9, this volume, for a discussion). Sociobiology may be a field with great potential, but psychology's contribution rests on the ability to provide explanations rather than description. In the absence of a method that allows the examination of mechanisms, comments about the specific claims of this evolutionary approach to gender must wait.

A Variation on a Psychoanalytic Theme

Freud's (1907/1953, 1925/1961, 1931/1961) ideas of gender development have remained central at least in psychoanalytic circles where gender development is discussed.

It is clear that as early as when Freud's theory was first proposed, critical reaction followed (see Chodorow, 1989), but it is also clear that feminist theory has posed among the more serious challenges to the core of the original psychoanalytic theory of gender development. Among such commentators, almost none is as well recognized as Chodorow (1989), who has persuasively argued that a critical advantage is gained by offering reformulations from within the confines of Freud's account of personality and gender development. Because I work far from the boundaries of psychodynamic theory, it is perhaps difficult for me to appreciate the significance of the dialogue in which feminist psychoanalysts are engaged. Yet, it is clear that a feminist psychoanalysis, whether one agrees with its tenets or not, has provoked critical questions about a ubiquitous theory of gender development.

Fast proposes a revision of Freud's account that, like other revisions, places greater importance on social and cognitive factors in development. Although such efforts result in more persuasive theories of development, they also create a dilemma. A "socializing" of psychoanalytic accounts of gender development makes such theories more plausible and testable than the original version. Yet, that same broadening also threatens the centrality of Freud's analysis of gender. For example, Fast (Chapter 7, this volume) notes:

> Although the infant itself does not yet experience its genitals in gender terms, they probably color patterns of child care in subtle but pervasive ways. The infant's activities—vigorous, languid, alert, tender, assertive, curious or angry—may be variously encouraged or discouraged by caregivers as sex appropriate. (p. 180)

Such statements raise legitimate questions about what remains of the psychoanalytic components of theories to retain them as viable accounts. Discoveries of a cognitive unconscious (Kihlstrom, 1990) will make social cognition accounts of gender development even more persuasive and accessible, and at some point, such alternative views inserted into dynamic theories will produce hybrids that contain the advantages of both accounts (psychoanalytic and social, cognitive) or a greater and greater shift in emphasis toward social learning and social cognition explanations.

TIME AND SPACE FRONTIERS OF GENDER

Two chapters in this volume are concerned primarily with gender development over time (Jacklin & Reynolds, Chapter 8) and across cultures (Best

& Williams, Chapter 9). Jacklin and Reynolds present a summary of major approaches to childhood socialization. While they review social learning, social–cognitive (schema), and behavioral–genetic accounts, two of which have been presented in other chapters in this volume, they bring a different perspective by focusing on childhood socialization, a component that is missing from the other accounts (with the exception of Best & Williams). In their discussion of the meaning of biological differences, Jacklin and Reynolds raise the issue of the attitude toward the meaning and influence of biological factors in gender differentiation. Their point about the misuse of biological theories to maintain differences is useful, as is their solution which emphasizes the need among psychologists to attend to findings from research on biological differences. This is an important issue and one that will be addressed only by the participation of feminist scientists who are able to explicitly challenge earlier theories of gender difference.

Best and Williams provide a useful account of the cross-cultural approach to gender. They educate readers about the purpose of cross-cultural research in particular to provide an analysis of the problems that confront traditional cross-cultural comparisons of group difference. Their experience with cross-cultural data is invaluable to those who must acquire the skills to conduct such research, especially because such knowledge is not a component of traditional graduate training. Their own cross-cultural research, demonstrating how culture can shape gender development, is shown by the greater variation between than within groups. A group for comparison purposes is identified as a nation state, classified along a continuum from traditional to modern. (Such a classification must be questioned given the continually changing face of national borders.) Best and Williams are appropriately cautious in reporting and interpreting findings, pointing out lack of differences obtained across nations (as in the case of masculinity and femininity) as well as the presence of difference (as in the case of the strength of incorporating sex stereotypes into definitions of self).

A difficulty with cross-cultural research in general is the absence of strong explanatory concepts coupled with the analysis of fixed variables such as culture and gender (the latter problem is noted by Best & Williams, Chapter 9, this volume, as well). Although we learn that "Western" cultures differ from "Eastern" cultures (e.g., Markus & Kitayama, 1991) and that "traditional" cultures differ from "modern" ones, it is not clear what mechanisms promote and maintain such differences. This approach is not wholly satisfactory because often "culture" or "nation" becomes a post hoc catchall for observed differences. The problem is symmetric to the one encountered in sociobiological analyses. It is no longer convincing to find differences across cultures and conclude that sociocultural forces have produced that difference, just as it is unconvincing that a lack of differences across culture can be considered evidence in support of sociobiological mechanisms. The strength of Best and Williams's chapter is their systematic effort at documenting cultural differences in spite of their obvious awareness of the difficulty in interpretation and the limits of the method.

It is interesting that cross-cultural psychologists tend not to heed historic events that may tie superficially discrepant cultures together (e.g., countries that have a shared history of colonialism), or dissociate superficially similar cultures (e.g., groups that are equivalent in socioeconomic status but considered racially discrepant) and ask what differences exist between them. Analyses of discrepant countries and cultures might be more meaningful if they were guided by new specifications for coding differences rather than traditional ones such as nation state boundaries or exclusively Western views of similarity and difference. In attempting to understand the underlying mechanisms by which culture and biology shape cognition and personality, the approach used by Best and Williams, of including a developmental perspective (within the cross-cultural one), may be useful.

Cross-cultural research will also be enriched if culture is sought closer to home than in protracted analyses of the unfamiliar customs of alien peoples. In the superbly successful segregation that has been effected in most of the urban United States, vast cultural differences (albeit less exotic ones) may be examined for questions about culture and gender. The culture of Yale students and faculty on my side of Prospect Street and the starkly distinct culture of New Haven residents on the other can yield a cross-cultural analysis that will be quite revealing about two distinct cultures, and one that is less prone to the hazards of foreign travel.

CONCLUSION

I began this chapter with words spoken by Aristotle some time ago and by Catharine MacKinnon more recently. There are many differences between these individuals, and I chose their comments to represent dissimilar views of gender difference. The distinction lies as much in the content of their comments (which is obvious enough) as in the implication of each. While Aristotle's comment provides a description of difference (truth of that description aside), MacKinnon attempts an explanation for gender differences. As in all sciences, this distinction between description and explanation is crucial in measuring psychology's progress on the question of gender. A variety of psychologists have presented their accounts of gender in this volume, and many have attempted to provide explanations within the framework of a preferred theory. A true measure of their contributions will lie in the extent to which explanation is sought at all and subsequently in the accuracy of the explanations in representing the nature of female and male.

ACKNOWLEDGMENTS

I thank R. Bhaskar for helpful comments. Preparation of this chapter was supported in part by the National Science Foundation Grant DBC 9120987. Correspondence concerning this chapter may be addressed to the author at Department of Psychology, Yale University, P.O. Box 11A Yale Station, New Haven, CT 06520-7447.

REFERENCES

Aristotle. (1992). *The politics* (T. A. Sinclair, Trans.) (revised and re-presented by T. J. Saunders). New York: Penguin Books.

Ashmore, R. D., & Del Boca, F. (1986). *The social psychology of female–male relations: A critical analysis of central concepts.* New York: Academic Press.

Banaji, M. R., Hardin, C., & Rothman, A. J. (in press). Implicit sterotyping in person judgment. *Journal of Personality and Social Psychology.*

Banaji, M. R., & Greenwald, A. G. (1993). Implicit stereotyping and prejudice. In M. P. Zanna & J. M. Olson (Eds.), *The psychology of prejudice: The Ontario symposium* (Vol. 7, pp. 55–76). Hillsdale, NJ: Erlbaum.

Banaji, M. R., LaFrance, M., & Beall, A. E. (1992). *Gender and the expression of emotional intensity.* Unpublished manuscript, Yale University, New Haven, CT.

Bem, S. L. (1983). Gender schema theory and its implications for child development: Raising gender-aschematic children in a gender-schematic society. *Signs: Journal of Women in Culture and Society, 8,* 4, 598–616.

Bem, S. (1993). *The lenses of gender.* New Haven, CT: Yale University Press.

Bleier, R. (1988). Sex differences research: Science or belief? In R. Bleier (Ed.), *Feminist approaches to science* (pp. 147–164). New York: Pergamon Press.

Brody, L. R. (1985). Gender differences in emotional development: A review of theories and research. In A. J. Stewart & M. B. Lykes (Eds.), *Gender and personality: Current perspectives on theory and research* (pp. 14–61). Durham, NC: Duke University Press.

Brown, V., & Geis, F. L. (1984). Turning lead into gold: Leadership by men and women and the alchemy of social consensus. *Journal of Personality and Social Psychology, 46,* 811–824.

Buss, D. M. (1989). Sex differences in human mate preferences: Evolutionary hypotheses tested in 37 cultures. *Behavioral and Brain Sciences, 12,* 1–49.

Campbell, D. T. (1986). Science's social system of validity-enhancing collective belief change and the problems of the social sciences. In D. W. Fiske & R. A. Shweder (Eds.), *Metatheory in social science: Pluralisms and subjectivities* (pp. 108–135). Chicago: University of Chicago Press.

Carrigan, R. A., & Trower, W. P. (1989). *Particle physics in the cosmas*. San Francisco: W. H. Freeman.

Chapman, R. (1931). *Animal ecology with special reference to insects*. New York: McGraw- Hill.

Conant, J. B. (1951). *On understanding science*. New York: New American Library of World Literature.

Chodorow, N. J. (1989). *Feminism and psychoanalytic theory*. New Haven, CT: Yale University Press.

Deaux, K. (1984). From individual differences to social categories. *American Psychologist, 39*, 2, 105–116.

Deaux, K., & Emswiller, T. (1974). Explanations of successful performance on sex-linked tasks: What is skill for the male is luck for the female. *Journal of Personality and Social Psychology, 29*, 80–85.

Desmond, A. (1989). *The politics of evolution: Morphology, medicine and reform in radical London*. Chicago: University of Chicago Press.

Dickemann, M. (1979). Female infanticide, reproductive strategies, and social stratification: A preliminary model. In N. Chagnon & W. Irons (Eds.), *Evolutionary biology and human social behavior: An anthropological perspective* (pp. 321–367). North Scituate, MA: Duxbury.

Dupre, J. (1990). Global versus local perspectives on sexual difference. In D. L. Rhode (Ed.), *Theoretical perspectives on sexual differences* (pp. 47–62). New Haven, CT: Yale University Press.

Eagly, A. H. (1983). Gender and social influence. A social psychological analysis. *American Psychologist, 38*, 971–981.

Eagly, A. H. (1987). *Sex differences in social behavior: A social-role interpretation*. Hillsdale, NJ: Erlbaum.

Eagly, A., H., & Carli, L. L. (1981). Sex of researchers and sex-typed communications as determinants of sex differences in influenceability: A meta-analysis of social influence studies. *Psychological Bulletin, 90*, 1–20.

Eagly, A. H., & Wood, W. (1982). Inferred sex differences in status as a determinant of gender stereotypes about social influence. *Journal of Personality and Social Psychology, 43*, 915–928.

Eiseley, L. (1961). *Darwin's century*. New York: Doubleday.

Eiseley, L. (1973). *The man who saw through time*. New York: Scribner.

Epstein, C. F. (1988). *Deceptive distinctions: Sex, gender, and the social order*. New Haven, CT: Yale University Press and New York: Sage.

Farganis, S. (1986). *The social reconstruction of the female character*. Totowa, NJ: Rowman & Littlefield.

Fausto-Sterling, A. (1985). *Myths of gender*. New York: Basic Books.

Fiske, D. W., & Shweder, R. A. (Eds.). (1986). *Metatheory in social science: Pluralisms and subjectivities*. Chicago: University of Chicago Press.

Feingold, A. (1988). Cognitive gender differences are disappearing. *American Psychologist, 43*, 2, 95–103.

Freize, I. H., Parsons, J. E., Johnson, P. B., Ruble, D. N., & Zellman, G. L. (1978). *Women and sex roles: A social psychological perspective*. New York: W. W. Norton.

Freud, S. (1953). The sexual enlightenment of children. In J. Strachey (Ed. and Trans.), *The standard edition of the complete psychological works of Sigmund Freud*

(Vol. 7, pp. 135–243). London: Hogarth Press. (Original work published 1907)

Freud, S. (1961). Female sexuality. In J. Strachey (Ed. and Trans.), *The standard edition of the complete psychological works of Sigmund Freud* (Vol. 21, pp. 223–243). London: Hogarth Press. (Original work published 1931)

Freud, S. (1961). Some psychical consequences of the anatomical distinction between the sexes. In J. Strachey (Ed. and Trans.), *The standard edition of the complete psychological works of Sigmund Freud* (Vol. 19, pp. 248–258). London: Hogarth Press. (Original work published 1925)

Geis, F. L. (1983). *Gender schemas and achievement: Performance and recognition.* Invited address to the convention of the Eastern Psychological Association, Philadelphia, PA.

Geis, F. L., Boston, M., & Hoffman, N. (1985). Sex of authority role models and achievement by men and women: Leadership performance and recognition. *Journal of Personality and Social Psychology, 49,* 636–653.

Geis, F. L., Brown, V., Jennings, J., & Porter, N. (1984). T. V. commercials as achievement scripts for women. *Sex Roles, 10,* 513–525.

Genova, J. (1989). Women and the mismeasure of thought. In N. Tuana (Ed.), *Feminism and science* (pp. 211–227). Bloomington, IN: Indiana University Press.

Gergen, K. J. (1985). The social constructionist movement in modern psychology. *American Psychologist, 40,* 255–265.

Gilligan, C. (1982). *In a difference voice: Psychological theory and women's development.* Cambridge, MA: Harvard University Press.

Goldberg, P. (1968). Are women prejudiced against women? *Transaction, 5,* 28–30.

Gould, S. J. (1981). *The mismeasure of man.* New York: W. W. Norton.

Hall, J. A. (1984). *Nonverbal sex differences.* Baltimore, MD: Johns Hopkins University Press.

Hansen, R. D., & O'Leary, V. E. (1985). Sex-determined attributions. In V. E. O'Leary, R. K. Unger, & B. S. Wallston (Eds.), *Women, gender, and social psychology* (pp. 67–99). Hillsdale, NJ: Erlbaum.

Haraway, D. (1989). *Primate visions: Gender, race, and nature in the world of modern science.* New York: Routledge.

Harding, S. (1986). *The science question in feminism.* Ithaca, NY: Cornell University Press.

Hare-Mustin, R. T., & Marecek, J. (1990a). *Making a difference: Psychology and the construction of gender.* New Haven, CT: Yale University Press.

Hare-Mustin, R. T., & Marecek, J. (1990b). Gender and the meaning of difference: Postmodernism and psychology. In R. T. Hare-Mustin & J. Marecek (Eds.), *Making a difference: Psychology and the construction of gender.* New Haven, CT: Yale University Press.

Hintzman, D. T. (1990). 25 years of learning and memory: Was the cognitive revolution a mistake? In D. E. Meyer & S. Kornblum (Eds.), *Attention and performance* (Vol. 14). Hillsdale, NJ: Erlbaum.

Hirt, E. R. (1990). Do I see only what I expect? Evidence for an expectancy-guided retrieval model. *Journal of Personality and Social Psychology, 58,* 937–951.

Hoppenstadt, F. C. (1982). *Mathematical methods of population biology.* Cambridge, England: Cambridge University Press.

Hubbard, R. (1988). Some thought about the masculinity of the natural sciences. In M. M. Gergen (Ed.), *Feminist thought and the structure of knowledge* (pp. 1–15). New York: New York University Press.

Hubbard, R. (1990). The political nature of "human nature." In D. L. Rhode (Ed.), *Theoretical perspectives on sexual difference.* New Haven, CT: Yale University Press.

Hyde, J. S. (1981). How large are cognitive gender differences? A meta-analysis using w and d. *American Psychologist, 36,* 892–901.

Hyde, J. S. (1984). How large are gender differences in aggression? A developmental meta-analysis. *Developmental Psychology, 20,* 722–736.

Keller, E. F. (1985). *Reflections on gender and science.* New Haven, CT: Yale University Press.

Kihlstrom, J. (1990). The psychological unconscious. In L. A. Pervin (Ed.), *Handbook of personality: Theory and research* (pp. 445–464). New York: Guilford.

Kitcher, P. (1990). *Vaulting ambition.* Cambridge, MA: MIT Press.

Kohlberg, L. (1981). *The philosophy of moral development.* San Francisco: Harper & Row.

LaFrance, M., & Banaji, M. (1992). Toward a reconsideration of the gender–emotion relationship. In M. S. Clark (Ed.), *Emotion and social behavior: Review of personality and social psychology,* (Vol. 14, pp. 178–201). London: Sage.

Lehrke, R. G. (1972). A theory of x-linkage of major intellectual traits. *American Journal of Mental Deficiency, 76,* 611–619.

Lewin, M. (Ed.). (1984). *In the shadow of the past: Psychology portrays the sexes.* New York: Columbia University Press.

Lewontin, R. C., Rose, S., & Kamin, L. J. (1984). *Not in our genes.* New York: Pantheon Books.

Lotka, A. J. (1956). *Elements of mathematical biology.* New York: Dover.

Lott, B. (1987). Sexist discrimination as distancing behavior: I. A laboratory demonstration. *Psychology of Women Quarterly, 11,* 47–58.

Maccoby, E. E., & Jacklin, C. N. (1974). *The psychology of sex differences.* Stanford, CA: Stanford University Press.

MacKinnon, C. A. (1990). Legal perspectives on sexual difference. In D. L. Rhode (Ed.), *Theoretical perspectives on sexual difference.* New Haven, CT: Yale University Press.

Markus, H. R., & Cross, S. (1990). The interpersonal self. In L. A. Pervin (Ed.), *Handbook of personality: Theory and research* (pp. 576–608). New York: Guilford Press.

Markus, H. R., & Kitayama, S. (1991). Culture and the self: Implications for cognition, emotion, and motivation. *Psychological Review, 98,* 2, 224–253.

Markus, H. R., & Oyserman, D. (1988). Gender and thought: The role of the self-concept. In M. Crawford & M. Hamilton (Eds.), *Gender and thought* (pp. 100–127). New York: Springer-Verlag.

McGuire, W. J., & McGuire, C. V. (1988). Content and process in the experience of self. *Advances in Experimental Social Psychology, 21,* 97–144.

Merton, R. K. (1973). *The sociology of science.* Chicago: University of Chicago Press.

Miller, D. T., & Turnbull, W. (1986). Expectancies and interpersonal processes. *Annual Review of Psychology, 37,* 233–256.

Miller, N. E. & Dollard, J. (1941). *Social learning and imitation.* New Haven: Yale University Press.

Nisbett, R., & Wilson, T. D. (1977). Telling more than we can know: Verbal reports on neural processes. *Psychological Review, 84,* 231–259.

O'Leary, V. E., Unger, R. K., & Wallston, B. S. (1985). *Women, gender, and social psychology.* Hillsdale, NJ: Erlbaum.

Pigelou, E. C. (1969). *An introduction to mathematical ecology.* New York: Wiley.

Porter, N., & Geis, F. L. (1981). Women and nonverbal leadership cues: When seeing is not believing. In C. Mayo & N. Henley (Eds.), *Gender and nonverbal behavior.* New York: Springer-Verlag.

Porter, N., Geis, F. L., Cooper, E., & Newman, E. (1985). Androgyny and leadership in mixed-sex groups. *Journal of Personality and Social Psychology, 49,* 803–823.

Reinharz, S. (1985). Feminist distrust: Problems of context and context in sociological work. In D. N. Berg & K. K. Smith (Eds.), *The self in social inquiry: Researching methods* (pp. 153–172). Newbury Park, CA: Sage.

Reinharz, S. (1992). *Feminist methods in social research.* Oxford: Oxford University Press.

Rhode, D. L. (1990). Definitions of difference. In D. L. Rhode (Ed.), *Theoretical perspectives on sexual differences* (pp. 197–212). New Haven, CT: Yale University Press.

Ridgeway, C. L. (1992). *Gender, interaction, and inequality.* New York: Springer-Verlag.

Riger, S. (1992). Epistemological debates, feminist voices. *American Psychologist, 47,* 6, 730–740.

Singh, J. (1964). *Great ideas in operations research.* New York: Dover.

Skrypnek, B. J., & Snyder, M. (1982). On the self-perpetuating nature of stereotypes about women and men. *Journal of Experimental Social Psychology, 18,* 277–291.

Smith, J. M. (1971). *Mathematical ideas in biology.* Cambridge, England: Cambridge University Press.

Snyder, M., & Swann, W. B., Jr. (1978). Behavioral confirmation in social interaction: From social perception to social reality. *Journal of Experimental Social Psychology, 14,* 148–162.

Spence, J. T., & Helmreich, R. L. (1978). *Masculinity and femininity.* Austin, TX: University of Texas Press.

Snyder, M., Tanke, E. D., & Berscheid, E. (1977). Social perception and interpersonal behavior: On the self-fulfilling nature of social sterotypes. *Journal of Personality and Social Psychology, 35,* 656–666.

Stern, M., Karraker, K. H. (1989). Sex stereotyping of infants: A review of gender labeling studies. *Sex Roles, 20,* 501–522.

Stewart, A. J., & Lykes, M. B. (1985), *Gender and personality: Current perspectives on theory and research.* Durham, NC: Duke University Press.

Swim, J., Borgida, E., Maruyama, G., & Myers, D. G. (1989). Joan T. McKay versus John T. MacKay: Do gender stereotypes bias evaluations? *Psychological Bulletin, 105,* 409–429.

Unger, R. K. (1988). Psychological, feminist, and personal epistemology: Transcending contradiction. In M. M. Gergen (Ed.), *Feminist thought and the structure of knowledge* (pp. 124–141). New York: New York University Press.

Wallston, B. S., & O'Leary, V. E. (1981). Sex makes a difference: Differential perceptions of women and men. In L. Wheeler (Ed.), *Review of personality and social psychology* (pp. 9–41). Newbury Park, CA: Sage.

Whitehead, A. N. (1975). *Science and the modern world*. Cambridge, MA: Cambridge University Press. (Original work published 1925)

Williams, J. E., & Best, D. L. (1990). *Measuring sex stereotypes: A multination study*. Newbury Park, CA: Sage.

Wood, W., & Karten, S. J. (1986). Sex differences in interaction style as a product of perceived sex differences in competence. *Journal of Personality and Social Psychology*, *50*, 341–347.

Index